CLASSICS
OF APPLIED
HISTORY

CLASSICS OF APPLIED HISTORY

EDITED BY
JOHN BEW, ANDREW EHRHARDT
AND MATTIAS HESSÉRUS

BOKFÖRLAGET STOLPE

CONTENTS

PREFACE

It is clear that the spectacular mechanical and scientific creations of modern man tend to conceal from him the nature of his own humanity and to encourage him in all sorts of Promethean ambitions and illusions. It is precisely this person who, as he gets carried along on the dizzy pace of technological change, needs most to be reminded of the nature of the species he belongs to, of the limitations that rest on him, of the essential elements, both tragic and helpful, of his own condition. It is these reminders that history, and history alone, can give.[1]
George Kennan, 1960

In recent years there has been something of a renaissance of 'applied history' in both the academy and policymaking circles, particularly in the realm of statecraft and foreign policy. Put simply, the champions of applied history advocate the use of historical methods and knowledge to help illuminate contemporary challenges and to improve the quality of analysis and decision-making. Sometimes this is done by analogy; on other occasions, by the learning of lessons from the past that are deemed directly relevant today. While advocates of applied history have varying levels of appetite for making precise policy prescriptions on the basis of historical knowledge, they all agree on the importance of a historical mindset – or 'sensibility' – as an aide to better-quality analysis and better-informed policymaking.

And yet the concept of applied history is nothing new. The idea that history has an applicable social and political purpose – above and beyond the study of the past for its own sake – goes back to the very foundations of the subject. It is no exaggeration to say that applied historians today represent the modern manifestation of an intellectual lineage which dates back to the historians of Ancient Greece. In each generation, historians have modelled their work on that of preceding thinkers while developing their own scholarship. Yet all the while a basic concept has remained central. It is one which, for many, constitutes the ultimate purpose of history: to understand the present by studying the past.

As the range of selections in this volume show, historians have grappled differently with the way that history interacts with the present. It was not until the twentieth century, when the professionalisation of historical methods combined with greater interest in the idea of 'public history', that the label 'applied history' was first used. It was initially coined by an American professor of political science, Benjamin F Shambaugh, who sought to articulate an operating concept in an effort to bridge the gap between scholarship and practical politics. But as Shambaugh understood, he was far from the first to wrestle with these dilemmas. Going back centuries, many scholars had not only pondered the existence and pertinence of applied history but also debated the methodology, philosophy and ethics around it. In bringing these past works to the fore and placing them together, side by side, this volume aims to introduce students, scholars and practitioners to the concept of applied history and to provide readers with a working foundation for future historical study and writing.

While applied history can take many forms – traversing all areas of policy, including social and economic history – its use in the world of diplomacy and statecraft has been particularly pronounced. Today's interest in applied history can be traced directly to great intellects of Western foreign policy during the Cold War, such as Henry Kissinger and George Kennan, who sought to place geopolitical dilemmas within a sense of the historical *longue durée*. Kissinger began his academic life with a thesis on the philosophy of history before moving into graduate work on nineteenth-century

European diplomacy. That learning would shape the time he spent in office. Kennan's biographer John Lewis Gaddis described how, on long overnight flights from Washington to Moscow, the diplomat immersed himself in Edward Gibbon's classic *The Decline and Fall of the Roman Empire.* Across those six volumes, Kennan absorbed countless insights, among them the tenuous nature of imperial control, especially when extended over distant, conquered societies.[2]

Yet the fortunes of applied historians have undulated in the decades since. The period following the end of the Cold War was not, it is now agreed, a golden era for the use of history as a lens through which to view the world. Both in the academy and in the core business of national security, at least in the perception of applied historians, the premium on traditional historical knowledge was deemed to be somewhat diluted.

In the early 2000s, one of Kennan's successors as Director of Policy Planning at the State Department, Dennis Ross, complained of a lack of historical knowledge within the upper echelons of American foreign policy.[3] As Francis Fukuyama's idea of the 'end of history' was subject to growing critique – not necessarily with full recognition of the subtlety of his thesis – so the idea of a much-needed and overdue 'return of history' began to gather pace.

In October 2016, professors Graham Allison and Niall Ferguson launched the Applied History Project at Harvard's Belfer Centre. Noting a long-standing 'history deficit' within the United States, they called for a new movement among historians and political scientists to bring more historical study to bear on pressing contemporary political and economic questions. Echoing Kennan's remarks decades before, they wrote: 'Applied historians do not have crystal balls…[but] their study of previous sharp discontinuities encourages a "historical sensibility" that is attuned to the long-term rhythms, strategic surprise, and daring coups de main that run through history.'[4]

Since 2016, the Applied History initiative has grown to include a robust transatlantic network of scholars, commentators and practitioners. University programmes from Stanford, Harvard and Johns Hopkins to King's College London, Cambridge University and the Stockholm School of Economics now host postgraduate and undergraduate fellows specialising in the relationship between history and policy. The *Journal of Applied History* was launched in the Netherlands in 2018 and boasts an editorial board from across the globe.

Up till now, however, there is no single volume that aims to link the recent revival of interest in applied history to its pre-existing lineage. This collection is an attempt to correct this by bringing together a selection of the most important contributions in the applied history tradition, chosen and edited by scholars and practitioners who are sympathetic to the idea. All of the texts included in this book are supportive of a basic premise – namely that historical study is not only useful but *essential* to understanding the present and planning for the future. When Lord Acton writes in 1895 that 'The knowledge of the past, the record of truths revealed by experience, is eminently practical, as an instrument of action and a power that goes to the making of the future', his argument is echoed by the likes of Sir Michael Howard, who wrote almost a century later: 'Far more than poets can historians claim to be the unacknowledged legislators of mankind; for all we believe about the present depends on what we believe about the past.'

At a more fundamental level, the relevance of the past to the present is, according to a number of authors included in this study, an essence of human experience. Carl Becker's essay in this volume, 'Everyman His Own Historian', argues that all individuals, as part of their daily existence, engage with historical facts on a regular basis. This obvious but fundamental fact is one that many people, including historians, often take for granted. Furthermore, past experience provides individuals with indispensable insight. Though he is not featured in this collection, the philosopher and historian R G Collingwood perhaps stated it best: 'Knowing yourself means knowing what you can do; and since nobody knows what he can do until he tries, the only clue to what man can do is what man has done. The value of history, then, is that it teaches us what man has done and thus what man is.'[5]

While those in this volume all agree on the relevance of history, applied history is a long way from being an agreed methodology. The question of *how* one learns from the past is one in which there is little agreement. For example, one of the great debates across the applied history movement concerns the selection and relevance of particular historical case studies. Any individual interested in contemporary foreign policy has inevitably encountered the analogies of Munich 1938 and the Vietnam War. These analogies, though they can serve as a window into the past, must be treated with caution. As such, Margaret MacMillan warns: 'Using the wrong one not only can present an oversimplified picture of a complex situation in the present but can lead to wrong decisions.'[6]

Another major methodological question has to do with the way that historians collect and arrange disparate facts. For scholars such as Arnold Toynbee, a central responsibility of historians was to discover generalisations, ones that could illuminate larger trends operating across decades and even centuries. If one could come to recognise such phenomena through historical study, he believed, then this knowledge would be of immeasurable value to those looking to the future.

His approach was representative of what J H Hexter criticised as 'lumping' together facts at the expense of more specific detail. As David Martin Jones points out in his introduction to Hexter's work, the latter preferred what he termed 'splitting' – in other words, the tendency, common among historians, to break down larger theories of explanation and uncover more unique detail. Similarly, John Lewis Gaddis has distinguished between the general 'particularisation' which he considers the work of social scientists and the particular generalisation' which is more the habit of historians.

Like Hexter and Gaddis, Philip Zelikow has also offered a view on this perennial methodological issue. 'Inside every judgment there are generalizations,' he has written; but he clarifies the difference between so-called 'hard' and 'soft' generalisations. Where the former represents a statement rooted in fact, the latter is based on presumption. Historians, he points out, usually break down hard generalisations, while political scientists strive to solidify soft generalisations. Rather than gleaning specific or verifiable lessons from the past, applied history may best be conceived as a *way of thinking.* Francis J Gavin describes this as 'thinking historically'. A historical mindset encourages individuals to reflect on larger systemic trends as well as the significance of the individual and unique facts. Moreover, through these lenses, the role of the contingent in history – in other words, the role of chance – looms large, and helps one factor this into their assessments and planning.

As we hope this volume will show, the study of history does not provide answers as much as approaches to confronting the major political, economic, security and social questions of our time. A sound grasp of history – specifically how other individuals and societies have navigated the challenges of their own period – is, in many ways, the invaluable intellectual foundation for approaching the future with prudence and wisdom.

John Bew, Andrew Ehrhardt and Mattias Hessérus
London, January 2022

1. George Kennan, 'The Experience of Writing History', in Stephen Vaughan, ed., *The Vital Past: Writings on the Uses of History* (Athens, GA The University of Georgia Press, 1985), here 97.

2. John Lewis Gaddis, *George F. Kennan: an American Life* (New York: Penguin, 2012), 167–169; 175–176.

3. Referenced in Graham Allison and Niall Ferguson, 'Don't Know Much About History: Why the President Needs a Council of Historical Advisers', *The Atlantic* 318:2 (2016): 28–29

4. Graham Allison and Niall Ferguson. 'Applied History Manifesto'. Paper, Belfer Center for Science and International Affairs, Harvard Kennedy School, October 2016.

5. R G Collingwood, *The Idea of History*, (Oxford: Clarendon Press, 1946), 10; also quoted in Stephen Vaughan, 'History: Is It Relevant?', in Vaughan (ed.), *The Vital Past: Writings on the Uses of History* (Athens, GA: The University of Georgia Press, 1985), 1–14, here 7.

6. Margaret MacMillan, 'History as a Guide and Friend', in *The Uses and Abuses of History* (Toronto: Viking, 2008), 153–183, here 175.

THUCYDIDES:
THE SWORD HE FORGED

INTRODUCTION BY KORI SCHAKE

This selection from the opening of Thucydides's *History of the Peloponnesian War* is not its most famous passage. The most famous part is the Melian Dialogue, wherein a weak state attempts several lines of argument to forestall its destruction by an imperial state that is justifying its oppression by making no distinction between power and right. The Melian Dialogue includes a line favoured by those seeking to justify cynical approaches to power, that 'those in positions of power do what their power permits, while the weak have no choice but to accept it.'[1]

But the passage selected here is predominantly about the tradecraft of writing history. Thucydides explains his approach to the *History*, and why he considers that approach superior. He disparages both poets ('who exaggerate the importance of their themes') and prose chroniclers ('who are less interested in telling the truth than in catching the attention of their public'), and then describes his own method: Thucydides gathers evidence, weighs its credibility by examining the motives of its protagonists, offers varying perspectives for consideration, and constructs a narrative. Evidence, a story arc and conclusions transparently arrived at. He justifies his topic selection, answering the question of why he's writing about this subject, as every historian should. Thucydides's rationale is that 'this was the greatest disturbance in the history of the Hellenes, affecting also a large part of the non-Hellenic world.'

Part of what makes Thucydides so refreshing is his honesty about the limits of his sourcing and his judgment. He acknowledges that he cannot remember the speeches exactly: 'My method has been, while keeping as closely as possible to the general sense of the words that were actually used, to make the speakers say what, in my opinion, was called for by each situation.'

The History of the Peloponnesian War teaches us that history is not determined by fate but decided by the actions and judgments of humans. It contains contradictions that suggest Thucydides's views changed over the course of writing this unfinished manuscript. If there are summary lessons to be drawn from the fulgency of the *History*, they would probably be the importance of leadership in democracy, and the double-edged sword of alliances (because it is demagogues overcoming elites that dooms Athens, and the willingness to protect weaker states that enmeshes Sparta).

The selection closes with Thucydides's oft-quoted conclusion that 'what made war inevitable was the growth of Athenian power and the fear which this caused in Sparta', which has been trumpeted as the basis for a 'Thucydides Trap', given currency by the American political scientist Graham Allison, in which war between a hegemon and a rising challenger is axiomatic, with the dominant power in the international order being blamed rather than the challenger. Yet that pat conclusion is refuted by Thucydides' own account, in which both Athens and Sparta are pushed into war by domestic disputes and Sparta responds to the pleas of weak allies for protection from a predatory Athens.

His weary resignation is palpable in acknowledging the limits of the historian's influence, since 'most people, in fact, will not take trouble in finding out the truth, but are much more inclined to accept the first story they hear.' The 'trap' in Thucydides is constricting it to a narrow interpretation, presuming there is a single lesson to be drawn from an account with kaleidoscopic changes in colour and geometry. What Thucydides recounts is a history of changing perspectives: people retell history differently for their own purposes.

That Thucydides refutes his own conclusion circles back to the beginning of his opening sentence: 'Thucydides the Athenian wrote the history of the war.' Even that great founder of history as an academic discipline struggled for objectivity. Thucydides describes himself as an Athenian – a partisan in the conflict, a leader whose failure to protect Amphipolis consigned him to exile from his home. Thucydides himself taught us to weigh the motives of sources, so it is not surprising that his Athenian loyalty would see him blame Sparta for the outbreak of a war that his own history makes clear was much more contingent and complicated than his oft-quoted summation.

Thucydides's account of the Peloponnesian War remains a classic because he taught us how to be historians. In recounting the events of twenty years of conflict that destroyed the societies of both its principal antagonists, he illuminates enduring truths about human nature, governance and the behaviour of states. But his own conclusions about the history of the Peloponnesian War are struck down by the sword he forged, called into question by the very method that he taught us – namely that of examining the evidence and assessing the motives of sources when crafting history.

Washington, DC, February 2022

---

1.   Johanna Hanink translation, 2019.

THUCYDIDES
HISTORY OF THE
PELOPONNESIAN WAR

Book One

INTRODUCTION

1. Thucydides the Athenian wrote the history of the war fought between Athens and Sparta, beginning the account at the very outbreak of the war, in the belief that it was going to be a great war and more worth writing about than any of those which had taken place in the past. My belief was based on the fact that the two sides were at the very height of their power and preparedness, and I saw, too, that the rest of the Hellenic world was committed to one side or the other; even those who were not immediately engaged were deliberating on the courses which they were to take later. This was the greatest disturbance in the history of the Hellenes, affecting also a large part of the non-Hellenic world, and indeed, I might almost say, the whole of mankind. For though I have found it impossible, because of its remoteness in time, to acquire a really precise knowledge of the distant past or even of the history preceding our own period, yet, after looking back into it as far as I can, all the evidence leads me to conclude that these periods were not great periods either in warfare or in anything else.

[…]

20. In investigating past history, and in forming the conclusions which I have formed, it must be admitted that one cannot rely on every detail which has come down to us by way of tradition. People are inclined to accept all stories of ancient times in an uncritical way – even when these stories concern their own native countries.

Most people in Athens, for instance, are under the impression that Hipparchus, who was killed by Harmodius and Aristogeiton, was tyrant at the time, not realising that it was Hippias who was the eldest and the chief of the sons of Pisistratus, and that Hipparchus and Thessalus were his younger brothers. What happened was this: on the very day that had been fixed for their attempt, indeed at the very last moment, Harmodius and Aristogeiton had reason to believe that Hippias had been informed of the plot by some of the conspirators. Believing him to have been forewarned, they kept away from him, but, as they wanted to perform some daring exploit before they were arrested themselves, they killed Hipparchus when they found him by the Leocorium organising the Panathenaic procession.[1]

The rest of the Hellenes, too, make many incorrect assumptions not only about the dimly remembered past, but also about contemporary history. For instance, there is a general belief that the kings of Sparta are each entitled to two votes, whereas in fact they have only one; and it is believed, too, that the Spartans have a company of troops called 'Pitanate'. Such a company has never existed. Most people, in fact, will not take trouble in finding out the truth, but are much more inclined to accept the first story they hear.[2]

21. However, I do not think that one will be far wrong in accepting the conclusions I have reached from the evidence which I have put forward. It is better evidence than that of the poets, who exaggerate the importance of their themes, or of the prose chroniclers, who are less interested in telling the truth than in catching the attention of their public, whose authorities cannot be checked, and whose subject matter, owing to the passage of time, is mostly lost in the unreliable streams of mythology. We may claim instead to have used only the plainest evidence and to have reached conclusions which are reasonably accurate, considering that we have been dealing with ancient history, As for this present war, even though people are apt to think that the war in which they are fighting is the greatest of all wars and, when it is over, to relapse again

into their admiration of the past, nevertheless, if one looks at the facts themselves, one will see that this was the greatest war of all.

22. In this history I have made use of set speeches, some of which were delivered just before and others during the war. I have found it difficult to remember the precise words used in the speeches which I listened to myself and my various informants have experienced the same difficulty; so my method has been, while keeping as closely as possible to the general sense of the words that were actually used, to make the speakers say what, in my opinion, was called for by each situation.[3]

And with regard to my factual reporting of the events of the war I have made it a principle not to write down the first story that came my way, and not even to be guided by my own general impressions; either I was present myself at the events which I have described or else I heard of them from eyewitnesses whose reports I have checked with as much thoroughness as possible. Not that even so the truth was easy to discover: different eyewitnesses give different accounts of the same events, speaking out of partiality for one side or the other or else from imperfect memories. And it may well be that my history will seem less easy to read because of the absence in it of a romantic element. It will be enough for me, however, if these words of mine are judged useful by those who want to understand clearly the events which happened in the past and which (human nature being what it is) will, at some time or other and in much the same ways, be repeated in the future. My work is not a piece of writing designed to meet the taste of an immediate public, but was done to last for ever.

23. The greatest war in the past was the Persian War; yet in this war the decision was reached quickly as a result of two naval battles and two battles on land. The Peloponnesian War, on the other hand, not only lasted for a long time, but throughout its course brought with it unprecedented suffering for Hellas. Never before had so many cities been captured and then devastated, whether by foreign armies or by the Hellenic powers themselves (some of these

cities, after capture, were resettled with new inhabitants); never had there been so many exiles; never such loss of life – both in the actual warfare and in internal revolutions. Old stories of past prodigies, which had not found much confirmation in recent experience, now became credible. Wide areas, for instance, were affected by violent earthquakes; there were more frequent eclipses of the sun than had ever been recorded before; in various parts of the country there were extensive droughts followed by famine; and there was the plague which did more harm and destroyed more life than almost any other single factor. All these calamities fell together upon the Hellenes after the outbreak of war.

War began when the Athenians and the Peloponnesians broke the Thirty Years' Truce, which had been made after the capture of Euboca.[4] As to the reasons why they broke the truce, I propose first to give an account of the causes of complaint which they had against each other and of the specific instances where their interests clashed: this is in order that there should be no doubt in anyone's mind about what led to this great war falling upon the Hellenes. But the real reason for the war is, in my opinion, most likely to be disguised by such an argument. What made war inevitable was the growth of Athenian power and the fear which this caused in Sparta. As for the reasons for breaking the truce and declaring war which were openly expressed by each side, they are as follows.

Translated by Rex Warner

---

1. In vi, there is a lengthy digression on the assassination of Hipparchus in 514 BC.
2. See the Introduction.
3. See the Introduction.
4. In 446–445 B.C.

POLYBIUS:
THE FATHER OF PRAGMATIKÉ HISTORIA

INTRODUCTION BY ISKANDER REHMAN

Polybius was born around 200 BC in the town of Megalopolis into an aristocratic family of some repute. At the time, Megalopolis was part of the Achaean Confederacy, a grouping of Greek city states which, along with the Aetolian League in north-central Greece, had coalesced to counterbalance the might of a revitalised Macedonian monarchy. Polybius's father had served as the *strategos* – or top elected official – of the Achaean Confederacy several times throughout the 180s BC, and in 170 BC the 30-year-old future historian was elected to the position of *hipparchos*, or cavalry commander, the second highest office in the confederacy. While in office, he struggled to preserve a modicum of Achaean autonomy, gingerly walking a fine line between nominally supporting Rome's war efforts against Macedon, and a tacit policy of neutrality. This quest for an awkward equilibrium cruelly backfired when, at the end of the Third Macedonian War, he was accused of anti-Roman conduct and unceremoniously bundled, along with about a thousand other Achaeans, onto a ship bound for Italy.

It was over the course of his 17 years in captivity that Polybius set to the monumental task of writing his history of Rome's meteoric rise to prominence. As stated in this introductory excerpt, he initially intended to cover the period from 220 BC – the beginning of the so-called Social Wars (220 BC–217 BC) in Greece – to 167 BC and Rome's victory in the Third Macedonian War, which in his mind marked the final and definitive subjection of the patchwork of feuding Greek statelets to Roman primacy. Like many a scholar self-entangled in the thickening web of his own research design, Polybius soon realised that he needed to revise the scope of the project, both going further back and ranging further forward. The final version of *The Histories* thus commences in the years leading up to the First Punic War (264–241 BC), coming to a suitably climactic end a full 120 years later, with the grim destruction of both Carthage and Corinth in 146 BC. *The Histories* were undeniably a mammoth achievement – they comprised 40 volumes of which five books survive in full, along with portions, some still quite extensive, of other volumes.

Although Polybius was widely appreciated in the ancient world, his influence arguably reached its apogee in the wake of his rediscovery in early fifteenth-century Florence. Polybius came to be viewed not only as a precious source of knowledge on the Punic and Macedonian Wars, but also as an invaluable guide to 'prudence' in statecraft and, perhaps most importantly, to effective military strategy and organisation. With his lengthy, technical digressions on issues ranging from fire-signalling to regimental spacing, Polybius can be justly considered the finest 'military historian of not just Greece but of all of Antiquity'.[1]

Polybius's most significant and lasting legacy, however, lies in the realm of political theory. His organicist concept of *anacyclosis*, – a complex process which unfolds as a *politeia* rotates through three separate conditions – monarchy, aristocracy and democracy – along with each of their corrupted forms (tyranny, oligarchy and ochlocracy, or mob rule), was deemed hugely compelling, and its intellectual vestiges can be found strewn across the historiographical frameworks of thinkers as varied as Hegel, Marx or Toynbee.

In Book VI of *The Histories*, Polybius famously argued that Rome's unique constitutional compound, alloyed from the more untarnished elements of all three principal forms of government, had shielded it from the oxidising process of *anacyclosis*. For the historian, great power competition was fundamentally a two-level game, and Rome's imperial success was directly linked to the solidity of its internal political arrangement, which maintained it in a state of delicate equilibrium, 'like a well-trimmed boat'. To say that Polybius's theories on the virtues of a mixed constitution with checks and balances were impactful would be an understatement. Over the course of the centuries, they decisively shaped the writings of – among others – Machiavelli, Montesquieu and the American Founding Fathers.

For students of applied history and grand strategy, Polybius remains of enduring value, and this is for several reasons. First, and most obviously, because his works constitute by far the most reliable and granular repository of information on the Punic Wars – one of the earliest and best documented examples of a bipolar, protracted and genuinely cross-regional great power competition. And despite the occasionally crabbed character of his prose, which, one classicist quips, sometimes has the unadorned dryness of a memorandum hastily dispatched from a Hellenistic chancellery, *The Histories* make for a gripping and entertaining read.[2] Much of this has to do with Polybius's meticulous attention to detail, and with his famously nuanced approach to the study of human decision-making – an altogether rare combination of intellectual subtlety and psychological sensitivity which he shares with Thucydides.

Second, Polybius is worth reading for the sophistication of his multi-level analysis of causation, and most notably for his intense emphasis on the need for analysts to learn how to differentiate between a great power conflict's *prophasis* (πρόφασις), ie its simple pretexts or excuses and its *aitia* (αἰτία), ie its much deeper underlying causes. When seeking explanations or assigning blame for such dread conflagrations, the political historian must be clear-eyed, scrupulous and relentless in the pursuit of truth: rejecting parsimonious theories, charily weighing competing arguments and diving with unabashed relish into the meandering complexities of diplomatic history. It was this combination of moral even-handedness and sound judgment that so endeared Polybius to just war theorists such as Hugo Grotius, who memorably portrayed him as the first historian to establish clear-cut distinctions between a righteous cause for war and merely a persuasive argument.

Third, Polybius is perhaps the most unsparingly practical of all ancient historians, espousing a uniquely symbiotic approach to historical learning and statesmanship. Not only, as this excerpt demonstrates, did he view the study of *'pragmatiké historia'* as an essential prerequisite for any aspiring statesman, he would also later argue that all historians, prior to taking up their pens, should have had some experience in government, and preferably in waging war.

Finally, Polybius's concept of *symploke* (συμπλοκή) – literally the study of the *interweaving* of events – will resonate most deeply with contemporary students of grand strategy, already accustomed to scrying the riotous flow of world affairs with the hope of spotting, amid its eddying whirls, underlying currents of cause and effect. The historian famously notes in the opening to the *Histories* that with Rome's rise as the great power arbiter across the Mediterranean, he had witnessed the advent of a new form of *'universal'* history, one which had forcibly meshed formerly disparate sub-theatres together, and which therefore required the budding historian to take a more synoptic view of geopolitical developments.

Only a century earlier, Aristotle had argued that as history consisted all too often in a simple catalogue of disaggregated events, it was eternally condemned to remain an inferior genre to poetry, which possessed a more pleasingly unified structure and was thus vested with a greater degree of intellectual coherence. Major events in different theatres could certainly be synchronous, the Stagirite observed, but in a fractured, multipolar world this did not mean that they were interlinked in any way.

For example, it was commonly believed since Herodotus that the Battle of Himera (pitting the Western Mediterranean Greeks against the Carthaginians in Sicily) and the naval confrontation of Salamis (involving the Eastern Mediterranean Greeks versus the Persians) had unfolded on the very same day in 480 BC. And yet, Aristotle contended in *Poetics*, one would be hard pressed to point to both conflicts' interactive effects, as they had 'occurred simultaneously without in any way tending towards the same end; in exactly the same way one thing may follow another in succession over a period of time without their producing a single result'. For Polybius, however, these assertions no longer held true – while the world of his ancestors may have possessed a 'disseminated' or 'sporadic' character, with 'no more unity of conception and of execution than unity of place', history had now begun to reweave itself into a more 'organic whole'.

If a violent storm now erupted in one conflict-lashed corner of the Mediterranean basin, its chill wind would, sooner or later, reach the other. It was time for a new approach – one which eschewed siloed approaches and 'partial histories', and which also took care to record parallel events across interlocking theatres, which, 'as points of reference and comparison' would then allow historians 'to draw conclusions at a different level'.

And therein lies, no doubt, the most intriguing and stimulating aspect of Polybian thought for the reader of this volume: his clear focus on chains of causation, his close attention to the interconnections between theatres, actions and events, and his refreshing ability to analyse history horizontally as well as vertically. 'One can get some idea of a whole from a part,' he sagely avers, 'but never knowledge or exact opinion.' Whether one is a practically minded historian or a historically minded practitioner (and ideally for Polybius one should aspire over the course of one's lifetime to be both) one should be prepared to continuously sift through the warp and weft of historical events, with the aim of discerning amid its jumble of tangled threads the patterns of cause and effect.

Only then, he suggests, will one's intellectual efforts prove truly worthwhile, and of use to the broader *polis*.

Washington, DC, March 2022

---

1. William Kendrick Pritchett, *Studies in Ancient Greek Topography*, vol. 4 (University of California, Berkeley, CA, 1950), 37.

2. Craige Champion, *Cultural Politics in Polybius' Histories* (University of California Press, Berkeley, CA, 2004), 21.

POLYBIUS
THE HISTORIES

Book One

1. If earlier historians had failed to eulogise history itself, it would, I suppose, be up to me to begin by encouraging everyone to occupy himself in an open-minded way with works like this one, on the grounds that there is no better corrective of human behaviour than knowledge of past events. But in fact it is hardly an exaggeration to say that all of my predecessors (not just a few) have made this central to their work (not just a side issue), by claiming not only that there is no more authentic way to prepare and train oneself for political life than by studying history, but also that there is no more comprehensible and comprehensive teacher of the ability to endure with courage the vicissitudes of Fortune than a record of others' catastrophes.

Obviously, then, the general principle that no one should feel obliged to repeat what has often been well said before is particularly pertinent in my case. For the extraordinary nature of the events I decided to write about is in itself enough to interest everyone, young or old, in my work, and make them want to read it. After all, is there anyone on earth who is so narrow-minded or uninquisitive that he could fail to want to know how and thanks to what kind of political system almost the entire known world was conquered and brought under a single empire, the empire of the Romans, in less than fifty-three years[1] – an unprecedented event?

Or again, is there anyone who is so passionately attached to some other marvel or matter that he could consider it more important than knowing about this?

2. The extraordinary and spectacular nature of the subject I propose to consider would become particularly evident if we were to compare and contrast the most famous empires of the past – the ones that have earned the most attention from writers – with the supremacy of the Romans. The empires that deserve to be compared and contrasted in this way are the following.[2] The Persians once held sway over a huge realm, but whenever they endeavoured to go beyond the boundaries of Asia, they endangered not just their rule, but their very existence. The Spartans strove for leadership of the Greeks for a long time and achieved it, but maintained a secure grip on it for barely twelve years. Although in Europe Macedonian dominion extended only from the Adriatic region to the Danube – nothing but a tiny fraction, you might think, of this continent – they later gained control of Asia too, by overthrowing the Persian Empire; but despite the view that never had more places, nor greater power, been in the hands of a single state, they still left most of the known world in others' hands. They made not the slightest attempt, for example, to take over Sicily, Sardinia and Libya, and they were, to put it bluntly, completely unaware of the existence of the extremely warlike peoples of western Europe. The Romans, however, have made themselves masters of almost the entire known world, not just some bits of it, and have left such a colossal empire that no one alive today can resist it and no one in the future will be able to overcome it. My work will make it possible to understand more clearly how the empire was gained, and no reader will be left in doubt about the many important benefits to be gained from reading political history.

3. In terms of time, my work will start with the 140th Olympiad.[3] In terms of events, it will start with the so-called Social War in Greece,[4] the first war fought by Philip V, the son of Demetrius II and father of Perseus, in which he fought the Aetolians, with the

Achaeans as his allies; and it will start with the war for Coele Syria in Asia, fought between Antiochus III and Ptolemy IV Philopator; and with the clash between the Romans and Carthaginians in Italy and Libya, which is usually called the Hannibalic War. Aratus of Sicyon's book[5] ended just before these events.

Before this time, things happened in the world pretty much in a sporadic fashion, because every incident was specific, from start to finish, to the part of the world where it happened. But ever since then history has resembled a body, in the sense that incidents in Italy and Libya and Asia and Greece are all interconnected, and everything tends towards a single outcome. That is why I have made this period the starting point of my treatment of world events. For once the Romans had defeated the Carthaginians in the Hannibalic War, they came to think that they had completed the largest and most difficult part of their project of worldwide dominion, and so that was the first time when they ventured to reach out for what was left – to cross over with an army to Greece and Asia.

Now, if we were familiar and acquainted with the states that disputed universal rulership with each other, there would, I suppose, have been no need for me to go back in time and describe what their goals and resources were when they took on such an immense task. But since most Greeks are unfamiliar with the past history – the resources and achievements – of either Rome or Carthage,[6] I felt obliged to preface my history with this and the following book, to make sure that no one would have to interrupt his absorption in my account of events to wonder and enquire what the Romans' intentions were, or what forces and resources they had, when they committed themselves to this enterprise, which has given them dominion over all the land and sea in our part of the world. By means of these two books and the introduction they contain, I hope to make it clear to any reader that the whole process, from formulation of plans to their fulfilment in imperial rulership over the whole world, was based on very reasonable grounds.

4. The point is that the distinctive feature of my work (which is at the same time the remarkable feature of our epoch) is this: Fortune has turned almost all the events of the known world in a single direction and has forced everything to tend towards the same goal. A historian, then, should use his work to bring under a single conspectus for his readers the means by which Fortune has brought everything to this point. In fact, it was this in particular that originally prompted me to set about writing history – and then also the fact that no one else in our times has attempted to write a universal history, because otherwise I would have been far less inclined to do so. But I saw that most historians had concerned themselves with particular wars and with certain of the events that went along with them, while no one, as far as I knew, had even attempted to investigate the general, comprehensive organisation of events, in the sense of asking when and why this scheme of things started, and how it was realised. And so I came to believe that it was absolutely essential for me not to overlook or leave in obscurity the finest thing Fortune has ever achieved, and the one from which we can learn most. For although Fortune is a constant presence in people's lives, and though it is often creative, never before has it produced such an accessible piece or put on the kind of performance that it has in our time.

It is impossible to gain this comprehensive perspective from writers of partial histories. That is the same as thinking that all it takes instantly to grasp the form of the whole world, and its order and arrangement in their entirety, is to visit, one by one, each of its outstanding cities – or, indeed, to look at sketches of them! Imagine people who think that looking at the scattered parts of a once living and beautiful body is all they need to do to witness the energy and beauty of the actual living creature: it seems to me that those who are convinced that they can gain a comprehensive and general perspective with the help of partial histories are in pretty much the same situation. After all, if one could then and there put the living creature back together again and make it whole (in respect not just of its physical appearance, but also of its charm as an animate creature), and show it to these people, I am sure they would all quickly agree that before they had had as tenuous a grasp of reality as dreamers. For while it may be possible to get an *impression* of the whole from a part, it is impossible to gain knowledge and precise understanding. So we are bound to conclude that partial histories are more or less useless when it comes to gaining a comprehensive perspective, and are unreliable. On the contrary, it is only by connecting and comparing *all* the parts with one another, by seeing their similarities and differences – it is only such an overview that puts one in a position to derive benefit and pleasure from history.

[…]

Leaving aside the fact that this approach makes his work undignified and sentimental, let us consider the proper qualities and functions of history. A historian should not use his narrative to astound his readers with sensationalism, nor should he make up plausible speeches and list all the possible consequences of events. A historian should leave these things to tragic poets, and should focus exclusively on what was actually done and said, even if some of these facts are rather unexciting. History and tragedy do not serve the same purposes. On the contrary, it is the job of a tragic poet to astound and entertain his audience for a moment by means of the most convincing words he can find, but it is the job of a historian to instruct and persuade his readers for all time by means of deeds that actually took place and words that were actually spoken. The object in the first case is to create a plausible fiction in order to beguile an audience, in the second case to write what is true in order to educate the reader.

Translated by Robin Waterfield

1. *in less than fifty-three years*: Polybius is referring to the period from the beginning of the Second Punic War – which he thinks started with Hannibal's siege of Saguntum in 219 BC – to the end of the Third Macedonian War in 168/67 BC, when Rome defeated Perseus and abolished the Macedonian monarchy. Although there were many conquests still to come, Polybius had good grounds for regarding 167 BC as the date which marked the establishment of Roman rule in the Mediterranean.

2. *The empires that deserve to be compared…are the following*: the Persian Empire was established under Cyrus (559–529 BC) and overstepped its Asian boundaries, as Polybius says, when Darius invaded Greece in 490 BC and was defeated at the Battle of Marathon, and when Xerxes tried again in 480/79 BC, only to meet with disaster at the battles of Salamis and Plataea; Alexander the Great's victories, and accession as Great King in 330 BC, marked the end of the Persian Empire. Polybius dates Sparta's period of rule from her victory over the Athenians in the Peloponnesian War at the Battle of Aegospotami (405 BC) to her defeat by the Athenian admiral, Conon, at the Battle of Cnidus (394 BC). Macedonian supremacy, established by Philip and Alexander, is probably thought of as coming to an end with Rome's victory over the Seleucid king, Antiochus III, at the Battle of Magnesia in 189 BC.

3. *the 140th Olympiad*: the Olympiad dating system was based on the four years between celebrations of the Olympic Games, starting with Olympiad 1, 776–772 BC: Olympiad 1.1 = 776/5 (an Olympiad year did not coincide exactly with a modern year), Olympiad 1.2 = 775/4, Olympiad 1.3 = 774/3, Olympiad 1.4 = 773/2, Olympiad 2.1 = 772/1 etc.

4. *the so-called Social War in Greece*: the main protagonists in the largely indecisive Social War, which lasted from 220 to 217 BC, were, on one side, Philip V of Macedon with his Achaean allies, and, on the other, the Aetolian League (the federation of north-west Greek states that controlled central Greece). The Fourth Syrian War (219–217 BC), part of a continuing frontier dispute between the Seleucid and Ptolemaic empires – Coele Syria was roughly the area of modern Lebanon, southern Syria, northern Israel – was fought between Ptolemy IV Philopator of Egypt and Antiochus III of Syria: to everyone's surprise the indolent Philopator won a great victory at the Battle of Raphia in 217 BC.

5. *Aratus of Sicyon's book*: Aratus of Sicyon (271–213 BC) was one of the great leaders of the Achaean League. His *Memoirs* in at least thirty books do not survive, but were evidently used by Polybius for what he says about the earlier history of the League (2.38–70). It was traditional for a historian to identify himself as the continuator of a distinguished predecessor (as Xenophon did of Thucydides – Hellenica 1.1).

6. *But since most Greeks are unfamiliar with the past history…of either Rome or Carthage*: Polybius' justification for writing the first two introductory books is that his Greek audience would not know the Roman and Carthaginian background. He offers no explanation, however, for the fact that almost half of Book 2 is devoted to the earlier history of the Achaean League and Greek affairs.

NICCOLÒ MACHIAVELLI:
THE MORAL
CONSTITUTIONALIST

INTRODUCTION BY PHILIP BOBBITT

It is difficult to overstate the importance of publishing translations from Machiavelli's two great works, *The Prince* and the *Discourses on the First Ten Books of Livy*, side by side in one volume. Taken together in this way, they resolve many of the false paradoxes that have long characterised the misunderstanding of Machiavelli's work.

Like the *Discourses*, *The Prince* is fundamentally a constitutional treatise, composed at about the same time. The first book discusses republics; the second treats principalities. They should be seen as two parts of one great essay on the emerging modern state.

In both books, Machiavelli suggests that a state is best founded by a single leader, but the *Discourses* confirms that republics are Machiavelli's preferred form of regime. Indeed, Machiavelli began the *Discourses* as a defence of the republican form of government, a defence, that is, of the Florentine experiment of which he had been a senior official and which had collapsed. With the fortuitous advent of a Medici pope whose brother controlled Florence, however, Machiavelli saw the opportunity to unite the Papal States and the vicarages of the Romagna with Florence and its possessions, thus creating in the centre of Italy a state capable of resisting the invasions of Spain, France and the Empire. He therefore stopped work on the *Discourses* – evidence for which is his statement in *The Prince* that he will not deal with republics in that book, having already written on the subject – and began a shorter treatise not on princes but, as he tells us, on principalities.

Perhaps the most entrenched mischaracterisation of Machiavelli's writings is that they are the work of a committed lover of authoritarianism. Is not his most famous work, *The Prince*, named for the ruler? After all, who could be further from a republican constitutionalist than the author of 'it is better to be feared than loved'?

Except that Machiavelli did not title his book *The Prince*; that was done posthumously by a publisher. Machiavelli's title was *Of Principalities*. This is not an idle point: Machiavelli was writing a treatise on the different kinds of state, not chiefly a 'mirror book' meant to instruct princes about their manners and morals.

Seeing the two works as parts of the same whole leaves little doubt as to Machiavelli's preferred form of regime (which was also Livy's). If there remains any doubt as to his true convictions, one need only consult the two draft constitutions for Florence, written by Machiavelli at the requests of the Medici popes Leo X and Giulio de Medici, the latter of which who became Clement VII. Both proposals, written two years apart, are explicitly republican and indeed demand that the Medici relinquish their pre-eminent role in the governance of Florence – a rather brave refutation of the charge that *The Prince* is really no more than an employment application to the Medici.

Moreover, understanding Machiavelli's project as supremely constitutionalist – and Machiavelli as the prophet of the coming modern state – also helps us resolve some of the false impressions about Machiavelli's ethical and moral views. Among his contemporaries and for many centuries, the desired moral code of the ruler had depended upon the observance of the classical and Christian virtues. Following these would lead to political success. Departing from this idea earned Machiavelli a good deal of opprobrium as a kind of demon, but would an amoralist have written the following?

[It] cannot be called *virtu* to murder one's fellow citizens, to betray allies, to act without faith, pity or religion.[1]

The portrayal of Machiavelli as a 'teacher of evil' is grounded in his rejection of the classical moral ideal but also in a refusal to appreciate what Machiavelli wished to put in its place and why he felt it imperative to do so.

Machiavelli sought to reify the state as an entity with its own reality, a reality that was not simply the personal power of the prince. (Today the term 'state' is often used as little more than a synonym for government; how much is lost when we refuse to conceptualise the state as a distinct apparatus of power and when we fail to appreciate Machiavelli as the originator of this line of thought.) This led to Machiavelli's great insight that officials must disregard their personal moral codes in carrying out the duties of the state. This emphatically did not mean that rulers were unfettered. Both principalities and republics 'need to be regulated by laws, because a prince who can do simply as he wishes is crazed, and a people who can do whatever it wishes is imprudent'.[2] The moral duty of the republican constitutionalist arises from the responsibility that an official owes to protect the interests of the state and to carry out the decisions of the republic as expressed in constitutional forms. He must follow a precise moral code, one that subordinates his personal interests in favour of serving the public good.

In light of recent scholarship – I have in mind especially the work of Maurizio Viroli, and also Erica Benner – and what I hope will be greater study given to Machiavelli's two proposed constitutions, it ought to be easier now to resolve some of the famous debates about Machiavelli: Was he a forthright totalitarian or a rights-respecting republican? Was he a Christian or a pagan? Did he give priority to the lawgiver or the war fighter? Was he essentially an ethical writer or an unabashed amoralist? Was he attempting to do for statecraft what Galileo sought to do for cosmology or was he a committed sceptic where prediction is concerned? Did he believe that the affairs of mankind were cyclical or that there was a decisive role for individual free will?

Of course, Machiavelli was not the only thinker of his time to glimpse the future that would destroy feudal Europe. It is notable that Thomas More's *Utopia* and Martin Luther's *95 Theses* were published at about the same time as Machiavelli's great works. But for us today, despite the profound misunderstanding, even caricature, of Machiavelli that has prevailed for so long, it is he, above all his contemporaries, who speaks to us. Consider the claim that Machiavelli was an advocate for the idea that history repeats itself.

Many celebrated historians – Vico and Polybius, and in the twentieth century, Spengler, Toynbee and Kondratieff – are described as arguing that there are historical cycles. Polybius, for example, alarmed the framers of the American Constitution with his conclusion that inevitably democracies decay into anarchy, to be replaced by monarchies that deteriorate into tyrannies, that are replaced by aristocracies that become oligarchies and are removed in favour of democracies, and so on.

But this is not quite Machiavelli's view. He did believe in historical cycles,[3] but with one important caveat that marks him as a modern.

Consider the bicycle. Put a white dot on one of the tyres and then move the bicycle, thus rotating the tyre, and the white dot will always return to its original position. So it is with cyclical theories of history. But notice that the bicycle has to move – it has to go to a new place for the wheel to turn. For a cycle of history to return, it must take place in new circumstances. This was Machiavelli's theory of history. To rephrase Ovid, we might say, 'For nothing to perish, everything must change.'

Finally, there is a claim, generally accepted without demurrer, that *The Prince* is a 'mirror book', a treatise that prescribes the proper deportment of a prince. Cicero's *De Officiis* is the classical model, but there are countless examples. Much of *The Prince* can thus be described with some relish because Machiavelli appears to turn Cicero's advice on its head. But reading *The Prince* this way encourages us to ignore its more significant constitutional dimensions that comprise more than half the book, and its important relation to *The Discourses* (putting aside the awkward fact that, as Viroli has noted, there is no definitive evidence that Machiavelli ever read *De Officiis*).

That constitutionalism is the basis for Machiavelli's stated aim to establish 'new modes and orders',[4] and his warning that

> One always ought to remember that there is nothing more difficult to undertake, nor more dangerous to administer, nor more unlikely to succeed, than to introduce a new political order.[5]

Machiavelli's important and original insights about the constitutional order of the state – which were ignored in his lifetime and misconstrued so often since – rebut the false descriptions and the contradictions those mischaracterisations engender. Publishing these extracts from his greatest works side by side is a hopeful step in that direction.

London, July 2022

---

1. Niccolò Machiavelli, *The Prince*, Chapter 8.
2. Machiavelli, *Discourses on the First Ten Books of Livy I*, Chapter 58.
3. Ibid.
4. Ibid.
5. Machiavelli, *The Prince*, Chapter 6.

NICCOLÒ MACHIAVELLI
THE DISCOURSES

Book One

THE DEVELOPMENT OF ROME'S CONSTITUTION

The Preface

Although owing to the envy inherent in man's nature it has always been no less dangerous to discover new ways and methods than to set off in search of new seas and unknown lands because most men are much more ready to belittle than to praise another's actions, none the less, impelled by the natural desire I have always had to labour, regardless of anything, on that which I believe to be for the common benefit of all, I have decided to enter upon a new way, as yet untrodden by anyone else. And, even if it entails a tiresome and difficult task, it may yet reward me in that there are those who will look kindly on the purpose of these my labours. And if my poor ability, my limited experience of current affairs, my feeble knowledge of antiquity, should render my efforts imperfect and of little worth, they may none the less point the way for another of greater ability, capacity for analysis and judgment, who will achieve my ambition; which, if it does not earn me praise, should not earn me reproaches.

When, therefore, I consider in what honour antiquity is held, and how – to cite but one instance – a bit of an old statue has fetched a high price that someone may have it by him to give honour to his house and that it may be possible for it to be copied by those who are keen on this art; and how the latter then with great industry take pains to reproduce it in all their works; and when, on the other hand, I notice that what history has to say about the highly virtuous actions performed by ancient kingdoms and republics, by their kings, their generals, their citizens, their legislators, and by others who have gone to the trouble of serving their country, is rather admired than imitated; nay, is so shunned by everybody in each little thing they do, that of the virtue of bygone days there remains no trace, it cannot but fill me at once with astonishment and grief. The more so when I see that in the civic dispute which arise between citizens and in the diseases men get, they always have recourse to decisions laid down by the ancients and to the prescriptions they drew up. For the civil law is nothing but a collection of decisions, made by jurists of old, which the jurists of today have tabulated in orderly fashion for our instruction. Nor, again, is medicine anything but a record of experiments, performed by doctors of old, upon which the doctors of our day base their prescriptions. In spite of which in constituting republics, in maintaining states, in governing kingdoms, in forming an army or conducting a war, in dealing with subjects, in extending the empire, one finds neither prince nor republic who repairs to antiquity for examples.

This is due in my opinion not so much to the weak state to which the religion of today has brought the world, or to the evil wrought in many provinces and cities of Christendom by ambition conjoined with idleness, as to the lack of a proper appreciation of history, owing to people failing to realise the significance of what they read, and to their having no taste for the delicacies it comprises. Hence it comes about that the great bulk of those who read it take pleasure in hearing of the various incidents which are contained in it, but never think of imitating them, since they hold them to be not merely difficult but impossible of imitation, as if the heaven, the sun, the elements and man had in their motion, their order and potency become different from what they used to be.

Since I want to get men out of this wrong way of thinking, I have thought fit to write a commentary on all those books of Titus Livy which have not by the malignity of time had their continuity broken.[1] It will comprise what I have arrived at by comparing ancient with modern events, and think necessary for the better understanding of them, so that those who read what I have to say may the more easily draw those practical lessons which one should seek to obtain from the study of history. Though the enterprise is difficult, yet, with the help of those who have encouraged me to undertake the task, I think I can carry it out in such a way that there shall remain to another but a short road to traverse in order to reach the place assigned.

39. To Different Peoples the Same Sort of Thing Is Often Found to Happen

If the present be compared with the remote past, it is easily seen that in all cities and in all peoples there are the same desires and the same passions as there always were. So that, if one examines with diligence the past, it is easy to foresee the future of any commonwealth, and to apply those remedies which were used of old; or, if one does not find that remedies were used, to devise new ones owing to the similarity between events. But, since such studies are neglected and what is read is not understood, or, if it be understood, is not applied in practice by those who rule, the consequence is that similar troubles occur at all times.

Since the city of Florence after '94 lost part of its dominions, eg Pisa and other towns, it had to make war on those who had occupied them. And, because those who had occupied them were powerful, the result of the war was considerable expense and no fruit; from the expense there resulted heavy taxation; and from the heavy taxation endless complaints by the populace. Since this war was administered by a magistracy consisting of ten citizens, called 'the Ten of War', the public in general began to be disgusted with it in that it was responsible both for the war and for the expense. They were convinced that, if this magistracy was abolished, there would be an end to the war; so, when the time came to re-elect it, instead of making new appointments they let it lapse, and entrusted their affairs to the Signoria. This decision was so disastrous that not only did it fail to stop the war, as the public in general had expected, but it removed the very men who had been administering it wisely, and led to such confusion that, in addition to Pisa, Arezzo was lost, and many other places. Consequently the people repented their mistake, and since the cause of the trouble was the malady, not the doctor, they reappointed the magistracy of the Ten.

The same passion was aroused in Rome by the title of consul. For, when the people saw one war following on another, and that they never got any rest, they ought to have ascribed it to the ambition of neighbours who were seeking to crush them, whereas they thought it was due to the ambition of nobles who, unable to chastise the plebs within the state where they were protected by the power of the tribunes, were anxious for them to be led forth under consuls that they might oppress them where there was no one to help. For this reason they thought it necessary either to abolish the consuls, or so to regulate their power that they should have no authority over the populace either abroad or at home. The first to propose such a law was Terentillus, a tribune. He proposed that five men should be appointed to investigate the consular power and to set limits to it. This incensed the nobles not a little, for it looked to them as if the majesty of government would vanish altogether, and that to the nobility there would no longer remain any status in the republic. The obstinacy of the tribunes was none the less such that the title as consul was abolished, and, after certain other ordinances had been made, they were at length content to appoint tribunes with consular power instead of consuls, so that what they had really hated was the title rather than the authority of the consuls. This custom was observed for a long time, but at length, realising their mistake, they again appointed consuls, just as the Florentines returned to the 'Ten'.

Book Three

FURTHER REFLECTIONS BASED ON THE SAMNITE WARS

43. That Men Who Are Born in the Same Country Display throughout the Ages Much the Same Characteristics

Prudent men are wont to say – and this not rashly or without good ground – that he who would foresee what has to be, should reflect on what has been, for everything that happens in the world at any time has a genuine resemblance to what happened in ancient times. This is due to the fact that the agents who bring such things about are men, and that men have, and always have had, the same passions, whence it necessarily comes about that the same effects are produced. It is true that men's deeds are sometimes more virtuous in this country than in that, and in that than in some other, according to the type of education from which their inhabitants have derived their mode of life.

Knowledge of the future based on the past is also facilitated when we find a nation which for a long time has had the same customs, which has been, for instance, consistently grasping or consistently deceitful, or which has had any other such vice or virtue. Thus, whoever studies the past history of this our city of Florence and compares what happened then with what has happened in quite recent times will find the German and French peoples imbued with avarice, pride, ferocity and unreliability, for all these four characteristics of theirs have at different times done much harm to our city. In regard to untrustworthiness, for instance, everybody knows how often money was given to King Charles VIII, and how he promised to restore the fortresses of Pisa and never did so; whereby this king displayed alike his untrustworthiness and no small avarice.

But let us pass over these recent events. Everybody will have heard of what happened in the war which the Florentines waged against the Visconti, Dukes of Milan. Since the Florentines had no other expedient available, they considered bringing the emperor into Italy that his standing and his forces might be of avail in the attack on Lombardy. The emperor promised to come with a strong army to join them in their war with the Visconti, and to protect Florence against that power, on condition that the Florentines gave him a hundred thousand ducats on his starting out and another hundred thousand when he should arrive in Italy, to which terms the Florentines agreed. Having been paid the first instalment, and then the second, when he got to Verona he turned back without doing anything, pleading that he was held up by those who had not fulfilled the agreements he had made with them. So that, had Florence neither been driven to it by necessity nor overcome by passion, but had read about and become acquainted with the habits of barbarians in ancient times, she would not have been misled by them on this occasion and on many others, since they have always been the same and have behaved everywhere and to everybody in the same way.

This may be seen from what they did of old to the Tuscans. The latter were much harassed by the Romans, by whom they had often been put to flight and routed. It became clear to them that with their own forces they could not resist such attacks, so they made an agreement with the Gauls who had settled on the Italian side of the Alps whereby in return for a sum of money they were to join forces with them and to march against the Romans. The result was that, having accepted the money, the Gauls refused to take up arms on their behalf, alleging that they had accepted it not on the understanding that they should make war on the enemies of Tuscany but that they should abstain from pillaging Tuscan territory. So that, owing to the avarice and untrustworthiness of the Gauls, the Tuscan peoples at once lost their money and the help they had hoped to get from them.

Thus we see that in the case of the ancient Tuscans and in that of the Florentines, the Gauls adopted the same policy; from which it is easy to judge how much reliance rulers can place in them.

Translated by Leslie J Walker

---

1. This makes it clear that Machiavelli only intended to comment on Livy's first ten books, which were on the causes of Rome's rise to power by virtue, as he saw it, of her republican constitution. Machiavelli's republican bias in the *Discourses* is thus both moral and methodological.

NICCOLÒ MACHIAVELLI
THE PRINCE

VI. *Of New Principalities That Are Acquired through One's Own Arms and Virtue*

No one should marvel if, in speaking as I will do of principalities that are altogether new both in prince and in state, I bring up the greatest examples. For since men almost always walk on paths beaten by others and proceed in their actions by imitation, unable either to stay on the paths of others altogether or to attain the virtue of those whom you imitate, a prudent man should always enter upon the paths beaten by great men, and imitate those who have been most excellent, so that if his own virtue does not reach that far, it is at least in the odour of it. He should do as prudent archers do when the place they plan to hit appears too distant, and knowing how far the strength[1] of their bow carries, they set their aim much higher than the place intended, not to reach such height with their arrow, but to be able with the aid of so high an aim to achieve their plan.

I say, then, that in altogether new principalities, where there is a new prince, one encounters more or less difficulty in maintaining them according to whether the one who acquires them is more or less virtuous. And because the result of becoming prince from private individual presupposes either virtue or fortune, it appears that one or the other of these two things relieves in part many difficulties; nonetheless, he who has relied less on fortune has maintained himself more. To have the prince compelled to come to live there in person, because he has no other states, makes it still easier. But, to come to those who have become princes by their own virtue and not by fortune, I say that the most excellent are Moses, Cyrus, Romulus, Theseus and the like. And although one should not reason about Moses, as he was a mere executor of things that had been ordered for him by God, nonetheless he should be admired if only for that grace which made him deserving of speaking with God. But let us consider Cyrus and the others who have acquired or founded kingdoms: you[2] will find them all admirable; and if their particular actions and orders are considered, they will appear no different from those of Moses, who had so great a teacher. And as one examines their actions and lives, one does not see that they had anything else from fortune than the opportunity, which gave them the matter enabling them to introduce any form they pleased. Without that opportunity their virtue of spirit would have been eliminated, and without that virtue the opportunity would have come in vain.

It was necessary then for Moses to find the people of Israel in Egypt, enslaved and oppressed by the Egyptians, so that they would be disposed to follow him so as to get out of their servitude. It was fitting that Romulus not be received in Alba, that he should have been exposed at birth, if he was to become king of Rome and founder of that fatherland. Cyrus needed to find the Persians malcontent with the empire of the Medes, and the Medes soft and effeminate because of a long peace. Theseus could not have demonstrated his virtue if he had not found the Athenians dispersed. Such opportunities, therefore, made these men happy, and their excellent virtue enabled the opportunity to be recognised; hence their fatherlands were ennobled by and became very happy.

Those like these men, who become princes by the paths of virtue, acquire their principality with difficulty but hold it with ease; and the difficulties they have in acquiring their principality arise in part from the new orders and modes that they are forced to introduce so as to found their state and their security. And it should be considered that nothing is more difficult to handle, more doubtful of success, nor more dangerous to manage, than to put oneself at the head of introducing new orders. For the introducer has all those who benefit from the old orders as enemies, and he has lukewarm defenders in all those who might benefit from the new orders. This lukewarmness arises partly from fear of adversaries who have the laws on their side and partly from the incredulity of men, who do not truly believe in new things unless they come to have a firm experience of them. Consequently, whenever those who are enemies have opportunity to attack, they do so with partisan zeal, and the others defend lukewarmly so that one is in peril along with them.

It is however necessary, if one wants to discuss this aspect well, to examine whether these innovators stand by themselves or depend on others; that is, whether to carry out their deed they must beg[3] or indeed can use force. In the first case they always come to ill and never accomplish anything; but when they depend on their own and are able to use force, then it is that they are rarely in peril. From this it arises that all the armed prophets conquered, and the unarmed ones were ruined. For, besides the things that have been said, the nature of peoples is variable; and it is easy to persuade them of something, but difficult to keep them in that persuasion. And thus things must be ordered in such a mode that when they no longer believe, one can make them believe by force. Moses, Cyrus, Theseus and Romulus would not have been able to make their peoples observe their constitutions for long if they had been unarmed, as happened in our times to Brother Girolamo Savonarola. He was ruined in his new orders as soon as the multitude began not to believe in them, and he had no mode for holding firm those who had believed nor for making unbelievers believe.[4] Men such as these, therefore, find great difficulty in conducting their affairs; all their dangers are along the path, and they must overcome them with virtue.

But once they have overcome them and they begin to be held in veneration, having eliminated those who had envied them for their quality, they remain powerful, secure, honoured and happy.

To such high examples I want to add a lesser example, but it will have some proportion with the others and I want it to suffice for all other similar cases: this is Hiero of Syracuse. From private individual he became prince of Syracuse, nor did he receive anything more from fortune than the opportunity. For when the Syracusans were oppressed, they chose him as their captain, and from there he proved worthy of being made their prince. And he was of such virtue, even in private fortune, that he who wrote of him said 'that he lacked nothing of being a king except a kingdom'.[5] Hiero eliminated the old military and organised a new one; he left his old friendships and made new ones; and when he had friendships and soldiers that were his own, he could build any building on top of such a foundation; so he went through a great deal of trouble to acquire, and little to maintain.

XXVI. *Exhortation to Seize Italy and to Free Her from the Barbarians*
Thus, having considered everything discussed above, and thinking to myself whether in Italy at present the times have been tending to the honour of a new prince, and whether there is matter to give opportunity to someone prudent and virtuous to introduce a form that would bring honour to him and good to the community of men there, it appears to me that so many things are tending to the benefit of a new prince that I do not know what time has ever been more apt for it. And if, as I said,[6] it was necessary for anyone wanting to see the virtue of Moses that the people of Israel be enslaved in Egypt, and to learn the greatness of spirit of Cyrus, that the Persians be oppressed by the Medes, and to learn the excellence of Theseus, that the Athenians be dispersed, so at present to know the virtue of an Italian spirit[6] it was necessary that

Italy be reduced to the condition in which she is at present, which is more enslaved than the Hebrews, more servile than the Persians, more dispersed than the Athenians, without a head, without order, beaten, despoiled, torn, pillaged, and having endured ruin of every sort.

And although up to now a glimmer has shone in someone who could judge that he had been ordered by God for her redemption, yet later it was seen that in the highest course of his actions, he was repulsed by fortune. So, left as if lifeless, she awaits whoever it can be that will heal her wounds, and put an end to the sacking of Lombardy, to the taxes on the kingdom and on Tuscany, and cure her of her sores that have festered now for a long time. One may see how she prays God to send her someone to redeem her from these barbarous cruelties and insults. One may also see her ready and disposed to follow a flag, provided that there be someone to pick it up. Nor may one see at present anyone in whom she can hope more than in your illustrious house, which with its fortune and virtue, supported by God and by the Church of which it is now prince,[7] can put itself at the head of this redemption. This is not very difficult if you[8] summon up the actions and lives of those named above. And although these men are rare and marvellous, nonetheless they were men, and each of them had less opportunity than the present; for their undertaking was not more just than this one, nor easier, nor was God more friendly to them than to you. Here there is great justice, 'for war is just to whom it is necessary, and arms are pious when there is no hope but in arms'.[9] Here there is very great readiness, and where there is great readiness, there cannot be great difficulty, provided that your house keeps its aim on the orders of those whom I have put forth. Besides this, here may be seen extraordinary things without example, brought about[10] by God: the sea has opened; a cloud has escorted you along the way; the stone has poured forth water; here manna has rained;[11] everything has concurred in your greatness. The remainder you must do yourself God does not want to do every thing, so as not to take free will from us and that part of the glory that falls to us.

And it is not a marvel if none of the Italians named before has been able to do what it is hoped will be done by your illustrious house, and if in so many revolutions in Italy and in so many maneuvers of war, it always appears that military virtue has died out in her. This arises from the fact that er ancient orders were not good and that there has not been anyone who know how to find new ones; and nothing brings so much honour to a man rising newly as the new laws and the new orders found by him. When these things have been founded well and have greatness in them, they make him revered and admirable. And in Italy matter is not lacking for introducing every form; here there is great virtue in the limbs, if it were not lacking in the heads. Look how in duels and in encounters with few the Italians are superior in force, dexterity and ingenuity. But when it comes to armies, they do not compare. And everything follows from the weakness at the head, because those who know are not obeyed, and each thinks he knows, since up to now no one has been able to raise himself, both by virtue and by fortune, to a point where the others will yield to him. From this it follows that in so much time, in so many wars made in the last twenty years, when there has been an armyentirely Italian it has always proven to be bad. The first testimony to this is Taro, then Alessandria, Capua, Genoa, Vaili, Bologna, Mestre.[12]

Thus, if your illustrious house wants to follow those excellent men who redeemed their countries,[13] it is necessary before all other things, as the true foundation of every undertaking, to provide itself with its own arms; for one cannot have more faithful, nor truer, nor better soldiers. And although each of them may be good, all together become better when they see themselves commanded by their prince, and honored and indulged by him. It is necessary, therefore, to prepare such arms for oneself so as to be able with Italian virtue to defend oneself from foreigners. And although Swiss and Spanish infantry are esteemed to be terrifying, nonetheless there is a defect in both, by means of which a third order might not only oppose them but also be confident of overcoming them. For the Spanish cannot withstand horse, and the Swiss have to be afraid of infantry if they meet in combat any that are obstinate like themselves. Hence it has been seen, and will be seen by experience, that the Spanish cannot withstand French cavalry, and the Swiss are ruined by Spanish infantry. And although a complete experiment of this last has not been seen, yet an indication of it was seen in the Battle of Ravenna,[14] when the Spanish infantry confronted the German battalions, who use the same order as the Swiss. There the Spanish, with their agile bodies and aided by their bucklers, came between and under the Germans' pikes and attacked them safely without their having any remedy for it; and if it had not been for the cavalry that charged them, they would have worn out all the Germans. Having thus learned the defects of both of these infantry, one can order a new one that would resist horse and not be afraid of infantry; this will be done by a regeneration of arms and a change in orders. And these are among those things which, when newly ordered, give reputation and greatness to a new prince.

Thus, one should not let this opportunity pass, for Italy, after so much time, to see her redeemer. I cannot express with what love he would be received in all those provinces that have suffered from these floods from outside; with what thirst for revenge, with what obstinate faith, with what piety, with what tears. What doors would be closed to him? What peoples would deny him obedience? What envy would oppose him? What Italian would deny him homage? This barbarian domination stinks to everyone. Then may your illustrious house take up this task with the spirit and hope in which just enterprises are taken up, so that under its emblem this fatherland may be ennobled and under its auspices the saying of Petrarch's may come true:

Virtue will take up arms against fury,
and make the battle short,
because the ancient valour in Italian hearts
is not yet dead.[15]

Translated by Harvey C Mansfield

---

1. Lit: virtue.
2. The formal or plural you.
3. Or pray.
4. Savonarola (1452–98) was a Dominican friar who came to Florence to preach in 1481, and succeeded in convincing the Florentines, who thought themselves 'neither rude nor ignorant', that 'he spoke with God'. Cf. *Discourses on Livy I*, where Machiavelli praises this accomplishment and does not refer, as he does here, to Savonarola's terrible end by burning at the stake.
5. Possible sources: Polybius, I 8, 16; VII 8; Livy XX IV 4; Justin, XXIII 4; I Samuel 18: 8. Cf. the Dedicatory Letter to the Discourses on Livy.
6. See Chapter 6.
7. *spirito*, not *animo*.
8. Cardinal Giovanni di Lorenzo de Medici, Lorenzo's uncle, became Pope Leo X in 1513.
9. The formal or plural you.
10. Quoted in Latin from Livy IX. 1; see also Discourses on Livy III 12, and Florentine Histories vol 8, where the same quotation is used to emphasise necessity rather than justice.
11. Lit: conducted.
12. These are references to miracles that occurred as Moses led the Israelites to the promised land, just before the revelation at Mount Sinai. They are not given in the same order as in the Bible, Exodus 14:21, 13:21, 17:6, 16:4.
13. Seven battles that were Italian defeats, from 1495 to 1513.
14. Lit: provinces.
15. April I I, IS 12; see Chapter 3.
. Petrarch, 'Italia mia', 93–96.

LEOPOLD VON RANKE:
THE THEORY AND PRACTICE OF HISTORY

INTRODUCTION BY BRENDAN SIMMS

The German historian Leopold von Ranke is the great-grandfather not just of modern historiography but also of the study of global statecraft. His multivolume histories of England, Reformation Germany and the wider world may not receive much attention today but they still inspire respect, and Ranke's shorter pieces remain staples of reading lists on the science (or should that be the art?) of history. One of those iconic essays is *Die Idee der Universalhistorie*, penned in the early 1830s, which is generally translated, not altogether happily, as 'On the character of historical science'.[1]

The work was written when Europe was in turmoil after the Revolutions of 1830 and Ranke's career was at a crossroads. He was already a celebrated historian on account of his *Ottoman and the Spanish Empires in the Sixteenth and Seventeenth Centuries* (1827), which had set a new standard for historical scholarship through its close reading of primary sources. At the request of the Prussian foreign minister, Count Bernstorff, he had agreed to edit a new journal designed to counter what was regarded as subversive liberal thinking among the intelligentsia. 'I became a political journalist,' Ranke went on to recall, 'but on the basis of ideas which I had formed from the study of history and my experience in life.' It is this interplay between history, politics and philosophy which we see at work in 'On the character of historical science'.

Nearly 200 years later, Ranke's piece seems both remote and

relevant. We stumble, of course, over his claim that while 'India had philosophy…she did not have history.' And ditto when he writes that 'we can devote but scant attention to those peoples who still remain today in a kind of state of nature', by which he meant most of the extra-European world, including India and China. Clearly, we would not accept this kind of 'universal history' today!

We also envy, rather than share, Ranke's breezy belief that historians do not have to justify themselves because their 'effort is recognised as necessary, and it would be useless to speak about [the utility of history] since nobody doubts it'. Oh, happy days, when compared to the challenges that historians currently face from other disciplines, and indeed from within the profession itself.

That said, much of what Ranke was arguing still resonates today, or at least it should. In what was surely one of the first critiques of teleology in history, he demarcated the discipline from philosophy. The philosopher, Ranke writes, 'constructs all history for himself: how it must have taken place according to his concept of mankind'. This kind of history, Ranke lamented, was not falsifiable. The philosopher of history, he complained, 'recognises the truth of history only insofar as it subordinates itself to his idea'. Of course, we all know those kinds of historians.

Ranke's main objection to the teleological approach was that the a priori assumption made 'all that which is peculiarly interesting about history…disappear'. Historical facts and processes would be reduced to vindicating the underlying philosophical construct. Research would be pointless, since the answers were already known.

Here Ranke was articulating an important principle which goes to the heart of the study of history as a critical space-specific and time-specific subject. It should be focused on the particular, at least to begin with, and it is interested in the past primarily for its own sake. 'History sees the good and the beneficent in that which exists,' he wrote. 'It tries to comprehend [it] and looks to the past.' Ranke added that history 'recognises even in error its share in truth', and for this reason, 'it sees in the former rejected philosophies a part of eternal knowledge.' Philosophy, by contrast, 'is forever rejecting: it places the state of which it would approve into the remote future'.

Instead, Ranke said that the historian must have a 'pure love of truth' and a respect for bygone ages. The close engagement with the past through a 'documentary, penetrating, profound study' would provide this and enable historians to 'acquire a certain esteem for that which has transpired, passed or appeared'. They would also learn an understanding of causation, motivation and even-handedness. 'We judge the past too often by the present situation,' Ranke charged, which 'may be the way of proceeding in politics' but not in history. Instead, 'both parties must be viewed on their own ground, in their own environment, so to speak.' 'We must understand them,' Ranke argues, 'before we judge them.' He was aware, of course, that historians adopt their own standpoint, but believed that this should not be an obstacle to true understanding.

This made the historian a conservative of sorts, but not a reactionary. To be sure, Ranke 'oppose[d] change which negates the existing', but by this he meant the complete rejection of the past 'as if it were something completely dead and unusable'. Ranke not only knew that everything was subject to change – he was not obtuse – but actually welcomed the fact. The grim defence of the status quo, Ranke believed, meant trying to end history. After all, he pointed out, 'what exists [today] is derived from reform by struggles which destroyed what existed before.'

'History…recognises the principle of movement,' Ranke concluded, 'but as evolution and not as revolution.' Contrary to his fond belief, this is very much a political rather than a merely historical dictum, but it retains its freshness after the passage of almost two centuries.

Cambridge, May 2022

---

1. In German, the word *Wissenschaft* ('scholarship') can be used to refer to the sciences, the social sciences, and also the humanities.

LEOPOLD VON RANKE
ON THE CHARACTER OF
HISTORICAL SCIENCE

A Manuscript of the 1830s

History is distinguished from all other sciences in that it is also an art. History is a science in collecting, finding, penetrating; it is an art because it recreates and portrays that which it has found and recognised. Other sciences are satisfied simply with recording what has been found; history requires the ability to recreate.

As a science, history is related to philosophy, as an art, to poetry. The difference is that, in keeping with their nature, philosophy and poetry move within the realm of the ideal, while history has to rely on reality. If one assigned philosophy the task of penetrating the image which has appeared in time, it would be involved in discovering causality and conceptualising the core of existence: and is philosophy of history not also history? If philosophy of history would assign to poetry the task of reproducing past life, then it would to history.

History is distinguished from poetry and philosophy not with regard to its capacity but by its given subject matter, which imposes conditions and is subject to empiricism. History brings both together in a third element peculiar only to itself. History is neither the one nor the other, but demands a union of the intellectual forces active in both philosophy and poetry under the condition that the last two be directed away from their concern with the ideal to the real. There are nations which do not have the ability to master this element. India had philosophy; she did not have history.

It is strange how, among the Greeks, history developed out of poetry and then emancipated itself from poetry. The Greeks had a theory of history which, while not equal by far to their practice, was nevertheless significant. Some stressed the scientific character more, others the artistic, but nobody denied the necessity of uniting the two. Their theory moves between both elements and cannot decide for either. Quintilian still said: 'Historia est proxima poetis et quodammodo carmen solutum.'[1]

In modern times one has, in cases of doubt, dealt only with the element of reality or has insisted on science as the sole principle. One has gone so far as to make history disappear as a part of philosophy. However, as has been said, history must be science and art at the same time. History is never the one without the other. But it is possible for the one or the other to be more pronounced. In lectures history can, of course, appear only as a science. For just this reason it is necessary that we undertake presently to deal with the idea of history.

Art rests on itself: its existence proves its validity. On the other hand, science must be totally worked out to its very concept and must be clear to its core.

Therefore, I would like to clarify the idea of world history in some preliminary lectures – by dealing in succession with the historical principle, the scope, and the unity of world history.[2]

I. *Of the Historical Principle*

They talk about what it is that justifies the historian's efforts in themselves. Not with regard to life. His effort is recognised as necessary, and it would be useless to speak about its utility since nobody doubts it. Society, the interrelatedness of things, demands it. But we must raise ourselves to a higher level. To justify our science against the claims of philosophy, we seek to relate to the sublime. We search for a principle from which history would receive a unique life of its own. To grasp this principle we shall consider history in its struggle with philosophy. We are speaking of that type of philosophy which has reached its results by way of speculation and which claims to dominate history.

But what are these claims? Fichte, among others, expressed them thus:

> If the philosopher is to deduce the phenomena which are possible in experience from the unity of his presupposed concept, then it is clear that he needs no experience at all for his work. Remaining freely within the limits of philosophy without regard for any experience, he must be able *a priori* to describe all of time and all its possible epochs *a priori.*

He demands of philosophy:[3] a unified idea of all of life which is divided into various epochs, each of which is comprehensible abstractly or through the others, just as each of these special epochs is again a unified concept of a special age – which manifests itself in manifold phenomena.

It turns out that the philosopher, starting from a truth, which has been found elsewhere and in a way peculiar to him as a philosopher, constructs all of history for himself: how it must have taken place according to his concept of mankind. Not satisfied to test whether his idea is right or wrong, without deceiving himself, in terms of the course of events which have really occurred, he undertakes to subordinate the very events to his idea. Indeed, he recognises the truth of history only insofar as it subordinates itself to his idea. This is a mere construct of history.

Were this procedure correct, history would lose all independence. It would be ruled simply by a proposition derived from pure philosophy and would stand and fall with the latter's truth. All that which is peculiarly interesting about history would disappear. Everything worthy of knowledge would seek only to know to what extent the philosophic principle can be demonstrated in history: to what extent the progress (*Fortgang*) of mankind, seen a priori, takes place. But it would be of no interest at all to delve into the events which have taken place or even to want to know how men lived and thought at a certain time. Only the totality of the concept which had once been alive[4] in the observable history of man would be of interest. It would never be possible to reach certainty about the course of universal history through the study of history. The only possible variations would lie in splitting concepts, in deducing the lower from the higher. It suffices to say that history would become dependent, without an inherent interest of its own, and that the wellspring of its life would dry up. It would hardly be worthwhile to devote study to history since it would already be implicit in the philosophic concept.

These claims have in earlier times been raised by theology which, too, on the basis of what was unquestionably a misunderstanding, wanted to divide all of human history into a few periods based on sin, salvation and millennium, or into the four monarchies prophesied by Daniel. It thus sought to capture the totality of phenomena in a few propositions contained in revelation – as theology understood revelation.

In either way, history would lose all scientific footing and character: it would be impossible to speak of a principle of its own from which history would derive its life.

But we notice that history remains in steady opposition to these claims. Indeed, even philosophy has never yet been able to exercise its rule. As far as printed works are concerned, I have not found that any philosophy has given even the slightest appearance of having taken control or succeeded in deducing the diversity of phenomena from a speculative concept; for the reality of fact eludes and escapes the concept of speculation in all respects.

Besides, we find that history has always opposed those claims with its full, undiminished strength. Hereby, it proves the unique character of principle inherent in history, opposed to that of philosophy. Before giving expression to this principle, we ask first through what acts it manifests itself.

First of all, philosophy always reminds us of the claim of the supreme idea. History, on the other hand, reminds us of the conditions of existence. The former lends weight to the universal interest, the latter to the particular interest. The former considers the development (*Fortgang*) essential and sees every particular only as a part of the whole. History turns sympathetically also to the particular. Philosophy is forever rejecting: it places the state of which it would approve into the remote future. By its nature philosophy is prophetic, forward-directed. History sees the good and the beneficent in that which exists. It tries to comprehend them and looks to the past.

Indeed, in this opposition one science directly attacks the other. While, as we have seen, philosophy is intent on subjecting history to itself, history at times makes similar claims. It does not want to consider the results of philosophy as absolute, but only as phenomena in time. It assumes that the most exact philosophy[5] is contained in the history of philosophy, ie that the absolute truth recognisable to the human race is inherent in the theories which appear from time to time, no matter how much they contradict each other. History goes still one step further here; it assumes that philosophy, especially when it engages in definitions, is only the manifestation of national knowledge inherent in language. It thus denies philosophy any validity and comprehends it in its other manifestation.[6] In this, even the philosophers side with the historians for, as a rule, they accept all former systems only as steps, only as relative phenomena, and ascribe absolute validity only to their own systems.

I do not mean to say that the historian is right in so viewing philosophy; I only want to show that in the historic view of things there is an active principle which is always opposed to the philosophic view and which constantly expresses itself. The question is what this principle is that lies at the basis of such expression.

While the philosopher, viewing history from his vantage point, seeks infinity merely in progression, development and totality, history recognises something infinite in every existence: in every condition, in every being, something eternal, coming from God; and this is its vital principle.

How could anything be without the divine basis of its existence?

Therefore, as we have said, history turns with sympathy to the individual;[7] therefore it insists on the validity of the particular interest. It recognises the beneficent, the existing, and opposes change which negates the existing. It recognises even in error its share in truth. For this reason, it sees in the former rejected philosophies a part of eternal knowledge.

It is not necessary for us to prove at length that the eternal dwells in the individual. This is the religious foundation on which our efforts rest. We believe that there is nothing without God, and nothing lives except through God. By freeing ourselves from the claims of a certain narrow theology, we do, nevertheless, profess that all our efforts stem from a higher, religious source.

The idea that even historical efforts are directed solely towards the search for that higher principle in phenomena must be rejected, history would thereby come too close to philosophy, since it would presuppose rather than contemplate the principle. History elevates, gives significance to and hallows the phenomenal world, in and by itself, because of what it contains. It devotes its efforts to the concrete, not only to the abstract which might be contained therein.

Now that we have vindicated our supreme principle, we have to consider what demands result from it for historical practice.

1. The first demand is pure love of truth. By recognising something sublime in the event, the condition or the person we want to know about, we acquire a certain esteem for that which has transpired, passed or appeared. The first purpose is to recognise this. If we wanted to preempt this recognition with our imagination, we would counter our very purpose and would investigate only the reflection of our subjective notions and theories. By this, however, we do not mean that one should simply remain attached to the

appearance, to its when, where or how. For then we would take hold of only something external, although our own principle directs us inward.

2. Therefore, a documentary, penetrating, profound study is necessary. First of all, this study must be devoted to the phenomenon itself, to its condition, its surroundings, chiefly for the reason that we would otherwise be incapable of knowing it; then, to its essence, its content, for as in the last analysis every unity is a spiritual one, it can only be grasped through spiritual apperception. This apperception rests on the agreement of the laws in accordance with which the observing mind proceeds with those which determine the emergence of the object under observation. Here, it is already possible to be more or less gifted. All genius rests on the congruence of the individual and the species. The productive principle which formed and created nature confronts itself in the individual who recognises her and through him becomes clear to itself and attains self-understanding.

This gift is possible to a greater or lesser degree, but to a certain extent everybody has it. Intelligence, courage and honesty in telling the truth are sufficient. Everyone may hope to find out, to penetrate, that to which he has devoted his efforts if in his studies he remains free of prejudice and retains his humility. But what is lack of prejudice? This question leads us to the third demand issuing from our principle.

3. A universal interest. There are those who are interested only in civic institutions, in constitutions, in scientific progress, in artistic creations, or only in political entanglements. Most of history[8] thus far has dealt with war and peace. But since these aspects of society are never present separately but always together – indeed, determining each other – and since, for instance, the attitudes of science[9] often influence foreign policy and especially domestic politics, equal interest must be devoted to all of these factors. Otherwise we would render ourselves incapable of comprehending the one aspect without the other, and would work counter to

the purpose of cognition. Herein lies the freedom from prejudice which we mean. It is not a lack of interest, but rather an interest in pure cognition undulled by preconceived notions. But how? Will this penetrating truth-searching effort not merely dissect the whole field into individual parts, will we not occupy ourselves merely with a series of fragments?

4. Penetration of the causal nexus. Basically, we should be satisfied with simple information – satisfied that it merely corresponds to the object. Our original demand would have been satisfied if there were only a sequence among the various events. But there is a connection among them. Events which are simultaneous touch and affect each other; what precedes determines what follows; there is an inner connection of cause and effect. Although this causal nexus is not designated by dates, it exists nevertheless. It exists, and because it exists we must try to recognise it. This kind of observation of history, which derives effects from causes, is called pragmatic; but we would like to understand it not in the usual manner but according to our concepts.

Since the development of contemporary historiography, the pragmatic school of thought, as applied to actions, has introduced a system according to which selfishness and lust for power are the mainsprings of all affairs. What is usually required is to explain the observable actions of individuals as the result of passions which we derive deductively from our concept of man. The resulting point of view is tinged with an aridity, irreligiosity and lack of sensitivity which drive us to despair. I do not deny that selfishness and lust for power can be very powerful motives and have had a great influence, but I deny that they are the only ones. First and foremost, we have to investigate the genuine information as precisely as possible to determine whether we can discover the real motives. Doing so will be possible more frequently than one might think. Only when this path leads us no further are we permitted to conjecture. Let no one believe that this limitation would restrict freedom of observation; no, the more documentary, the more exact, and the more fruitful the research is, the more freely can our art unfold, which only flourishes in the element of immediate, undeniable truth! Only invented motives are dry. The true ones, derived from fresh observation, are diverse and profound. Thus, like knowledge in general, even our pragmatism is documentary.[10] It can even be very reticent and yet very essential. Where the events themselves speak, where the pure composition manifests the connection, it is not necessary to talk of this connection at length.

5. Impartiality. As a rule, two contending parties appear in world history. The struggles in which these parties are engaged are, to be sure, very different, but closely related. We always see one develop out of the other.

Let no one believe that they will be so easily forgotten in the course of time. There is in man a happy trust in the judgment of history and of posterity which is appealed to a thousand times. But rarely is this judgment passed objectively. There is not alive within us[11] an interest similar to that of the past. We judge the past too often by the present situation. Perhaps this trait was never worse than at present, when a few interests which permeate all of world history occupy general opinion more than ever and split it into a great pro and con.

This may be the way of proceeding in politics, but it is not truly historical. We, who search for truth, even in error, who view every existence as permeated with original life, must above all avoid this error. Where there is any similar struggle, both parties must be viewed on their own ground, in their own environment, so to speak, in their own particular inner state. We must understand them before we judge them.

The objection will be raised that the writer, too, the one who describes, must have his opinion, his religion, from which he cannot separate himself.

This objection would be justified if we would presume to say who is right in every dispute. It is easily possible that, even in the midst of a dispute, we already know clearly which side we would support, in favour of which opinion we would decide. It is also possible that that impartiality which, in a conflict between two divergent opinions, often sees[12] the truth in the middle, becomes impossible for the historian since he is very definitely devoted to his opinion. But this is not all that matters. We can see the error, but where is there no error? This will not lead us to deny the realities of the existence. Next to the good we recognise evil, but this is an evil which is inherent in the situation.

It is not opinions which we examine. We are dealing with existence, which has often the most decisive influence in political and religious disputes. Here we rise to contemplate the essential character of the opposing, conflicting elements, and see how complex and entangled they are. It is not up to us to judge about error and truth as such. We merely observe one figure (*Gestalt*) arising side by side with another figure; life side by side with life; effect side by side with counter-effect. Our task is to penetrate them to the bottom of their existence and to portray them with complete objectivity.

At present two great parties are engaged in a struggle for which the words movement and resistance have become a watchword. History marks itself off from the party who desires eternal preservation as well as from the one who favours continual movement onwards. Some consider preservation to be the legitimate principle. They find a legality in the preservation of a recognised status quo, of a definite law. They do not want to notice that what exists is derived from reform by struggles which destroyed what existed before. But then history would cease. It would somewhere reach its goal. There would be, so to speak, no illegal condition, none which reason could attack – an impossible conclusion. But history can just as little approve of the overthrow of the old, as if it were something completely dead and unusable, without regard to locality and particular interests. If history shuns violence in observation, how much more will it shun violence in execution. This demolishing and changing and again demolishing is not the way of nature. It is a state of inner ruin which manifests itself in this way. It is an organism which has come into conflict with itself, certainly curious to observe but not pleasing. History, of course, recognises the principle of movement, but as evolution and not as revolution. This is the very reason why it recognises the principle of resistance. Only where movement and resistance balance each other without getting into these violent, all-devouring battles can mankind prosper. Only because history recognises both can history be just towards both. It is not up to history even to pass judgment in theory on the struggle which the past teaches it. History knows very well that the struggle will be decided according to God's will.

6. Conception of the totality. Just as there exists the particular, the connection of the one to the other, so there finally exists totality. If it is a life, we grasp its appearance. We perceive the sequence by which one factor follows another. But that is not enough. There is also something total in each life; it becomes, it exerts an effect, it acquires influence, it passes away. This totality is as certain at each moment as every expression. We must devote all our attention to it. If we are dealing with a people, we are not interested only in the individual moments of its living expressions. Rather, from the totality of its development, its deeds, its institutions and its literature, the idea speaks to us so that we simply cannot deny our attention. The further we go, the harder it is, of course, to get at the idea – for here, too, we can accomplish something only through exact research, through step-by-step understanding,[13] and through the study of documents. If this process proceeds through induction from the well known, it is intuitive knowledge (*Divination*); if it proceeds from the little-known, it takes the form of abstract philosophic propositions. One sees how infinitely difficult things become with universal history. What an infinite amount of material! What diverse efforts! How difficult it is only to grasp the particular. Since, moreover, there is much that we do not know, how

are we to understand the causal nexus everywhere, not to mention getting to the bottom of the essence of totality? I consider it impossible to solve this problem entirely. God alone knows world history. We recognise the contradictions – 'the harmonies,' as an Indian poet says, 'known to the Gods, but unknown to men'; we can only divine, only approach from a distance. But there exists clearly for us a unity, a progression, a development.

So by way of history we arrive at a definition of philosophy's task. If philosophy were what it ought to be, if history were perfectly clear and complete, then they would fully coincide with each other. Historical science would permeate its subject matter with the spirit of philosophy. If historical art would then succeed in giving life to this subject matter and in reproducing it with that part of poetic power which does not think up new things but mirrors in its true character that which has been graved and comprehended, it would, as we said in the beginning, unite in its own peculiar manner science and art at the same time.

II. *Of The Scope of World History*

In three ways – with regard to (1) sequence, (2) simultaneity and (3) individual developments.[14]

1. Sequence – in the abstract, history would embrace all of the life of mankind appearing in time. But too much of it is lost and unknown. The first period of its existence as well as the connecting links are lost without any hope of ever finding them again.

We can note what significance history has. If authors of another kind are lost, one misses the expression of one single individual. In a historical book, however, not only the existence and the view of an author is expressed; the historical book rather interests us because of the lives of others it contains. Much that was described has been lost; some has never been described. All this is threatened by death. Only those whom history remembers have not entirely died; their character and their existence continue to exist insofar as they remain in the consciousness of men. Only with the extinction of memory does actual death set in.

We are fortunate where documentary traces remain. At least these can be grasped. But what happens where there are none, for instance in prehistory? I am in favour of excluding this period from history because it contradicts the historical principle, which is documentary research.

One should exclude entirely that which usually is taken over in world history from geological deduction and from the results of natural history about the first creation of the world, the solar system and the earth. By our method we find out nothing about these topics; it is permissible to confess our ignorance.

As for myths, I do not want to deny categorically that they contain perhaps an occasional historical element. But the most important thing is that they express the view of a people of itself, its attitude towards the world etc. They are important insofar as the subjective character of a people or its thoughts may have been expressed in them, not because of any objective facts they may contain. In the former respect they possess a firm foundation and are very reliable for historical research, but not in the latter.

Finally, we can devote but scant attention to those peoples who still remain today in a kind of state of nature and who lead us to assume that they have been in this state from the beginning; that the prehistoric condition has been preserved in them. India and China claim an old age and have a lengthy chronology. But even the cleverest chronologists cannot understand it. Their antiquity is legendary, but their condition is rather a matter for natural history.

Translated by Wilma A Iggers and Konrad von Moltke

1. Institutio Oratoria X. i. 31: 'History is akin to the poets and is, so to speak, a prose poem.' *Solutum* in this context means free of metrical restrictions.
2. The passage beginning 'by dealing…' is garbled in Kessel's reading and has been translated here from Fuchs's reading.
3. Fuchs's reading: 'He demands of the philosopher'.
4. Fuchs's reading: 'which had become alive'.
5. Fuchs's reading: 'It assumes that the true (wahrhafte) philosophy'.
6. begreift sie unter der anderen Erscheinung – meaning not clear.
7. Fuchs inserts a phrase here: 'Therefore it likes to attach itself to the conditions of appearance (Erscheinung)'.
8. Fuchs's reading: 'Most histories'.
9. die wissenschaftlichen Richtungen – meaning not quite clear in this context.
10. Fuchs's reading: 'even our pragmatism is only (nur) documentary'.
11. Fuchs's reading reverses the meaning: 'There is also alive within us'.
12. Fuchs's reading: 'often seeks'.
13. Kessel's reading: 'understanding (Apprehendiren)'; Fuchs's reading: 'approximation (Approximieren)'.
14. This is an incomplete sentence in the German original.

JOHANN GUSTAV DROYSEN:
PRUSSIAN POLITICS AND THE POINT OF HISTORY

INTRODUCTION BY KATJA HOYER

'What is the point of history?' is a timeless question, asked wherever a teacher pontificates about dead kings and fallen empires. Johann Gustav Droysen was one such teacher, but, unlike many before him, he did not dismiss the question with a raised, learned eyebrow in the unshakable belief that historical studies are self-justifying. To him, history had potential outside its own remit, propelling human progress. Thus, he spent much of the nineteenth century attempting to bring rigour and purpose to the young academic discipline. His seminal text, *Outline of the Principles of History*, continues to divide opinion.

Droysen was not a detached theorist. At the beginning of the 1830s, fresh out of the Friedrich Wilhelm University of Berlin and equipped with infectious enthusiasm, he worked as a teacher at Berlin's oldest *Gymnasium*, Graues Kloster. Years later, one of his former students, the historian Rochus Freiherr von Liliencron, still gushed: 'Nobody remembered ever having heard such a beautifully constructed and sparklingly lively lecture, such a fresh perspective on ancient history.'[1] The young teacher took the educational dimensions of history seriously, engaging and inspiring his captive audiences.

A quarter of a century later, Droysen had begun to formalise his convictions about the nature of history in *Outline of the Principles of History*: 'The political events of today, tomorrow belong to history.'

He thought of past and present as poles on the same continuum – no wonder, given the brushes his early life had with so many events and people that can still be found in our textbooks today. Droysen's childhood was coloured by the Napoleonic Wars. Reading philosophy and philology at university, he heard lectures by the influential philosopher Georg Wilhelm Friedrich Hegel. From 1827 to 1829, he worked as a private tutor to Felix Mendelssohn, who was to become a close friend and one of the most important musicians of the early Romantics. Through him, he also encountered many other influential figures, like the poet Heinrich Heine. Otto von Bismarck completed his A levels at the Graues Kloster while Droysen was a teacher there. It is easy to see how the young man from a humble background came to regard the present as history in the making.

However, the currents of then and now flow in both directions. *Outline* also states that 'every point in the present is one which has come to be.' In other words, what we observe in the present is a result of the past. But 'only...the insight of investigation is able to resuscitate [such processes]'. To understand and shape the events of today, one must study how they came about. This thought gave history a political dimension and Droysen his *raison d'être*.

In order to widen the national appeal of this political approach to history, Droysen switched his specialism from Ancient to Modern and applied his findings in political activism. As professor at the Kiel University, he got involved in the complex tussle between Denmark and the German states over the territories of Schleswig and Holstein, whereby the Prussian historian naturally opposed Danish claims. To support his views, he produced a history of the duchies' interrelationship with Denmark since 1800.

Droysen was also elected as a member of the Frankfurt parliament during the 1848 revolutions and vociferously campaigned to bring about German unification. In many ways a typical National-Liberal of his time, he championed Prussian hegemony within an all-German constitutional monarchy and directed his later historical work entirely towards the pursuit of this aim. Accordingly, his magnum opus, *The History of Prussian Politics*, which he began in 1855 and worked upon until his death in 1884, attempted to show in meticulous detail how Prussia's influence had grown steadily. This in turn lent justification to a Prussian-led *kleindeutsch* unification without Austria.

In order to gain enough gravitas to shape politics, however, history needed to be established as an academic discipline with validity and prestige equivalent to but distinct from the other humanities and the sciences. It is in this context that his *Outline* should be read.

Droysen lived in a time where history was only just coming into its own rather than being treated as a sub-strand of philosophy, philology and theology. He sketched out the distinct set of skills historians required – the critical and interpretative study of sources, hermeneutics, good writing and positivist research. *Outline* thus laid vital groundwork for the professionalisation of the discipline. The first edition in 1858 was based on a lecture he gave while a professor at the University of Jena, where the circle of young scholars around him had begun to build academic routines that resemble modern ones. They met at the Historical Society to dissect sources and discuss – a format not unlike the seminar-type meetings of today. At the universities of Kiel, Jena and Berlin, Droysen worked tirelessly towards the professionalisation of history, not just its politicisation.

Today, historians sometimes criticise Droysen for yoking history to politics, dismissing him as a founding member of the 'Prussian School' and a supporter of 'Great Man Theory'. Wilfried Nippel's Droysen biography states that the political approach undermined his work's longevity. After all, what was the point of historical studies designed to bring about German unification once this goal had been achieved in 1871, well within Droysen's lifetime?

But ultimately, it is naive to assume that historians are ever free from ideology, or that they can produce 'pure' history which will be considered valid throughout the ages. Even if that were possible, others could never be compelled to follow suit. History is drawn upon by everyone from state leaders to the man on the bar stool to justify contemporary views and actions. Droysen's contribution to the field was to lay claim to a legitimacy of professional academic history above and beyond that of the casual utilisation of the past.

As access to half-information is now readily available to everyone and all the time, the disciplined approach to applied history described in Droysen's *Outline* still has much to offer – not least as a signpost down the steps of the ivory tower. The point of history is not mere academic indulgence. Done well, it can help explain the present and inform decisions for the future.

Sussex, February 2022

---

1   Eberhard Fromm, 'Zwischen Emanzipation und Tradition. Johann Gustav Droysen', *Deutsche Denker,* 7/1998, 57–62. Translated from German by the author.

JOHANN GUSTAV DROYSEN

OUTLINE OF THE PRINCIPLES OF HISTORY

No one will withhold from historical studies the recognition of having, like others, their place in the living scientific movement of our age. New historical discoveries are busily making, old beliefs are examined afresh, and the results presented in appropriate form.

But if we demand a scientific *raison d'être* for these studies, if we wish to know their relation to other forms of human knowledge, and the underlying reason why they take the course they do, they are not in condition to give satisfactory information.

Not that they regard themselves logically above such questions, or incompetent to solve them. Now and then an attempt has been made to do this, the solution having been sometimes put forward within the very circle of historical studies, sometimes borrowed from other branches of learning. By some the history of the world is assigned a place in the encyclopedia of philosophy. Writers of a different tendency, sceptical about logical necessities, all the more confidently on this account recommend us to develop history out of material conditions, out of the figures put down in statistics. Another – and he only expresses in the form of a theory what men without number are thinking or have thought – questions the very existence of 'so-called history'. 'Peoples exist purely in the abstract; the individual is the real thing. The history of the world is strictly a mere accidental configuration, destitute of metaphysical significance.' Elsewhere, pious zeal – pious, of course, more in appearance than in reality, insists upon substituting the miraculous workings of God's power under His unsearchable decree, for the natural causal connection of human things, a doctrine having this advantage, at least, that, being stated, it is under no further indebtedness to the understanding.

Within the sphere of historical studies, even so early as the close of the eighteenth century, the Göttingen school of that day had busied itself with these general questions; and they have been handled afresh from time to time ever since. Writers have undertaken to show that history is 'essentially political history', and that the many sorts of elementary, auxiliary and other sciences belonging to our department group themselves around this kernel. Then the essence of history has been recognised as consisting in method, and this characterised as a 'criticism of the sources', as a setting forth of the 'pure fact'. Others have found the definitive task of our science in artistic exposition, 'the work of the historical artist', and even celebrate as the greatest historian of our time him whose exposition approaches nearest to Sir Walter Scott's romances.

The historical sense is too active in human nature not to have been forced to find its expression early, and, wherever conditions were fortunate, in appropriate forms; and it is this natural tact which points out the way and gives the form to our studies even at the present time. But the pretensions of the science could not be satisfied with this. It must make clear to itself its aims, its means, its foundations. Only thus can it exalt itself to the height of its task; only thus, to use expressions from Bacon, can it set aside the preconceptions now governing its procedure, the idols of the theatre, tribe, forum and den, for whose maintenance just as powerful interests are active now as once interposed in favour of astrology, of lawsuits against witches, and of belief in pious and impious witchcraft. By thus becoming conscious, history will make good its jurisdiction over an incomparably wider realm of human interests than it is likely or possible that the science should master otherwise.

The need of attaining clear conceptions touching our science and its problem, every instructor who has to introduce youth into the study will feel, just as I have, though others will have found out how to satisfy it in a different manner. I for my part was urged to such investigations especially by the sort of questions which are usually passed over because in our daily experience they seem to have been solved long ago.

The political events of today, tomorrow belong to history. The business transaction of today, if of consequence enough, takes rank after a generation, as a piece of history. How is it that these mere affairs turn into history?[1] What criterion is to determine whether they become history or not? The contract of purchase concluded today between private individuals – is it the thousand years that transforms it into a historical document?

Everyone declares history to be an important means of culture; and in the education of today it certainly is a weighty element. But why is it thus? In what form? Did not history render the same service to the Greeks of the age of Pericles? To be sure the form was different then – probably that of the Homeric Songs. And how can national poems have had to Greeks and to Germany under the Hohenstaufen the educational value of historical instruction?

Observation of the present teaches us how, from different points of view, every matter of fact is differently apprehended, described and connected with others; how every transaction in private as well as in public life receives explanations of the most various kinds. A man who judges carefully will find it difficult to gather out of the plenitude of utterances so different, even a moderately safe and permanent picture of what has been done and of what has been purposed. Will the correct judgment be any more certain to be found after a hundred years, out of the so soon lessened mass of materials? Does criticism of the sources lead to anything more than the reproduction of views once held? Does it lead to the 'pure fact'?

And if such querying is possible as to the 'objective' content of history, what becomes of historical truth? Can history be in any sense characterised by truth without being correct? Are those right who speak of history in general as a fable agreed upon? A certain natural feeling, as well as the undoubting and agreeing judgment of all times tells us that it is not so, that there is in human things a unity, a truth, a might, which, the greater and more mysterious it is, so much the more challenges the mind to fathom it and to get acquainted with it.

Right here another list of questions presented itself, questions touching the relation of this potency in history to the individual, touching his position between this and the moral potencies which bear him on and bring him to self-realisation, touching his duties and his highest duty; considerations leading far beyond the immediate compass of our study, and of course convincing us that the problem by them presented was to be investigated only in its most general connections. Could one venture to undertake such investigation with only the circle of information and attainments that grow out of the historian's studies? Could these studies presume, as the studies of nature have done with so splendid a result, to make themselves their own foundation? One thing was clear: that if the historian, with his merely historical cognizance of what philosophy, theology, the observation of nature etc, have wrought out, was to take hold of these difficult problems, he must have no inclination to speculate, but must in his own empirical way proceed from the simple and solid basis of what has been done and discovered.

I found in William von Humboldt's investigations the thought which, so I believed, opened the way to a sort of a solution to these problems. He seemed to me to be for the historical sciences a Bacon. We cannot speak of a philosophical system of Humboldt's, but what the ancient expression ascribes to the greatest of historians, 'political understanding and the power of interpretation',[2] these he possessed in remarkable harmony. His thinking, his investigations, likewise the wonderful knowledge of the world won through that active life of his, led him to a view of the world which had its centre of gravity in his own strong and thoroughly cultivated sense of the ethical. As he traced out the practical and the ideal creations of the human race, languages in particular, he became acquainted with the at once spiritual and sensuous nature of the race, as well as with the perpetually creative power which, as men mutually impart and receive, belongs to the expression of this nature; these, the nature and the power, being the two elements in which the moral world, producing, so to speak, ever new electric currents in ever new polarisations, moves by creating forms and creates forms by moving.

It appeared to me possible by the aid of these thoughts to pierce deeper into the question of our science, to explain its problem and its procedure, and, from a true recognition of its nature, to develop in a general way its proper form.

In the following paragraphs I have endeavoured to do this. They have grown out of lectures delivered by me upon the encyclopedia and methodology of history. My aim has been to give in this 'Outline' a general view of the whole subject, and to hint at particulars only so far as seemed necessary to make clear the sense and connection.

Introduction: I. *History*

§1

Nature and history are the widest conceptions under which the human mind apprehends the world of phenomena. And it apprehends them thus, according to the intuitions of time and space, which present themselves to it as, in order to comprehend them, it analyzes for itself in its own way the restless movement of shifting phenomena.

Objectively, phenomena do not separate themselves according to space and time; it is our apprehension that thus distinguishes them, according as they appear to relate themselves more to space or to time. The conceptions of time and space increase in definiteness and content in the measure in which the side-by-side character of that which is and the successive character of that which has become, are perceived, investigated and understood.

§ 2

The restless movement in the world of phenomena causes us to apprehend things as in a constant development, this transition on the part of some seeming merely to repeat itself periodically, in case of others to supplement the repetition with ascent, addition, ceaseless growth, the system continually making, so to speak, 'a contribution to itself'.[3] In those phenomena in which we discover an advance of this kind, we take the successive character, the element of time, as the determining thing. These we grasp and bring together as history.

§ 3

To the human eye, only what pertains to man appears to partake of this constant upward and onward motion, and of this, such motion appears to be the essence and the business. The *ensemble* of this restless progress upward is the moral world. Only to this does the expression 'History' find its full application.

§ 4

The science of history is the result of empirical perception, experience and investigation, ἱστορία. All empirical knowledge depends upon the 'specific energy' of the nerves of sense, through the excitation of which the mind receives, not 'images' but signs of things without, which signs this excitation has brought before it. Thus it develops for itself systems of signs in which the corresponding external things present themselves to it, constituting a world of ideas. In these the mind, continually correcting, enlarging and building up *its* world, finds itself in possession of the external world, that is, so far as it can and must possess this in order to grasp it, and, by knowledge, will and formative power, rule it.

§5

All empirical investigation governs itself according to the data to which it is directed, and it can only direct itself to such data as are immediately present to it and susceptible of being cognised through the senses. The data for historical investigation are not past things, for these have disappeared, but things which are still present here and now, whether recollections of what was done, or remnants of things that have existed and of events that have occurred.

§6

Every point in the present is one which has come to be. That which it was and the manner whereby it came to be – these have passed away. Still, ideally, its past character is yet present in it. Only ideally, however, as faded traces and suppressed gleams. Apart from knowledge these are as if they existed not. Only searching vision, the insight of investigation, is able to resuscitate them to a new life and thus cause light to shine back into the empty darkness of the past. Yet what becomes clear is not past events as past. These exist no longer. It is so much of those past things as still abides in the now and the here. These quickened traces of past things stand to us in the stead of their originals, mentally constituting the 'present' of those originals.

The finite mind possesses only the now and the here. But it enlarges for itself this poverty-stricken narrowness of its existence, forward by means of its willing and its hopes, backward through the fullness of its memories. Thus, ideally locking together in itself both the future and the past, it possesses an experience analogous to eternity. The mind illuminates its present with the vision and knowledge of past events, which yet have neither existence nor duration save in and through the mind itself. 'Memory, that mother of Muses, who shapes all things',[4] creates for it the forms and the materials for a world which is in the truest sense the mind's own.

§7

It is only the traces which *man* has left, only what man's hand and man's mind has touched, formed, stamped, that thus lights up before us afresh. As he goes on fixing imprints and creating form and order, in every such utterance the human being brings into existence an expression of his individual nature, of his 'I'. Whatever residue of such human expressions and imprints is anywise, anywhere, present to us, that speaks to us and we can understand it.

Translated by E Benjamin Andrews

---

1. 'Geschäfte' into 'Geschichte'.
2. ἡ σύνεσις πολιτική καί ἡ δύναμις ἑρμηνευτική.
3. 'ἐπίδοσις εἰς αὐτό'. Aristotle, de anima, II, 5, 7. Appendix II at the end of this 'Outline' is an amplification of §§ 1 and 2 here.
4. μνήμην ἀ'πάντων μουσομήτορ' ἐργάνην. Æschylus, Prometheus, 466.

FRIEDRICH NIETZSCHE:
HISTORY, HISTORICISM AND MYTH

INTRODUCTION BY CHRISTOPHER COKER

The four *Untimely Meditations*, of which this essay is the most widely read, has a history. Nietzsche's writings following the hostile reception of his *The Birth of Tragedy* (1872) are marked by his self-imposed isolation from formal academic life; his break with Richard Wagner, and perhaps more important, his distancing from Schopenhauerian pessimism. The essay on history is also a response not only to a personal crisis in his life, but also a political one. Nietzsche was increasingly sceptical of the new German state that had come into existence after the Franco–Prussian War (1870–71). He was especially anxious about the intensification of nationalist feelings which he himself had experienced in the early months of the conflict. Thirdly, in his essay on history, we can find themes that crystallised in his later works such as *Human, All Too Human* (1878) and *Daybreak* (1881). The mission he set himself was to understand modernity on its own terms, to dismiss the Enlightenment's universalistic claims of reason, and to see the modern age as a distinctive historical era that required new ways of thinking about politics and history.

What is the importance of the essay for an understanding of history itself? Its opening line is famous: 'Observe the herd as it grazes past you/it cannot distinguish yesterday from today…' All animals have a biology, only humans have a history. Of all animals, we are the ones that display an unbelievable degree of behavioural plasticity, and the reason – we know now, though

Nietzsche did not – is that our genetic underdetermination is itself genetically determined. Our behaviour is determined as much by culture as it is by biology, or rather by the interaction of the two. We have escaped, in other words, being governed entirely by the Darwinian dynamic of natural selection.

Nietzsche's essay cautions against an 'ahistorical' mind which makes us no better than the beasts grazing in the fields. But he also warns that the 'suprahistorical' mind takes history much too seriously, and for that reason is life-denying. An example might be present-day Russia and the Russian language, which lacks a pluperfect. It is an unfortunate grammatical loss, for nothing in the country's history ever becomes history. Like a stubborn page in a new book, it refuses to be turned over by the reader. It is impossible to draw a line under events and start anew. Everything seems to happen again. Tsars reappear as Stalin or Putin; dissidents continue to be locked up; the Russian Bear continues to menace its neighbours. The country would seem to be locked in an endless 'past imperfect'.

Nietzsche also cautions us against two other kinds of historical thinking. The first he calls 'antiquarianism', the wish to freeze the past, or to restore it. A contemporary example might be today's Islamists who dream of recreating the Caliphate – the great era in the history of Islam when the empire of the faithful stretched from the Pyrenees to the Hindu Kush. For some fundamentalist groups it can be physically recreated, for others it is the 'once and future utopia' – it is the journey, not the arrival that matters.

The second kind of historical thinking, 'monumentalism', offers a mythical past which, as Nietzsche writes, exults greatness selectively and deceives by analogies, 'amus[ing] rashness in those who are courageous and fanaticism in those who are inspired.' Nietzsche was fighting against an idea increasingly popular in Germany after 1871, that the unification of the German people was the inevitable expression of their 'primordial' spirit; in other words, the German people had a historical destiny. But there are examples of monumentalism in democracies too. A striking example is the United States' belief in its own historical exceptionalism. Writing in the early 1970s, the historian Jack Plumb predicted that metaphors such as 'Manifest Destiny' had already become 'the threadbare refuge for the ageing rulers of a society in which all strong emotion is rapidly draining away'.[1] But the fact that such myths are still entrenched in the American imagination is testament to the tenacity of what Plumb called 'the Past', not history. Nietzsche famously criticised the 'monumentalist' historians for looking to the ancestors too much, to those at the top of the 'totem pole', not recognising that much more interesting were the broad horizons beyond, the future which is determined by what we do in the present.

Nietzsche's preference was for 'critical history', which he considered to be life-affirming. Every nation should look at its own past with a critical eye. Today, however, others are doing quite the opposite. In China, Patriotic History courses remind the young of 'the century of humiliation' visited upon their ancestors by the Europeans in the nineteenth century. In Putin's Russia, since 2013, history textbooks have set out to eliminate 'internal contradictions' and 'distortions' of Russian history. In democracies, we teach history for a reason – to foster the critical faculties which allow us to challenge people who are not self-critical. This includes the conspiracy theorists, populists, nationalists and charlatans who peddle 'alternative facts', like the belief that our ancestors were not clever enough to build the pyramids without alien assistance. Equally dangerous is the trashing of our own history, as statues are toppled in atonement for past injustices and the young are encouraged to be ashamed of their ancestors. Nietzsche's insight was that an ability to be self-critical is indeed central to a productive life, but that a predisposition for self-criticism is only healthy when balanced by some measure of self-belief.

The fundamental lesson Nietzsche leaves us with in his essay is that the true study of history is about life. We must understand the past without becoming prisoners of it like the monumentalists; and we must avoid the fate of the antiquarians who are steeped so deeply in the past that they can't see beyond it. And we must avoid the fate of the presentists, who have no interest in what happened before they came of age. It is up to each reader to decide which of these groups poses the greatest challenge.

London, November 2022

---

1   J H Plumb, *The Death of the Past* (Penguin, London, 1972), 149.

FRIEDRICH NIETZSCHE
ON THE UTILITY AND LIABILITY
OF HISTORY FOR LIFE

I.

Observe the herd as it grazes past you: it cannot distinguish yesterday from today, leaps about, eats, sleeps, digests, leaps some more, and carries on like this from morning to night and from day to day, tethered by the short leash of its pleasures and displeasures to the stake of the moment, and thus it is neither melancholy nor bored. It is hard on the human being to observe this, because he boasts about the superiority of his humanity over animals and yet looks enviously upon their happiness – for the one and only thing that he desires is to live like an animal, neither bored nor in pain, and yet he desires this in vain, because he does not desire it in the same way as does the animal. The human being might ask the animal: 'Why do you just look at me like that instead of telling me about your happiness?' The animal wanted to answer, 'Because I always immediately forget what I wanted to say' – but it had already forgotten this answer and hence said nothing, so that the human being was left to wonder.

But he also wondered about himself and how he was unable to learn to forget and always clung to what was past; no matter how far or how fast he runs, that chain runs with him. It is cause for wonder; the moment, here in a flash, gone in a flash, before it nothing, after it nothing, does, after all, return as a ghost once more and disturbs the peace of a later moment. Over and over a leaf is loosened from the scroll of time, falls out, flutters away – and suddenly flutters back into the human being's lap. Then the human being says 'I remember', and he envies the animal that immediately forgets and that sees how every moment actually dies, sinks back into fog and night and is extinguished forever. Thus the animal lives *ahistorically*, for it disappears entirely into the present, like a number that leaves no remainder; it does not know how to dissemble, conceals nothing, and appears in each and every moment as exactly what it is, and so cannot help but be honest. The human being, by contrast, braces himself against the great and ever-greater burden of the past; it weighs him down or bends him over, hampers his gait as an invisible and obscure load that he can pretend to disown, and that he is only too happy to disown when he is among his fellow human beings in order to arouse their envy. That is why the sight of a grazing herd or, even closer to home, of a child, which, not yet having a past to disown, plays in blissful blindness between the fences of the past and the future, moves him as though it were the vision of a lost paradise. And yet the child's play must be disturbed; all too soon it will be summoned out of its obliviousness. Then it will come to understand the phrase 'it was', that watchword that brings the human being strife, suffering and boredom, so that he is reminded what his existence basically is – a never to be perfected imperfect. When death finally brings him the much longed for oblivion, it simultaneously also suppresses the present; and with this, existence places its seal on the knowledge that existence itself is nothing but an uninterrupted having-been, something that lives by negating, consuming and contradicting itself.

If happiness, if striving for new happiness, is in any conceivable sense what binds the living to life and urges them to live on, then perhaps no philosopher is closer to the truth than the cynic, for the happiness of the animal, who is, after all, the consummate cynic, provides living proof of the truth of cynicism. The smallest happiness, if it is uninterruptedly present and makes one happy, is an incomparably greater form of happiness than the greatest happiness that occurs as a mere episode, as a mood, so to speak, as a wild whim, in the midst of sheer joylessness, yearning and privation. But in the case of the smallest and the greatest happiness, it is always just one thing alone that makes happiness happiness: the ability to forget, or, expressed in a more scholarly fashion, the capacity to feel ahistorically over the entire course of its duration. Anyone who cannot forget the past entirely and set himself down on the threshold of the moment, anyone who cannot stand, without dizziness or fear, on one single point like a victory goddess, will never know what happiness is; worse, he will never do anything that makes others happy. Imagine the most extreme example, a human being who does not possess the power to forget, who is damned to see becoming everywhere; such a human being would no longer believe in his own being, would no longer believe in himself, would see everything flow apart in turbulent particles, and would lose himself in this stream of becoming; like the true student of Heraclitus, in the end he would hardly even dare to lift a finger. All action requires forgetting, just as the existence of all organic things requires not only light, but darkness as well. A human being who wanted to experience things in a thoroughly historical manner would be like someone forced to go without sleep, or like an animal supposed to exist solely by rumination and ever repeated rumination. In other words, it is possible to live almost without memory, indeed, to live happily, as the animals show us; but without forgetting, it is utterly impossible to live at all. Or, to express my theme even more simply: *There is a degree of sleeplessness, of rumination, of historical sensibility, that injures and ultimately destroys all living things, whether a human being, a people or a culture.*

In order to determine this degree and thereby establish the limit beyond which the past must be forgotten if it is not to become the gravedigger of the present, we would have to know exactly how great the *shaping power* of a human being, a people, a culture is; by shaping power I mean that power to develop its own singular character out of itself, to shape and assimilate what is past and alien, to heal wounds, to replace what has been lost, to recreate broken forms out of itself alone. There are people who possess so little of this power that they bleed to death from a single experience, a single pain, particularly even from a single mild injustice, as from a tiny little cut. On the other hand, there are those who are so little affected by life's most savage and devastating disasters, and even by their own malicious actions, that, while these are still taking place, or at least shortly thereafter, they manage to arrive at a tolerable level of well-being and a kind of clear conscience. The stronger the roots of a human being's innermost nature, the more of the past he will assimilate or forcibly appropriate; and the most powerful, most mighty nature would be characterised by the fact that there would be no limit at which its historical sensibility would have a stifling and harmful effect; it would appropriate and incorporate into itself all that is past, what is its own as well as what is alien, transforming it, as it were, into its own blood. Such a nature knows how to forgot whatever does not subdue it; these things no longer exist. Its horizon is closed and complete, and nothing is capable of reminding it that beyond this horizon there are human beings, passions, doctrines, goals. And this is a universal law: every living thing can become healthy, strong and fruitful only within a defined horizon; if it is incapable of drawing a horizon around itself and too selfish, in turn, to enclose its own perspective within an alien horizon, then it will feebly waste away or hasten to its timely end. Cheerfulness, good conscience, joyous deeds, faith in what is to come – all this depends, both in the instance of the individual as well as in that of a people, on whether there is a line that segregates what is discernible and bright from what is unilluminable and obscure; on whether one knows how to forget things at the proper time just as well as one knows how to remember at the proper time; on whether one senses with a powerful instinct which occasion should be experienced historically, and which ahistorically. This is the preposition the reader is invited to consider: *the ahistorical and the historical are equally necessary for the health of an individual, a people and a culture.*

Everyone has made at least this one simple observation: a human being's historical knowledge and sensitivity can be very limited, his horizon as narrow as that of the inhabitant of an isolated alpine valley; each of his judgments may contain an injustice, each experience may be marked by the misconception that he is the first to experience it – yet in spite of all these injustices and all these misconceptions, he stands there, vigorously healthy and robust, a joy to look at. At the same time, someone standing close beside him who is far more just and learned grows sick and collapses because the lines of his horizon are restlessly redrawn again and again, because he cannot extricate himself from the much more fragile web of his justice and his truths and find his way back to crude wanting and desiring. By contrast, we saw the animal, which is wholly ahistorical and dwells within a horizon almost no larger than a mere point yet still lives in a certain kind of happiness, at the very least without boredom and dissimulation. We will therefore have to consider the capacity to live to a certain degree ahistorically to be more significant and more originary, insofar as it lays the foundation upon which something just, healthy and great, something that is truly human, is able to grow at all. The ahistorical is like an enveloping atmosphere in which alone life is engendered, and it disappears again with the destruction of this atmosphere. It is true: only when the human being, by thinking, reflecting, comparing, analysing, and synthesising, limits that ahistorical element, only when a bright, flashing, iridescent light is generated within that enveloping cloud of mist – that is, only by means of the power to utilise the past for life and to reshape past events into history once more – does the human being become a human being; but in an excess of history the human being ceases once again, and without that mantle of the ahistorical he would never have begun and would never have dared to begin. What deeds could a human being possibly accomplish without first entering that misty region of the ahistorical? Or, to put metaphors aside and turn instead to an illustrative example: imagine a man seized and carried away by a vehement passion for a woman or for a great idea; how his world changes! Looking backward he feels he is blind, listening around him he hears what is unfamiliar as a dull, insignificant sound; and those things that he perceives at all he never before perceived in this way; so palpably near, colourful, resonant, illuminated, as though he were apprehending it with all his senses at once. All his valuations are changed and devalued; many things he can no longer value because he can scarcely feel them any more; he asks himself whether all this time he was merely duped by the words and opinions of others; he marvels that his memory turns inexhaustibly round and round in a circle and yet is still too weak and exhausted to make one single leap out of this circle. It is the most unjust condition in the world, narrow, ungrateful to the past, blind to dangers, deaf to warnings; a tiny whirlpool of life in a dead sea of night and oblivion; and yet this condition – ahistorical, anti-historical through and through – is not only the womb of the unjust deed but of every just deed as well; and no artist will create a picture, no general win a victory and no people gain its freedom without their having previously desired and striven to accomplish these deeds in just such an ahistorical condition. Just as anyone who acts, in Goethe's words, is always without conscience, so is he also without knowledge: he forgets most things in order to do one thing, he is unjust to whatever lies behind him and recognises only one right, the right of what is to be. Thus, everyone who acts loves his action infinitely more than it deserves to be loved, and the best deeds occur in such an exuberance of love that, no matter what, they must be unworthy of this love, even if their worth were otherwise incalculably great.

If in many cases any one person were capable of sniffing out and breathing once again this ahistorical atmosphere in which every great historical event is born, then such a person, as a cognitive being, would be able to elevate himself to a *suprahistorical* standpoint, something Niebuhr once depicted as the possible result of historical reflections. He says:

when understood clearly and fully, [history] is at least useful for one thing: so that we might recognise how even the greatest and loftiest intellects of the human race do not know how fortuitously their eye has taken on its manner of seeing and forcibly demanded that all others see in this same manner; forcibly, because the intensity of their consciousness is exceptionally great. Anyone who has not recognised and understood this fully and in many individual instances will be enslaved by the presence of any powerful intellect that places the loftiest passion into a given form.

Such a standpoint could be called suprahistorical because anyone who occupies it could no longer be seduced into continuing to live on and take part in history, since he would have recognised the single condition of all events: that blindness and injustice dwelling in the soul of those who act. From that point onward he would be cured of taking history overly seriously. For he would have learned, for every human being, for every experience – regardless of whether it occurred among the Greeks or the Turks, or in the first or the nineteenth century – to answer the question: Why and to what purpose do people live? Anyone who asks his acquaintances whether they would like to relive the last ten or twenty years will easily recognise which of them are suited for that suprahistorical standpoint. To be sure, they will all answer 'No!', but they will give different reasons for this answer. Some, perhaps, by consoling themselves with the claims 'but the next twenty will be better'. Of such people David Hume once said derisively:

And from the dregs of life hope to receive,
What the first sprightly running could not give.

We shall call them historical human beings; a glance into the past drives them on towards the future, inflames their courage to go on living, kindles their hope that justice will come, that happiness is waiting just the other side of the mountain they are approaching. These historical human beings believe that the meaning of existence will come ever more to light in the course of a *process*; they look backward only to understand the present by observation of the prior process and to learn to desire the future even more keenly; they have no idea how ahistorically they think and act despite all their history, nor that their concern with history stands in the service not of pure knowledge but of life.

But that question, whose first answer we have just heard, can also be answered differently. Of course, once again with a 'No!', but for different reasons: with the No of the suprahistorical human being, who does not seek salvation in a process but for whom instead the world is complete and has arrived at its culmination in every individual moment. What could ten new years possibly teach that the past ten could not!

Suprahistorical human beings have never agreed whether the substance of this doctrine is happiness or resignation, virtue or atonement; but, contrary to all historical modes of viewing the past, they do arrive at unanimity with regard to the statement: the past and the present are one and the same. That is, in all their diversity, they are identical in type, and as the omnipresence of imperishable types they make up a stationary formation of unalterable worth and eternally identical meaning. Just as the hundreds of different languages conform to the same constant types of human needs, so that anyone who understood these needs would be able to learn nothing new from these languages, the suprahistorical thinker illuminates the entire history of peoples and individuals from the inside, clairvoyantly divining the primordial meaning of the different hieroglyphs and gradually even exhaustedly evading this constantly rising flood of written signs: for, given the infinite superabundance of events, how could he possibly avoid being satiated, oversatiated, indeed even nauseated! Ultimately, perhaps the rashest of these suprahistorical human beings will be prepared to say to his heart, as did Giacomo Leopardi:

Nothing exists that is worthy
of your emotions, and the earth deserves no sighs.
Our being is pain and boredom, and the world
is excrement – nothing else.
Calm yourself.

But let us leave the suprahistorical human beings to their nausea and their wisdom: today we instead want to rejoice with all our hearts in our unwisdom and to make things easier for ourselves by playing the roles of those active and progressive people who venerate process. Our evaluation of what is historical might prove to be nothing more than an occidental prejudice, but let us at least move forward and not simply stand still in these prejudices. If we could at least learn how to pursue history better for the purpose of *life*! Then we would gladly concede that suprahistorical human beings possess more wisdom than we do; at least, as long as we are certain of possessing more life, for that, at least, our unwisdom would have more of a future than their wisdom. And so as to banish all doubts about the meaning of this antithesis between life and wisdom, I will come to my own aid by employing a long-standing practice and propound, without further ado, some theses.

A historical phenomenon, when purely and completely understood and reduced to an intellectual phenomenon, is dead for anyone who understands it, for in it he understands the delusion, the injustice, the blind passion, and in general the whole darkened earthly horizon of that phenomenon, and from this simultaneously its historical power. At this point this power becomes powerless for him as someone who understands it, but perhaps it is not yet powerless for him as someone who lives.

History, conceived as a pure science and accorded sovereignty, would be for humanity a kind of conclusion to life and a settling of accounts. But historical cultivation is beneficial and holds out promise for the future only when it follows in the wake of a powerful new torrent of life, for example, an evolving culture; that is, only when it is governed and guided by a superior power instead of governing and guiding itself.

Insofar as it stands in the service of life, history also stands in the service of an ahistorical power, and because of this subordinate position, it neither could nor should become a pure science on the order of mathematics, for example. But the question about the degree to which life needs the service of history at all is one of the supreme questions and worries that impinges on the health of a human being, a people or a culture. For at the point of a certain excess of history, life crumbles and degenerates – as does, ultimately, as a result of this degeneration, history itself as well.

II.

That life requires the service of history must be comprehended, however, just as clearly as the proposition that will subsequently be proved – that an excess of history is harmful to life. History pertains to the living person in three respects: it pertains to him as one who acts and strives, as one who preserves and venerates, and as one who suffers and is in need of liberation. These three relations correspond to three kinds of history: insofar as it is permissible to distinguish between a *monumental*, an *antiquarian* and a *critical* kind of history.

Above all, history pertains to the active and powerful human being, to the person who is involved in a great struggle and who needs exemplars, teachers and comforters but is unable to find them among his contemporaries and in the present age. This is how it pertained to Schiller, for, as Goethe observed, our age is so wretched that the poet encounters no useful qualities in the lives of the human beings around him. Polybius, for example, was thinking of the person who takes action when he called political history the proper preparation for governing a state and the best teacher, who admonishes us steadfastly to endure the vicissitudes of fortune by reminding us of the misfortunes of others. Anyone who has come to recognise in this the meaning of history cannot help but be annoyed to see curious tourists or meticulous micrologists climbing about on the pyramids of great past ages; where he finds inspiration to emulate and to improve, he does not wish to encounter the idler who, longing for diversion or excitement, saunters about as though among the painted treasures in a gallery. So as not to experience despair and disgust amid these weak and hopeless idlers, amid these excited and fidgety contemporaries, who in fact only appear to be active, the person who takes action must, in order to catch his breath, glance backward and interrupt the progress towards his goal. However, his goal is some kind of happiness – not necessarily his own, but often that of a people or of all of humanity; he shrinks from resignation and uses history as a means to combat it. For the most part, he can hope for no reward other than fame, that is, the expectation of a place of honour in the temple of history, where he can, in turn, serve later generations as a teacher, comforter and admonisher. For his commandment reads: Whatever was once capable of extending the concept of 'the human being' and of giving it a more beautiful substance must be eternally present in order for it perpetually to have this effect. That the great moments in the struggles of individuals form links in one single chain; that they combine to form a mountain range of humankind through the millennia; that for me the highest point of such a long-since-past moment is still alive, bright and great – this is the fundamental thought in the belief in humanity that expresses itself in the demand for a *monumental* history. Precisely this demand that what is great be eternal sparks the most terrible struggle, however. For every other living thing cries out: 'No! The monumental shall not come into being' – this is the watchword of those who oppose it. Dull habit, the trivial and the common, fill every nook and cranny of the world, gather like a dense earthly fog around everything great, throw themselves in the path that greatness must travel to attain immortality so as to obstruct, deceive, smother and suffocate it. But this path leads through human minds! Through the minds of frightened and short-lived animals who constantly return to the same needs and only with great effort ward off destruction for a short time. For first and foremost they want only one thing: to live at all costs. Who could possibly imagine that they would run the difficult relay race of monumental history that greatness alone can survive! And yet again and again a few awaken who, viewing past greatness and strengthened by their observation of it, feel a sense of rapture, as if human life were a magnificent thing and as if the most beautiful fruit of this bitter plant were the knowledge that in an earlier time some person once passed through this existence with pride and strength, another pensively, a third helpfully and with compassion – all of them leaving behind the single lesson that the most beautiful life is led by those who do not hold existence in high regard. While the common human being clutches to this span of time with such greed and gloomy earnest, those who were on the way to immortality and to monumental history at least knew how to treat it with Olympian laughter, or at least with sublime derision; often they went to their graves with a sense of irony – for what was left of them to bury! Certainly only that which as waste, refuse, vanity and animality had always oppressed them, something that now would fall into oblivion after long being the object of their contempt. But one thing will live on: the signature of their most authentic being, a work, a deed, a rare inspiration, a creation; it will live on because posterity cannot do without it. In this, its most transfigured form, fame is something more than just the tastiest morsel of our self-love, as Schopenhauer called it; it is the belief in the coherence and continuity of what is great in all ages, it is a protest against the change of generations and against transitoriness.

Of what utility to the contemporary human being, then, is the monumental view of the past, the occupation with the classical and rare accomplishments of earlier times? From it he concludes that the greatness that once existed was at least *possible* at one time, and that it therefore will probably be possible once again; he goes his way with more courage, for the doubt that befalls him in his weaker moments – is he not, in fact, striving for the impossible? – is now banished. Suppose someone believed that no more than one hundred productive human beings, educated and working in the same spirit, would be needed to put an end to the cultivatedness that has just now become fashionable in Germany; would he not be strengthened by the recognition that the culture of the Renaissance was borne on the shoulders of just such a band of one hundred men?

And yet – so that we might immediately learn something new from the same example – how fluid and tentative, how imprecise that comparison would be! If it is to be effective, how many differences must be overlooked, with what violence the individuality of what is past must be forced into a general form, its sharp edges and its lines broken in favour of this conformity. Basically, in fact, what was possible once could only become possible a second time if the Pythagoreans were correct in believing that when an identical constellation of the heavenly bodies occurs, identical events – down to individual, minute details – must repeat themselves on the earth as well; so that whenever the stars have a particular relation to each other, a Stoic will join forces with an Epicurean to murder Caesar, and whenever they are in another configuration Columbus will discover America. Only if the earth always began its drama all over again after the conclusion of the fifth act, only if it were certain that the same entanglement of motives, the same *deus ex machina*, the same catastrophe would recur at fixed intervals, could the powerful human being possibly desire monumental history in its absolute iconic *veracity*, that is, with every fact depicted in all its peculiarity and uniqueness. This is unlikely to happen until astronomers have once again become astrologers. Until then, monumental history will have no need for that absolute veracity: it will continue to approach, generalise , and ultimately identify non-identical things, it will continue to diminish the differences between motives and causes in order to present, to the detriment of the *causae*, the *effectus* as monumental – that is, as exemplary and worthy of emulation. As a result, since it disregards all causes, one would with little exaggeration be able to call monumental history a collection of 'effects in themselves', of events that will have an effect on every age. What is celebrated at popular festivals and at religious or military commemorations is really just such an 'effect in itself': this is what disturbs the sleep of the ambitious, what lies like an amulet on the heart of the enterprising – not the true historical *connexus* of causes and effects, which, once fully comprehended, would only prove that the dice game of the future and of chance would never again produce something wholly identical to what it produced in the past.

As long as the soul of historiography lies in the great stimuli that a powerful person derives from it, as long as the past must be described as worthy of imitation, as capable of imitation and as possible a second time, it is in danger of becoming somewhat distorted, of being reinterpreted more favourably, and hence of approaching pure fiction. Yes, there are ages that are entirely incapable of distinguishing between a monumental past and a mythical fiction, because they could derive the very same stimuli from the one as from the other. Thus, if the monumental view of the past *prevails* over other modes of viewing it, over the antiquarian and the critical views, then the past itself is *damaged*: entire large parts of it are forgotten, scorned and washed away as if by a grey, unremitting tide, and only a few individual, embellished facts rise as islands above it. There seems to be something unnatural and wondrous about those rare persons who become visible at all, much like the golden hip by which the disciples of Pythagoras claimed to recognise their master. Monumental history deceives by means of analogies: with seductive similarities it amuses rashness in those who are courageous and fanaticism in those who are inspired; and if one imagines this history in the hands and heads of talented egoists and wicked fanatics, then empires will be destroyed, princes murdered, wars and revolutions incited, and the number of historical 'effects in themselves' – that is, of effects without sufficient causes – will further increase. So much as a reminder of the damage that monumental history can cause among powerful and active human beings, regardless of whether they are good or evil: just imagine the effect it would have if it were seized and exploited by the powerless and inactive!

Let's take the simplest and most common example. Just picture to yourself the unartistic and insufficiently artistic natures clad and armoured in the monumental history of art: against whom will they now turn their weapons! Against their arch-enemies, the strong artistic spirits; in other words, against those who alone are capable of truly learning – that is, learning with an eye to life – from history and of translating what they have learned into a higher form of praxis. Their path is obstructed; their air is darkened when zealous idolators dance around the shrine at some half-understood monument of a great past, as if they wanted to say: 'Look, this is the only true and real art; of what concern to you is art that is just coming into being or has not yet been realised!' Apparently this dancing mob even has the privilege of determining what 'good taste' is, for anyone who himself actually creates has always been at a disadvantage to those who merely observe and do not themselves take a hand in creation; just as in all ages the bar-stool politician is more intelligent, just and reflective than the governing statesman. But if one insists on transposing the custom of popular referendum and majority rule into the realm of art and thereby forcing, as it were, the artist to defend himself before a jury of aesthetic do-nothings, then you can bet that he will be condemned; and this not despite the fact that, but precisely *because*, his judges have ceremoniously proclaimed the canon of monumental art – that is, according to our earlier explanation, of the art that in all ages 'produced an effect': whereas for the appreciation of all art that is non-monumental simply because it is contemporary, these judges lack, first, the need, second, the genuine inclination, and third, precisely that authority of history. On the other hand, their instinct tells them that art can be murdered by art: the monumental should by no means come into being again, and to prevent this they deploy the authority of the monumental derived from the past. Thus they are connoisseurs of art because they want to do away with art altogether; thus they masquerade as physicians while in fact they intend to administer a poison; thus they cultivate their tongue and their taste in order to explain from their position of fastidiousness why they so persistently reject all the nourishing artistic dishes offered them. For they don't want great art to come into being: their strategy is to say: 'Look, great art already exists!' In truth, however, they are as little concerned with this great art that already exists as they are with that art that is coming into being; their lives bear witness to this. Monumental history is the costume under which their hatred of all the great and powerful people of their age masquerades as satiated admiration for the great and powerful people of past ages, the costume in which they surreptitiously turn the actual meaning of the monumental view of history into its opposite; whether they are clearly aware of it or not, they act as though their motto were 'Let the dead bury the living.'

Each of these three types of history is valid only in one soil and in one climate; in any other it develops into the most devastating weed. If the human being who wants to create something great needs the past at all, then he takes control of it by means of monumental history; those, on the other hand, who wish to remain within the realm of the habitual and the time-honoured, foster the past in the manner of antiquarian historians; and only those who are oppressed by the affliction of the present and who wish to throw off this burden at all costs sense the need for critical history – that is, for history that judges and condemns. Much harm stems from the thoughtless transplanting of these plants: the critic without affliction, the antiquarian without piety, the connoisseur of greatness unable to create something great are just such plants that, alienated from the natural soil that nurtures them, have degenerated and shot up as weeds.

[…]

VII.

The historical sensibility, when it rules *uncontrolled* and is allowed to realise all its consequences, uproots the future because it destroys illusions and robs existing things of that atmosphere in which they alone are able to live. Historical justice, even if it is really practised with the purest of intentions, is a terrible virtue for the simple reason that it always undermines and destroys living things; its verdict is always a death sentence. If no constructive impulse is at work behind the historical impulse, if things are not destroyed and swept away so that a future that is already alive in our hopes can erect its house on cleared ground, if justice alone rules, then the creative instinct is enfeebled and discouraged. A religion, for example, that is supposed to be transformed under the rule of pure justice into historical knowledge, a religion that is supposed to be understood scientifically through and through, will be destroyed as soon as it reaches this goal. The reason for this is that every historical audit always brings to light so much falsehood, coarseness, inhumanity, absurdity and violence that the pious atmosphere of illusion, in which alone everything that wants to live is actually capable of life, vanishes, However, only in love, only in the shadow of the illusion of love, does the human being create – that is, only in the unconditional belief in perfection and justness. Everyone who is forced no longer to love unconditionally has been cut off from the roots of his strength; he cannot help but wither, that is, become dishonest. In such effects art is the antithesis of history, and only when history allows itself to be transformed into a work of art, into a pure aesthetic structure, can it perhaps retain or even arouse instincts. However, this type of historiography would run wholly counter to the analytical and unartistic temper of our age; indeed, our age would view it as a counterfeit. But a history that only destroys without being guided by an inner constructive impulse in the long run makes its instruments blasé and unnatural, for such human beings destroy illusions, and 'anyone who destroys illusions in himself and others is punished by nature, the sternest of all tyrants'.

[…]

But they are utilised against youth so as to make it fit the mould of that mature manhood of egoism to which the whole world aspires; they are utilized so as to overcome youth's natural aversion to that manly-unmanly egoism by transfiguring it so that it appears in a magically scientific light. It is well known – indeed, too well known – what a certain excess of history is capable of: namely of uprooting the strongest instincts of youth, its fire, defiance, self-oblivion and love; of smothering the ardour of its passion for justice; of repressing or suppressing its desire to mature slowly by supplanting it with the opposite desire to be quickly finished, quickly useful and quickly productive; of infecting youth's honesty and boldness of feeling with doubt. Indeed, it is even capable of cheating youth out of its most beautiful privilege, out of the power to plant, overflowing with faith, a great thought within itself and letting it grow into an even greater thought. A certain excess of history is capable of doing all of this, as we have seen, and it accomplishes this by constantly shifting the human being's horizons and perspectives, by removing the atmosphere that envelops him, thereby preventing him from feeling and acting *ahistorically*. He then retreats from an infinite horizon into himself, into the tiniest egoistical realm, and is doomed to wither there and dry up. It is probable that he will attain cleverness, but he will never attain wisdom. He compromises, calculates and accommodates himself to the facts; he does not seethe but merely blinks and knows how to seek his own or his party's advantage in the advantage or disadvantage of others; he unlearns superfluous shame and thereby arrives successively at the stages of Hartmann's 'man' and 'old man'. But that is what he is *supposed to* become, precisely this is the meaning of that 'total surrender of personality to the world process' that is so cynically demanded today – for the sake of his goal, the redemption of the world, as E von Hartmann assures us. Now the will and the goal of Hartmann's 'men' and 'old men' is hardly world redemption, but certainly the world would be even more redeemed if it were redeemed of these men and old men. For then the kingdom of youth would be at hand.

X.

Thinking of *youth* at this point, I call out 'Land ho!, Land ho!' Enough, more than enough, of this passionately seeking but fruitless voyage on strange, dark seas! Now, at least, we see a shore: regardless of what it is like, this is where we must land, and even the poorest haven is better than being swept back into this infinite hopelessness and scepticism. Our first task is to make land; later on we will find the good harbours and make landing easier for those who follow us.

This voyage was dangerous and exciting. How far we now are from the calm contemplation with which we first watched our ship set out to sea. Going out in search of the dangers of history, we found ourselves exposed to all of them in the most acute manner; we ourselves bear the marks of those sufferings that afflict human beings of the modern age as a consequence of an excess of history, and this very treatise exhibits, as I freely admit, in the immoderation of its criticism, in the immaturity of its humaneness, in its frequent shifts from irony to cynicism, from pride to skepticism, its thoroughly modern character, the character of the weak personality. And yet I still have faith in the inspirational power that, in lieu of genius, has guided my vessel; I have faith in *youth*, and I have faith that it has steered me correctly by forcing me into a position of *protest against the historical education of the modern human being in his youth*, and by forcing this protester to demand that human beings above all learn to live and to employ history only *in the service of the life they have learned to live.* It is necessary to be young in order to understand this protest; indeed, given the premature greyness of our youth today, one can scarcely be young enough and still be able to sense exactly what I am protesting against. Let me turn to an example for help. It has been little over a century since a natural instinct for what is called poetry awoke in some of the young people in Germany. Are we to suppose that prior generations and even their own contemporaries never spoke at all about that art that was inwardly alien and unnatural to them? We know the opposite to be true, namely that they reflected, wrote and argued about 'poetry' with all the energy at their disposal, producing words about words about words about words. That incipient awakening of the word to life did not immediately spell the death of these word producers; in a certain sense they live on yet today. For if it is true, as Gibbon claims, that the demise of a world takes nothing but time, albeit a great deal of time, then it will take nothing but time, albeit even a great deal more time, for a false notion to perish in Germany, the 'land of the gradual'. And yet: today there are perhaps a hundred more people than there were a hundred years ago who know what poetry is; perhaps a hundred years from now there will be a hundred more who meanwhile will also have learned what culture is, and will have learned that the Germans, no matter how much they might speak of it and flaunt it, to this day simply have had no culture. In their eyes, the general satisfaction of the Germans with their 'cultivation' will appear just as unbelievable and foolish as Gottsched's once widely acknowledged classicism or Ramler's status as the German Pindar now seem to us. They will perhaps conclude that this cultivation is a kind of knowledge about cultivation, and a false and superficial knowledge at that. False and superficial because the Germans tolerated the contradiction between life and knowledge, because they utterly failed to perceive what was characteristic about the cultivation of truly cultured nations: that culture can only grow and flourish out of life, whereas in the case of the Germans it is always pinned on like an artificial flower or put on like a sugar-coating, and for that reason can never be anything but mendacious and unfruitful. But the education of German youth proceeds from precisely this false and unfruitful concept of culture; its aim, conceived purely and loftily, is by no means the independent cultivated person but rather the scholar, the scientifically oriented person, a person, moreover, who is useful at the earliest possible age and places himself outside life in order to recognise it more clearly. Its result, when viewed in a vulgar, empirical manner, is the historically and aesthetically cultivated philistine, the quickly dated up-to-date babbler about the state, the Church and art, the *sensorium* for a thousand second-hand sensations, an insatiable stomach that does not even know the meaning of genuine hunger and thirst. That an education with that aim and with this result is unnatural can only be sensed by those who have not yet been fully shaped by it; only the instincts of youth can sense this, because youth still possesses the instincts of nature that are artificially and violently broken by that education. However, anyone who, in turn, seeks to break this education must help youth express itself, must help illuminate, with the lucidity of concepts, the path of their unconscious resistance against this education and transform it into an aware and outspoken consciousness. But how can such an unusual goal be achieved? –

Above all by destroying one superstition, the belief in the *necessity* of this type of education. It is still commonly believed that there is no alternative to our present, extremely distressing reality. With this question in mind, we need only examine the literature on secondary and higher education that has appeared over the past few decades: we will discover to our dismay just how uniformly the entire aim of education has been conceived, despite the great divergence of opinions and the vehemence of the controversies; we will discover just how unswervingly the previous product of education, the 'cultivated human being' as he is conceived today, is accepted as the necessary and rational foundation of all further education. This is more or less the substance of that monotonous educational canon: the young person must begin with knowledge about cultivation, not with knowledge about life, and even less so with life and experience themselves. Moreover, this knowledge about cultivation is instilled or inculcated in the youth in the form of historical knowledge; that means that his head is jammed with an enormous number of concepts that are derived not from the immediate perception of life but from the extraordinarily mediate acquaintance with past ages and peoples. Any desire to experience something for himself and to sense how his own experiences grow inside him into an integrated and organic system is numbed and, as it were, intoxicated by the illusory promise that in the span of a few short years it will be possible to collect in himself the highest and most remarkable experiences of older ages, especially the greatest of these. It is exactly the same insane method that drives our young painters into the art museums and galleries instead of into the workshop of a master, and above all into the singular workshop of the singular master, nature. It is as though on a fleeting stroll through history we could pick up the skills and artistry of the past, the actual fruits of past lives; indeed, as though life itself were not a craft that has constantly to be learned from the ground up and relentlessly practised if it is supposed to produce anything but bunglers and babblers! –

Plato thought it necessary that the first generation of his new society (in the perfect state) be educated with the aid of a powerful *necessary lie*; children should learn to believe that they had all lived for some time in a dream state beneath the earth, where they were shaped and formed by the demiurge of nature. It would be impossible to rebel against this past! It would be impossible to oppose the work of the gods! It was to be regarded as an inviolable law of nature: those born to be philosophers have bodies of gold; those born to be guardians, bodies only of silver; and those born to be labourers, bodies of iron and bronze. Just as it is not possible to mix these metals, Plato asserts, so should it not be possible ever to intermix or overturn these caste divisions; the belief in the *aeterna veritas* of this order is the foundation of the new form of education and therewith of the new state. The modern German now has the same belief in the *aeterna veritas* of his education, of his type of culture; and yet this belief would collapse, just as the Platonic state would have collapsed, if its necessary lie were ever confronted with a *necessary truth*: that the German has no culture for the simple reason that his education makes it impossible for him to have one. He seeks to have the flower without the roots and stem; he therefore seeks it in vain. That is a simple truth, an unpleasant and crude but genuinely necessary truth.

But *our first generation* must be educated in this necessary truth; it will certainly suffer the most under it, for it has to educate itself – educate itself, moreover, against itself – by means of this necessary truth in order to acquire new habits and a new nature and leave its old habits and its first nature behind. Thus it could address itself with the classical Spanish phrase *Defienda me Dios de my*, Lord protect me from myself, that is, from that nature acquired through my upbringing. It must sip this truth drop by drop, sip it like a bitter yet powerful medicine, and every individual of this generation must overcome himself in order to pass judgment on himself, something that would be easier to endure in the form of a general judgment on the entire age.

We have no cultivation; what is worse, we are ruined and incapable of living, of correct and simple seeing and hearing, of happily seizing what is nearest and natural; and to date we do not even possess the foundation of a culture, because we ourselves are not convinced that there is a true life within us. Fragmented and disintegrated, our totality half-mechanically divided into an interior and an exterior, littered with concepts as with dragon's teeth, producing concept dragons; suffering, furthermore, from the sickness of words and mistrustful of every individual feeling that does not yet bear the stamp of words: as such a non-living and yet incredibly active factory of concepts and words, I perhaps am still justified in saying *cogito, ergo sum*, but not *vivo, ergo cogito*. I am granted empty 'being', but not full, green 'life'; my original feeling only vouches for the fact that I am a thinking, but not a living creature, that I am no *animal*, but at the very most a *cogital*. First grant me life, and then I will create a culture from it!

This is what the individual of this first generation cries out, and all these individuals will recognise one another by this call. Who will grant them this life?

No god and no human being: only their own *youth*. Unshackle this youth and with it you will have liberated life. For it merely lay hidden, in prison, it has not yet withered and died out – just ask yourselves!

But it is sick, this unshackled life, and must be cured. It is sick with many ills and does not merely suffer from the memory of its chains; it suffers – and this is of special concern to us – from the *historical sickness*. The excess of history has attacked the shaping power of life, it no longer understands how to utilize the past as a powerful nourishment. This illness is horrible, but nevertheless: if youth did not possess the prophetic gift of nature, then no one would even know that it is an illness and that a paradise of health has been lost. However, this same youth divines with the healing instinct of this same nature how paradise is to be regained; it is acquainted with the balms and remedies effective against the historical sickness, against the excess of history. What are the names of these remedies?

Well, don't be surprised to find out that they are the names of poisons: the antidotes to the historical are *the ahistorical and the suprahistorical.* With these names we return to the beginning of our observations and to its calm tenor.

With the term 'the ahistorical' I designate the art and power to be able to *forget* and to enclose oneself in a limited *horizon*; I term 'suprahistorical' those powers that divert one's gaze from what is in the process of becoming to what lends existence the character of something eternal and stable in meaning, to *art* and *religion. Science* – for it is science that here would speak of 'poisons' – views in this strength, in these antagonistic powers and strengths, for it considers the mere observation of things to be true and correct, that is, to be scientific observation, which everywhere perceives only what has already become something, something historical, and nowhere does it perceive something being, something eternal. Science lives in an internal contradiction with the eternalising powers of art and religion, just as it hates oblivion, the death of knowledge; it seeks to suspend all the limitations placed on horizons and to catapult the human being into an infinite, unlimited lightwave sea of known becoming.

If only he could live in it! Just as in an earthquake cities collapse and are destroyed and human beings build their houses but fearfully and fleetingly on volcanic ground, so life caves in on itself and becomes feeble and discouraged when the *concept-quake* unleashed by science robs the human being of the foundation for all his security and tranquillity, his belief in what is lasting and eternal. Should life rule over knowledge and science, or should knowledge rule over life? Which of these forces is higher and more decisive? No one will doubt: life is the higher, the ruling force; for any knowledge that destroyed life would simultaneously destroy itself. Knowledge presupposes life; hence it has the same interest in the preservation of life that every creature has in its own continued existence. This is the reason why science needs the supervision and surveillance of a higher power; a *hygiene of life* occupies a place close by the side of science; and one proposition of this hygiene would be: the ahistorical and the suprahistorical are the natural antidotes to the stifling of life by the historical, to the historical sickness. It is likely that we, the historically sick, will also have to suffer from these antidotes. But the fact that we suffer from them provides no evidence that could call the correctness of the chosen therapy into question.

And it is in this that I recognise the mission of that *youth* of which I have spoken, of that first generation of fighters and dragon slayers who will advance a happier, more beautiful cultivation and humanness without themselves ever having more than a promising inkling of this future happiness and coming beauty. This youth will suffer simultaneously from the illness and the cure, but despite this they believe that they can boast better health and even a more natural nature than the generations that preceded them, the cultivated 'men' and 'old men' of the present. But it is their mission to shatter the conceptions that this present age has of 'health' and 'cultivation', and to arouse scorn and hatred against these monstrous conceptual hybrids. And the symptom that will vouch for their greater health will be that this youth will be able to use no concepts, no party slogans from among the verbal and conceptual coins that are currently in circulation, to designate their own being. Rather, their conviction will derive only from a power active within them that struggles, discriminates and analyzes, and from a feeling for life that is constantly heightened in every good hour. Some may disagree with the claim that this youth will already have cultivation – but what youth would consider this a reproach? We may accuse them of being crude and intemperate – but they are not yet old and wise enough to moderate their demands. But above all, they do not need either to feign or defend a ready-made cultivation, and they enjoy all the consolations and privileges of youth, especially the privilege of courageous, unreflected honesty and the inspiring consolation of hope.

I know that these hopeful individuals have a concrete understanding of these generalisations and will translate them by means of their own experience into a doctrine that is personally meaningful. In the meantime, others may perceive nothing but covered dishes that could possibly even be empty, until one day they are surprised to see with their own eyes that these dishes are full and that assaults, demands, life drives and passions that could not remain concealed for very long are packed into and compressed within these same generalizations. Calling the attention of these sceptics to time, which brings everything to light, I will conclude by turning to that society of hopeful individuals, in order to relate to them by means of a parable the course and progress of their cure, their redemption from the historical sickness, and hence their own personal history up to that point at which they will once again be healthy enough to pursue history anew and to make use of the past in the service of life in the sense of the three historical modes described above, namely the monumental, the antiquarian and the critical. At that moment they will be less knowledgeable than the 'cultivated people' of the present, for they will have forgotten much of what they learned and will even have lost all desire to attend at all to the things that those cultivated persons want to know. Seen from the perspective of these cultivated persons, their distinguishing marks are precisely their 'lack of cultivation', their indifference and reserve with regard to many things that are otherwise celebrated, even with regard to many things that are good. But when they have arrived at the conclusion of their cure, they have once again become *human beings* and have ceased to be humanlike aggregates – that's quite an accomplishment! There is still hope. Don't your hearts rejoice at this, you hopeful individuals?

'And how will we arrive at this goal?', you will ask. At the very beginning of your journey to that goal the God of Delphi will call out to you his imperative, 'Know thyself.' It is a difficult imperative, for this God, as Heraclitus has said, 'neither conceals nor reveals, but merely alludes'. What does he allude to?

There were centuries in which the Greeks found themselves threatened by a danger similar to the one we face today, the danger, namely, of perishing in a flood of things alien and past, of perishing of 'history'. They never lived in proud isolation; on the contrary, their 'cultivation' was for many years a chaos of foreign – Semitic, Babylonian, Lydian and Egyptian – forms and concepts, and their religion represented a veritable struggle among the gods of the entire Orient. This is similar to the manner in which today 'German cultivation' and religion represent an internally struggling chaos of all foreign lands and all prior history. But despite this, and thanks to that Apollonian imperative, Hellenic culture did not become an aggregate. The Greeks gradually learned how *to organize this chaos* by concentrating – in accordance with this Delphic doctrine – on themselves, that is, on their genuine needs, and by letting those pseudo-needs die out. They thereby took possession of themselves again; they did not long remain the glutted heirs and epigones of the entire Orient; based on the practical interpretation of Apollo's imperative, they themselves became, after a difficult struggle with themselves, the happiest enrichers and increasers of that inherited treasure; they became the first cultured people, and hence the model for all future cultured peoples.

This is a parable for every individual among us: he must organize the chaos within him by concentrating on his genuine needs. His honesty, his sound and truthful character, must at some point rebel against the constant imitation – imitation of speech and imitation of learning – that he finds everywhere around him. He then will begin to grasp that culture can be something other than the *decoration of life* – that is, at bottom always only mere dissimulation and disguise, for all ornaments have the purpose of concealing what they adorn. In this way the Greek concept of culture – as opposed to the Roman – will be disclosed to him, the concept of culture as a new and improved *physis*, without interior and exterior, without dissimulation and convention, a concept of culture as the harmony of life, thought, appearance and will. He thus will learn from his own experience that it was the higher power of *moral* nature that made the Greeks' victory over other cultures possible, and that every increase in truthfulness is always a necessary step towards the furthering of *true* cultivation – even though this truthfulness may sometimes do serious harm to that cultivatedness that is held in esteem at the time, even though it may hasten the downfall of an entire decorative culture.

Translated by Richard T Gray

JOHN ROBERT SEELEY:
THE SCHOOL OF STATEMANSHIP

INTRODUCTION BY ROBERT CROWCROFT

Sir John Robert Seeley was one of the most distinguished scholars of the late nineteenth century. Regius Professor of Modern History at the University of Cambridge, he is best known as the author of a seminal 1883 account of British imperialism, *The Expansion of England*. Yet 13 years prior to the publication of that justly famous book – during his 1870 inaugural lecture at Cambridge, 'The Teaching of Politics' – Seeley offered perhaps one of the most provocative arguments ever made about the benefits, and power, of reflecting deeply on the past. He did this by posing a simple question of his audience: 'Why should history be studied?' In attempting to answer this, Seeley ventured that there was one reason above all others. 'History is the school of statesmanship,' he boldly declared.

This may be the statement that best exemplifies the value and potential of applied history. In Seeley's mind, history was not about leafing through stacks of dusty documents and then assembling accounts that were of purely antiquarian interest. Just the opposite. History was something living and vital. It was a discipline of practical utility, one that trained the mind by exposing its students to a vast repository of previous action and decision. To explore past politics was to mine human experience itself.

History, then, represented nothing less than a master key for political leaders, a key that unlocked both the present and the future. And there was a reason why it was so important. Those who engaged in statecraft were dabbling in the most arduous of all endeavours. The rigours and uncertainties of leadership taxed, and usually defeated, even the most capable of individuals. Seeley believed that intuition gleaned from the past might prepare us for these trials. If one knew history and cultivated its insights, one would be in a stronger position to navigate the currents of the present. It might even help us avoid coming to grief on the reefs of the future.

The young men gathered in that Cambridge lecture hall to listen to Seeley intone on the purpose of the past were the best and the brightest of Britain at the apex of its global wealth and influence. Soon enough, they would take their place in governing the richest, most powerful nation in the international system. For these future policymakers and high officials to be informed that, in taking a degree in history, they were *actually* attending an advanced training centre for statecraft itself must have been extraordinarily exciting. And Seeley was clear that, even for the great majority of the public who found themselves in rather more modest stations, it was still essential that the responsible citizen possess knowledge of 'great events' in the past, in order to discharge their duties and comprehend their place in the rich tapestry of mankind. To this end, he described history as 'the school of public feeling and patriotism', for 'without at least a little knowledge of history no man can take a rational interest in politics.' Yet it was for leaders and officials, engaged in staggeringly difficult practical tasks, that reflection on the past was so imperative: 'If it is an important study to every citizen, it is the one important study to the legislator and ruler.' And so it remains.

If political history is to ever reclaim the position of intellectual ascendancy that it once held, and ought never have surrendered to other sub-disciplines, its practitioners should take Seeley's maxims, and his admonitions, to heart. They might conceptualise their work, like Seeley did his, as being to help prepare people for the challenges of decision-making in high-stakes environments of pervasive, inescapable uncertainty. Only through this process can future leaders be encouraged to cultivate the insights, and humility, that are the proper inheritance of the human past.

Edinburgh, January 2022

JOHN ROBERT SEELEY
THE TEACHING OF POLITICS

An Inaugural Lecture Delivered at Cambridge in 1870

It is natural to me on this occasion to call to mind the lectures on modern history of Sir James Stephen, to which I listened in this place seventeen years ago. I recollect the professor and his audience, the merit of his lectures and the degree of attention with which they were heard. The recollection is discouraging. I do not hope to give better lectures than Sir James Stephen. I remember that he was master of his subject, skilful in the exposition of it, and not sparing of pains. Yet, of his audience, most were there by compulsion; few of them were what we called 'reading men'; I myself only went because I was ill and had been recommended not to study too hard. It was – and I think the professor felt it – a painful waste of power. There was teaching of the highest and rarest kind, and no demand for it, or only such artificial demand as can be created by a protective system.

I do not suppose that matters are quite the same now; I have heard that Professor Kingsley was able to command an audience worthy of his earnestness and eloquence. But the causes which were at work in Sir James Stephen's time to depress the study of modern history have not quite ceased to operate, though they may operate less powerfully; and, therefore it is in no sanguine spirit that I commence my labours.

After this day, my words will only reach those who have already elected to study modern history; but it is possible that I have before me now many who have never fairly considered the claims of this subject upon their attention. For this reason, and also because, in my opinion, the theory of education, apart from practical educational details, is too little discussed in Cambridge, I will propose the question of the value of modern history in education.

The reason why this subject is not taken up by most undergraduates in this university is not, I may take it for granted, to be found in any conviction of their own that other subjects in themselves deserve the preference. The question is settled for them, partly by the competitions and prizes of the place, which give an artificial value to classics and mathematics, partly by the advice of their elders and teachers. These two influences taken together are nearly overwhelming, but that of the two which deserves to have the least weight has, I fear, the most. I must always regard it as a misfortune that prizes and fellowships, which have been admitted into education under the notion of incentives to industry or aids to deserving poverty, should be practically used so as to produce other and more questionable effects, and should be converted into a protection of particular studies and a prohibition of others.

The other influence – advice of elders and teachers – I certainly am not interested to discredit. The undergraduate who deviates from the ordinary course of study in this place may indeed deserve praise if he prefers his own intellectual progress to material rewards; but his conduct is much more questionable if he merely prefers his own opinion to that of wiser people. I can remember well the doubts that disturbed me when I was an undergraduate, as they must have disturbed many others, in considering the course of studies prescribed by usage in the university. What should a student do who doubts whether this course of studies is really the best for him? Is he to sacrifice his own judgment to that of the men who have prescribed this course, or is he to try the hazardous experiment of chalking out a course for himself? I do not intend here to offer any hasty solution of this delicate question. But it seems to me that both teachers in advising particular studies, and students in receiving such advice, should carefully separate in their minds their educational value from their pecuniary value. Let not a subject which is useful towards winning a fellowship be confounded with a subject that is useful in developing the mind. The two things may chance to be different; nay, we have only to consider the process by which fellowships are awarded to perceive that they can only by accident be the same. Let the student by all means elect for himself which path he will follow. If he cannot secure at once distinction in the university and a good education, let him make his choice between these objects, or let him study, if he will, to reconcile them; but in any case let him not mistake the one for the other.

I must venture to suggest to the student another reason for not sacrificing his own judgment too readily. To the unanimous opinion of good authorities it would certainly be presumptuous in him not to yield, but when those authorities differ he must, whether he will or not, make himself arbiter between them; and it is mere laziness, not modesty, to abandon himself to the guidance of those advisers who happen to be in a majority in his immediate neighbourhood. A few years ago no student here had any strong reason to think he could go far wrong in devoting himself to classics or mathematics. But the case is very different now. Let a man thumb his Thucydides to pieces, and fill his *Poetæ Scenici* from the first page to the last with annotations; all this zeal and enthusiasm will not save him, when he goes out into the world, from being treated, and that by men whose ability he cannot deny, as a mere ignoramus – as a man who has acquired no knowledge, though he may have gained some cultivation. The mathematician hardly fares better. He had always to endure some contempt from the scholar as uncultivated; then philosophy fell upon him, represented by Sir William Hamilton, and attempted to prove that his studies were ruinous to the intellect; and now physical science includes him in the sweeping condemnation it passes upon all who do not make observations and try experiments.

Let me not exaggerate the difference of opinion that prevails. There is no school that does not hold both classical and mathematical studies in respect as far as they go. The student who has a pronounced taste for either is still safe in indulging his taste. Every student may feel convinced that, if he brings a sufficiently liberal spirit to either study, he will acquire at least something valuable, if not the most valuable thing. But beyond this, whether he will or not, he must decide for himself. Between those who attach a great value to the study of words and those who cast contempt on words in comparison with things; between those who value the abstract sciences and those who rate the sciences of experiment far higher; between those who would study man and those who would study nature; between those who would study the ancient world – whether in language, literature or history – and those who would study the modern; the student must inevitably choose for himself. He does not escape the necessity by devolving the choice upon advisers, for those advisers themselves have to be chosen.

So long as education is in its transition state in this country, there must be some confusion and some perplexity in the minds of students. This is unavoidable; but if he frankly accepts the situation, the student may discover that it offers compensations. While so many studies are competing with each other, the student's mental range will be widened; the comparison of sciences will become familiar to him; the world of knowledge will be revealed to him as a whole, and each part of it will be better known when it is known as a part. This university, if it abandons its old simple routine of classics and mathematics, may perhaps seem to become for a time a scene of confusion – science struggling with science, and tripos elbowing tripos. The change has already advanced some way, and I cannot plead the cause of modern history today with any effect without advancing it further. The old boast of Cambridge, a certain modest thoroughness, exactness within a narrow range, will perhaps suffer when we try, as we are beginning to do, to teach and to learn everything; but even during the transition there will be no small compensation in enlargement of ideas, and when the transition is complete it may be found possible to recover the old exactness within a wider range. Lastly, the new obligation which falls upon the student of deciding for himself between several courses of study calls him to make an effort which may certainly be very beneficial to him. The old uniformity which was so tranquillising to the mind, when if a man would know it seemed as if he must apply himself to one of two sets of things – to Greeks and Romans on the one hand, or to magnitudes and numbers on the other – and no third department of knowledge anywhere existed, this uniformity deprived the student of one of the most wholesome mental exercises, the exercise of appraising or valuing knowledge. To know the value of a science, the relation it bears to life, the utility of it – I use the word utility in no sordid sense – is quite a different thing from knowing the science itself. It is not only a different but a very separable thing, and from this separation come two great evils – pedantry in the learned, and contempt for knowledge in the ignorant. If by the new variety of our studies, and the new difficulty of choosing between several courses, students should be led to a habit of intelligently comparing the different departments of knowledge, a great gain would accrue from a temporary embarrassment.

I turn now to the question of the place of history in education. Why should history be studied? Mathematics may teach us precision in our thoughts, consecutiveness in our reasonings, and help us to raise general views into propositions accurately qualified and quantified. Classics may train in us the gift of speech, and at the same time elevate our minds with the thoughts of great men and accustom us to exalted pleasures. Physical science may make us at home in nature, may educate the eye to observe, and reveal to us the excellent order of the universe we live in. Philosophy may make us acquainted with ourselves, may teach us to wonder in the difficult contemplation of that 'dark fluxion, all unfixable by thought', the personal subject, and to watch its varied activities of apprehending, doubting, believing, knowing, desiring, loving, praising, blaming. Such are the manifest claims of these great subjects. Does history recommend itself by less obvious uses? Are its claims upon our attention less urgent? Are they obscure, difficult to state or make good?

On the contrary, in discussing them I should feel embarrassed by the very easiness of my task, by the too glaring obviousness of the thesis I have to maintain, if I did not remember that after all the claims of history are practically very little admitted, not only in this university, but in English education generally. Let me say, then, that history is the school of statesmanship. If I were not addressing the students of Cambridge, I might take lower ground. I should choose rather to say, that as in a free country every citizen must be at least remotely interested in public affairs, it is desirable both for the public good and for the self-respect of each individual that great events and large interests should make part of the studies which are to prepare the future citizen for his duties, in order that he may follow with some intelligence the march of contemporary history, and may at least take an interest in the great concerns of his generation, even though he may not be called to take any considerable part in them, or to exert any great influence upon them. This more modest view is well worthy of consideration even here. The mass of those that are educated here will work in after-life in some very limited sphere. They will be compelled to concentrate themselves upon some humble task, to tread diligently some obscure routine. In these circumstances, their views are likely to become narrow, their thoughts paltry and sordid, if their education received here has not given them eyes to see whatever is largest and most elevating in life. Who has not met with some hard-working country curate, living remote from all intellectual society, and clinging with fondness to the remembrance of some college study which seems still to connect him with the world in which thinkers live? Who has not wished that he had some stouter rope to cling to than such reminiscences as college studies generally furnish – that he could remember something better, something more fruitful and suggestive, than scraps of Virgil or rules of gender and prosody? The most secluded man is living in the midst of momentous social changes, whether he can interpret them or not; the most humble task upon which any man is engaged makes part, even though he forgets it, of a total of human work by which a new age is evolved out of the old; the smallest individual life belongs to a national life which is great, to a universal life of the race which is illimitably great. There are studies which show a man the whole of which he is a part, and which throw light upon the great process of which his own life is a moment; the course along which the human race travels can be partially traced, and still more satisfactorily can the evolution of particular nations during limited periods be followed. Studies like this leave something more behind them than a refinement imparted to the mind, or even than faculties trained for future use; they furnish a theory of human affairs, a theory which is applicable to the phenomena with which life has to deal, and which serves the purpose of a chart or a compass. The man that has even a glimpse of such a theory, if the theory be itself a hopeful one, cannot but feel tranquillised and reassured; his life, from being a wandering or a drifting, becomes a journey or a voyage to a definite port; the changes that go on around him cease to appear capricious, and he is more often able to refer them to laws: hence his hopes become more measurable, and his plans more reasonable, and it may be that where his own efforts fail he is supported by faith in a law of Good, of which he has traced the workings. Such a study – teaching each man his place in the republic of man, the post at which he is stationed, the function with which he is invested, the work that is required of him – such a study is history when comprehensively pursued.

History, then, I might well urge, is the school of public feeling and patriotism. Without at least a little knowledge of history no man can take a rational interest in politics, and no man can form a rational judgment about them without a good deal. There is no one here, however humble his prospects, who does not hope to do as much as this. There are, it is true, men who, without any knowledge of history, are hot politicians, but it would be better for them not to meddle with politics at all: there are men who, knowing something of history, are indifferentists in politics; it is because they do not know history enough. But what I choose rather to say here, is not that history is the school of public feeling, but that it is the school of statesmanship. If it is an important study to every citizen, it is the one important study to the legislator and ruler. There are many things, doubtless, which it is desirable for the politician to know. It is so much the better if he acquires the cultivation that characterised the older race of our statesmen, the literary and classical taste of Fox and Canning. In the same way a lawyer or a clergyman will be the better for being a man of letters and scholarship. But as the indispensable thing for a lawyer is a knowledge of law, and for a clergyman the indispensable thing is a knowledge of divinity, so I will venture to say that the indispensable thing for a politician is a knowledge of political economy and of history. And, though perhaps we seldom think of it, our university is, and must be, a great seminary of politicians.

Here are assembled to prepare themselves for life the young men from whom the legislators and statesmen of the next age must be taken. In this place they will begin to form the views and opinions which will determine their political career. During the years they spend here, and through influences that operate here – perhaps not in the lecture room, but at any rate in the meetings of friends, or in the Union – their preparation for political life is made. It may seem a somewhat exaggerated view of my function, but I cannot help regarding myself as called to join with the Professor of Political Economy in presiding over this preparation. What will at any rate be learned *at* the university it should be possible, I hold, to learn *from* the university, and I shall consider it to be in great part my own fault if this does not prove to be the case.

If Professor Smyth delivered his inaugural lecture in this hall, it is very possible that among his hearers sat the young Lord Palmerston. It is possible that at this moment someone sits there who will occupy the position of Lord Palmerston in the last years of this century. In Professor Symond's lecture-room I dare say there may sometimes have been seen, wearing a Pembroke gown,[1] an undergraduate named William Pitt. It would be hard, certainly, to trace in the career either of Lord Palmerston or Pitt the influence of any of my predecessors. The influence of Cambridge upon Pitt is discernible rather in the command of finished language which his classical studies gave him, and the strong precision of thought which he got from mathematics, than in any wide historical views. But history was not then the practical study that it is now, and the kindred subject of political economy was not then taught in this university. The acquirement which more even than his eloquence or his mathematical knowledge raised Pitt above the other politicians of his time was one which, though it was not made here, might, had the university been in a more efficient state, have been made here, and could most certainly be made here now; it was his knowledge of Adam Smith.

But when I say that a knowledge of history is indispensable to the statesman, there will rise up in the minds of many a doubt which it is desirable to lay. Political economy is indispensable, yes! but is history so necessary? After all, how easy for a profound historian to be a very shallow politician! The light which is shed upon contemporary affairs by the experience of remote ages and quite different states of society is surely faint enough. How utterly inapplicable seem inferences drawn from Ancient Rome or Athens to the disputed political questions of the present day! Even less connection is there between medieval barbarism and the complicated civilisation we live in the midst of. Cannot high authorities be quoted to prove the uselessness of history in politics? No statesman ever towered above his contemporaries, not only in power but in statesmanlike qualities, more decidedly than Sir Robert Walpole, who was a contemner of every kind of learning. On the other hand, Carteret, full of historical knowledge, makes but a poor figure. The most influential politician of the last age, Cobden, was never tired of sneering at the pedants who busied themselves with the affairs of other ages. Can we avoid suspecting him to have been in the right when we remark the evident superiority as a statesman of a man so unlearned and so moderately gifted as Cobden, to such a prodigy both of ability and historical acquirement as Macaulay? Outmatched in eloquence, in acuteness, in cultivation, and most of all in knowledge of history, how did Cobden succeed in winning the race at last? Was it not evidently by occupying himself exclusively with the questions of the time and the place, by encumbering himself with no useless knowledge, by not obscuring plain matters with ambitious illustrations, curious parallels and obsolete authorities?

There is a very simple answer to all this. It is an argument that presupposes that history refers only to what is long past. Now it is not unnatural to give this meaning to the word history. We often in common parlance use the word so. We say that a thing belongs to history when it is past and gone. The title of history is given to books which contain narratives of occurrences that are past, and in most instances long past; it would not be given to a simple account of existing institutions or communities. We must remember, however, that the language of common life is one thing, and scientific language another. I do not intend on this occasion to give an exact definition of history as I understand it. The attempt to do so would lead me too far. But, however we determine the province of history, it must be understood that I use the word, and shall throughout use it, without any thought of time past or present. There are multitudes of past occurrences which do not belong, in my view, to history, and there are multitudes of phenomena belonging to the present time which do. Phenomena are classed together in science according to resemblances in kind, not according to date. If history were taken to have for its subject matter all that has happened in the world, it would not be a single science but the inductive basis of all sciences whatever. Evidently it must be taken scientifically to deal only with occurrences and phenomena of a certain kind, and this being so it is evident that vice versa phenomena of that particular kind must be reckoned as historical, to whatever period they belong. Now, whatever phenomena we exclude, it is evident that we must include political institutions within the limits of historical phenomena. Everone, therefore, who studies political institutions, whether in the past or in the present, studies history.

It is therefore a misconception to think that a politician disregards history because he disregards the remote past. It is misleading to call Macaulay a student of history and Cobden a contemner of history. Both men evidently were occupied with phenomena of the same kind; they laboured at perfectly similar problems. The power and weakness of states, their advance and decline, their chances of success in war, their political and social institutions, the stability or transience of their order, the state of civilization, the influences promoting it and the influences retarding it, the character and qualifications of public men – these and similar questions occupied both. However you describe the studies of the one, you must give the same name to the studies of the other. It cannot be just to rank them among the students of different sciences because the one examined the power of Louis XIV and the other that of the Emperor Nicholas, the one studied the struggle of political freedom with despotism and the other the struggle of commercial freedom with monopoly, or because the one was rather too much disposed to measure a country by its eminence in literature and the other by its activity in manufactures and trade.

But after this explanation you will perhaps be disposed to think me guilty of a truism; for it now appears that when I said that the study of history is indispensable to the politician, all I meant was that a politician must needs study politics. But is it a truism to say this? Is it a truism to say that a politician must study politics? I fear not. I fear that there is just as much unwillingness in this profession as in the other professions in England to acknowledge any general principles or build on any scientific basis. As in England your lawyer seldom knows jurisprudence, your clergyman is seldom a theologian, your medical man seldom a physiologist, so is it with the politician. He may know a great deal, but what he knows is not in the proper sense politics. He has much knowledge that is useful for a politician, but little of the knowledge that is indispensable and fundamental. He stores his memory with information about persons – how so-and-so voted on this question or on that. He becomes acute in party tactics, ready in popular arts, skilful in scaling the ladder of power. He watches perhaps the tides of opinion, knows what measure it is safe to propose or support, and what measure is inopportune, however salutary in itself. But for a politician who is serious in his profession, and who has higher ends than mere success or power for himself, all these things are secondary. What is primary is a solid knowledge of political and social well-being in its nature and its causes, and more particularly a strong apprehension of the place of government in human affairs, of its capacities and the limits of its capacities. Finesse, adroitness, eloquence, it may be desirable to have; but after all they are useful principally for those who have nothing better. A grain of real knowledge, of genuine uncontrollable conviction, will outweigh a bushel of adroitness, and to produce persuasion there is one golden principle of rhetoric not put down in the books – to understand what you are talking about. Now anyone who knows how much study it takes in the present complication of human affairs to arrive at solid political convictions, and how much taste for study there is in the ordinary Englishman, whether he belongs to the class of politicians or not, will arrive at the conclusion that our politicians must be insufficiently educated, from the mere fact that political science is so little taught in schools and colleges. An Englishman often extends in after-life his knowledge of the subjects to which he has been introduced at school or college, but does not very often travel into quite new regions of knowledge; and perhaps a political career, once begun, is too absorbing to leave much leisure or tranquillity for abstract investigation. In these days, when we are all more alive than our fathers were to the difficulty of the science of government, I may venture, perhaps, to make the assertion that we shall never have a supply of competent politicians until political science – that is, roughly, political economy and history together – is made a prominent part of the higher education.

But what are we to think of that difference of opinion among statesmen on the subject of history? For Walpole and Carteret, Cobden and Macaulay, though they do not really differ about the importance of history, do certainly differ about the proper way of studying it. What, then, is the exact point of difference between them, and to which of the two parties ought we to attach ourselves? Now, remembering the perpetual sneers of Cobden's school against classical studies, we may be inclined to answer the question by saying that they measure the importance of historical phenomena by their nearness to ourselves, while the opposite school measure them by their intrinsic greatness; so that the one school cares for nothing that is not modern, while the other, considering that some of the most memorable things happened in remote times, gives a great prominence in historical studies to antiquity. If this were really the difference, I for one should have little hesitation in siding against the modernists. Dr Arnold maintained that we allow ourselves to be misled by the word ancient, and that much of what we call ancient history is, for all practical purposes, more modern than most of that which is commonly called modern history. I agree with him heartily. I think that we shall derive more useful lessons to guide us in politics from Thucydides than from Froissart; and even times much more modern than those chronicled by Froissart seem to me barren of instruction compared to some periods of the ancient world. I feel more at home at Rome in the times of Cicero than at Paris in the disturbances of the Fronde. If, then, the school of Cobden maintain that historical phenomena deserve study in proportion to their nearness to the present time, I have no agreement with them. Men and things and occurrences are not memorable in proportion to their chronological relation to ourselves; some which are very near to our own times we cannot too soon forget, and some few we ought always to remember, however far we drift away from them upon the stream of time.

But you will observe that Dr. Arnold's own argument tacitly assumes that there is a historical period more important than even the most memorable periods of ancient history. For why does he attach so much importance to the classical periods? Because of their likeness to our own time; because of the light they throw upon our own time. It is implied in this that contemporary history is, in Dr. Arnold's opinion, more important than either ancient or modern; and in fact superior to it by all the superiority of the end to the means. Now, if after making this observation we reconsider the language of the Cobden school, we shall see that it is of contemporary history, and not merely of modern history, that they are thinking; and that they are not advocates of modern times against ancient, but of the present against the past. In his famous sneer at Thucydides, Cobden did not compare him with Froissart, or even with Clarendon, but with the *Times* newspaper. And in spite of all his contempt for Athens and the Ilissus, I think it very likely that he might have agreed with Arnold that Pericles and Demosthenes are better worth remembering and studying than Cœur de Lion or the Black Prince, and even than the Stuarts or Louis XIV. But then he would have added were he among us now, and Arnold we have seen tacitly agrees, that time spent upon either period, upon the fifth century before Christ or the seventeenth century after Christ, would be equally wasted if it did not lead to a clearer comprehension of the age of Queen Victoria, the Emperor Napoleon III, the Czar Alexander II and President Grant. Here, again, there is agreement. This is not the point of difference between the two schools, for no school denies, or can deny, that the especial business of the politician is to understand not some other age but the age he himself lives in. It is necessary, therefore, to ask once more, what is the point of difference?

Evidently the difference is here, that the school of Cobden are for attacking the problem directly, while the other school approach it by a circuitous route. Cobden scarcely sees any difference between the proposition that the present time ought to be understood and the proposition that the knowledge of it ought to be imparted in schools and colleges. He would have the student buckle to at once, occupy himself without the least delay in collecting and classifying and analysing the facts of the time. In his view other ages are of quite secondary importance, intrinsically indeed of no importance whatever, but not altogether to be despised on account of the illustrations that may occasionally be drawn from them. The opposite school, the school in possession, have precisely the same end in view, but approach it in quite a different way. To them the present time is like a fortified city, which must be attacked by opening trenches, working underground and gradually stealing nearer and nearer. They think it necessary, before introducing the student to the phenomena which he is ultimately to consider, to set before him analogous phenomena drawn from other ages. He is to store up a mass of facts which he will afterwards find useful as illustrations. While he is acquiring them it is of course impossible for him to appreciate their illustrative value, because he has not yet been acquainted with the phenomena which they illustrate, but when this is done it is supposed that they will at once recur to his memory – that all the dead knowledge will suddenly become alive, the dry facts give up their kernel of philosophical truth. And such vast importance is attached to this preparatory process that absolutely the whole time at command is spent upon it, and the day never comes in our course of education when the phenomena themselves, which it is the object of the whole process to explain and teach, are even in the most summary way stated to the student.

Here, then, are the two views. It is not necessary to accept either without qualification. Cobden, I think, greatly underrated the instruction to be derived from the past, and he had probably no idea of that philosophy of universal history which, if a number of great thinkers appearing in succession, from Vico and Herder to Comte and Buckle, are sufficient indications of the set of thought, will sooner or later be worked out. But, on the other hand, I earnestly urge that in preferring the direct method to the indirect in the teaching of political science or contemporary history he is right. I will give my reasons.

First let me point out that, though an indirect method may sometimes have its advantages, the presumption must always be against it. For it multiplies the number of things to be learnt, it increases the tax upon memory and time. The history of an age is composed of a vast mass of minute facts, which again are substantiated by other minute facts which we call evidence. To learn the history of an age is to commit to memory this whole mass and to weigh all the evidence. If, then, there is some age of which it is urgently important that the student should master the history – and such an age always is the age that is present – it is surely a serious matter to double or quadruple for him this already formidable task, by requiring him, as a mere preliminary exercitation, to master the history of two or three other periods. It may not indeed be a great burden upon a man whose life is passed among books; to him the additional labour thus imposed may be merely delightful; but for the man whom an active life awaits – we are thinking principally of the politician – as soon as his education is over it is such a burden that the very object of imposing it is defeated. If we will look facts in the face, we shall confess that the student commonly breaks off his historical course in the middle. He learns, more or less perfectly, those periods of remote history, whether ancient or modern, which are so rich in illustrations of our own time; but when the comparison between the present and the past comes to be made, when the analogies are to be traced and the results of the whole complicated process to be obtained, the student is tired, or has not energy to enter upon the new task, or the business of life has come upon him and left him no more leisure.

This danger, however, may be unavoidable; and if so, it must, of course, be faced. If the knowledge of the political world around us cannot be come at by the direct route, we must, of course, make a circuit, in spite of the risk that some of our pupils will grow weary before they reach the goal. But is it so? Is there any insuperable difficulty in the direct route? I do not believe it, and I think that we have here an example of the prevailing vice of English education, which is just this indirectness. Indirectness in education is a great evil. It is an evil not merely because it wastes time and energy, but still more because it conceals from the student the end of his studies. The student's interest in his studies will always be very much in proportion to the progress he perceives himself to be making, while it is impossible for him to perceive his progress at all unless he has his goal in sight. It is, therefore, most desirable that studies should have an object not merely good but visibly and plainly good. Compare in your minds the student who studies politics in the living time and he who studies them in the mirror of remote history. Think which of the two will bring the greater ardour or earnestness to the pursuit. There is indeed for drowsy imaginations a certain charm about the remote past which the present wants. It is so romantic, people say; that is to say, the characters are all in stage costume, and speak in quaint language; the rhetoric and literary art of succeeding generations have given an artificial dignity to the persons and incidents, and all the more prominent personages appear (as they never appeared to their contemporaries) with the halo round their heads of posthumous renown. No doubt, in that peaceful world of the past you escape all that is most uncomfortable in the present – the bustle, the petty detail, the slovenliness, the vulgarity, the hot discomfort, the bewildering hubbub, the humiliating spites and misconstructions, the ceaseless brawl of objurgation and recrimination, the painfulness of good men hating each other, the perplexingness of wise men flatly contradicting each other, the perpetual sight of failure, or of success soon regretted, of good things turning out to have a bad side, of new sores breaking out as fast as old ones are healed, the laboriousness and the littleness of all improvement, and in general the commonness and dullness and uneasiness of life. We escape from all this in the past, but after all we escape from it only by an illusion; and in truth he who desires pleasing and fascinating pictures for his imagination should have recourse to poetry, which expressly undertakes to furnish them, and not to history, where, if they are admitted, it is most commonly through the weakness of the historian. After all, it is another kind of interest that the present time has, in spite of all its discomfort; it is the interest of reality, the interest that our own private affairs have for us, an interest at least scarcely less keen and personal, and more ennobling, because connecting us with grander issues. Nay, to one who is to be a politician – and it is this case that I am principally considering – contemporary history not only resembles a personal affair but actually is a personal affair. Can anyone question the eagerness with which such a student would apply himself to this subject when introduced to him by his teachers, remembering that for him – in addition to its speculative interest which it shares with the rest of history, in addition to the interest which it must have for all people, because it concerns persons and things of which, as being contemporary, they must needs know a good deal and have thought a good deal beforehand – it would have the close and special interest of being the subject of all subjects which it would be most useful and most advantageous to him in after-life to understand?

That the history of the past is useful the student takes upon trust; that contemporary history is useful must needs be palpably evident to him. It is useful, like past history, for the lessons it gives, the principles it illustrates; but, unlike past history, it is also indispensable to the politician for its own sake. He who studies contemporary history, therefore, at the same time masters the principles and becomes familiar with the age, while he who studies the past learns only the principles and remains a stranger to the age. The latter, therefore, at the end of the process has still a necessary stage to traverse which the former has left behind him. They may have acquired an equal amount of historical information, have stored up an equal number of facts; but the one is still unprepared for want of knowledge which is indispensable while the other has all the knowledge which is necessary to start with. And this advantage, being felt from the beginning, cannot fail to give the student of contemporary history an ardour and an interest in his work which the student of the past must want. For he not only makes progress, but feels and knows that he makes progress. What he learns is not merely stored up for future use, but tells immediately upon his views and judgments of things around him. It sheds at once upon the political world, the world of states, nationalities, parliaments, armies, parties and interests, an illumination like that which natural science sheds upon the world of physical and vital forces, of light and heat, the plant and the animal. Studied in the past, history is rather entertaining than stimulating, except to those who have a natural inclination for it, or who come to it specially prepared. Studied in the present, I doubt not that it would be among the most stimulating and fascinating of studies. Like natural science, it is a study which a man may always carry about with him and prosecute in almost all circumstances. 'Pernoctat nobiscum, peregrinatur, rusticatur.' If the botanist and geologist cannot walk across the fields or along the high road without being reminded of their favourite studies, neither can the man who studies his age ever be in want of stimulants to reflection. To him, too, the fields and the roads read lessons, though of a different kind – lessons about the division of property, about the progress of industry. Meanwhile the town is his almost exclusively. He has the clue to the whole human movement; he is at home in the world of purpose and utility; all human activities he watches with a curious eye, and sees laws where others may see only a dull and bewildered confusion. He finds sermons in streets, and good in newspapers.

To turn history away from the past to the present is in fact to give it the interest of an experimental study. Our knowledge of both is necessarily imperfect. Of the past much is unrecorded, and many records have perished. The present has not yet been recorded perfectly, and the records have not been collected or made accessible. But in the present there is more room than in the past for the original and independent inquiries of the student. In ancient history, what can any student here do beyond reading intelligently his Grote and his Mommsen? To make new combinations is not to any important degree within his power. And in the past generally, though there remains much to be done for laborious investigators exploring archives and for great thinkers generalising the newly acquired facts, there is wanting a field in which the ordinary student, who has neither exceptional opportunities nor exceptional gifts, may without presumption make his own observations and venture upon original speculations. Yet no study which does not afford such a field can be in the highest degree stimulating or improving. Now contemporary history affords such a field. Ἀκήρατός ἐστ᾽ ἔτι λειμών. Anyone may join the reapers in that harvest. The phenomena are not hidden away in libraries, but are before our eyes. To everyone of us a certain proportion of them, a larger one perhaps than we sometimes think, are within the range of personal observation. Another large section lies scattered about the journals and magazines of Europe. Neither collected nor compared nor classified they lie, and there is no one who might not do for himself some work in sorting them – work which, though, like the collections of the private botanist or geologist, it may do nothing ultimately to advance the science, may yet do much towards improving the student's mind, and making his studies delightful to him.

Again, the past is a less stimulating contemplation than the present, because it is a thing complete and finished. It consists of controversies for good or for evil closed, questions answered whether rightly or wrongly, problems together with their solutions. But the present consists of problems which still await their solution, questions which the time is still struggling to answer, controversies in which we are called on to take a side. Now the mind is roused and stimulated by questions, not by answers. In education the essential thing is to offer problems of some kind to the student, and the solution must not be given along with them. The student's own solution is what it is important to get – some genuine exertion of his own faculty; and this it is barely possible to get when a solution is already before him. Everone can take an interest in divining what will happen next, for that is still unknown, and the issue will confirm or confound the prophecy; but it seems idle to stand guessing what might have happened next when the next page of the history tells you what did actually happen. We read in one sentence of the distress of the Roman peasantry, and of the agrarian law by which Tiberius Gracchus tried to relieve them; and few readers pause to consider what were the possible solutions out of which Gracchus made his choice. Surely it is much more stimulating to the intellect to consider, as we have been doing for some months, the distress of the Irish peasantry, and to conjecture the provisions of that agrarian law by which Mr Gladstone yesterday evening proposed to relieve it.

In short, past history is a dogmatist, furnishing for every doubt ready-made and hackneyed determinations. Present history is a Socrates, knowing nothing but guiding others to knowledge by suggestive interrogations.

All this is said in no spirit of disparagement of the past. Though I have several times mentioned the name of Cobden, it is not because I have any sympathy with that contempt for the old learning which is generally, and for all I know justly, attributed to him. Let us reverence the past, say I; let us cherish the records of it; let us often revert to it. What I urge is not that it is less instructive than is commonly supposed; what I wish to see is not a neglect of past history, whether contemptuous or respectful. I would rather that we realised the past less drowsily, that something better prevailed among us than what I may call the Waverley view of other times!

The past is in my eyes the best commentary on the present. What is it, then, that I urge? This: that the text should be put before the commentary, and the present before the past. Illustrations are valuable, but only when there is something to be illustrated; the analogies of past and present are full of interest, but not to one who is ignorant of the present. It is for this reason that the taste for history is commonly observed to come late. Not till people have seen the world a little, and have had some experience of affairs, are they able to realise, except in the theatrical spurious-poetical fashion, the order of phenomena with which historians are concerned. But this knowledge of the world, this experience of affairs, might be given earlier if the student were brought at once face to face with the living present, encouraged to follow the drama which is now being enacted on the stage which is all the world; accustomed, not in his hours of recreation, but as part of his education, to thread the maze of the world's affairs, to take the measure of public men before the world is unanimous about them, study tendencies before they have reached their limit, predict the growth of power not yet mature, or calculate the stages of its decline; accustomed, in fact, to work out for himself at his desk the very problems which are awaiting the solution of Time.

History the school of statesmanship! This was what I began with. It is a maxim which to many practical men sounds, I know, somewhat hollow. To give it another sound, to vindicate it as a sober maxim in this university, is a task to which I feel very unequal; nevertheless it is what I understand myself to be called upon to attempt. If I succeed in any measure, I hope to do so by the method I have now indicated, by giving due precedence in the teaching of history to the present over the past.

THE END

---

1.   I am told that this is a mistake, and that in Pitt's time the undergraduates' gown was the same for all the colleges.

LORD ACTON:
'POWER TENDS TO CORRUPT AND ABSOLUTE POWER CORRUPTS ABSOLUTELY'

INTRODUCTION BY ANDREW LAMBERT

John Emerich Edward Dalberg Acton, Lord Acton, (1834–1902), occupies a significant position in the study of applied history. An aristocrat with pan-European connections, born in Naples, raised in England and educated in Germany, his peripatetic upbringing combined the Catholic faith of his German mother with the progressive Liberalism of his stepfather, Earl Granville, a long-serving Liberal foreign secretary. Acton sat briefly in the House of Commons before being translated to the Lords by Liberal leader William Gladstone in the 1870s. Acton became a junior minister in Gladstone's last ministry, advising on European and religious issues while acting as lord-in-waiting to Queen Victoria, who shared his fascination with the genetic history of German royalty. Acton could not resist the temptation to play the 'Philosopher King' in politics, urging Gladstone to stick to his principles of liberal progress and avoid expedients. Within months of Gladstone's final resignation he would transition from political turmoil to academic eminence. His famous line about power and corruption may reflect personal experience.

Acton combined his political career with historical scholarship, which he saw as key to shaping understanding and educating judgement in the present, helping British history achieve academic credibility. His enduring fascination with historiography reflected a powerful sense that historians were the key to history.

Acton's approach to history focused on the interaction of politics, history and the abuse of power. If his aims were contemporary, he recognised the critical role of the past in establishing precedent and illuminating current issues. It was no accident that this powerful essayist and critic never published a book; he preferred the 'applied history' formats of essay and article, which could influence contemporary debates, to academic exchange. He targeted contemporary policymakers, including Gladstone. He created an overarching concept for a 'History of Liberty' in two essays on the 'History of Freedom' in 1877 and 1878, linked to Gladstone's attack on Disraeli's 'immoral' foreign policy. The common assumption that the project faltered because Acton attempted to read and list every relevant text is implausible. The 'Madonna of the Future' was a conceptual repository for the evidence he needed to address emerging political issues, imposing a progressive pattern on uncertain pasts, moulding hand-picked fragments to sustain his agenda. This was history with a purpose, sacrificing scholarly precision to contemporary effect. The concept may also have salved a troubled conscience while he remained focused on the world of politics.

Acton's inaugural lecture as Regius Professor of History at Cambridge, delivered on 11 June 1895, was a major intellectual event. Acton distilled a complex of ideas and agendas into relatively manageable form. Even so, the published version occupied 142 pages, dominated by footnotes, combining a philosophy of history, a personal manifesto and a guide to scholarly practice. His theme was progress, tracing the forces and ideas that had shaped the modern world, overcoming the stasis of authoritarian regimes in politics and faith, a process that conveniently opened the archives to historians. Weighty references and pan-European perspectives stressed the breadth and profundity of the discipline, highlighting the scale and range of contemporary historiography. Historians, he believed, were the key to history; they must be cross-examined and their motives judged. The emphasis on academic professionalism and 'scientific' method were calculated to secure audiences within and without the university, shaping the best minds of the rising generation before they entered the world of politics. He wanted to educate judgement, not shape opinion, an argument he sustained by referencing publications by an eminent scientist and a controversial theologian.[1] His 'Study of History' was deeply immersed in the wider culture of Western Europe, a critical aspect of intellectual maturity and the foundation of progress.

Having stressed the synergy of history and politics, Acton anticipated the development of contemporary history, citing a French precedent. The limits of access to contemporary evidence would be the point at which modern and contemporary history would divide. He approved the argument of positivist historian Frederic Harrison: 'All our hopes of the future depend upon a sound understanding of the past.'[2]

For Acton modern history was 'a narrative told of ourselves, the record of a life which is our own…weighty with inestimable lessons that we must learn by experience and at a great price, if we know not how to profit by the example and teaching of those who have gone before us, in a society largely resembling the one we live in'. Ultimately, history 'makes us wiser' because 'historical thinking… is better than historical learning.'[3] That phrase encapsulated a complex intellectual life and offered the ultimate justification for study: knowledge that could not be applied had little value, and little future beyond the academy. He understood that how individuals use the past would remain profoundly contingent, and endlessly fluid.

Acton's obsession with historiography, which many dismissed as a waste of time better used to write a book or two, was critical. Before using the work of any historian, they should be cross-examined at the bar of history, and he set high moral standards. His famous slips of paper were briefs for the prosecution, while the overpowering display of historiographical prowess was neither vainglory nor padding, merely a reminder that history is not easy, and historical judgments are never secure.

When it came to scholarly methods, Acton emphasised Ranke's critical comparison of sources, a recent innovation by a man he had known, but his judgments were altogether different. Despite stressing the need for balance, he made morality the key element of analysis. Much as he admired the technical skill and delivery of the leading historians of the age, Heinrich von Treitschke and Theodor Mommsen, he emphasised that lesser men should not conflate their opinions on current affairs with scholarship.[4] It was a mark of his scholarly detachment that he awarded such plaudits.[5] Acton hated the aggressive militarised nationalism of the age, and the concomitant crushing of confessional plurality, not least in Prussian-dominated, post-1871 Germany, condemning Johann Gustav Droysen's deification of militarism as a monstrous abuse of (historical) power, and regretted that the 'Prussian School' 'held Berlin like a fortress'.[6] He would not, one suspects, have been surprised by the terrible consequences of turning history into an overture to *Weltpolitik*, or the malign legacy of state-funded history in the twentieth century.

Acton's public lectures changed the fortunes of history in Britain; the inaugural lecture sold well, providing a suitable guide for teachers and students across the Anglophone world, an inspiration to advanced studies and an education for budding statesmen, but his time would be limited. Disabled by a stroke in April 1901, he died the following June. His legacy endured, along with an oracular reputation that led many to assume he had achieved the detachment he had urged on others. Always an applied historian, Acton's history served the present, challenging those who blocked the path of liberty and conscience in human affairs. Ironically, the Chair at Cambridge persuaded the Roman Church to overlook past differences on doctrine, man and faith reconciled by ignoring fundamental differences. This pan-European intellectual had no time for present-mindedness, or the nation state. The triumph of nationalism, however secured, was no cause for celebration, while victory and conquest did not offer *ex post facto* validation of violence and dishonesty.

For Acton history was both an intellectual training for active roles in the contemporary world and a moral education in the unstoppable progress of liberty. Although he valued morality and ethics above religious orthodoxy, he chose to remain within a Church he had publicly accused of abusing its power. Attempting to reconcile that paradox led him to place an ethical imperative at the core of his 'philosophy of history': it was a confession of weakness.[7] His triumph lay in turning personal failings into the analytical key to understanding the development of the modern world, integrating conflicting ideas and experience that could help policymakers to plot a course into the future.

Kew, London, December 2021

1. Lord Acton, 'A Lecture on the Study of History' (Macmillan, London, 1895), 24, 83.
2. Acton, 'Lecture', 12 and 80 reference to Frederic Harrison, *The Meaning of History: and Other Historical Pieces* (Macmillan, London, 1894), 6.
3. Acton, 'Lecture', 19–20.
4. Acton, 'Lecture', 30.
5. Owen Chadwick, 'Acton, Döllinger and History',German Historical Institute, London Annual Lecture, 1986, 15.
6. Hugh Tulloch, *Acton* (Weidenfeld & Nicholson, London, 1988), 94–96.
7. Gertrude Himmelfarb; 'Introduction' to Lord Acton, *Essays on Freedom and Power* (Thames and Hudson, London, 1956), 23. Tulloch, *Acton*, 60–62.

LORD ACTON
ON THE STUDY OF HISTORY

An Inaugural Lecture Delivered at Cambridge in June 1895

Fellow students – I look back today to a time before the middle of the century, when I was reading at Edinburgh and fervently wishing to come to this university. At three colleges I applied for admission, and, as things then were, I was refused by all. Here, from the first, I vainly fixed my hopes, and here, in a happier hour, after five-and-forty years, they are at last fulfilled.

I desire, first, to speak to you of that which I may reasonably call the unity of modern history, as an easy approach to questions necessary to be met on the threshold by anyone occupying this place, which my predecessor has made so formidable to me by the reflected lustre of his name.

You have often heard it said that modern history is a subject to which neither beginning nor end can be assigned. No beginning, because the dense web of the fortunes of man is woven without a void; because, in society as in nature, the structure is continuous, and we can trace things back uninterruptedly, until we dimly descry the Declaration of Independence in the forests of Germany. No end, because, on the same principle, history made and history making are scientifically inseparable and separately unmeaning.

'Politics,' said Sir John Seeley, 'are vulgar when they are not liberalised by history, and history fades into mere literature when it loses sight of its relation to practical politics.' Everybody perceives the sense in which this is true. For the science of politics is the one science that is deposited by the stream of history, like grains of gold in the sand of a river; and the knowledge of the past, the record of truths revealed by experience, is eminently practical, as an instrument of action and a power that goes to the making of the future. In France, such is the weight attached to the study of our own time that there is an appointed course of contemporary history, with appropriate textbooks. That is a chair which, in the progressive division of labour by which both science and government prosper, may some day be founded in this country. Meantime, we do well to acknowledge the points at which the two epochs diverge. For the contemporary differs from the modern in this, that many of its facts cannot by us be definitely ascertained. The living do not give up their secrets with the candour of the dead; one key is always excepted, and a generation passes before we can ensure accuracy. Common report and outward seeming are bad copies of the reality, as the initiated know it. Even of a thing so memorable as the war of 1870, the true cause is still obscure; much that we believed has been scattered to the winds in the last six months, and further revelations by important witnesses are about to appear. The use of history turns far more on certainty than on abundance of acquired information.

Beyond the question of certainty is the question of detachment. The process by which principles are discovered and appropriated is other than that by which, in practice, they are applied; and our most sacred and disinterested convictions ought to take shape in the tranquil regions of the air, above the tumult and the tempest of active life. For a man is justly despised who has one opinion in history and another in politics, one for abroad and another at home, one for opposition and another for office. History compels us to fasten on abiding issues, and rescues us from the temporary and transient. Politics and history are interwoven, but are not commensurate. Ours is a domain that reaches farther than affairs of state, and is not subject to the jurisdiction of governments. It is our function to keep in view and to command the movement of ideas, which are not the effect but the cause of public events; and even to allow some priority to ecclesiastical history over civil, since, by reason of the graver issues concerned, and the vital consequences of error, it opened the way in research and was the first to be treated by close reasoners and scholars of the higher rank.

In the same manner, there is wisdom and depth in the philosophy which always considers the origin and the germ, and glories in history as one consistent epic. Yet every student ought to know that mastery is acquired by resolved limitation. And confusion ensues from the theory of Montesquieu and of his school, who, adapting the same term to things unlike, insist that freedom is the primitive condition of the race from which we are sprung. If we are to account mind not matter, ideas not force, the spiritual property that gives dignity and grace and intellectual value to history, and its action on the ascending life of man, then we shall not be prone to explain the universal by the national, and civilisation by custom. A speech of Antigone, a single sentence of Socrates, a few lines that were inscribed on an Indian rock before the Second Punic War, the footsteps of a silent yet prophetic people who dwelt by the Dead Sea and perished in the fall of Jerusalem, come nearer to our lives than the ancestral wisdom of barbarians who fed their swine on the Hercynian acorns.

For our present purpose, then, I describe as modern history that which begins four hundred years ago, which is marked off by an evident and intelligible line from the time immediately preceding, and displays in its course specific and distinctive characteristics of its own. The modern age did not proceed from the medieval by normal succession, with outward tokens of legitimate descent. Unheralded, it founded a new order of things, under a law of innovation, sapping the ancient reign of continuity. In those days Columbus subverted the notions of the world and reversed the conditions of production, wealth and power; in those days Machiavelli released government from the restraint of law; Erasmus diverted the current of ancient learning from profane into

Christian channels; Luther broke the chain of authority and tradition at the strongest link; and Copernicus erected an invincible power that set for ever the mark of progress upon the time that was to come. There is the same unbound originality and disregard for inherited sanctions in the rare philosophers as in the discovery of Divine Right and the intruding imperialism of Rome. The like effects are visible everywhere, and one generation beheld them all. It was an awakening of new life; the world revolved in a different orbit, determined by influences unknown before. After many ages persuaded of the headlong decline and impending dissolution of society, and governed by usage and the will of masters who were in their graves, the sixteenth century went forth armed for untried experience, and ready to watch with hopefulness a prospect of incalculable change.

That forward movement divides it broadly from the older world; and the unity of the new is manifest in the universal spirit of investigation and discovery which did not cease to operate, and withstood the recurring efforts of reaction until, by the advent of the reign of general ideas which we call the Revolution, it at length prevailed. This successive deliverance and gradual passage, for good and evil, from subordination to independence is a phenomenon of primary import to us, because historical science has been one of its instruments. If the Past has been an obstacle and a burden, knowledge of the Past is the safest and the surest emancipation. And the earnest search for it is one of the signs that distinguish the four centuries of which I speak from those that went before. The Middle Ages, which possessed good writers of contemporary narrative, were careless and impatient of older fact. They became content to be deceived, to live in a twilight of fiction, under clouds of false witness, inventing according to convenience and glad to welcome the forger and the cheat. As time went on, the atmosphere of accredited mendacity thickened, until, in the Renaissance, the art of exposing falsehood dawned upon keen Italian minds. It was then that history as we understand it began to be understood, and the illustrious dynasty of scholars arose to whom we still look both for method and material. Unlike the dreaming prehistoric world, ours knows the need and the duty to make itself master of the earlier times, and to forfeit nothing of their wisdom or their warnings, and has devoted its best energy and treasure to the sovereign purpose of detecting error and vindicating entrusted truth.

In this epoch of full-grown history men have not acquiesced in the given conditions of their lives. Taking little for granted they have sought to know the ground they stand on, and the road they travel, and the reason why. Over them, therefore, the historian has obtained an increasing ascendancy. The law of stability was overcome by the power of ideas, constantly varied and rapidly renewed; ideas that give life and motion, that take wing and traverse seas and frontiers, making it futile to pursue the consecutive order of events in the seclusion of a separate nationality. They compel us to share the existence of societies wider than our own, to be familiar with distant and exotic types, to hold our march upon the loftier summits, along the central range, to live in the company of heroes, and saints, and men of genius, that no single country could produce. We cannot afford wantonly to lose sight of great men and memorable lives, and are bound to store up objects for admiration as far as may be; for the effect of implacable research is constantly to reduce their number. No intellectual exercise, for instance, can be more invigorating than to watch the working of the mind of Napoleon, the most entirely known as well as the ablest of historic men. In another sphere, it is the vision of a higher world to be intimate with the character of Fénelon, the cherished model of politicians, ecclesiastics and men of letters, the witness against one century and precursor of another, the advocate of the poor against oppression, of liberty in an age of arbitrary power, of tolerance in an age of persecution, of the humane virtues among men accustomed to sacrifice them to authority, the man of whom one enemy says that his cleverness was enough to strike terror, and another, that genius poured in torrents from his eyes. For the minds that are greatest and best alone furnish the instructive examples. A man of ordinary proportion or inferior mettle knows not how to think out the rounded circle of his thought, how to divest his will of its surroundings and to rise above the pressure of time and race and circumstance, to choose the star that guides his course, to correct, and test, and assay his convictions by the light within, and, with a resolute conscience and ideal courage, to remodel and reconstitute the character which birth and education gave him.

For ourselves, if it were not the quest of the higher level and the extended horizon, international history would be imposed by the exclusive and insular reason that parliamentary reporting is younger than parliaments. The foreigner has no mystic fabric in his government, and no *arcanum imperii*. For him the foundations have been laid bare; every motive and function of the mechanism is accounted for as distinctly as the works of a watch. But with our indigenous constitution, not made with hands or written upon paper but claiming to develop by a law of organic growth; with our disbelief in the virtue of definitions and general principles and our reliance on relative truths, we can have nothing equivalent to the vivid and prolonged debates in which other communities have displayed the inmost secrets of political science to every man who can read. And the discussions of constituent assemblies, at Philadelphia, Versailles and Paris, at Cadiz and Brussels, at Geneva, Frankfurt and Berlin, above nearly all, those of the most enlightened states in the American Union, when they have recast their institutions, are paramount in the literature of politics, and proffer treasures which at home we have never enjoyed.

To historians the later part of their enormous subject is precious because it is inexhaustible. It is the best to know because it is the best known and the most explicit. Earlier scenes stand out from a background of obscurity. We soon reach the sphere of hopeless ignorance and unprofitable doubt. But hundreds and even thousands of the moderns have borne testimony against themselves, and may be studied in their private correspondence and sentenced on their own confession. Their deeds are done in the daylight. Every country opens its archives and invites us to penetrate the mysteries of state. When Hallam wrote his chapter on James II, France was the only Power whose reports were available. Rome followed, and The Hague; and then came the stores of the Italian States, and at last the Prussian and the Austrian papers, and partly those of Spain. Where Hallam and Lingard were dependent on Barillon, their successors consult the diplomacy of ten governments. The topics indeed are few on which the resources have been so employed that we can be content with the work done for us and never wish it to be done over again. Part of the lives of Luther and Frederic, a little of the Thirty Years' War, much of the American Revolution and the French Restoration, the early years of Richelieu and Mazarin, and a few volumes of Mr. Gardiner, show here and there like Pacific islands in the ocean. I should not even venture to claim for Ranke, the real originator of the heroic study of records, and the most prompt and fortunate of European pathfinders, that there is one of his seventy volumes that has not been overtaken and in part surpassed. It is through his accelerating influence mainly that our branch of study has become progressive, so that the best master is quickly distanced by the better pupil. The Vatican archives alone, now made accessible to the world, filled 3,239 cases when they were sent to France; and they are not the richest. We are still at the beginning of the documentary age, which will tend to make history independent of historians, to develop learning at the expense of writing, and to accomplish a revolution in other sciences as well.

To men in general I would justify the stress I am laying on modern history neither by urging its varied wealth, nor the rupture with precedent, nor the perpetuity of change and increase of pace, nor the growing predominance of opinion over belief, and of knowledge over opinion, but by the argument that it is a narrative told of ourselves, the record of a life which is our own, of efforts not yet abandoned to repose, of problems that still entangle the feet and vex the hearts of men. Every part of it is weighty with inestimable lessons that we must learn by experience and at a great price, if we know not how to profit by the example and teaching of those who have gone before us, in a society largely resembling the one we live in. Its study fulfils its purpose even if it only makes us wiser, without producing books, and gives us the gift of historical thinking, which is better than historical learning. It is a most powerful ingredient in the formation of character and the training of talent, and our historical judgments have as much to do with hopes of heaven as public or private conduct. Convictions that have been strained through the instances and the comparisons of modern times differ immeasurably in solidity and force from those which every new fact perturbs, and which are often little better than illusions or unsifted prejudice.

The first of human concerns is religion, and it is the salient feature of the modern centuries. They are signalised as the scene of Protestant developments. Starting from a time of extreme indifference, ignorance and decline, they were at once occupied with that conflict which was to rage so long, and of which no man could imagine the infinite consequences. Dogmatic conviction – for I shun to speak of faith in connection with many characters of those days – dogmatic conviction rose to be the centre of universal interest, and remained down to Cromwell the supreme influence and motive of public policy. A time came when the intensity of prolonged conflict, when even the energy of antagonistic assurance abated somewhat, and the controversial spirit began to make room for the scientific; and as the storm subsided, and the area of settled questions emerged, much of the dispute was abandoned to the serene and soothing touch of historians, invested as they are with the prerogative of redeeming the cause of religion from many unjust reproaches, and from the graver evil of reproaches that are just. Ranke used to say that Church interests prevailed in politics until the Seven Years' War, and marked a phase of society that ended when the hosts of Brandenburg went into action at Leuthen, chaunting their Lutheran hymns. That bold proposition would be disputed even if applied to the present age. After Sir Robert Peel had broken up his party, the leaders who followed him declared that no popery was the only basis on which it could be reconstructed. On the other side may be urged that, in July 1870, at the outbreak of the French war, the only government that insisted on the abolition of the temporal power was Austria; and since then we have witnessed the fall of Castelar, because he attempted to reconcile Spain with Rome.

Soon after 1850 several of the most intelligent men in France, struck by the arrested increase of their own population and by the telling statistics from Further Britain, foretold the coming preponderance of the English race. They did not foretell, what none could then foresee, the still more sudden growth of Prussia, or that the three most important countries of the globe would, by the end of the century, be those that chiefly belonged to the conquests of the Reformation. So that in Religion, as in so many things, the product of these centuries has favoured the new elements; and the centre of gravity, moving from the Mediterranean nations to the Oceanic, from the Latin to the Teuton, has also passed from the Catholic to the Protestant.

Out of these controversies proceeded political as well as historical science. It was in the Puritan phase, before the restoration of the Stuarts, that theology, blending with politics, effected a fundamental change. The essentially English reformation of the seventeenth century was less a struggle between churches than between sects, often subdivided by questions of discipline and self-regulation rather than by dogma. The sectaries cherished no purpose or prospect of prevailing over the nations; and they were concerned with the individual more than with the congregation, with conventicles, not with state churches. Their view was narrowed, but their sight was sharpened. It appeared to them that governments and institutions are made to pass away, like things of earth, whilst souls are immortal; that there is no more proportion between liberty and power than between eternity and time; that, therefore, the sphere of enforced command ought to be restricted within fixed limits, and that which had been done by authority, and outward discipline, and organised violence, should be attempted by division of power, and committed to the intellect and the conscience of free men. Thus was exchanged the dominion of will over will for the dominion of reason over reason. The true apostles of toleration are not those who sought protection for their own beliefs, or who had none to protect; but men to whom, irrespective of their cause, it was a political, a moral and a theological dogma, a question of conscience involving both religion and policy. Such a man was Socinus; and others arose in the smaller sects, the Independent founder of the colony of Rhode Island and the Quaker patriarch of Pennsylvania. Much of the energy and zeal which had laboured for authority of doctrine was employed for liberty of prophesying. The air was filled with the enthusiasm of a new cry; but the cause was still the same. It became a boast that religion was the mother of freedom, that freedom was the lawful offspring of religion; and this transmutation, this subversion of established forms of political life by the development of religious thought, brings us to the heart of my subject, to the significant and central feature of the historic cycles before us. Beginning with the strongest religious movement and the most refined despotism ever known, it has led to the superiority of politics over divinity in the life of nations, and terminates in the equal claim of every man to be unhindered by man in the fulfilment of duty to God – a doctrine laden with storm and havoc, which is the secret essence of the Rights of Man and the indestructible soul of Revolution.

When we consider what the adverse forces were, their sustained resistance, their frequent recovery, the critical moments when the struggle seemed for ever desperate, in 1685, in 1772, in 1808, it is no hyperbole to say that the progress of the world towards self-government would have been arrested but for the strength afforded by the religious motive in the seventeenth century. And this constancy of progress, of progress in the direction of organised and assured freedom, is the characteristic fact of modern history and its tribute to the theory of Providence. Many persons, I am well assured, would detect that this is a very old story, and a trivial commonplace, and would challenge proof that the world is making progress in aught but intellect, that it is gaining in freedom, or that increase in freedom is either a progress or a gain. Ranke, who was my own master, rejected the view that I have stated; Comte, the master of better men, believed that we drag a lengthening chain under the gathered weight of the dead hand; and many of our recent classics – Carlyle, Newman, Froude – were persuaded that there is no progress justifying the ways of God to man, and that the mere consolidation of liberty is like the motion of creatures whose advance is in the direction of their tails. They deem that anxious precaution against bad government is an obstruction to good, and degrades morality and mind by placing the capable at the mercy of the incapable, dethroning enlightened virtue for the benefit of the average man. They hold that great and salutary things are done for mankind by power concentrated, not by power balanced and cancelled and dispersed, and that the Whig theory, sprung from decomposing sects, the theory that authority is legitimate only by virtue of its checks, and that the sovereign is dependent on the subject, is rebellion against the divine will manifested all down the stream of time.

I state the objection not that we may plunge into the crucial controversy of a science that is not identical with ours, but in order to make my drift clear by the defining aid of express contradiction. No political dogma is as serviceable to my purpose here as the historian's maxim to do the best he can for the other side, and to avoid pertinacity or emphasis on his own. Like the economic precept *laissez-faire*, which the eighteenth century derived from Colbert, it has been an important, if not a final step in the making of method. The strongest and most impressive personalities, it is true, like Macaulay, Thiers, and the two greatest of living writers,

Mommsen and Treitschke, project their own broad shadow upon their pages. This is a practice proper to great men, and a great man may be worth several immaculate historians. Otherwise there is virtue in the saying that a historian is seen at his best when he does not appear. Better for us is the example of the Bishop of Oxford, who never lets us know what he thinks of anything but the matter before him; and of his illustrious French rival, Fustel de Coulanges, who said to an excited audience: 'Do not imagine you are listening to me; it is history itself that speaks.' We can found no philosophy on the observation of four hundred years, excluding three thousand. It would be an imperfect and a fallacious induction. But I hope that even this narrow and disedifying section of history will aid you to see that the action of Christ who is risen on mankind whom He redeemed fails not, but increases; that the wisdom of divine rule appears not in the perfection but in the improvement of the world; and that achieved liberty is the one ethical result that rests on the converging and combined conditions of advancing civilisation. Then you will understand what a famous philosopher said, that history is the true demonstration of Religion.

But what do people mean who proclaim that liberty is the palm, and the prize, and the crown, seeing that it is an idea of which there are two hundred definitions, and that this wealth of interpretation has caused more bloodshed than anything, except theology? Is it democracy as in France, or federalism as in America, or the national independence which bounds the Italian view, or the reign of the fittest, which is the ideal of Germans? I know not whether it will ever fall within my sphere of duty to trace the slow progress of that idea through the chequered scenes of our history, and to describe how subtle speculations touching the nature of conscience promoted a nobler and more spiritual conception of the liberty that protects it, until the guardian of rights developed into the guardian of duties which are the cause of rights, and that which had been prized as the material safeguard for treasures of earth became sacred as security for things that are divine. All that we require is a workaday key to history, and our present need can be supplied without pausing to satisfy philosophers. Without enquiring how far Sarasa or Butler, Kant or Vinet, is right as to the infallible voice of God in man, we may easily agree in this, that where absolutism reigned, by irresistible arms, concentrated, possessions, auxiliary churches and inhuman laws, it reigns no more; that commerce having risen against land, labour against wealth, the state against the forces dominant in society, the division of power against the state, the thought of individuals against the practice of ages, neither authorities, nor minorities, nor majorities can command implicit obedience; and, where there has been long and arduous experience, a rampart of tried conviction and accumulated knowledge, where there is a fair level of general morality, education, courage and self-restraint, there, if there only, a society may be found that exhibits the condition of life towards which, by elimination of failures, the world has been moving through the allotted space. You will know it by outward signs: representation, the extinction of slavery, the reign of opinion and the like; better still by less apparent evidences: the security of the weaker groups and the liberty of conscience, which, effectually secured, secures the rest.

Here we reach a point at which my argument threatens to abut on a contradiction. If the supreme conquests of society are won more often by violence than by lenient arts, if the trend and drift of things is towards convulsions and catastrophes, if the world owes religious liberty to the Dutch Revolution, constitutional government to the English, federal republicanism to the American, political equality to the French and its successors, what is to become of us, docile and attentive students of the absorbing Past? The triumph of the revolutionist annuls the historian. By its authentic exponents, Jefferson and Sieyès, the Revolution of the last century repudiates history. Their followers renounced acquaintance with it, and were ready to destroy its records and to abolish its inoffensive professors. But the unexpected truth, stranger than fiction, is that this was not the ruin but the renovation of history. Directly and indirectly, by process of development and by process of reaction, an impulse was given which made it infinitely more effectual as a factor of civilisation than ever before, and a movement began in the world of minds which was deeper and more serious than the revival of ancient learning. The dispensation under which we live and labour consists first in the recoil from the negative spirit that rejected the law of growth, and partly in the endeavour to classify and adjust the Revolution, and to account for it by the natural working of historic causes. The Conservative line of writers, under the name of the Romantic or Historical school, had its seat in Germany, looked upon the Revolution as an alien episode, the error of an age, a disease to be treated by the investigation of its origin, and strove to unite the broken threads and to restore the normal conditions of organic evolution. The Liberal School, whose home was France, explained and justified the Revolution as a true development, and the ripened fruit of all history. These are the two main arguments of the generation to which we owe the notion and the scientific methods that make history so unlike what it was to the survivors of the last century. Severally, the innovators were not superior to the men of old. Muratori was as widely read, Tillemont as accurate, Leibniz as able, Fréret as acute, Gibbon as masterly in the craft of composite construction. Nevertheless, in the second quarter of this century, a new era began for historians.

I would point to three things in particular, out of many, which constitute the amended order. Of the incessant deluge of new and unsuspected matter I need say little. For some years, the secret archives of the papacy were accessible at Paris; but the time was not ripe, and almost the only man whom they availed was the archivist himself. Towards 1830 the documentary studies began on a large scale, Austria leading the way. Michelet, who claims, towards 1836, to have been the pioneer, was preceded by such rivals as Mackintosh, Bucholtz and Mignet. A new and more productive period began thirty years later, when the war of 1859 laid open the spoils of Italy. Every country in succession has now allowed the exploration of its records, and there is more fear of drowning than of drought. The result has been that a lifetime spent in the largest collection of printed books would not suffice to train a real master of modern history. After he had turned from literature to sources, from Burnet to Pocock, from Macaulay to Madame Campana, from Thiers to the interminable correspondence of the Bonapartes, he would still feel instant need of enquiry at Venice or Naples, in the Ossuna library or at the Hermitage.

These matters do not now concern us. For our purpose, the main thing to learn is not the art of accumulating material, but the sublimer art of investigating it, of discerning truth from falsehood and certainty from doubt. It is by solidity of criticism more than by the plenitude of erudition that the study of history strengthens, and straightens, and extends the mind. And the accession of the critic in the place of the indefatigable compiler, of the artist in coloured narrative, the skilled limner of character, the persuasive advocate of good, or other, causes, amounts to a transfer of government, to a change of dynasty, in the historic realm. For the critic is one who, when he lights on an interesting statement, begins by suspecting it. He remains in suspense until he has subjected his authority to three operations. First, he asks whether he has read the passage as the author wrote it. For the transcriber, and the editor, and the official or officious censor on the top of the editor, have played strange tricks, and have much to answer for. And if they are not to blame, it may turn out that the author wrote his book twice over, that you can discover the first jet, the progressive variations, things added and things struck out. Next is the question where the writer got his information. If from a previous writer, it can be ascertained, and the inquiry has to be repeated. If from unpublished papers, they must be traced, and when the fountainhead is reached, or the track disappears, the question of veracity arises. The responsible writer's character, his position, antecedents and probable motives have to be examined into; and this is what, in a different and adapted sense of the word, may be called the higher criticism, in comparison with the servile and often mechanical work of pursuing statements to their root. For a historian has to be treated as a witness, and not believed unless his sincerity is established. The maxim that a man must be presumed to be innocent until his guilt is proved, was not made for him.

For us, then, the estimate of authorities, the weighing of testimony, is more meritorious than the potential discovery of new matter. And modern history, which is the widest field of application, is not the best to learn our business in; for it is too wide, and the harvest has not been winnowed as in antiquity, and further on to the Crusades. It is better to examine what has been done for questions that are compact and circumscribed, such as the sources of Plutarch's *Pericles*, the two tracts on Athenian government, the origin of the *Epistle to Diognetus*, the date of the life of St. Antony; and to learn from Schwegler how this analytical work began. More satisfying because more decisive has been the critical treatment of the medieval writers, parallel with the new editions, on which incredible labour has been lavished, and of which we have no better examples than the prefaces of Bishop Stubbs. An important event in this series was the attack on Dino Compagni, which, for the sake of Dante, roused the best Italian scholars to a not unequal contest. When we are told that England is behind the continent in critical faculty, we must admit that this is true as to quantity, not as to quality of work. As they are no longer living, I will say of two Cambridge professors, Lightfoot and Hort, that they were critical scholars whom neither Frenchman nor German has surpassed.

The third distinctive note of the generation of writers who dug so deep a trench between history as known to our grandfathers and as it appears to us, is their dogma of impartiality. To an ordinary man the word means no more than justice. He considers that he may proclaim the merits of his own religion, of his prosperous and enlightened country, of his political persuasion, whether democracy, or liberal monarchy, or historic conservatism, without transgression or offence, so long as he is fair to the relative, though inferior, merits of others, and never treats men as saints or as rogues for the side they take. There is no impartiality, he would say, like that of a hanging judge. The men who, with the compass of criticism in their hands, sailed the uncharted sea of original research proposed a different view. History, to be above evasion or dispute, must stand on documents, not on opinions. They had their own notion of truthfulness, based on the exceeding difficulty of finding truth and the still greater difficulty of impressing it when found. They thought it possible to write, with so much scruple, and simplicity, and insight, as to carry along with them every man of good will, and, whatever his feelings, to compel his assent. Ideas which, in religion and in politics, are truths, in history are forces. They must be respected; they must not be affirmed. By dint of a supreme reserve, by much self-control, by a timely and discreet indifference, by secrecy in the matter of the black cap, history might be lifted above contention, and made an accepted tribunal, and the same for all. If men were truly sincere, and delivered judgment by no canons but those of evident morality, then Julian would be described in the same terms by Christian and pagan, Luther by Catholic and Protestant, Washington by Whig and Tory, Napoleon by patriotic Frenchman and patriotic German.

I speak of this school with reverence, for the good it has done, by the assertion of historic truth and of its legitimate authority over the minds of men. It provides a discipline which everyone of us does well to undergo, and perhaps also well to relinquish. For it is not the whole truth. Lanfrey's essay on Carnot, Chuquet's wars of the Revolution, Ropes's military histories, Roget's Geneva in the time of Calvin, will supply you with examples of a more robust impartiality than I have described. Renan calls it the luxury of an opulent and aristocratic society, doomed to vanish in an age of fierce and sordid striving. In our universities it has a magnificent and appointed refuge; and to serve its cause, which is sacred, because it is the cause of truth and honour, we may import a profitable lesson from the highly unscientific region of public life. There a man does not take long to find out that he is opposed by some who are abler and better than himself. And, in order to understand the cosmic force and the true connection of ideas, it is a source of power, and an excellent school of principle, not to rest until, by excluding the fallacies, the prejudices, the exaggerations which perpetual contention and the consequent precautions breed, we have made out for our opponents a stronger and more impressive case than they present themselves. Excepting one to which we are coming before I release you, there is no precept less faithfully observed by historians.

Ranke is the representative of the age which instituted the modern study of history. He taught it to be critical, to be colourless, and to be new. We meet him at every step, and he has done more for us than any other man. There are stronger books than any one of his, and some may have surpassed him in political, religious, philosophic insight, in vividness of the creative imagination, in originality, elevation and depth of thought; but by the extent of important work well executed, by his influence on able men, and by the amount of knowledge which mankind receives and employs with the stamp of his mind upon it, he stands without a rival. I saw him last in 1877, when he was feeble, sunken and almost blind, and scarcely able to read or write. He uttered his farewell with kindly emotion, and I feared that the next I should hear of him would be the news of his death. Two years later he began a Universal History, which is not without traces of weakness, but which, composed after the age of eighty-three, and carried, in seventeen volumes, far into the Middle Ages, brings to a close the most astonishing career in literature.

His course had been determined, in early life, by *Quentin Durward*. The shock of the discovery that Scott's Louis XI was inconsistent with the original in Commynes made him resolve that his object thenceforth should be above all things to follow, without swerving, and in stern subordination and surrender, the lead of his authorities. He decided effectually to repress the poet, the patriot, the religious or political partisan, to sustain no cause, to banish himself from his books, and to write nothing that would gratify his own feelings or disclose his private convictions. When a strenuous divine, who, like him, had written on the Reformation, hailed him as a comrade, Ranke repelled his advances. 'You,' he said, 'are in the first place a Christian: I am in the first place a historian. There is a gulf between us.' He was the first eminent writer who exhibited what Michelet calls *le désintéressement des morts.* It was a moral triumph for him when he could refrain from judging, show that much might be said on both sides, and leave the rest to Providence. He would have felt sympathy with the two famous London physicians of our day, of whom it is told that they could not make up their minds on a case and reported dubiously. The head of the family insisted on a positive opinion. They answered that they were unable to give one, but he might easily find fifty doctors who could.

Niebuhr had pointed out that chroniclers who wrote before the invention of printing generally copied one predecessor at a time, and knew little about sifting or combining authorities. The suggestion became luminous in Ranke's hands, and with his light and dexterous touch he scrutinised and dissected the principal historians, from Machiavelli to the *Mémoires d'un Homme d'État,* with a rigour never before applied to moderns. But whilst Niebuhr dismissed the traditional story, replacing it with a construction of his own, it was Ranke's mission to preserve, not to undermine, and to set up masters whom, in their proper sphere, he could obey. The many excellent dissertations in which he displayed this art, though his successors in the next generation matched his skill and did still more thorough work, are the best introduction from which we can learn the technical process by which within living memory the study of modern history has been renewed. Ranke's contemporaries, weary of his neutrality and suspense, and of the useful but subordinate work that was done by beginners who borrowed his

wand, thought that too much was made of these obscure prelimi-
naries which a man may accomplish for himself, in the silence of
his chamber, with less demand on the attention of the public. That
may be reasonable in men who are practised in these fundamental
technicalities. We who have to learn them must immerse ourselves
in the study of the great examples.

Apart from what is technical, method is only the reduplication
of common sense, and is best acquired by observing its use by the
ablest men in every variety of intellectual employment. Bentham
acknowledged that he learned less from his own profession than
from writers like Linnaeus and Cullen; and Brougham advised the
student of Law to begin with Dante. Liebig described his *Organic
Chemistry* as an application of ideas found in Mill's *Logic,* and a
distinguished physician, not to be named lest he should overhear
me, read three books to enlarge his medical mind; and they were
Gibbon, Grote and Mill. He goes on to say, 'An educated man
cannot become so on one study alone, but must be brought under
the influence of natural, civil and moral modes of thought.' I quote
my colleague's golden words in order to reciprocate them. If men
of science owe anything to us, we may learn much from them that
is essential. For they can show how to test proof, how to secure
fullness and soundness in induction, how to restrain and to employ
with safety hypothesis and analogy. It is they who hold the secret of
the mysterious property of the mind by which error ministers to
truth, and truth slowly but irrevocably prevails. Theirs is the logic
of discovery, the demonstration of the advance of knowledge and
the development of ideas, which, as the earthly wants and passions
of men remain almost unchanged, are the charter of progress and
the vital spark in history. And they often give us invaluable counsel when they attend to their own subjects and address their own
people. Remember Darwin taking note only of those passages that
raised difficulties in his way; the French philosopher complaining
that his work stood still because he found no more contradicting
facts; Baer, who thinks error treated thoroughly nearly as

remunerative as truth, by the discovery of new objections; for, as Sir Robert Ball warns us, it is by considering objections that we often learn. Faraday declares that 'in knowledge, that man only is to be condemned and despised who is not in a state of transition.' And John Hunter spoke for all of us when he said: 'Never ask me what I have said or what I have written; but if you will ask me what my present opinions are, I will tell you.'

From the first years of the century we have been quickened and enriched by contributors from every quarter. The jurists brought us that law of continuous growth which has transformed history from a chronicle of casual occurrences into the likeness of something organic. Towards 1820 divines began to recast their doctrines on the lines of development, of which Newman said, long after, that evolution had come to confirm it. Even the economists, who were practical men, dissolved their science into liquid history, affirming that it is not an auxiliary but the actual subject matter of their inquiry. Philosophers claim that, as early as 1804, they began to bow the metaphysical neck beneath the historical yoke. They taught that philosophy is only the amended sum of all philosophies, that systems pass with the age whose impress they bear, that the problem is to focus the rays of wandering but extant truth, and that history is the source of philosophy, if not quite a substitute for it. Comte begins a volume with the words that the preponderance of history over philosophy was the characteristic of the time he lived in. Since Cuvier first recognised the conjunction between the course of inductive discovery and the course of civilisation, science had its share in saturating the age with historic ways of thought, and subjecting all things to that influence for which the depressing names historicism and historical-mindedness have been devised.

There are certain faults which are corrigible mental defects on which I ought to say a few denouncing words, because they are common to us all. First: the want of an energetic understanding of the sequence and real significance of events, which would be fatal to a practical politician, is ruin to a student of history, who is the politician with his face turned backwards. It is playing at study to see nothing but the unmeaning and unsuggestive surface, as we generally do. Then we have a curious proclivity to neglect, and by degrees to forget, what has been certainly known. An instance or two will explain my idea. The most popular English writer relates how it happened in his presence that the title of Tory was conferred upon the Conservative Party. For it was an opprobrious name at the time, applied to men for whom the Irish government offered head money; so that if I have made too sure of progress, I may at least complacently point to this instance of our mended manners. One day, Titus Oates lost his temper with the men who refused to believe him, and, after looking about for a scorching imprecation, he began to call them Tories. The name remained; but its origin, attested by Defoe, dropped out of common memory, as if one party were ashamed of their godfather and the other did not care to be identified with his cause and character. You all know, I am sure, the story of the news of Trafalgar, and how, two days after it had arrived, Mr. Pitt, drawn by an enthusiastic crowd, went to dine in the city. When they drank the health of the minister who had saved his country, he declined the praise. 'England,' he said, 'has saved herself by her own energy; and I hope that after having saved herself by her energy, she will save Europe by her example.' In 1814, when this hope had been realised, the last speech of the great orator was remembered, and a medal was struck upon which the whole sentence was engraved, in four words of compressed Latin: *Seipsam virtute, Europam exemplo.* Now it was just at the time of his last appearance in public that Mr. Pitt heard of the overwhelming success of the French in Germany, and of the Austrian surrender at Ulm. His friends concluded that the contest on land was hopeless, and that it was time to abandon the continent to the conqueror, and to fall back upon our new empire of the sea. Pitt did not agree with them. He said that Napoleon would meet with a check whenever he encountered a national resistance; and he declared that Spain was the place for it, and that then England would intervene. General Wellesley, fresh from India, was present. Ten years later, when he had accomplished that which Pitt had seen in the lucid prescience of his last days, he related at Paris what I scarcely hesitate to call the most astounding and profound prediction in all political history, where such things have not been rare.

I shall never again enjoy the opportunity of speaking my thoughts to such an audience as this, and on so privileged an occasion a lecturer may well be tempted to bethink himself whether he knows of any neglected truth, any cardinal proposition, that might serve as his selected epigraph, as a last signal, perhaps even as a target. I am not thinking of those shining precepts which are the registered property of every school; that is to say – Learn as much by writing as by reading; be not content with the best book; seek sidelights from the others; have no favourites; keep men and things apart; guard against the prestige of great names; see that your judgments are your own, and do not shrink from disagreement; no trusting without testing; be more severe to ideas than to actions; do not overlook the strength of the bad cause or the weakness of the good; never be surprised by the crumbling of an idol or the disclosure of a skeleton; judge talent at its best and character at its worst; suspect power more than vice, and study problems in preference to periods; for instance: the derivation of Luther, the scientific influence of Bacon, the predecessors of Adam Smith, the medieval masters of Rousseau, the consistency of Burke, the identity of the first Whig. Most of this, I suppose, is undisputed, and calls for no enlargement. But the weight of opinion is against me when I exhort you never to debase the moral currency or to lower the standard of rectitude, but to try others by the final maxim that governs your own lives, and to suffer no man and no cause to escape the undying penalty which history has the power to inflict on wrong. The plea in extenuation of guilt and mitigation of punishment is perpetual. At every step we are met by arguments which go to excuse, to palliate, to confound right and wrong, and reduce the just man to the level of the reprobate. The men who plot to baffle and resist us are, first of all, those who made history what it has become. They set up the principle that only a foolish Conservative judges the present time with the ideas of the past; that only a foolish Liberal judges the past with the ideas of the present.

The mission of that school was to make distant times, and especially the Middle Ages, then most distant of all, intelligible and acceptable to a society issuing from the eighteenth century. There were difficulties in the way; and among others this, that, in the first fervour of the Crusades, the men who took the Cross, after receiving communion, heartily devoted the day to the extermination of Jews. To judge them by a fixed standard, to call them sacrilegious fanatics or furious hypocrites, was to yield a gratuitous victory to Voltaire. It became a rule of policy to praise the spirit when you could not defend the deed. So that we have no common code; our moral notions are always fluid; and you must consider the times, the class from which men sprang, the surrounding influences, the masters in their schools, the preachers in their pulpits, the movement they obscurely obeyed and so on, until responsibility is merged in numbers and not a culprit is left for execution. A murderer was no criminal if he followed local custom, if neighbours approved, if he was encouraged by official advisers or prompted by just authority, if he acted for the reason of state or the pure love of religion, or if he sheltered himself behind the complicity of the law. The depression of morality was flagrant; but the motives were those which have enabled us to contemplate with distressing complacency the secret of unhallowed lives. The code that is greatly modified by time and place will vary according to the cause. The amnesty is an artifice that enables us to make exceptions, to tamper with weights and measures, to deal unequal justice to friends and enemies.

It is associated with that philosophy which Cato attributes to the gods. For we have a theory which justifies Providence by the event, and holds nothing so deserving as success, to which there can be no victory in a bad cause; prescription and duration legitimate; and whatever exists is right and reasonable; and as God manifests His will by that which He tolerates, we must conform to the divine decree by living to shape the future after the ratified image of the past. Another theory, less confidently urged, regards history as our guide, as much by showing errors to evade as examples to pursue. It is suspicious of illusions in success, and, though there may be hope of ultimate triumph for what is true, if not by its own attraction, by the gradual exhaustion of error, it admits no corresponding promise for what is ethically right. It deems the canonisation of the historic past more perilous than ignorance or denial, because it would perpetuate the reign of sin and acknowledge the sovereignty of wrong, and conceives it the part of real greatness to know how to stand and fall alone, stemming, for a lifetime, the contemporary flood.

Ranke relates, without adornment, that William III ordered the extirpation of a Catholic clan, and scouts the faltering excuse of his defenders. But when he comes to the death and character of the international deliverer, Glencoe is forgotten, the imputation of murder drops, like a thing unworthy of notice. Johannes Müller, a great Swiss celebrity, writes that the British constitution occurred to somebody, perhaps to Halifax. This artless statement might not be approved by rigid lawyers as a faithful and felicitous indication of the manner of that mysterious growth of ages, from occult beginnings, that was never profaned by the invading wit of man; but it is less grotesque than it appears. Lord Halifax was the most original writer of political tracts in the pamphleteering crowd between Harrington and Bolingbroke; and in the Exclusion struggle he produced a scheme of limitations which, in substance if not in form, foreshadowed the position of the monarchy in the later Hanoverian reigns. Although Halifax did not believe in the plot, he insisted that innocent victims should be sacrificed to content the multitude. Sir William Temple writes:

We only disagreed in one point, which was the leaving some priests to the law upon the accusation of being priests only, as the House of Commons had desired; which I thought wholly unjust. Upon this point Lord Halifax and I had so sharp a debate at Lord Sunderland's lodgings, that he told me, if I would not concur in points which were so necessary for the people's satisfaction, he would tell everybody I was a Papist. And upon his affirming that the plot must be handled as if it were true, whether it were so or no, in those points that were so generally believed.

In spite of this accusing passage, Macaulay, who prefers Halifax to all the statesmen of his age, praises him for his mercy: 'His dislike of extremes, and a forgiving and compassionate temper which seems to have been natural to him, preserved him from all participation in the worst crimes of his time.'

If, in our uncertainty, we must often err, it may be sometimes better to risk excess in rigour than in indulgence, for then at least we do no injury by loss of principle. As Bayle has said, it is more probable that the secret motives of an indifferent action are bad than good; and this discouraging conclusion does not depend upon theology, for James Mozley supports the sceptic from the other flank, with all the artillery of Tractarian Oxford. 'A Christian,' he says,

is bound by his very creed to suspect evil, and cannot release himself... He sees it where others do not; his instinct is divinely strengthened; his eye is supernaturally keen; he has a spiritual insight, and senses exercised to discern... He owns the doctrine of original sin; that doctrine puts him necessarily on his guard against appearances, sustains his apprehension under perplexity, and prepares him for recognising anywhere what he knows to be everywhere.

There is a popular saying of Madame de Staël, that we forgive whatever we really understand. The paradox has been judiciously pruned by her descendant, the Duke de Broglie, in the words: 'Beware of too much explaining, lest we end by too much excusing.' History, says Froude, does teach that right and wrong are real distinctions. Opinions alter, manners change, creeds rise and fall, but the moral law is written on the tablets of eternity. And if there are moments when we may resist the teaching of Froude, we have seldom the chance of resisting when he is supported by Mr. Goldwin Smith:

> A sound historical morality will sanction strong measures in evil times; selfish ambition, treachery, murder, perjury, it will never sanction in the worst of times, for these are the things that make times evil – Justice has been justice, mercy has been mercy, honour has been honour, good faith has been good faith, truthfulness has been truthfulness from the beginning.

The doctrine that, as Sir Thomas Browne says, morality is not ambulatory, is expressed as follows by Burke, who, when true to himself, is the most intelligent of our instructors:

> My principles enable me to form my judgement upon men and actions in history, just as they do in common life; and are not formed out of events and characters, either present or past. History is a preceptor of prudence, not of principles. The principles of true politics are those of morality enlarged; and I neither now do, nor ever will admit of any other.

Whatever a man's notions of these later centuries are, such, in the main, the man himself will be. Under the name of History, they cover the articles of his philosophic, his religious, and his political creed. They give his measure; they denote his character: and, as praise is the shipwreck of historians, his preferences betray him more than his aversions. Modern history touches us so nearly, it is so deep a question of life and death, that we are bound to find our own way through it, and to owe our insight to ourselves. The historians of former ages, unapproachable for us in knowledge and in talent, cannot be our limit. We have the power to be more rigidly impersonal, disinterested and just than they; and to learn from undisguised and genuine records to look with remorse upon the past, and to the future with assured hope of better things; bearing this in mind, that if we lower our standard in history, we cannot uphold it in Church or State.

Editor's note: All footnotes in the original text have been removed.

J B BURY:
STRIPPING THE BANDAGES OF ERROR FROM THE EYES OF MEN

INTRODUCTION BY T G OTTE

J B Bury's inaugural lecture as Regius Professor of Modern History at the University of Cambridge marked a further step towards greater professionalisation of historical scholarship in Britain. The occasion itself – especially Bury's assertion 'that history is a science, no less and no more' – elicited a mixed response.[1] It was either accepted as an expression of an obvious truth or it was vigorously attacked, most notably by G M Trevelyan, to whom such 'scientism' was anathema.[2] Neither that label, nor that of positivism, nor that of 'mere historical empiricism', in fact, seems appropriate.[3] And yet such persistent stereotypes have turned the ideas of a major historian into dusty relics in 'the museum of historiographical antiquities', so much so that a recent writer magisterially dismissed the lecture as 'that over-celebrated inaugural'.[4]

The Anglo-Irish historian John Bagnell Bury (1861–1927) was a classical philologist by training and inclination, a fact to which his major works on the late Roman Empire and Byzantium testify.[5] Like so many of his contemporaries, he was deeply influenced by German idealism in his early years, especially by Hegel, though the latter's attraction palled over time.[6] A strong interest in the philosophical problems of historical study, however, remained. In 1902, he succeeded Lord Acton as Regius Professor of Modern History at Cambridge. With some justification, he may be said to

197

have been 'the greatest historian' to have occupied the Cambridge chair until then.[7] His clerical ancestry notwithstanding, Bury held strongly rationalist beliefs, not unlike those of Gibbon, whose *Decline and Fall* he edited just before his translation to the Fen country.[8] His Cambridge inaugural marked a sharp contrast in approach to his three immediate predecessors, none of whom had pursued history entirely for its own sake. For Charles Kingsley it was a form of Protestant theology (with an erratic admixture of Norse mythology); for Sir John Robert Seeley it was the hand-maiden of politics; and for Acton it was about morality. To Bury it was a science.

The nomenclature may jar, and it readily lends itself to all man-ner of misunderstandings. His 'science' corresponded to the German *Wissenschaft*, historical scholarship which established and presented facts about the past according to exacting standards and in a systematic fashion.[9] No longer was history the manservant of other disciplines. It was autonomous – a science. The rigorous han-dling of sources and their careful contextualisation allowed for the reconstruction of facts; embracing what Bury called the 'genetic' approach to the past made possible order and comprehensibility.[10]

Central to this was the idea of development, of history as a pro-cess of growth. This was 'the great transforming concept'. Histori-cal phenomena could now be recognised as coherent, causal sequences in time, capable of examination by the scholar.[11] It was this that made history as a 'science' possible. Bury was neverthe-less wary of the notion of linearity, and in its stead emphasised 'historical relativity', noting: 'All events in the past…were relative to their historical conditions.'[12] More, history was saturated with contingency: 'The logical consequences may be facilitated or upset, accelerated or retarded, by contingencies; and it is this which makes history so interesting and so baffling.'[13]

The notion of sequences provides the necessary link to Bury's reflections about the direction of the historical process itself: '"Progress" involves a judgment of value, which is not involved in the concept of history as a genetic process...Nevertheless it is closely related to the ideas which revolutionised history at the beginning of the last century...and it helped effectively to establish the notion of history as a continuous process.'[14] Progress, then, was not so much the process of change as the meaning with which that process was invested by the observer. That meaning reflected assumptions about human nature and the course of history which were not amenable to verification. It was 'a theory which involves a synthesis of the past and a prophecy of the future'. As such, it was the product of a specific historical location; it could only have relative value. To pretend otherwise was to fall for 'the illusion of finality', of an absolute truth, belief in which was 'an act of faith'.[15]

Bury's liberalism accepted open-ended progress but abjured the notion that progress was providential or immanent in the historical process. His general insistence on scholarly autonomy notwithstanding, it was inseparably entwined with his acceptance that history served broader ends than simply the advancement of learning. The 'practical value of history' did not consist 'in lessons and examples, but in the fact that it explains the present, and that without it the present, in which we have to act, would be incomprehensible'.[16] By rendering to the present an account of its own past, scholarship played an important role in clarifying choices for future action. In that sense, scholarship served society, tying together past and present into a unity that provided meaning for the present and the future: 'For us...because we have grasped the idea of development...the reconstruction of history has become a necessity.'[17] There was a latitudinal aspect to this effort. The narrower Rankean idea of *Staatengeschichte* had to be broadened by 'a more comprehensive definition [of history] which embraces all records, whatever their nature may be, of the material and spiritual development, of the culture and the works, of man in society, from the stone age onwards'.[18] In his own writings, for instance, Bury emphasised the importance of geography.[19] A broader scope of historical enquiry meant that larger questions could be tackled:

'If, year by year, history is to become a more and more powerful force for stripping the bandages of error from the eyes of men…she will best prepare her disciples for the performance of that task…by remembering always that…she is herself simply a science, no less and no more.'[20]

Bury's programme for deepening and widening historical scholarship remained largely that, a prospectus. His own studies of the Roman and Byzantine empires were principally concerned with their administrative, constitutional and political aspects.[21] And yet that prospectus, leavened by a humane breadth of vision and sceptical pragmatism, is worth reconsidering. So is his insistence that 'the furtherance of research…is the highest duty of universities, [which] requires ways and means.' In 'promoting and prosecuting such [scientific] research we are not indulging in a luxury but doing a thoroughly practical work and performing a great duty to posterity'.[22] 'Research', Bury added on another occasion, 'might move the world' – words that should be written in the skies.[23]

Norfolk, January 2022

---

1. J B Bury, 'The Science of History: an Inaugural Lecture Delivered in the Divinity School Cambridge on January 26, 1903' (Cambridge, 1903), 7 and 42.
2. G M Trevelyan, 'Clio, a Muse', in *Clio, a Muse and Other Essays* (Literary and Pedestrian, London, 1914), 1–55. The piece was first published in 1903 as a direct riposte to Bury's lecture; see D Cannadine, *G.M. Trevelyan: a Life in History* (London, 1993 (pb)), 214–15.
3. F Stern, 'Introduction', in Stern, ed., *The Varieties of History: from Voltaire to the Present*, 2nd edn (Red Globe Press, London, 1970), 20.
4. D S Goldstein, 'JB Bury's Philosophy of History: a Reappraisal', *American Historical Review* lxxxii/4 (1977), 916; and M Bentley, *Modernizing England's Past: English Historiography in the Age of Modernism, 1870–1970* (Cambridge University Press, Cambridge, 2005), 97.

5. For an assessment see G Huxley, 'The Historical Scholarship of John Bagnell Bury', *Greek, Roman and Byzantine Studies* xvii/1 (1976), 81–104.

6. H Temperley, 'Introduction: the Historical Ideas of J.B. Bury', in Temperley, ed., *Selected Essays of J.B. Bury* (Cambridge University Press, Cambridge, 1930), xviii; for a biographical sketch see N H Baynes, *A Bibliography of the Works of JB Bury, Compiled with a Memoir* (The Unviersity Press, Cambridge, 1929).

7. G P Gooch, 'The Cambridge Chair of Modern History', in *Studies in Modern History* (Longmans, London, 1931), 319.

8. E Gibbon, *The Decline and Fall of the Roman Empire*, 7 vols, ed. J B Bury (London, 1896–1900).

9. Bury, *The Life of St. Patrick: and His Place in History*, viii (Macmillan, London, 1905); and *The Ancient Greek Historians* (Harvard Lectures) (Macmillan, New York, 1909), 258.

10. Bury, 'Darwinism and History [1909]', *Selected Essays*, 23 *et passim*.

11. Bury, 'Inaugural Lecture', 17–18.

12. Bury, *Greek Historians*, 250.

13. Bury, 'Cleopatra's Nose [1916]', *Selected Essays*, 68. He also suggested that, with the growth of democracy, social organisation and knowledge, the scope for contingency declined – shades of Max Weber's 'iron cage'.

14. Bury, 'Darwinism and History', 27.

15. Bury, *The Idea of Progress: an Inquiry into Its Origin and Growth* (London, 1920; Dover Publications, New York, repr. 1955), 4–5 and 351.

16. Bury, 'The Place of Modern History in the Perspective of Knowledge [1904]', *Selected Essays*, 57. Bury delivered this paper at the rightly famed Congress of Arts and Sciences at St. Louis, Missouri.

17. Bury, *The Ancient Greek Historians*, 257–58

18. Bury, 'Inaugural Lecture', 35–36. Bury was sympathetic to Karl Lamprecht's Kulturgeschichte but remained sceptical of his claims that it was capable of producing scientific laws.

19. Bury, 'Russia (1462–1682)' in *The Cambridge Modern History*, v: eds AW Ward, GW Prothero and S Leathes (Cambridge University Press, Cambridge, 1907), 478.

20. Bury, 'Inaugural Lecture', 41–42.

21. This may well reflect his interest in the continuities between the Greek, Roman and post-Roman polities, and the fact that these manifested themselves above all in politics and administration, see Bury, *A History of Greece to the Death of Alexander the Great* (Macmillan, London, 1900), v; also *The Invasion of Europe by the Barbarians* (Macmillan, London, 1928; repr. 2017), 200–07 *et passim*.

22. Bury, 'Inaugural Lecture', 24 and 35.

23. As recalled by Temperley in 'Introduction', *Selected Essays*, xxxii.

J B BURY
THE SCIENCE OF HISTORY

An Inaugural Lecture Delivered in the Divinity School,

Cambridge, on January 26, 1903

In saying that I come before you today with no little trepidation, I am not uttering a mere conventional profession of diffidence. There are very real reasons for misgiving. My predecessor told you how formidable he found this chair, illuminated as it is by the lustre of the distinguished historian whom he succeeded. But if it was formidable then, how much more formidable is it today! The terrors which it possessed for Lord Acton have been enhanced for his successor.

In a home of historical studies where so much thought is spent on their advancement, one can hardly hope to say any new thing touching those general aspects of history which most naturally invite attention in an inaugural lecture. It may be appropriate and useful now and again to pay a sort of solemn tribute to the dignity and authority of a great discipline or science by reciting some of her claims and her laws, or by reviewing the measures of her dominion; and on this occasion, in this place, it might perhaps seem to be enough to honour the science of history in this formal way, sprinkling, as it were, with dutiful hands some grains of incense on her altar.

Yet even such a tribute might possess more than a formal significance, if we remember how recently it is – within three generations, three short generations – that history began to forsake her old irresponsible ways and prepared to enter into her kingdom.

In the story of the nineteenth century, which has witnessed such far-reaching changes in the geography of thought and in the apparatus of research, no small nor isolated place belongs to the transformation and expansion of history. That transformation, however, is not yet complete. Its principle is not yet universally or unreservedly acknowledged. It is rejected in many places, or ignored, or unrealised. Old envelopes still hang tenaciously round the renovated figure, and students of history are confused, embarrassed and diverted by her old traditions and associations. It has not yet become superfluous to insist that history is a science, no less and no more; and some who admit it theoretically hesitate to enforce the consequences which it involves. It is therefore, I think, almost incumbent on a professor to define, at the very outset, his attitude to the transformation of the idea of history which is being gradually accomplished; and an inaugural address offers an opportunity which, if he feels strongly the importance of the question, he will not care to lose.

And moreover I venture to think that it may be useful and stimulating for those who are beginning historical studies to realise vividly and clearly that the transformation which those studies are undergoing is itself a great event in the history of the world – that we are ourselves in the very middle of it, that we are witnessing and may share in the accomplishment of a change which will have a vast influence on future cycles of the world. I wish that I had been enabled to realise this when I first began to study history. I think it is important for all historical students alike – not only for those who may be drawn to make history the special work of their lives, but also for those who study it as part of a liberal education – to be fully alive and awake to the revolution which is slowly and silently progressing. It seems especially desirable that those who are sensible of the importance of the change and sympathise with it should declare and emphasise it; just because it is less patent to the vision and is more perplexed by ancient theories and traditions than those kindred revolutions which have been effected simultaneously in other branches of knowledge. History has really been enthroned and ensphered among the sciences; but the particular nature of her influence, her time-honoured association with literature, and other circumstances, have acted as a sort of vague cloud, half concealing from men's eyes her new position in the heavens.

The proposition that before the beginning of the last century the study of history was not scientific may be sustained in spite of a few exceptions. The works of permanent value, such as those of Muratori, Ducange, Tillemont, were achieved by dint of most laborious and conscientious industry, which commands our highest admiration and warmest gratitude: but it must be admitted that their criticism was sporadic and capricious. It was the criticism of sheer learning. A few stand on a higher level insofar as they were really alive to the need of bringing reason and critical doubt to bear on the material, but the systemised method which distinguishes a science was beyond the vision of all, except a few like Mabillon. Erudition has now been supplemented by scientific method, and we owe the change to Germany. Among those who brought it about, the names of Niebuhr and Ranke are pre-eminent. But there is another name which historical students should be slow to forget, the name of one who, though not a historian but a philologist, nevertheless gave a powerful stimulus to the introduction of critical methods which are now universally applied. Six years before the eighteenth century closed a modest book appeared at Halle, of which it is perhaps hardly a grave exaggeration to say that it is one of half a dozen which in the last three hundred years have exercised most effective influence upon thought. The work I mean is Wolf's *Prolegomena to Homer*. It launched upon the world a new engine – *donum exitiale Minervae* – which was soon to menace the walls of many a secure citadel. It gave historians the idea of a systematic and minute method of analysing their sources, which soon developed into the microscopic criticism now recognised as indispensable.

All truths (to modify a saying of Plato) require the most exact methods; and closely connected with the introduction of a new method was the elevation of the standard of truth. The idea of a scrupulously exact conformity to facts was fixed, refined and canonised; and the critical method was one of the means to secure it. There was indeed no historian since the beginning of things who did not profess that his sole aim was to present to his readers untainted and unpainted truth. But the axiom was loosely understood and interpreted, and the notion of truth was elastic. It might be difficult to assign to puritanism and rationalism and other causes their respective parts in crystallising that strict discrimination of the true and the false which is now so familiar to us that we can hardly understand insensibility to the distinction. It would be a most fruitful investigation to trace from the earliest ages the history of public opinion in regard to the meaning of falsehood and the obligation of veracity. About twenty years ago a German made a contribution to the subject by examining the evidence for the twelfth, thirteenth and fourteenth centuries, and he showed how different were the views which men held then as to truth-telling and lying from those which are held today. Moreover, so long as history was regarded as an art, the sanctions of truth and accuracy could not be severe. The historians of ancient Rome display what historiography can become when it is associated with rhetoric. Though we may point to individual writers who had a high ideal of accuracy at various ages, it was not till the scientific period began that laxity in representing facts came to be branded as criminal. Nowhere perhaps can we see the new spirit so self-conscious as in some of the letters of Niebuhr.

But a stricter standard of truth and new methods for the purpose of ascertaining truth were not enough to detach history from her old moorings. A new transfiguring conception of her scope and limits was needed, if she was to become an independent science. Such a conception was waiting to intervene, but I may lead up to it by calling to your recollection how history was affected by the political changes of Europe.

It was a strange and fortunate coincidence that the scientific movement in Germany should have begun simultaneously with another movement which gave a strong impetus to historical studies throughout Europe and enlisted men's emotions in their favour. The saying that the name of hope is remembrance was vividly illustrated, on a vast scale, by the spirit of resurgent nationality which you know has governed, as one of the most puissant forces, the political course of the last century, and is still unexhausted. When the peoples, inspired by the national idea, were stirred to mould their destinies anew, and, looking back with longing to the more distant past, based upon it their claims for independence or for unity, history was one of the most effective weapons in their armouries; and consequently a powerful motive was supplied for historical investigation. The inevitable result was the production of some crude uncritical histories, written with national prejudice and political purpose, redeemed by the genuine pulse of national aspiration. But in Germany the two movements met. Scientific method controlled, while the national spirit quickened, the work of historical research. One of the grave dangers was the temptation to fix the eyes exclusively on the inspiring and golden periods of the past, and it is significant to find Dahlmann, as early as 1812, warning against such a tendency, and laying down that the statesman who studies national history should study the whole story of his forefathers, the whole development of his people, and not merely chosen parts.

But the point which concerns us now is that the national movements of Europe not only raised history into prominence and gave a great impulse to its study, but also partially disclosed where the true practical importance of history lies. When men sought the key of their national development not in the immediate but in the remoter past, they had implicitly recognised in some measure the principles of unity and continuity. That recognition was a step towards the higher, more comprehensive and scientific estimation of history's practical significance, which is only now beginning to be understood.

Just let me remind you what used to be thought in old days as to the utility of history. The two greatest of the ancient historians, Thucydides and Polybius, held that it might be a guide for conduct, as containing examples and warnings for statesmen; and it was generally regarded in Greece and at Rome as a storehouse of concrete instances to illustrate political and ethical maxims. Cicero called history in this sense *magistra vitae*, and Dionysius designated it 'Philosophy by examples'. And this view, which ascribed to it at best the function of teaching statesmen by analogy, at worst the duty of moral edification, prevailed generally till the last century. Of course it contained a truth which we should now express in a different form by saying that history supplies the material for political and social science. This is a very important function; but, if it were the only function, if the practical import of history lay merely in furnishing examples of causes and effects, then history, in respect of practical utility, would be no more than the handmaid of social science.

And here I may interpolate a parenthesis, which even at this hour may not be quite superfluous. I may remind you that history is not a branch of literature. The facts of history, like the facts of geology or astronomy, can supply material for literary art; for manifest reasons they lend themselves to artistic representation far more readily than those of the natural sciences; but to clothe the story of a human society in a literary dress is no more the part of a historian as a historian than it is the part of an astronomer as an astronomer to present in an artistic shape the story of the stars. Take, for example, the greatest living historian. The reputation of Mommsen as a man of letters depends on his *History of Rome*; but his greatness as a historian is to be sought far less in that dazzling work than in the *Corpus* and the *Staatsrecht* and the *Chronicles*.

This by way of parenthesis; and now to resume. A right notion of the bearing of history on affairs, both for the statesman and for the citizen, could not be formed or formulated until men had grasped the idea of human development. This is the great transforming conception, which enables history to define her scope. The idea was first started by Leibnitz, but, though it had some exponents in the interval, it did not rise to be a governing force in human thought till the nineteenth century, when it appears as the true solvent of the anti-historical doctrines which French thinkers and the French Revolution had arrayed against the compulsion of the past. At the same time, it has brought history into line with other sciences, and, potentially at least, has delivered her from the political and ethical encumbrances which continued to impede her after the introduction of scientific methods. For notwithstanding those new engines of research, she remained much less, and much more, than a science in Germany, as is illustrated by the very existence of all those bewildering currents and cross-currents, tendencies and counter-tendencies, those various schools of doctrine, in which Lord Acton was so deeply skilled. The famous saying of Ranke – *Ich will nur sagen wie es eigentlich gewesen ist* – was widely applauded, but it was little accepted in the sense of a warning against transgressing the province of facts; it is a text which must still be preached, and when it has been fully taken to heart, though there be many schools of political philosophy, there will no longer be divers schools of history.[1]

The world is not yet alive to the full importance of the transformation of history (as part of a wider transformation) which is being brought about by the doctrine of development. It is always difficult for those who are in immediate proximity to realise the decisive steps in intellectual or spiritual progress when those steps are slow and gradual; but we need not hesitate to say that the last century is not only as important an era as the fifth century BC in the annals of historical study, but marks, like it, a stage in the growth of man's self-consciousness. There is no passage, perhaps, in the works of the Greek tragedians so instructive for the historical student as that song in the *Antigone* of Sophocles, in which we seem to surprise the first amazed meditation of man when it was borne in upon him by a sudden startling illumination, how strange it is that he should be what he is and should have wrought all that he has wrought – should have wrought out, among other things, the city state. He had suddenly, as it were, waked up to realise that he himself was the wonder of the world. Οὐδέυ δεινότερου πέλει.[2] That intense expression of a new detached wondering interest in man, as an object of curiosity, gives us the clue to the inspiration of Herodotus and the birth of history. More than two thousand years later human self-consciousness has taken another step, and the 'sons of flesh' have grasped the notion of their upward development through immense cycles of time. This idea has recreated history. Girded with new strength she has definitely come out from among her old associates, moral philosophy and rhetoric; she has come out into a place of liberty; and has begun to enter into closer relations with the sciences which deal objectively with the facts of the universe.

The older view, which we may call the politico-ethical theory, naturally led to eclecticism. Certain periods and episodes, which seemed especially rich in moral and political lessons, were picked out as pre-eminently and exclusively important, and everything else was regarded as more or less the province of antiquarianism. This eclectic and exclusive view is not extinct, and can appeal to recent authority. It is remarkable that one of the most eminent English historians of the latter half of the last century, whose own scientific work was a model for all students, should have measured out the domain of history with the compasses of political or ethical wisdom, and should have protested as lately as 1877 against the principle of unity and continuity. That inconsistency is an illustration of the tenacity with which men cling to predilections that are incongruous with the whole meaning of their own life work. But it is another great Oxford historian to whom perhaps more than to any other teacher we owe it that the Unity of History is now a commonplace in Britain. It must indeed be carried beyond the limits within which he enforced it, but to have affirmed and illustrated that principle was not the least useful of Mr Freeman's valuable services to the story of Europe. In no field, I may add, have the recognition of continuity and the repudiation of eclecticism been more notable or more fruitful than in a field in which I happen to be specially interested, the history of the Eastern Roman Empire, the foster mother of Russia.

The principle of continuity and the higher principle of development lead to the practical consequence that it is of vital importance for citizens to have a true knowledge of the past and to see it in a dry light, in order that their influence on the present and future may be exerted in right directions. For, as a matter of fact, the attitude of men to the past has at all times been a factor in forming their political opinions and determining the course of events. It would be an instructive task to isolate this influence and trace it from its most rudimentary form in primitive times, when the actions of tribes were stimulated by historical memories, through later ages in which policies were dictated or confirmed by historical judgments and conceptions. But the clear realisation of the fact that our conception of the past is itself a distinct factor in guiding and moulding our evolution, and must become a factor of greater and increasing potency, marks a new stage in the growth of the human mind. And it supplies us with the true theory of the practical importance of history.

It seems inevitable that, as this truth is more fully and widely though slowly realised, the place which history occupies in national education will grow larger and larger. It is therefore of supreme moment that the history which is taught should be true; and that can be attained only through the discovery, collection, classification and interpretation of facts – through scientific research. The furtherance of research, which is the highest duty of universities, requires ways and means. Public money is spent on the printing and calendaring of our own national records; but we ought not to be satisfied with that. Every little people in Europe devotes sums it can far less well afford to the investigation of its particular history.

We want a much larger recognition of the necessity of historical research; a recognition that it is a matter of public concern to promote the scientific study of any branch of history that any student is anxious to pursue. Some statesmen would acknowledge this; but in a democratic state they are hampered by the views of unenlightened taxpayers. The wealthy private benefactors who have come forward to help universities, especially in America, are deplorably short-sighted; they think too much of direct results and immediate returns; they are unable to realise that research and the accumulated work of specialists may move the world. In the meantime, the universities themselves have much to do; they have to recognise more fully and clearly and practically and preach more loudly and assiduously that the advancement of research in history, as in other sciences, is not a luxury, subsidiary though desirable, but is a pressing need, a matter of inestimable concern to the nation and the world.

It must also be remembered that a science cannot safely be controlled or guided by a subjective interest. This brings me to the question of perspective in ecumenical history. From the subjective point of view, for our own contemporary needs, it may be held that certain centuries of human development are of a unique and predominant importance, and possess, for purposes of present utility, a direct value which cannot be claimed for remoter ages.

---

1. '*Ich will nur sagen wie es eigentlich gewesen ist*': I only aim to say how it really was.
2. 'Οὐδέυ δειυότερου πέλει': There is no second chance.

BENJAMIN F SHAMBAUGH: THE HISTORIAN'S LABORATORY

INTRODUCTION BY MATTIAS HESSÉRUS

When we think of 'applied history' today it is works like *Destined for War* by Graham Allison that come to mind. We think of historians who use historical analogies when analysing problems of geopolitics and international relations. However, applied history as a field did not start that way. Actually, the first writers calling themselves 'applied historians' were mostly concerned with local history and a rather defined set of problems of public administration.

The term 'applied history' was coined in 1909 by Benjamin Franklin Shambaugh (1871–1940), an American historian and political scientist. Shambaugh's professional life is intertwined with the American progressive era and his thinking is formed by the ideals of the liberal movement of the time. The issues that he was most concerned with were questions of good governance, higher education and social welfare. Shambaugh is arguably the first applied historian in the sense that he is the first scholar who creates and defines, if loosely, a theory and method for the field of applied history. Shambaugh also founded the first applied history project under the name of The State Historical Society of Iowa. From 1912 to the mid 1920s, 52 scholars and associates would hold positions.[1] They worked together and applied history to solve contemporary problems in a kind of history laboratory.

Even though Shambaugh coined the term, he is humble regarding the originality of the idea, writing: 'I do not know that the phrase "Applied History" is one that has thus far been employed by students of history and politics…But I believe that the time has come when it can be used with both propriety and profit.'[2]

Shambaugh, of course, understood that applying history was not new, it had been done since at least Thucydides. And Shambaugh's writings also echo that Thucydidean ideal of a history that could be 'judged useful by those who want to understand clearly the events which happened in the past and which (human nature being what it is) will, at some time or other and in much the same ways, be repeated in the future'[3]. Yet what he wanted to do was to systematise the way historians applied history to enhance its usefulness for governance. In the 'Editor's Introduction' of *Applied History, vol. 1*, republished in this anthology, Shambaugh is trying to create a framework to do exactly that. He believed that history belonged to the sciences rather than the arts. He defines applied history as 'the use of the scientific knowledge of history and experience in efforts to solve present problems of human betterment'[4].

Shambaugh had a strong belief in the scientific method and the progress of mankind. It was the advancement through science he had noticed in other fields that led him to believe that historical knowledge could also improve politics and public administration. He writes:

Applied History is simply the use of the creative power of scientific knowledge in politics and administration. Scientific farming has greatly increased the yield of the soil. Scientific mining has greatly increased the output of the mine. Scientific forestry has greatly conserved the woodlands. Scientific hygiene has greatly conserved the health and life of the people. Scientific engineering has overcome the most stubborn obstacles of nature. Can anyone doubt that some day scientific history, scientific legislation and scientific administration will be able to boast of a similar record of accomplishment?[5]

This naive enthusiasm is of the kind that was probably only possible before the First World War. In *The World of Yesterday*, Stefan Zweig describes the progressive mindset in Europe at the turn of the century:

> There was a grave and dangerous arrogance in this touching confidence that we had barricaded ourselves to the last loophole against any possible invasion of fate…[And] now it was merely a matter of decades until the last vestige of evil and violence would finally be conquered, and this faith in an uninterrupted and irresistible 'progress' truly had the force of a religion for that generation. One began to believe more in this 'progress' than in the Bible.[6]

Every age has its illusions. Shambaugh's applied history project was certainly fuelled by the almost romantic idealism of the progressive era. Yet it was also shaped by Leopold von Ranke's dry German empiricism. According to Shambaugh, the practice of applied history was to be defined by two things: scientific methods and interdisciplinary research. Its purpose was to provide 'reliable and complete information concerning the public questions which now confront us and which we are called upon to solve' and to link 'the public with results of scientific research in political and social science'.[7]

Shambaugh succeeded in bringing his ideas to fruition, and his applied history project was quite an achievement. He managed to bring together professional historians and give them great resources like a reference library, research facilities and travel funds. For more than a decade his scholars took on problems, applied history and made the results available to the public, just as Shambaugh had envisioned. His biographer Rebecca Conard cites a 1912 newspaper report which read:

Lights gleam every evening from the third floor of the hall of liberal arts, where are located the offices, library and research rooms of the State Historical Society of Iowa. Here from 8 o'clock in the morning until 10 o'clock at night or later, a group of professors and scholars…are engaged in careful, scientific research in Iowa history and allied subjects.[8]

Through his history lab, Shambaugh tried to solve local problems for the Iowans of the time. He was probably too humble to ever imagine that his vision of applied history would inspire a global research field. Still, as the reader of the following excerpt will see, much of what applied historians do today carries the hallmark of Shambaugh's original idea: that history can be applied in the pursuit of a better society.

Withington, January 2022

1. Rebecca Conard, *Benjamin Shambaugh and the Intellectual Foundations of Public History* (University of Iowa Press, Iowa City, IA, 2002), 81.
2. Conard, *Benjamin Shambaugh and the Intellectual Foundations*, 33.
3. Thucydides, *History of the Peloponnesian War*, trans Rex Warner (Penguin Classics, New York, 1985), 48.
4. Benjamin F Shambaugh (ed), *Applied History*, vol I, (The State Historical Society of Iowa, Iowa City, IA, 1912), vii.
5. Shambaugh (ed), *Applied History*, viii.
6. Stefan Zweig, *The World of Yesterday: an Autobiography* (Cassell and Company Ltd., London, 1943; orig. *Die Welt von Gestern*, Stockholm, 1942), 14.
7. Shambaugh (ed), *Applied History*, vi, xiii.
8. Conard, *Benjamin Shambaugh and the Intellectual Foundations*, 81.

BENJAMIN F SHAMBAUGH
APPLIED HISTORY

Among citizens, lawmakers and public officials there is a widespread desire for better roads, better schools, better methods of taxation, better labour laws, better safety appliances in hazardous occupations, better insurance against work accidents, better regulation of public utilities, better banking laws, better corrupt practices legislation, better court procedure and better methods of public administration in general.

As citizens, lawmakers and public officials we are all alike deeply concerned in these vital questions of political, industrial and social welfare. We may confess ignorance in regard to some of these matters; and at times we may feel that, along with the rest of the world, we are hopelessly groping in the dark. But not one of us is at heart really indifferent to the problems of human betterment – although it is true that our desire for better things, both for ourselves and for others, invariably outruns our knowledge of how wisely to bring them to pass.

Real advancement is so elaborately slow that we find it difficult at times to resist the temptation to take shortcuts to progress. There are so many obstacles on the road to permanent betterment, so many petty mistakes and so many temporary failures on the journey, that we sometimes lose heart and despair of ever reaching the goal. Fortunately, however, no amount of delay and no number of mistakes can ever wholly extinguish our zeal for real progress; and healthy-minded men and women will continue to view failures as the inevitable accompaniment of forward movements. To them every step, whether on the greensward or among the thorns, is a goal attained.

As practical, common-sense people we are eager to know more about this journey towards social betterment upon which we find our generation embarked. What are the problems of the way? On what stage of the journey are we at this moment? How far have we gone? Whither are we tending? What were the experiences of those who preceded us? How fares it with others who are now travelling towards the same goal? And finally, how in the light of all these facts may we improve our means of travel, overcome obstacles and accelerate our speed?

To speak more directly, as practical citizens, lawmakers and public officials we demand reliable and complete information concerning the public questions which now confront us and which we are called upon to solve as best we can. For example, we desire exact and full information on such questions as road administration, tax reform, the regulation of urban utilities, employers' liability and workmen's compensation, the extension of industrial education and the prevention of corrupt practices.

Moreover, the data and other information sought with reference to these questions are, first of all, the plain facts gathered through careful investigation from the history of our own state, from contemporary experience in other states, and from selected foreign sources; second, the expert interpretation of all the facts collected; third, the expert definition of regulation, legislation and administration; and, finally, the application of these standards of legislation and administration to existing needs and conditions.

It is to supply citizens, lawmakers and public officials with just such data and other information that The State Historical Society of Iowa has undertaken to compile and publish a series of papers under the title of 'Applied History' – which may be defined as the use of the scientific knowledge of history and experience in efforts to solve present problems of human betterment. As thus defined applied history comprehends impartial investigation, scientific interpretation and expert definition and application of standards: it frankly recognises the fact that public service to be efficient must be guided by open-minded experts – by men governed by knowledge, reason and high-mindedness.

Applied history views the past as a vast social laboratory in which experiments in politics and human welfare are daily being set and tested on a most elaborate scale. Moreover, in this human laboratory the conditions are *real* conditions, the factors are *real* men and women, and the varied relations and combinations or conditions and factors are always those of *real* life.

Now it is evident that nowhere have the conditions for social and political experimentation been more varied nor the results more accessible than in our own American commonwealths. Here the records are marvellously rich in experiments in civil and criminal law, in the application of constitutional limitations, in labour legislation, in the regulation of common carriers and public utilities, in taxation, in the administration of roads, in domestic relations, in the protection of women and children, in the conservation of health, in the maintenance of order, in the exploitation of natural resources, in the promotion of industry and in the democratisation of education and politics. To wisely use the results of all these experiments in efforts to solve the problems which confront each generation is to carry out a programme of applied history.

Applied history is simply the use of the creative power of scientific knowledge in politics and administration. Scientific farming has greatly increased the yield of the soil. Scientific mining has greatly increased the output of the mine. Scientific forestry has greatly conserved the woodlands. Scientific hygiene has greatly conserved the health and life of the people. Scientific engineering has overcome the most stubborn obstacles of nature. Can anyone doubt that some day scientific history, scientific legislation and scientific administration will be able to boast of a similar record of accomplishment?

The foundation upon which applied history rests is the scientific law of the continuity of history – a law which asserts that 'every human institution, every generally accepted idea, every important invention, is but the summation of long lines of progress'. Indeed, it is the recognised validity of this law that affords substantial assurance that applied history is not a dream but a sound and intelligent method of interrogating the past in the light of the conditions of the present and the obvious needs of the immediate future to the end that a rational programme of progress may be outlined and followed in legislation and administration.

Applied history is, indeed, the natural outcome of scientific history, itself the inevitable result of the development of the newer anthropological studies – especially archaeology, ethnology, sociology, politics and administration, economics, comparative religion and social psychology. In fact, these social sciences, which have developed so marvellously under the inspiration of the doctrine of evolution, have involved historical study in a revolutionary process which is giving birth to a 'New History'.

The first advances of the social sciences were opposed by the more orthodox historians: they seemed fearful lest the encroachments of anthropology, archaeology, sociology, politics and economics should turn them out of doors. But it is now apparent that, upon second thought, they are wisely resolving not to resist but to make use of the new sciences in the development of new viewpoints in history.

It is commonplace to say that we are in the midst of new conditions: Everone seems to be more or less conscious of the fact that times have changed. Moreover, with a knowledge of man and of the world immensely greater than ever before, 'society is today engaged in a tremendous and unprecedented effort to better itself in manifold ways'. Mankind has, indeed, embarked upon a career of social readjustment in the course of which history is to serve as 'a guidepost to betterment' rather than a 'barrier cast across the way of progress'.

Henceforth the new history, leavened and enriched by the products of political and social science, promises to play a much more important role in the intellectual life and progress of mankind. The past will be brought into direct relations with the present; and the 'fitting intervals' by which historians have separated their studies from the near at hand will disappear. The present, which 'has hitherto been the willing victim of the past', will now 'turn on the past and exploit it in the interests of advance'; and historians who have hitherto entertained 'other notions of their functions' will 'furnish us with what lies behind our great contemporaneous task of human betterment'.[1]

History, like all other studies, has constantly undergone changes – changes in subject matter, changes in methods of investigation, changes in presentation, changes in viewpoint and changes in interpretation. Indeed, it may be said that no phase of man's record has been fully and finally written. Even the manuscripts of the most critical are already worn with erasures or blurred with corrections. Old versions are revised, and new chapters are added; and the latest chapter in the history of historical study is what has above been defined as applied history.

For untold ages of biologic time man's progress was recorded only in his animal body – a most fascinating sourcebook of origins but recently discovered. Moreover, it is a remarkable fact that the discovery of this record of man's earliest and most ancient history was made not in the library by historians, but in the laboratory by students of natural science – by Darwin and Haeckel, by Wallace and Weismann, by Spencer and Huxley: names still unknown to the literature of much orthodox history.

With the development of the art of language, history first appears as oral tradition; then as a literature of story and mythology; and finally as a more prosaic record of things that actually occurred. In recent times historical study has become more and more scientific: not content with finding out what has actually transpired, historians have seriously endeavoured to explain how in fact things have come about. And now in our own day – as if in response to the spirit of an age that likes to call itself practical – history becomes up to date by bringing itself down to date, and ventures to suggest a programme of what should come to pass on the morrow. That is to say, it is now proposed to apply the scientific knowledge of history in working out a rational programme of human progress in government and administration.

Nor should the relations of education and applied history as joint agents of social betterment be overlooked; for the battles of real progress have always been won by the forces of education – especially higher education. In this connection it is worth remembering that the statesmanship of modern Germany has been guided by the scholarship of the German universities; and that not only the inspiration for advance but the details of the programme of social betterment which is now attracting the attention of the world came from these same universities. In Germany it is not simply the privilege but indeed – as an official report puts it – the duty of the university to give opinions on all kinds of problems touching the public welfare.

In Iowa we have a state-supported university with a college of applied science, and a state-supported college of acriculture and mechanic arts with an experiment station and a highway commission. Is there any good reason why we should not have in this state a college of applied political and social science with a department for the extension of political education? The successful operation of such a college would certainly help to make our State a better place to live in politically and socially. Moreover, such a college, with courses correlated with the applied sciences of engineering and medicine, would be in a position to furnish the trained experts whose services are so necessary to efficiency in public administration. Why should the State afford special facilities for training lawyers, doctors, engineers, agriculturists and dairymen, and at the same time neglect the training of men and women for public service?

It is utterly futile for us to talk about high-minded citizenship and ideals in public service without seriously endeavouring to provide that special training which will make men really capable and efficient public servants. Fieldwork is as important and short courses as practicable in politics and administration as in agriculture and the industrial arts.

State institutions, like high-minded citizens, should be dominated by a zeal for public service: they should show a lively interest in the public welfare. And so, in bringing the history of our commonwealth down to the present hour, in conducting scientific researches along lines of political, economic and social developments, and in projecting a series of publications on applied history, in which the language of the scientific investigator is translated into more popular form, The State Historical Society of Iowa aims to make a direct contribution to the public welfare by linking the public with the results of scientific research in political and social science.

To outline and conduct investigations for purposes of applied history is a difficult and exacting task. Research is always serious business. But when the results may possibly be used as a basis of constructive legislation, the investigation must be thorough, impartial, accurate and scientific to the last degree. There must be no superficial examination of the sources, no intellectual juggling with complex data, no smothering of undesirable facts, no partisan presentation of the truth or shallow expediency in handling difficult and delicate problems.

---

1. See James Harvey Robinson, 'The New History' in *Proceedings of the American Philosophical Society*, vol 50, no 199 (American Philosophical Society, Philadelphia, PA, 1911).

CARL BECKER:
THE SOCIAL OBLIGATION OF
THE HISTORIAN

INTRODUCTION BY KATHLEEN BURK

Professor Carl L Becker (1873–1945) was an eminent twentieth-century American historian, whose writings focused primarily on eighteenth-century European and American history and particularly on the Enlightenment. He was also concerned about the contemporary political and economic situation in the United States.

He was a very influential critic of the traditional doctrine of objectivity; he was sceptical of the ideal of a neutral, disinterested approach to finding out about the past, and was critical of the belief that the duty of a historian was to find out what had actually happened without any concern as to how it related to the present. The belief of many historians of the late nineteenth and early twentieth centuries was that they should find out the objective and permanent truth about a historical event on which their interpretations should be based. Becker believed, as did most historians, that a historian searched for scholarly truth, but he did not believe that a definitive, objective, impartial reconstruction of the past is possible. He argued that a historian does not merely go to a set of documents with no idea of what they expect to find. Rather, the historian has a considered idea or question and selects the documents which will enable the question to be answered.

The focus was traditionally on constitutional and political history, and Becker believed that the range and scope of the types of history which it was proper to investigate should be extended to include social and economic history – and indeed, other historians proposed, to intellectual history. He argued that there were problems which needed to be addressed and that perhaps a knowledge of history might help. The difficulty with that, according to more traditional historians, is that bias can easily creep in, and that the historian's own ideas were likely to mask the objective truth.

Becker thought that historians should be more concerned with present problems, that they had a social as well as a historical responsibility, that history could be useful, and that the questions they formulated and the documents they selected to explore should be relevant to society's current needs. This did not preclude the search for scholarly truth – ie one did not massage the evidence. Consider Mr Everyman. He had a problem that he needed to solve, which was to determine to whom of two merchants he should pay for the coal that had been delivered. To do this he used his memory; when that turned out to be wrong, he consulted the relevant documents; when their information conflicted, he compared them critically; and once he had ascertained the answer, he was able to pay his bill. Mr Everyman thus used the same methodology as an academic historian, although he would not be considered by them to be a 'historian'. But, Becker says, he was.

Furthermore, the nature of both questions and answers changed as time and circumstances changed. Some called this presentism or relativism, which openly invited or allowed the historian to impose their own ideas as to the questions they wished to ask, to select the types of evidence that they found most useful, and to discover the evidence needed to answer those questions, rather than somehow allowing the facts to be found and an interpretation to emerge. In any case, going into research blindfolded is not the normal process; and, furthermore, a narrow focus can limit the facts that emerge. Every historian has an ideological commitment, whether or not they recognise this. Becker's main point was that it is the historian's responsibility to provide an account of the past that is appropriate to society's current needs. They have a social as well as a scholarly obligation. As time passes and society changes, as circumstances change, so might these needs also change and the questions that should be asked.

Of course, there was no dividing line between two clear schools of thought. No more than cats can historians be herded into an enclosure. But Becker's 1931 presidential address to the American Historical Association, titled 'Everyman His Own Historian', did provide something of a line over which to argue. History, which is 'the memory of things said and done', does not provide either permanent questions or permanent answers. As Becker argued, 'Mr Everyman is stronger than we [historians] are, and sooner or later we must adapt our knowledge to his necessities…We do not impose our version of the human story on Mr Everyman; in the end it is rather Mr Everyman who imposes his version on us.' History, in short, is relative. It also has a pendulum. Relativism became the primary, although not the sole, approach to research and writing history until after the Second World War, when a modified idea of objectivity appeared again on historians' horizons.

Oxford, February 2022

CARL BECKER
EVERYMAN HIS OWN HISTORIAN

Presidential Address Delivered before the American

Historical Association at Minneapolis,

on December 29, 1931

I.

Once upon a time, long long ago, I learned how to reduce a fraction to its lowest terms. Whether I could still perform that operation is uncertain; but the discipline involved in early training had its uses, since it taught me that in order to understand the essential nature of anything it is well to strip it of all superficial and irrelevant accretions – in short, to reduce it to its lowest terms. That operation I now venture, with some apprehension and all due apologies, to perform on the subject of history.

I ought first of all to explain that when I use the term history, I mean knowledge of history. No doubt throughout all past time there actually occurred a series of events which, whether we know what it was or not, constitutes history in some ultimate sense. Nevertheless, much the greater part of these events we can know nothing about, not even that they occurred; many of them we can know only imperfectly; and even the few events that we think we know for sure we can never be absolutely certain of, since we can never revive them, never observe or test them directly. The event itself once occurred, but as an actual event it has disappeared; so that in dealing with it the only objective reality we can observe or test is some material trace which the event has left – usually a written document. With these traces of vanished events, these documents, we must be content since they are all we have; from them we infer what the event was, we affirm that it is a fact that the event was so and so. We do not say 'Lincoln is assassinated'; we say 'it is a fact that Lincoln was assassinated'. The event *was*, but is no longer; it is only the affirmed fact about the event that *is* that persists, and will persist until we discover that our affirmation is wrong or inadequate. Let us then admit that there are two histories: the actual series of events that once occurred; and the ideal series that we affirm and hold in memory. The first is absolute and unchanged – it was what it was whatever we do or say about it; the second is relative, always changing in response to the increase or refinement of knowledge. The two series correspond more or less, it is our aim to make the correspondence as exact as possible; but the actual series of events exists for us only in terms of the ideal series which we affirm and hold in memory. This is why I am forced to identify history with knowledge of history. For all practical purposes, history is, for us and for the time being, what we know it to be.

It is history in this sense that I wish to reduce to its lowest terms. In order to do that I need a very simple definition. I once read that 'History is the knowledge of events that have occurred in the past'. That is a simple definition, but not simple enough. It contains three words that require examination. The first is knowledge. Knowledge is a formidable word. I always think of knowledge as something that is stored up in the *Encyclopedia Britannica* or the *Summa Theologica*; something difficult to acquire, something at all events that I have not. Resenting a definition that denies me the title of historian, I therefore ask what is most essential to knowledge. Well, memory, I should think (and I mean memory in the broad sense, the memory of events inferred as well as the memory of events observed); other things are necessary too, but memory is fundamental: without memory no knowledge. So our definition becomes 'History is the memory of events that have occurred in the past'. But events – the word carries an implication of something grand, like the taking of the Bastille or the Spanish–American War. An occurrence need not be spectacular to be an event. If I drive a motor car down the crooked streets of Ithaca, that is an event – something done; if the traffic cop bawls me out, that is an event – something said; if I have evil thoughts of him for so doing, that is an event – something thought. In truth anything done, said, or thought is an event, important or not as may turn out. But since we do not ordinarily speak without thinking, at least in some rudimentary way, and since the psychologists tell us that we can not think without speaking, or at least not without having anticipatory vibrations in the larynx, we may well combine thought events and speech events under one term; and so our definition becomes 'History is the memory of things said and done in the past'. But the past – the word is both misleading and unnecessary: misleading, because the past, used in connection with history, seems to imply the distant past, as if history ceased before we were born; unnecessary, because after all everything said or done is already in the past as soon as it is said or done. Therefore, I will omit that word, and our definition becomes 'History is the memory of things said and done'. This is a definition that reduces history to its lowest terms, and yet includes everything that is essential to understanding what it really is.

If the essence of history is the memory of things said and done, then it is obvious that every normal person, Mr. Everyman, knows some history. Of course, we do what we can to conceal this invidious truth. Assuming a professional manner, we say that so and so knows no history, when we mean no more than that he failed to pass the examinations set for a higher degree; and simple-minded persons, undergraduates and others, taken in by academic classifications of knowledge, think they know no history because they have never taken a course in history in college, or have never read Gibbon's *The Decline and Fall of the Roman Empire*. No doubt the academic convention has its uses, but it is one of the superficial accretions that must be stripped off if we would understand history reduced to its lowest terms. Mr. Everyman, as well as you and I, remembers things said and done, and must do so at every waking moment. Suppose Mr. Everyman to have awakened this morning unable to remember anything said or done. He would be a lost soul indeed. This has happened, this sudden loss of all historical knowledge. But normally it does not happen. Normally the memory of Mr. Everyman, when he awakens in the morning, reaches out into the country of the past and of distant places and instantaneously recreates his little world of endeavour, pulls together as it were things said and done in his yesterdays, and coordinates them with his present perceptions and with things to be said and done in his to-morrows. Without this historical knowledge, this memory of things said and done, his today would be aimless and his tomorrow without significance.

Since we are concerned with history in its lowest terms, we will suppose that Mr. Everyman is not a professor of history but just an ordinary citizen without excess knowledge. Not having a lecture to prepare, his memory of things said and done, when he awakened this morning, presumably did not drag into consciousness any events connected with the Liman von Sanders mission or the Pseudo-Isidorian Decretals; it presumably dragged into consciousness an image of things said and done yesterday in the office, the highly significant fact that General Motors had dropped three points, a conference arranged for ten o'clock in the morning, a promise to play nine holes at 4.30 in the afternoon, and other historical events of similar import. Mr. Everyman knows more history than this, but at the moment of awakening this is sufficient: memory of things said and done, history functioning, at 7.30 in the morning, in its very lowest terms, has effectively oriented Mr. Everyman in his little world of endeavour.

Yet not quite effectively after all, perhaps; for unaided memory is notoriously fickle; and it may happen that Mr. Everyman, as he drinks his coffee, is uneasily aware of something said or done that he fails now to recall. A common enough occurrence, as we all know to our sorrow – this remembering, not the historical event, but only that there was an event which we ought to remember but cannot. This is Mr. Everyman's difficulty, a bit of history lies dead and inert in the sources, unable to do any work for Mr. Everyman because his memory refuses to bring it alive in consciousness. What then does Mr. Everyman do? He does what any historian would do: he does a bit of historical research in the sources. From his little private record office (I mean his vest pocket) he takes a book in MS, volume XXXV it may be, and turns to page 23, and there he reads: 'December 29, pay Smith's coal bill, 20 tons, $1,017.20.' Instantaneously a series of historical events comes to life in Mr. Everyman's mind. He has an image of himself ordering twenty tons of coal from Smith last summer, of Smith's wagons driving up to his house, and of the precious coal sliding dustily through the cellar window. Historical events these are, not so important as the forging of the Isidorian Decretals, but still important to Mr. Everyman: historical events which he was not present to observe, but which, by an artificial extension of memory, he can form a clear picture of, because he has done a little original research in the manuscripts preserved in his private record office.

The picture Mr. Everyman forms of Smith's wagons delivering the coal at his house is a picture of things said and done in the past. But it does not stand alone, it is not a pure antiquarian image to be enjoyed for its own sake; on the contrary, it is associated with a picture of things to be said and done in the future; so that throughout the day Mr. Everyman intermittently holds in mind, together with a picture of Smith's coal wagons, a picture of himself going at four o'clock in the afternoon to Smith's office in order to pay his bill. At four o'clock Mr. Everyman is accordingly at Smith's office. 'I wish to pay that coal bill', he says. Smith looks dubious and disappointed, takes down a ledger (or a filing case), does a bit of original research in his private record office, and announces: 'You don't owe me any money, Mr. Everyman. You ordered the coal here all right, but I didn't have the kind you wanted, and so turned the order over to Brown. It was Brown delivered your coal: he's the man you owe.' Whereupon Mr. Everyman goes to Brown's office; and Brown takes down a ledger, does a bit of original research in his private record office, which happily confirms the researches of Smith; and Mr. Everyman pays his bill, and in the evening, after returning from the country club, makes a further search in another collection of documents, where, sure enough, he finds a bill from Brown, properly drawn, for twenty tons of stove coal, $1,017.20. The research is now completed. Since his mind rests satisfied, Mr. Everyman has found the explanation of the series of events that concerned him.

Mr. Everyman would be astonished to learn that he is a historian, yet it is obvious, isn't it, that he has performed all the essential operations involved in historical research. Needing or wanting to do something (which happened to be, not to deliver a lecture or write a book, but to pay a bill; and this is what misleads him and us as to what he is really doing), the first step was to recall things said and done. Unaided memory proving inadequate, a further step was essential – the examination of certain documents in order to discover the necessary but as yet unknown facts. Unhappily the documents were found to give conflicting reports, so that a critical comparison of the texts had to be instituted in order to eliminate error. All this having been satisfactorily accomplished, Mr. Everyman is ready for the final operation – the formation in his mind, by an artificial extension of memory, of a picture, a definitive picture let us hope, of a selected series of historical events – of himself ordering coal from Smith, of Smith turning the order over to Brown, and of Brown delivering the coal at his house. In the light of this picture Mr. Everyman could, and did, pay his bill. If Mr. Everyman had undertaken these researches in order to write a book instead of to pay a bill, no one would think of denying that he was a historian.

II.

I have tried to reduce history to its lowest terms, first by defining it as the memory of things said and done, second by showing concretely how the memory of things said and done is essential to the performance of the simplest acts of daily life. I wish now to note the more general implications of Mr. Everyman's activities. In the realm of affairs Mr. Everyman has been paying his coal bill; in the realm of consciousness he has been doing that fundamental thing which enables man alone to have, properly speaking, a history: he has been re-enforcing and enriching his immediate perceptions to the end that he may live in a world of semblance more spacious and satisfying than is to be found within the narrow confines of the fleeting present moment.

We are apt to think of the past as dead, the future as non-existent, the present alone as real; and prematurely wise or disillusioned counsellors have urged us to burn always with 'a hard, gemlike flame' in order to give 'the highest quality to the moments as they pass, and simply for those moments' sake'. This no doubt is what the glow-worm does; but I think that man, who alone is properly aware that the present moment passes, can for that very reason make no good use of the present moment simply for its own sake. Strictly speaking, the present doesn't exist for us, or is at best no more than an infinitesimal point in time, gone before we can note it as present. Nevertheless, we must have a present; and so we create one by robbing the past, by holding on to the most recent events and pretending that they all belong to our immediate perceptions. If, for example, I raise my arm, the total event is a series of occurrences of which the first are past before the last have taken place; and yet you perceive it as a single movement executed in one present instant. This telescoping of successive events into a single instant philosophers call the 'specious present'. Doubtless they would assign rather narrow limits to the specious present; but I will wilfully make a free use of it, and say that we can extend the specious present as much as we like. In common speech we do so:

we speak of the 'present hour', the 'present year', the 'present generation'. Perhaps all living creatures have a specious present; but man has this superiority, as Pascal says, that he is aware of himself and the universe, can as it were hold himself at arm's length and with some measure of objectivity watch himself and his fellows functioning in the world during a brief span of allotted years. Of all the creatures, man alone has a specious present that may be deliberately and purposefully enlarged and diversified and enriched.

The extent to which the specious present may thus be enlarged and enriched will depend upon knowledge, the artificial extension of memory, the memory of things said and done in the past and distant places. But not upon knowledge alone; rather upon knowledge directed by purpose. The specious present is an unstable pattern of thought, incessantly changing in response to our immediate perceptions and the purposes that arise therefrom. At any given moment each one of us (professional historian no less than Mr. Everyman) weaves into this unstable pattern such actual or artificial memories as may be necessary to orient us in our little world of endeavour. But to be oriented in our little world of endeavour we must be prepared for what is coming to us (the payment of a coal bill, the delivery of a presidential address, the establishment of a League of Nations or whatever); and to be prepared for what is coming to us it is necessary not only to recall certain past events but to anticipate (note I do not say predict) the future.

Thus from the specious present, which always includes more or less of the past, the future refuses to be excluded; and the more of the past we drag into the specious present, the more a hypothetical, patterned future is likely to crowd into it also. Which comes first, which is cause and which effect, whether our memories construct a pattern of past events at the behest of our desires and hopes, or whether our desires and hopes spring from a pattern of past events imposed upon us by experience and knowledge, I shall not attempt to say. What I suspect is that memory of past and anticipation of future events work together, go hand in hand as it were in a friendly way, without disputing over priority and leadership.

At all events they go together, so that in a very real sense it is impossible to divorce history from life: Mr. Everyman can not do what he needs or desires to do without recalling past events; he can not recall past events without in some subtle fashion relating them to what he needs or desires to do. This is the natural function of history, of history reduced to its lowest terms, of history conceived as the memory of things said and done: memory of things said and done (whether in our immediate yesterdays or in the long past of mankind), running hand in hand with the anticipation of things to be said and done, enables us, each to the extent of his knowledge and imagination, to be intelligent, to push back the narrow confines of the fleeting present moment so that what we are doing may be judged in the light of what we have done and what we hope to do. In this sense all *living* history, as Croce says, is contemporaneous: insofar as we think the past (and otherwise the past, however fully related in documents, is nothing to us) it becomes an integral and living part of our present world of semblance.

It must then be obvious that living history, the ideal series of events that we affirm and hold in memory, since it is so intimately associated with what we are doing and with what we hope to do, can not be precisely the same for all at any given time, or the same for one generation as for another. History in this sense can not be reduced to a verifiable set of statistics or formulated in terms of universally valid mathematical formulae. It is rather an imaginative creation, a personal possession which each one of us, Mr. Everyman, fashions out of his individual experience, adapts to his practical or emotional needs, and adorns as well as may be to suit his aesthetic tastes. In thus creating his own history, there are, nevertheless, limits which Mr. Everyman may not overstep without incurring penalties. The limits are set by his fellows. If Mr. Everyman lived quite alone in an unconditioned world he would be free to affirm and hold in memory any ideal series of events that struck his fancy, and thus create a world of semblance quite in accord with the heart's desire. Unfortunately, Mr. Everyman has to live in a world of Browns and Smiths; a sad experience, which has taught him the expediency of recalling certain events with much exactness. In all the immediately practical affairs of life Mr. Everyman is a good historian, as expert, in conducting the researches necessary for paying his coal bill, as need be. His expertness comes partly from long practice, but chiefly from the circumstance that his researches are prescribed and guided by very definite and practical objects which concern him intimately. The problem of what documents to consult, what facts to select, troubles Mr. Everyman not at all. Since he is not writing a book on 'Some Aspects of the Coal Industry Objectively Considered', it does not occur to him to collect all the facts and let them speak for themselves. Wishing merely to pay his coal bill, he selects only such facts as may be relevant; and not wishing to pay it twice, he is sufficiently aware, without ever having read Bernheim's *Lehrbuch*, that the relevant facts must be clearly established by the testimony of independent witnesses not self-deceived. He does not know, or need to know, that his personal interest in the performance is a disturbing bias which will prevent him from learning the whole truth or arriving at ultimate causes. Mr. Everyman does not wish to learn the whole truth or to arrive at ultimate causes. He wishes to pay his coal bill. That is to say, he wishes to adjust himself to a practical situation, and on that low pragmatic level he is a good historian precisely because he is not disinterested: he will solve his problems, if he does solve them, by virtue of his intelligence and not by virtue of his indifference.

Nevertheless, Mr. Everyman does not live by bread alone; and on all proper occasions his memory of things said and done, easily enlarging his specious present beyond the narrow circle of daily affairs, will, must inevitably, in mere compensation for the intolerable dullness and vexation of the fleeting present moment, fashion for him a more spacious world than that of the immediately practical. He can readily recall the days of his youth, the places he has lived in, the ventures he has made, the adventures he has had – all the crowded events of a lifetime; and beyond and around this central pattern of personally experienced events, there will be embroidered a more dimly seen pattern of artificial memories, memories of things reputed to have been said and done in past times which he has not known, in distant places which he has not seen. This outer pattern of remembered events that encloses and completes the central pattern of his personal experience, Mr. Everyman has woven, he could not tell you how, out of the most diverse threads of information, picked up in the most casual way, from the most unrelated sources – from things learned at home and in school, from knowledge gained in business or profession, from newspapers glanced at, from books (yes, even history books) read or heard of, from remembered scraps of newsreels or educational films or *ex cathedra* utterances of presidents and kings, from fifteen-minute discourses on the history of civilization broadcast by the courtesy (it may be) of Pepsodent, the Bulova Watch Company or the Shepard Stores in Boston. Daily and hourly, from a thousand unnoted sources, there is lodged in Mr. Everyman's mind a mass of unrelated and related information and misinformation, of impressions and images, out of which he somehow manages, undeliberately for the most part, to fashion a history, a patterned picture of remembered things said and done in past times and distant places. It is not possible, it is not essential, that this picture should be complete or completely true: it is essential that it should be useful to Mr. Everyman; and that it may be useful to him he will hold in memory, of all the things he might hold in memory, those things only which can be related with some reasonable degree of relevance and harmony to his idea of himself and of what he is doing in the world and what he hopes to do.

In constructing this more remote and far-flung pattern of remembered things, Mr. Everyman works with something of the freedom of a creative artist; the history which he imaginatively recreates as an artificial extension of his personal experience will inevitably be an engaging blend of fact and fancy, a mythical adaptation of that which actually happened. In part it will be true, in part false; as a whole perhaps neither true nor false, but only the most convenient form of error. Not that Mr. Everyman wishes or intends to deceive himself or others. Mr. Everyman has a wholesome respect for cold, hard facts, never suspecting how malleable they are, how easy it is to coax and cajole them; but he necessarily takes the facts as they come to him, and is enamoured of those that seem best suited to his interests or promise most in the way of emotional satisfaction. The exact truth of remembered events he has in any case no time, and no need, to curiously question or meticulously verify. No doubt he can, if he be an American, call up an image of the signing of the Declaration of Independence in 1776 as readily as he can call up an image of Smith's coal wagons creaking up the hill last summer. He suspects the one image no more than the other; but the signing of the Declaration, touching not his practical interests, calls for no careful historical research on his part. He may perhaps, without knowing why, affirm and hold in memory that the Declaration was signed by the members of the Continental Congress on 4 July. It is a vivid and sufficient image which Mr. Everyman may hold to the end of his days without incurring penalties. Neither Brown nor Smith has any interest in setting him right; nor will any court ever send him a summons for failing to recall that the Declaration, 'being engrossed and compared at the table, was signed by the members' on 2 August. As an actual event, the signing of the Declaration was what it was; as a remembered event it will be, for Mr. Everyman, what Mr. Everyman contrives to make it: will have for him significance and magic, much or little or none at all, as it fits well or ill into his little world of interests and aspirations and emotional comforts.

III.

What then of us, historians by profession? What have we to do with Mr. Everyman, or he with us? More, I venture to believe, than we are apt to think. For each of us is Mr. Everyman too. Each of us is subject to the limitations of time and place; and for each of us, no less than for the Browns and Smiths of the world, the pattern of remembered things said and done will be woven, safeguard the process how we may, at the behest of circumstance and purpose.

True it is that although each of us is Mr. Everyman, each is something more than his own historian. Mr. Everyman, being but an informal historian, is under no bond to remember what is irrelevant to his personal affairs. But we are historians by profession. Our profession, less intimately bound up with the practical activities, is to be directly concerned with the ideal series of events that is only of casual or occasional import to others; it is our business in life to be ever preoccupied with that far-flung pattern of artificial memories that encloses and completes the central pattern of individual experience. We are Mr. Everybody's historian as well as our own, since our histories serve the double purpose, which written histories have always served, of keeping alive the recollection of memorable men and events. We are thus of that ancient and honourable company of wise men of the tribe, of bards and storytellers and minstrels, of soothsayers and priests, to whom in successive ages has been entrusted the keeping of the useful myths. Let not the harmless, necessary word 'myth' put us out of countenance. In the history of history a myth is a once valid but now discarded version of the human story, as our now valid versions will in due course be relegated to the category of discarded myths. With our predecessors, the bards and storytellers and priests, we have therefore this in common: that it is our function, as it was theirs, not to create, but to preserve and perpetuate the social tradition; to harmonise, as well as ignorance and prejudice permit, the actual and the remembered series of events; to enlarge and enrich the specious present common to us all to the end that 'society' (the tribe, the nation or all mankind) may judge of what it is doing in the light of what it has done and what it hopes to do.

History as the artificial extension of the social memory (and I willingly concede that there are other appropriate ways of apprehending human experience) is an art of long standing, necessarily so since it springs instinctively from the impulse to enlarge the range of immediate experience; and however camouflaged by the disfiguring jargon of science, it is still in essence what it has always been. History in this sense is story, in aim always a true story; a story that employs all the devices of literary art (statement and generalisation, narration and description, comparison and comment and analogy) to present the succession of events in the life of man, and from the succession of events thus presented to derive a satisfactory meaning. The history written by historians, like the history informally fashioned by Mr. Everyman, is thus a convenient blend of truth and fancy, of what we commonly distinguish as 'fact' and 'interpretation'. In primitive times, when tradition is orally transmitted, bards and storytellers frankly embroider or improvise the facts to heighten the dramatic import of the story. With the use of written records, history, gradually differentiated from fiction, is understood as the story of events that actually occurred; and with the increase and refinement of knowledge the historian recognises that his first duty is to be sure of his facts, let their meaning be what it may. Nevertheless, in every age history is taken to be a story of actual events from which a significant meaning may be derived; and in every age the illusion is that the present version is valid because the related facts are true, whereas former versions are invalid because based upon inaccurate or inadequate facts.

Never was this conviction more impressively displayed than in our own time – that age of erudition in which we live, or from which we are perhaps just emerging. Finding the course of history littered with the *debris* of exploded philosophies, the historians of the last century, unwilling to be forever duped, turned away

(as they fondly hoped) from 'interpretation' to the rigorous examination of the factual event, just as it occurred. Perfecting the tech-
nique of investigation, they laboriously collected and edited the
sources of information, and with incredible persistence and ingenuity ran illusive error to earth, letting the significance of the Middle Ages wait until it was certainly known 'whether Charles the Fat
was at Ingelheim or Lustnau on July 1, 887', shedding their 'life-
blood', in many a hard-fought battle, 'for the sublime truths of Sac
and Soc'. I have no quarrel with this so great concern with hoti's
business. One of the first duties of man is not to be duped, to be
aware of his world; and to derive the significance of human experience from events that never occurred is surely an enterprise of
doubtful value. To establish the facts is always in order, and is
indeed the first duty of the historian; but to suppose that the facts,
once established in all their fullness, will 'speak for themselves' is
an illusion. It was perhaps peculiarly the illusion of those historians of the last century who found some special magic in the word
'scientific'. The scientific historian, it seems, was one who set forth
the facts without injecting any extraneous meaning into them. He
was the objective man whom Nietzsche described – 'a mirror:
accustomed to prostration before something that wants to be
known…he waits until something comes, and then expands himself sensitively, so that even the light footsteps and gliding past of
spiritual things may not be lost in his surface and film'.[1] 'It is not I
who speak, but history which speaks through me,' was Fustel's
reproof to applauding students. 'If a certain philosophy emerges
from this scientific history, it must be permitted to emerge naturally, of its own accord, all but independently of the will of the historian.'[2] Thus the scientific historian deliberately renounced philosophy only to submit to it without being aware. His philosophy
was just this, that by not taking thought a cubit would be added to
his stature. With no other preconception than the will to know, the
historian would reflect in his surface and film the 'order of events
throughout past times in all places'; so that, in the fullness of time,

when innumerable patient expert scholars, by 'exhausting the sources', should have reflected without refracting the truth of all the facts, the definitive and impregnable meaning of human experience would emerge of its own accord to enlighten and emancipate mankind. Hoping to find something without looking for it, expecting to obtain final answers to life's riddle by resolutely refusing to ask questions – it was surely the most romantic species of realism yet invented, the oddest attempt ever made to get something for nothing!

That mood is passing. The fullness of time is not yet, overmuch learning proves a weariness to the flesh, and a younger generation that knows not von Ranke is eager to believe that Fustel's counsel, if one of perfection, is equally one of futility. Even the most disinterested historian has at least one preconception, which is the fixed idea that he has none. The facts of history are already set forth, implicitly, in the sources; and the historian who could restate without reshaping them would, by submerging and suffocating the mind in diffuse existence, accomplish the superfluous task of depriving human experience of all significance. Left to themselves, the facts do not speak; left to themselves they do not exist, not really, since for all practical purposes there is no fact until some one affirms it. The least the historian can do with any historical fact is to select and affirm it. To select and affirm even the simplest complex of facts is to give them a certain place in a certain pattern of ideas, and this alone is sufficient to give them a special meaning. However 'hard' or 'cold' they may he, historical facts are after all not material substances which, like bricks or scantlings, possess definite shape and clear, persistent outline. To set forth historical facts is not comparable to dumping a barrow of bricks. A brick retains its form and pressure wherever placed; but the form and substance of historical facts, having a negotiable existence only in literary discourse, vary with the words employed to convey them. Since history is not part of the external material world but an imaginative reconstruction of vanished events, its form and substance are inseparable: in the realm of literary discourse substance, being an idea, *is* form; and form, conveying the idea, *is* substance. It is thus not the undiscriminated fact, but the perceiving mind of the historian that speaks: the special meaning which the facts are made to convey emerges from the substance-form which the historian employs to recreate imaginatively a series of events not present to perception.

In constructing this substance-form of vanished events, the historian, like Mr. Everyman, like the bards and storytellers of an earlier time, will be conditioned by the specious present in which alone he can be aware of his world. Being neither omniscient nor omnipresent, the historian is not the same person always and everywhere; and for him, as for Mr. Everyman, the form and significance of remembered events, like the extension and velocity of physical objects, will vary with the time and place of the observer. After fifty years we can clearly see that it was not history which spoke through Fustel, but Fustel who spoke through history. We see less clearly perhaps that the voice of Fustel was the voice, amplified and freed from static as one may say, of Mr. Everyman; what the admiring students applauded on that famous occasion was neither history nor Fustel, but a deftly coloured pattern of selected events which Fustel fashioned, all the more skilfully for not being aware of doing so, in the service of Mr. Everyman's emotional needs – the emotional satisfaction, so essential to Frenchmen at that time, of perceiving that French institutions were not of German origin. And so it must always be. Played upon by all the diverse, unnoted influences of his own time, the historian will elicit history out of documents by the same principle, however more consciously and expertly applied, that Mr. Everyman employs to breed legends out of remembered episodes and oral tradition.

Berate him as we will for not reading our books, Mr. Everyman is stronger than we are, and sooner or later we must adapt our knowledge to his necessities. Otherwise he will leave us to our own devices, leave us it may be to cultivate a species of dry professional arrogance growing out of the thin soil of antiquarian research. Such research, valuable not in itself but for some ulterior purpose, will be of little import except insofar as it is transmuted into common knowledge. The history that lies inert in unread books does no work in the world. The history that does work in the world, the history that influences the course of history, is living history, that pattern of remembered events, whether true or false, that enlarges and enriches the collective specious present, the specious present of Mr. Everyman. It is for this reason that the history of history is a record of the 'new history' that in every age rises to confound and supplant the old. It should be a relief to us to renounce omniscience, to recognise that every generation, our own included, will, must inevitably, understand the past and anticipate the future in the light of its own restricted experience, must inevitably play on the dead whatever tricks it finds necessary for its own peace of mind. The appropriate trick for any age is not a malicious invention designed to take anyone in, but an unconscious and necessary effort on the part of 'society' to understand what it is doing in the light of what it has done and what it hopes to do. We, historians by profession, share in this necessary effort. But we do not impose our version of the human story on Mr. Everyman; in the end it is rather Mr. Everyman who imposes his version on us – compelling us, in an age of political revolution, to see that history is past politics, in an age of social stress and conflict to search for the economic interpretation. If we remain too long recalcitrant Mr. Everyman will ignore us, shelving our recondite works behind glass doors rarely opened. Our proper function is not to repeat the past but to make use of it, to correct and rationalise for common use Mr. Everyman's mythological adaptation of what actually happened. We are surely under bond to be as honest and as intelligent as human frailty permits; but the secret of our success in the long run is in conforming to the temper of Mr. Everyman, which we seem to guide only because we are so sure, eventually, to follow it.

Neither the value nor the dignity of history need suffer by regarding it as a foreshortened and incomplete representation of the reality that once was, an unstable pattern of remembered things redesigned and newly coloured to suit the convenience of those who make use of it. Nor need our labours be the less highly prized because our task is limited, our contributions of incidental and temporary significance. History is an indispensable even though not the highest form of intellectual endeavour, since it makes, as Santayana says, a gift of 'great interests…to the heart. A barbarian is no less subject to the past than is the civic man who knows what the past is and means to be loyal to it; but the barbarian, for want of a transpersonal memory, crawls among superstitions which he cannot understand or revoke and among people whom he may hate or love, but whom he can never think of raising to a higher plane, to the level of a purer happiness. The whole dignity of human endevor is thus bound up with historic issues, and as conscience needs to be controlled by experience if it is to become rational, so personal experience itself needs to be enlarged ideally if the failures and successes it reports are to touch impersonal interests.'[3]

I do not present this view of history as one that is stable and must prevail. Whatever validity it may claim, it is certain, on its own premises, to be supplanted; for its premises, imposed upon us by the climate of opinion in which we live and think, predispose us to regard all things, and all principles of things, as no more than 'inconstant modes or fashions', as but the 'concurrence, renewed from moment to moment, of forces parting sooner or later on their way'. It is the limitation of the genetic approach to human experience that it must be content to transform problems since it can never solve them. However accurately we may determine the 'facts' of history, the facts themselves and our interpretations of them, and our interpretation of our own interpretations, will be seen in a different perspective or a less vivid light as mankind moves into the unknown future. Regarded historically, as a process of becoming, man and his world can obviously be understood only tentatively, since it is by definition something still in the making, something as yet unfinished. Unfortunately for the 'permanent contribution' and the universally valid philosophy, time passes; time, the enemy of man as the Greeks thought; tomorrow and tomorrow and tomorrow creeps in this petty pace, and all our yesterdays diminish and grow dim: so that, in the lengthening perspective of the centuries, even the most striking events (the Declaration of Independence, the French Revolution, the Great War itself; like the Diet of Worms before them, like the signing of the Magna Carta and the coronation of Charlemagne and the crossing of the Rubicon and the Battle of Marathon) must inevitably, for posterity, fade away into pale replicas of the original picture, for each succeeding generation losing, as they recede into a more distant past, some significance that once was noted in them, some quality of enchantment that once was theirs.

1.   Friedrich Nietzsche, *Beyond Good and Evil: Prelude to a Philosophy of the Future*, (orig. *Jenseits von Gut und Böse: Vorspiel einer Philosophie der Zukunft* [C. G. Naumann, Leipzig, 1886]), 140.

2.   Quoted in *English Historical Review*, vol 1 (Oxford Academic, Oxford, 1886).

3.   George Santayana, *The Life of Reason*, vol 68 (MIT Press, Cambridge, MA, 1906).

HERBERT BUTTERFIELD:
HISTORIAN WHO WRESTLED WITH THE TRAGEDY OF INTERNATIONAL POLITICS

INTRODUCTION BY ALBERTO R COLL

No twentieth-century historian was more earnest than Sir Herbert Butterfield about the historian's need to maintain the craft's integrity in the face of the historian's bias. Yet he was just as curious to explore the implications of historiography for the practice of international relations and statecraft. In classics such as *The Whig Interpretation of History*, *The Origins of Modern Science* and his posthumous *The Origins of History*, Butterfield argued strenuously against those like Thomas Babington Macaulay and George Macaulay Trevelyan who injected their 'Whig', English liberal outlook into their interpretation of historical events.

Yet this was the same Butterfield who authored a wide range of works such as *Christianity, Diplomacy and War*, *Christianity and History*, and numerous papers for the British Committee on the Theory of International Politics (which he co-chaired with Martin Wight) probing the implications of Christian faith for one's philosophy of history and for the conduct of diplomacy and foreign affairs. Sceptical about bringing one's philosophical and teleological assumptions into a reading of the past, he also explored the relationship between the study of history and Christianity, thereby making an important contribution to a vigorous revival of political realism (typified by other major writers such as George Kennan, Reinhold Niebuhr and Hans Morgenthau) that gained salience in the 1940s and 1950s. While these simultaneous facets of his work seem paradoxical when juxtaposed side by side, they also help to explain why some consider him the twentieth century's most original English-speaking historian.

Butterfield was highly aware that history can be dangerous. Although best known for his critiques of 'Whig' historiography, in his lifetime he witnessed in both Nazi Germany and Soviet Russia the disastrous culmination of other currents of historicism that had built up during the nineteenth century, all of them underpinned by the belief that history was moving in a particular direction congruent with a specific ideological vision. He was conscious of the myriad ways in which historians easily stray from telling the *story* of what actually happened, veering off into efforts to fit a specific event into a larger historical narrative supportive of a grand philosophical world view. He called this 'bad history', and it was dangerous because it tended to confirm people's contemporary prejudices and preconceived notions instead of challenging them.

History was especially dangerous because the people who 'made' politics – in other words, the 'great actors' in political life who made policy and had some real influence over the course of events, including, most worryingly, over international politics – often followed some grand historical vision supported by specific interpretations of certain historical events. He had in mind Niccolo Machiavelli, Napoleon Bonaparte and Vladimir Lenin. Were he alive today, Butterfield might have added to that famous roster the Russian president, Vladimir Putin, who preceded his invasion of Ukraine with a 5,000-word historical essay drawing on a particular version of history to make his case that the 44-million-strong nation of Ukraine should be part of Russia. 'A little history,' warned Butterfield, 'may make people mentally rigid.'

Somewhat paradoxically, the antidote to the dangers of history was 'to study more and more history'. Taking in a wide range of history from many perspectives and across different periods could help a person 'acquire the right feeling for the texture of events' and make that person more intellectually open-minded and flexible. From Butterfield's viewpoint, some of the most successful practitioners of foreign policy in terms of achieving lasting results of strategic value for their country were people such as Otto von Bismarck who were characterised by high levels of flexibility and pragmatism, and who were unencumbered by specific assumptions about the course of history. Lesser political talents might acquire a similar 'elasticity of mind' by steeping themselves deeply enough in history, so that in time, as Butterfield phrased it, they might 'unlearn' the 'bad history'. The key was to read lots of history, of different periods, from many different angles, and at different levels of detail. This process might give someone a deeper sense of the complexity of politics, the unpredictability of human behaviour, the interaction between human will and larger social and economic forces over which political actors have little control, and thereby make individuals more reflective, more deliberative, and essentially humbler in their analyses and prescriptions.

None of this stopped Butterfield from writing numerous books and essays in which he wrestled with the implications that his own Christian faith might have for his work as a historian, as well as for his views on foreign policy, diplomacy and war. However, he was always careful to distinguish between his commitments to his faith, on the one hand, and his specific judgments as a historian. Ultimately, for Butterfield, one of the chief contributions that the Christian faith could make to either a student of history or a practitioner of foreign policy was precisely that virtue of existential humility that he found salutary as a possible fruit of historical study. As a keen student of the sixteenth century's religious wars, he understood there was nothing automatic or universal about this connection. Plenty of Christians had been every bit as arrogant and destructive as the secular historicists he criticised. But in a world obsessed with the power and limitless possibilities of modern science and technology, Christian faith and the awareness that all human beings were under God's judgment might act as a source of restraint on some of the most hubristic illusions a historian or a statesman might be tempted to entertain.

Chicago, IL, March 2022

HERBERT BUTTERFIELD
THE DANGERS OF HISTORY

[…]

We are now in a position to survey the influence which something like a hundred and fifty years of historical study has exercised on the development of modern Europe. It is not clear that as yet we have learned all that there is to learn from this particular aspect of the history of historical science, or fathomed all the effects that the study of the past has itself had on nations and their policies. Concerning historians as interpreters and guides in the affairs of their own generation, I have read some severe things that Englishmen have written about German scholars, and there are similar things that the Germans have said about us. But the world still waits for the wag who will scientifically examine the nineteenth and twentieth-century writers of history and show us how far their studies and researches really did raise them above the fevers and prejudices of their time – how far in reality it is plausible to argue that historians are wiser than the rest of their contemporaries on political matters. And a more scientific age than ours may even find materials for an analytical treatment of associated questions; for, to take one example, it would be interesting to see it demonstrated whether it is always prudent to rely for political advice on the kind of 'expertness' which the 'regional historian' possesses – at any rate the one who, through the knowledge of one of the obscurer languages, has happened to acquire something approaching a monopoly in his field, without having to face any great clash of scholarship in his own country. And if we say that a given expert on Ruritania must be right provided he is accepted by the Ruritanians themselves, the history of historiography will be able no doubt to raise a debate even on this issue.

At any rate it is possible even now to make certain comments on the part which historical reflection has played in the development of the errors that have been so tragic for the twentieth century. And in this connection there is one law which makes itself apparent if we examine the events of the last one hundred and fifty years; and that is the paradox that a great deal of what people regard as the teaching or the lessons of history is really an argument in a circle. In reality the historian is in the habit of inserting some of his present-day prejudices into his reconstructions of the past; or unconsciously he sets out the whole issue in terms of some contemporary experience – he has what we might call the modern 'set-up' in his mind. In this way English writers once tended to see the ancient Greeks as modern Whigs; the Germans would read something of modern Prussia even into ancient Rome. Magna Carta would be interpreted in the nineteenth century in the light of modern English constitutional problems. Those who dealt with the medieval Holy Roman Empire too often envisaged it with the nineteenth-century conflict of Austria and Prussia in their minds. Sometimes there has been a tendency to project the prejudices of the present day into the structure of the past as it was envisaged in long periods and in general terms – the tendency for the British to say, when France was the enemy, that France had been the 'eternal enemy of mankind'. In England the view once prevailed that German history was particularly the history of freedom, for it was a story that comprised federation, parliament, autonomous cities, Protestantism and a law of liberty carried by German colonists to the Slavonic east. In those days it was the Latin states which were considered to be congenial to authoritarianism, clinging to the papacy in Italy, the Inquisition in Spain and the Bonapartist dictatorships in militaristic France. The reversal of this view in the twentieth century, and its replacement by a common opinion that Germany had been the aggressor and the enemy of freedom throughout all the ages, will no doubt be the subject of historical research itself some day, especially as it seems to have coincided so closely with a change in British foreign policy. The historian, then, can even deepen and magnify present-day prejudices by the mere fact that he so easily tends to throw them back and project them on to the canvas of all the centuries. And the more the historian seeks to please his generation or serve his government or support any cause save that of truth, the more he tends to confirm his contemporaries in whatever they happen to want to believe, the more he hardens the age in its favourite and fashionable errors.

Before 1919 I was taught a kind of history which saw in the sovereignty of national states the culmination of the progress of centuries – the very end towards which history was moving. I remember how the Reformation itself would be applauded for having released the nation states from 'the fetters of internationalism' and it was the custom to show that history, especially in the nineteenth century (the 'Holy Alliance', for example), had demonstrated the folly and futility of attempts to form anything like a League of Nations. From 1919, however, one saw the teaching of history reorganised and text-books rewritten – the events of the past now marshalled to serve a different purpose, and in particular the course of nineteenth-century European history reshaped – this time for the purpose of proving that all the centuries had been pointing to a different kind of consummation altogether, namely the League of Nations. I am not concerned with the question which of these views was the true one. But I should have been more impressed if on both those occasions the historian had not been so inclined to ordain and dispose his subject matter, and lay out the whole course of centuries, for the purpose of ratifying the prejudice that already prevailed for other reasons at the time. It can easily be seen, therefore, that the historian who most desires to please his age – the historian whom we most applaud because he chimes in with our views – may be betraying us, and may rob us of one of the possible benefits of historical study, namely the advantage of an escape from merely contemporary views and short-range perspectives. On the other hand, Burckhardt and Acton gave the nineteenth century certain warnings which the lapse of time has proved to be of great significance. It appears, however, that a generation does not take much notice of a message that it happens to dislike.

The things which happened in England have taken place in the historiography of all other countries; and of course the Englishman sees the error when German historians make it, and the German sees the error in the foreigner too, but none of us seem able to jump out of our own skins and to see our own position with a certain relativity. And for the most part there is much too little disposition even to attempt the task. Sometimes historical students take tremendous trouble with the details of their researches, but when they come to the important point where they build up the larger framework of their story or draw their final conclusions, or pretend to extract from the narrative its teaching value, they are liable to become very casual and to be totally unaware of the processes that are taking place in their minds. They do not realise that very often they are smuggling into history the things they eventually imagine themselves to be extracting from it – the penny that they draw out of the slot machine is the very penny that they first put in. Even after the historian has collected data and sifted his materials with industry and discrimination, a very minute addition of wishful thinking may deflect the whole organisation of the results. A desire for self-justification may set the historian at a slightly wrong angle; and the extension of the lines of the picture may mean that this apparently small deflection will ultimately have the effect of carrying him far away from the central course. Indeed, history can be very dangerous unless it is accompanied by severe measures of self-discipline and self-purification – unless we realise that there is something that we must do with our personalities. Let us note, then, that historians have developed a remarkable scientific apparatus for the discovery, handling and sifting of historical evidence. They have not always remembered that this leaves vast areas of historical reconstruction and historical thinking which have not yet been brought under the same scientific control, though the history of historiography may enable us to make further advances even here.

The situation is more serious than anything that has so far been stated, however; for I think it is true to say that in the European politics of the last two centuries certain errors are discoverable which were born out of historical reflection as such – errors which would not have been made if people had not been so interested in the past and so concerned with it. The influence of historical study in the nineteenth century led to the creation of what we can only regard as new kinds of myths – things which came with the mysterious halo of religion about them and were almost made to serve as substitutes for religion. Amongst these I should put the myth of romantic nationalism, the modern religion of exaggerated nationalism, which is a perversion of such principle of nationality as had existed hitherto. That myth had historians as its high priests, while its prophets were a particular type of student of the past who enquired into the history of languages and interested themselves in early folk literature. Moreover, ideas which are introduced into historical scholarship at a high level soon become degraded into myths. Instead of being developed in a flexible manner with the passage of time, they are repeated with rigidity, dragged into different contexts, tossed to and fro in the marketplace and generally hardened and coarsened in the rough-and-tumble of the world's affairs. Historical memories, especially in Eastern Europe – and also in Ireland – have engendered much of the national animosity of modern times. In a far wider sense than this the overstressing of the historical argument in modern European politics has been unfortunate both for historical study and for diplomacy. One must wonder sometimes whether it would not have been better if men could have forgotten the centuries long ago, and thrown off the terrible burden of the past, so that they might face the future without encumbrances. And above all, when history has been accompanied by a tendency to regard the past as an independent source of rights, or when it has been accompanied by a tendency to worship the primitive stages of one's national culture and the uniqueness of a national mentality, it has made its contribution even to that serious drift of the modern world in the direction of irrationalism – the flight from the old ideal of a universal human reasonableness.

It would seem that history possesses certain initial attractions which will prevent it from being overlooked in any consideration of a scheme of general education. It is one of the subjects which purport to produce a 'well-informed mind', and it answers many of the requirements of ordinary curiosity. It is capable of easy discussion across a table without necessary resort to any long-term intellectual system. It gives an extension to the material which the mind can gather for the purpose of manufacturing into experience. And it imparts the kind of knowledge which throws light on the problems of the present day, and which can be used to broaden our consciousness of citizenship, whether in a nation or in the world.

On the other hand, against mathematics (for example), it has the disadvantage that mere progress from one chapter to another – the mere perusal of a larger area of the subject matter – does not in itself constitute or impose an intellectual discipline. The mere reading of history, the mere process of accumulating more information, in this field, does not necessarily give training to a mind that was initially diffuse. For this reason it is not wise to learn history by a hasty accumulation of information, so that the mass of data clutters up the memory and the growth of knowledge too greatly outstrips the general development of the mind. Furthermore, in the case of mathematics we start with our feet on the hard earth, learning the simplest things first, firmly establishing them at each point before we go any further, and making our argument good and watertight at each step of the way. In other words, we begin with strong foundations of concrete, and we gradually build our skyscrapers on the top of this. In the case of history, on the other hand, we start up in the clouds, at the very top of the highest skyscraper. We start with an abridged story, seen in the large and constructed out of what in reality are broad generalisations. It is only much later, when we reach the actual work of research, that we really come down to earth and arrive at the primary facts and primary materials. Only at the end of many years of training do we come to know what it means genuinely to establish the assertions that we make. For this reason, history is dangerous as an educational subject; and the best kind of history teacher is not the one who tells us most clearly what to believe – not the one who seeks merely to transfer a body of knowledge from his head into the heads of his pupils. The best kind of history teacher is the one who realises the danger of the subject itself and construes it as his function to redeem and rescue it as far as possible.

[...]

History, in fact, is so dangerous a subject – and so often it is the sinister people like a Machiavelli or a Napoleon or a Lenin who learn 'tricks of the trade' from it, before the majority of people have thought of doing so – that we might wonder whether it would not be better for the world to forget all of the past, better to have no memories at all, and just to face the future without ever looking back. We must teach history, however, precisely because so much bad history exists in the world already. Bad history is in the air we breathe, and even those who do not pretend to know any history behind the days of their grandfathers are dangerous sometimes, for they too are the slaves of unconscious assumptions or concealed perversities on the subject of the past. From one point of view we must say that none of us learns history – none of us ever attains a final understanding or the kind of knowledge in which he can safely rest. From another point of view, however, we may say that there is great need for history all the same, provided we conceive it as a process of unlearning. Something can be achieved if we can sweep away only a single layer of the tremendous crust of error that already has the world under its grip. Perhaps we may say that we sweep away one layer of error from our minds when we are at school; another layer when we study history at the university; and a further layer still if we reach so far as actual research. Indeed, supposing we continue the study of history all our lives we may sweep away a further layer of this crust of error every ten years, if we can keep our freshness of mind. But we do not complete the process. We do not reach the stage when we can say that we comprehend a particular subject in a final manner. For this reason it is better that men, when they leave the university, should forget the history of Louis XIV as they learned it there, unless they are prepared to continue the process of 'unlearning'. It is better that they should not allow the knowledge to freeze in their minds while the world changes and historical science changes – better that they should not thirty years later be holding too rigidly in their memory the things learned so long before. For historical knowledge is valuable only while it is, so to speak, liquid – it is worse than lumber if it freezes and hardens in the mind. We may say, then, that it is better for men to forget what they have actually learned of Louis XIV and cling rather to the experience they gained in the study of history and in historical exercises. History is more useful when transmuted into a deeper wisdom that melts into the rest of experience and is incorporated in the fabric of the mind itself.

The dangers of history are liable to become much greater if we imagine that the study of this subject qualifies us to be politicians or provides us with patterns which we can immediately transpose into the context of contemporary politics. It is not even clear that English people are wise in teaching a knowledge of Tudor government if their ultimate objective is to show young people how their country is governed in the twentieth century. I once read a detective story written with the intention of showing precisely the movements and operations that take place at Scotland Yard after a murder has been reported. If our object is to show future voters how the wheels of government work, some such method applied to the Cabinet or any other part of the constitutional system would seem to me to be more appropriate than the study of history, as the Schools section of the bbc have apparently discovered.

The argument that history qualifies men for the practice of politics is one which had a certain relevance and validity when it was used by the aristocrats who ruled England in the eighteenth century; but they were thinking of history as an additional acquirement for people who were supposed to have had their real education already. In any case, those English gentlemen of the eighteenth century were brought up from their very childhood to be rulers and politicians. They saw the practice of administration, heard political discussion, learned the arts of management in their local estates and observed the conduct of public affairs at first hand from their earliest days – they were being educated all the time in the actual practice of politics. For these people history came in its proper context – it was the one additional thing which would widen their horizon. Since they knew so much about the practical working of current affairs they were politicians already, and the study of history was calculated to make them better ones precisely because it broadened their horizon. I should seriously question the validity of a parallel argument for the modern democratic world and our modern educational system. We are wrong to think that the study of history itself is sufficient to turn us into competent politicians. And it is perhaps a tragedy that nowadays so many people – even if unconsciously – are in reality building up their political outlook from what they have read in books.

Some of the best diplomatic historians I ever met were almost the worst diplomats in the world when it came to transacting business in real life. It is often said in England that history is useful, and that it qualifies people to take part in politics, because it enables them to see how such things as politics and diplomacy work. I once had to induce the governing body of my college in Cambridge to try to come to an agreement on the colour of a carpet for a college library. A person who has had to undertake such a task and who has discovered all the manoeuvrings, all the delicate tactics, the persuasions, the whole science of give and take, that are necessary to get twelve men to agree on the colour of a carpet – such a person may be said to have had his first lesson in diplomacy. A person who merely reads a life of Bismarck is liable to be deceived a hundred times over, owing to the sheer fact of unavoidable abridgements, even if for no other reason. In our condensed version of the story a host of little shiftings and successive adjustments and minute manoeuvrings made by Bismarck over the course of a number of weeks get compressed and telescoped together – so that they cake and solidify into one big thing, a mighty instantaneous act of volition, a colossal piece of Bismarckism. My teacher, Professor Temperley, once reminded us in Cambridge that when the research student goes to manuscript sources, to the original diplomatic correspondence, for example, he does not go merely in order to have a scoop and to uncover some surprising secret; he goes to the sources primarily in order that by an actual day-today study of the whole correspondence he shall learn the way in which diplomacy works and decisions are arrived at. Only the research student really studies things at close enough quarters to understand the complexity of these processes. Indeed, abridged history – through the mere fact that it is necessarily so abridged – is having the effect of leaving the world with many serious misconceptions. By foreshortening the picture and making Bismarckian strokes of policy more trenchant than they really were, abridged history gives men a greater appearance of sovereignty over events than they actually possess; and it tends to magnify the controlling power of governments over the next stage in the story. With the decline of religion, and in the absence of anything else that seems authentic, men and nations rely on the abridged history they have learned to give them their impression of their place in the sun, their purposeful intent, and their idea of what they can do with their destiny. They acquire an academic dream-impression of what statesmen can do in the world, what governments achieve, what their national mission is, and what can be brought about by sheer self-assertion and will.

In any case, the world rarely remembers to what a degree the pretended 'lessons' which are extracted by politicians from history are judgments based on the assumption that we know what would have happened if some statesman in the past had only acted differently. When historians so often assert that the Congress of Vienna made a mistake in neglecting the 'principle of nationality', we may wonder whether they have really faced for a single moment the question: what would have happened in Europe if the Congress of Vienna had followed the twentieth-century view? There was much talk in 1919 of the necessity of 'avoiding the mistakes of 1815'; and when a person has been fed with the apparently self-evident verdicts of abridged history, it is difficult to convince him that in any event this is a fallacious formula for policy. What you have to avoid in 1919 are not the mistakes of 1815 but the mistakes of 1919. What you have to avoid is too blind an immersion in the prejudices of your own time. Those who talked of 'avoiding the mistakes of 1815' were using history to ratify the prejudices they had already. In any case, men are slow to count their blessings and quick to see the faults and shortcomings of the world into which they are born, and in 1919 it was the general cry that Europe must not be saddled with the burden of a settlement as unsatisfactory as that of the Congress of Vienna. It took our knowledge of the difficulties, weaknesses and ephemerality of the Versailles settlement to make us realise that the state of the question is entirely different. What we want to learn now is why the Congress of Vienna was so much more successful than we have known how to be.

Not only do historical judgments rest so often on an assumption concerning what would have happened if a certain statesman had acted differently – if only Metternich had done *the other thing*, for example – but there is a rigidity that occurs in our treatment of the possible alternatives, for we so often imagine that there was only one alternative, when in reality there was a great range of them.

We overlook, therefore, the complexity of the mathematics that will be required to work out the displacements which a different event would have produced, as in the case of the problem of what would have happened if Napoleon had won the Battle of Waterloo. So from an armchair every Tom, Dick and Harry in England can conduct a facile course of reasoning which will satisfy him that he could easily have thwarted Hitler at an earlier point in the story, because he, for his part, would have done *the other thing*; as though in such a case a man like Hitler would not have done something different too at the next remove, and a host of other factors would have to be altered, the historical process quickly complicating all the calculations that require to be made. Indeed, history adds to the errors of a rigid mind and only serves us when we use it to increase our elasticity.

[...]

One of the dangers of history lies in the ease with which these apparently self-evident judgments can be extracted from it, provided one closes one's eyes to certain facts. The person who is incapable of seeing more than one thing at once – incapable of holding two factors in his mind at the same time – will reach results all the more quickly and will feel the most assured in the judgments that he makes.

I imagine that if we wish to study the effect of historical study on the actual conduct of affairs, one of the appropriate fields in which we can pursue the enquiry is that of military strategy. In general, it is not possible to have a war just for the purpose of training the leaders of an army, and it has been the case that the teaching of strategy was for a long time carried on by means of historical study – for a hundred years by a continual study of the methods of Napoleon. Since the time when Machiavelli inaugurated the modern science of war there have been grave misgivings about this use of history. Machiavelli himself was open to the reproach that since he required the detailed imitation of the methods of the Romans, he refused to believe in artillery. Similarly, it would appear to be the case that if men shape their minds too rigidly by a study of the last war, they are to some degree unfitting themselves for the conduct of the next one. If a nation decides conversely that it will set out with the particular purpose of avoiding the mistakes of the last war, it is still liable to be the slave of history and to be defeated by another nation that thinks of new things. Historical study, therefore, has sometimes had a deadening effect on military strategists; and it has often been a criticism of them that they were too prone to conduct the present war on the method of the previous one, forgetting how times had changed.

It seems true, however, that many of the errors which spring from a little history are often corrected as people go on to study more and more history. If a man had a knowledge of many wars and of the whole history of the art of war, studying not merely the accounts of battles and campaigns but relating the weapons of a given period to the conditions of the time, relating policies to circumstances, so that he came to have an insight into the deep causes of things, the hidden sources of the changes that take place – if he allowed this knowledge not to lie heavily on his mind, not to be used in a narrow and literal spirit, but to sink into the walls of his brain so that it was turned into wisdom and experience – then such a person would be able to acquire the right feeling for the texture of events, and would undoubtedly avoid becoming the mere slave of the past. I think he would be better able to face a new world, and to meet the surprises of unpredictable change with greater flexibility. A little history may make people mentally rigid. Only if we go on learning more and more of it – go on 'unlearning' it – will it correct its own deficiencies gradually and help us to reach the required elasticity of mind.

E H CARR:
A HISTORIAN FOR ALL SEASONS

INTRODUCTION BY MICHAEL COX

E H Carr (1892–1982) not only wrote a lot of history, including 14 volumes on the early years of Soviet Russia, four biographies and at least seven books on international relations which were just as much diplomatic history as they were pure 'IR', he also composed what possibly remains even today the most popular study on how to think about the historian's craft: namely *What is History?*, which was published in 1961.

Carr also made history during his twenty-year sojourn in the Foreign Office between 1916 and 1936. He was, quite literally, 'present at creation' during the Paris Peace Conference in 1919, advising the British government on how to deal with the emerging new states in Europe, an experience that forever turned him against nationalism. He was still a member of 'the Office' when Stalin set out to transform the Soviet Union through his first Five-Year Plan, and indeed under an assumed name (John Hallett) wrote a number of articles which recognised the historical significance of this first real experiment in planning. By the time Hitler came to power and began redrawing the map of Europe, Carr then became one of the foremost foreign policy experts advising officials in London to come to terms with Germany's territorial demands – appeasement by any other name.

Yet for someone who was so obviously an insider with friends in high places (he played an important role for a while in Chatham

House and later secured a fellowship at Trinity College, Cambridge), he very soon became one of the more controversial figures on the British intellectual scene. A towering presence he may well have become; according to his close friend A J P Taylor he was nothing less than 'the greatest British historian of his age', yet despite this acclaim, he was never considered 'safe'.

This was, in part, because he found himself on the wrong side in the Cold War. Certainly, his long-term relationship with the Marxist Isaac Deutscher – the biographer of both Stalin and Trotsky – could hardly reassure more conventional figures that he was really 'one of us'. Added to this was Carr's position as one of the great polemicists of his age. Indeed, over a long and very argumentative career, he managed to upset nearly every liberal of note – Arnold Toynbee and Alfred Zimmern being the most prominent, not to mention a whole raft of influential historians from Herbert Butterfield to Geoffrey Elton. Nor did his praise for Soviet economic achievements or his less than sympathetic attitude towards the nations of Eastern Europe win him many friends in the West either.

But it was just as much his approach to history as his defence of what he believed had been achieved in the Soviet Union that made him the controversial figure he became. As his granddaughter Helen Carr (herself a historian) has pointed out, he was not a historian 'by traditional standards', never having studied the subject at university. On the other hand, his approach as outlined early on in *The New Society* in 1951 and ten years later in *What is History?* could not but irritate many in the history establishment.

There were many reasons for this. One was that instead of being hostile to revolutions and revolutionaries in general, he tended in the main to be sympathetic to both. Nor did he accept the view that history was just a series of random events, or, to use his own term, 'patternless'. In fact, according to Carr, not only were there patterns and trends which it was up to the historian to uncover, there was also something called 'progress'. Historians moreover should stop thinking of their subject as if it was something sacrosanct which could not draw inspiration from other disciplines, including the social sciences. For most modern historians, drawing inspiration from other subject areas would seem to present no problem. In more conservative times, it appeared to sound like an attack on the very subject itself.

Finally, Carr upset more than a few of his peers by suggesting that history was not just about the accumulation of 'facts' – and even facts were not quite what they appeared to be, he insisted – but rather about how the historian assembled those facts. As he famously put it, in order to understand history, one must first study the historian and his times, a dangerous intellectual move according to critics, which seemed to imply there was no such thing as objectivity. Nor was this enough. One then had to go on and look for the cause or causes of what happened in history and not just tell a story. Indeed, merely telling a story based on 'an ocean of facts' was, in Carr's view, simply not history.

In our own age, which has gone through all sorts of intellectual challenges, from postmodernism to postcolonialism, this may all sound very tame. But Carr's radical way of thinking about the creative role of the historian, and that there may in fact be no such thing as a single narrative we call 'history', proved to be 'intellectual dynamite' at the time. It also had a major impact on an up-and-coming generation of historians. As one of his many contemporary admirers, Richard Evans, has reminded us, Carr's *What is History?* played a pivotal role in the historiographical revolution in Britain in the 1960s, one which challenged 'the kind of history' he had been taught at school. This older historical tradition, he noted, had been dominated by 'high politics and diplomacy, bereft of theory, and entirely innocent of any consciousness that it might be serving some kind of ideological or political purpose'. At a single stroke, Carr undermined this approach for ever.

Ironically, the reputation of this immensely important figure, who according to Evans changed the way that history was thought about at the time, has suffered greatly since the collapse of the system he devoted over 30 years of his professional life to writing about. That 'shocking old Soviet apologist', as one reviewer called him after the fall of the Soviet Union in 1991. 'The most overrated thinker of the century', according to another less than generous critic. History, it seems, has not been kind to Carr.

Yet much of what he wrote about history more generally still has relevance today, which may in large part explain why his *What is History?* is still widely read and why the book itself (now translated into over 25 languages) continues to be discussed by historians. Carr was certainly short-sighted when it came to the USSR, and he was clearly wrong to think it represented the future. Yet if he were alive today he might perhaps take some comfort from the fact that a 2020 poll found that 75% of Russians believed that the Soviet era was the greatest time in the country's history! As a good empirical historian who worked in more archives than most of his peers, Carr never believed in public polling. Nor did he think one could turn back the clock of history. The best one could do, as he made clear, was 'to cast the beam of the past over the issues which dominate present and future' and, by so doing, increase man's mastery of the real world in which he has to live. Many historians would insist that history should not have a purpose. Carr thought otherwise.

London, March 2022

E H CARR
THE NEW SOCIETY

Twenty-five years or so ago, when I was very young indeed and the world was not yet so uncomfortable a place as it has since become, I remember hearing a wise old gentleman remark that, in his opinion, the French Revolution was a great mistake and that everything that had happened since had only made it worse. This view struck me then as novel and shocking. It has since become almost a commonplace; and while I shall reserve for my last lecture my attempt to enquire whether the French revolution – together with its concomitant phenomena the American Revolution and the Industrial Revolution, which my friend would certainly have included in the category of events that had better not have happened – was or was not the starting point of a process of decline, I shall assert here and now that it was, so far as anything ever has a starting point in history, the starting point of something, and that in order to understand the problems of the 'new society' in which we live today we shall have to go back at least as far as the French, the American and the Industrial revolutions.

This assertion commits me to the historical approach to the contemporary world. Modern man is beyond all precedent 'history-conscious'. What philosophy was to Classical Greece and Rome, what theology was to the Middle Ages, what science was to the eighteenth century, that history is to our own time. The modern world is under no temptation to return to the monolithic aloofness of Thucydides, who opened his *History of the Peloponnesian War* with an expression of his belief that no great things had ever happened either in war or in peace before the events which he set out to describe, and evidently saw little reason to expect that any great things were likely to happen thereafter. The stoutest rationalist today finds cold comfort in the famous argument of Lucretius, the Roman sceptic: 'Consider how that past ages of eternal time before our birth were no concern of ours. This is a mirror which nature holds up to us of future time after our death.'

We have lost this capacity to isolate ourselves in time; we have become incorrigibly historical in our outlook. In the Middle Ages, it was the function of history to illustrate and justify God's ways to man. After the Renaissance, history got a new start out of the process of comparing the modern with the ancient world, which was held up as a model not since attained by a degenerate posterity; Gibbon's masterpiece was the high-water mark of this school. But it was left for the French revolution to enthrone history in her own right. Condorcet, while in prison awaiting the guillotine, rejected the consolations of religion in favour of those of history, and wrote *The Outline of a Table of Progress of the Human Spirit*, in which history was seen for the first time as a progressive advance towards a future utopia. Modern history begins when history becomes concerned with the future as well as with the past. Modern man peers eagerly back into the twilight out of which he has come, in the hope that its faint beams will illuminate the obscurity into which he is going; conversely his aspirations and anxieties about the path which lies before him sharpen his insight into what lies behind. No consciousness of the future, no history. In that nineteenth-century conglomeration of nations and potential nations, the Habsburg Empire, it was the so-called 'unhistorical peoples' who were unconcerned about their future; once they began to have aspirations for the future they discovered or invented histories of their past. Between past and future, action and interaction are constant. Past, present and future are woven together in an endless chain.

The birth of modern history was bound up with the belief that the path to knowledge is the discovery of certain laws and principles whose operation is exemplified in particular phenomena. This belief had its origin in the metaphysical rationalism of Descartes and the scientific rationalism of Newton. Its application to the processes of history began in France about 1750, when Montesquieu wrote in the preface to *De l'esprit des lois*: 'I have set forth the principles, I have seen particular cases conform to them as of their own accord, I have seen how the histories of all nations are nothing but their results.' In the nineteenth century, belief became general in a principle of progress whose laws were exemplified in the events of history; the study of history was the key to an understanding of these laws. The laws of history were thus strictly analogous to the laws of science. After Darwin it was even thought that they were substantially the same laws: Darwin had proved that evolution proceeded through the struggle for existence, the elimination of the unfit and the survival of the fittest. It suddenly became obvious that these forces were also at work in the advance of mankind through history.

[…]

The difference turns on fundamental conceptions of the nature of history. Toynbee's view, like Spengler's, rests on the analogy between history and science in which historical thought has been enmeshed for nearly two centuries. The analogy is false. In science the drama repeats itself over and over again because the *dramatis personae* are creatures unconscious of the past or inanimate objects. In history the drama cannot repeat itself because the *dramatis personae* at the second performance are already conscious of the prospective *denouement*; the essential condition of the first performance can never be reconstituted. Between the two world wars a well-known military critic, having studied the conditions of land warfare between 1914 and 1918 and decided that these conditions still held, predicted that in the next war the defensive would once more triumph over the offensive. His objective reasoning may have been perfectly correct. But he omitted one factor. The German generals were determined not to repeat the unfortunate *denouement* of 1918 at the second performance. They were thus enabled to introduce new elements into the chain of causation and to produce in 1940 directly opposite results to those predicted. Human consciousness of the past prevented history from repeating itself. Before the middle of the nineteenth century so-called bourgeois revolutions had put the middle class into power in most countries of western Europe. One result of this was a rapid expansion of the ruling middle class, and, as a result, an equally rapid expansion of the proletariat, so that Marx was emboldened to predict a proletarian revolution as the natural corollary of the bourgeois revolution. But, once this sequence of events had penetrated human consciousness, history could not repeat itself. The German middle class was by this time so frightened of the potential *denouement* that it refused to perform the drama of the bourgeois revolution in Germany and preferred to come to terms with Bismarck.

In history the presumption is not that the same thing will happen again, but that the same thing will not happen again. All analogies between history and science, all cyclical theories of history, are tainted with the fundamental error of neglecting human consciousness of the past. You cannot look forward intelligently into the future unless you also are prepared to look back attentively into the past. But this does not mean that you will find there either laws to obey or precedents to guide you. If I am deeply concerned in these lectures with the history of the last 150 years, this is not because I expect anything that happened then to happen again (this is the kind of lesson which history does not teach), but because history deals with a line or procession of events, half of which lies in the past and half in the future, and you cannot have an intelligent appreciation of one half unless you also concern yourself with the other half.

[…]

History is therefore a process of interaction between the historian and the past of which he is writing. The facts help to mould the mind of the historian. But the mind of the historian also, and just as essentially, helps to mould the facts. History is a dialogue between past and present, not between dead past and living present, but between living present and a past which the historian makes live again by establishing its continuity with the present; and, among recent writers on the subject, I find myself most indebted to Collingwood, who has insisted most strongly on this continuity and on this process of interaction. It is an old trouble that the word 'history', which by its derivation and in its proper use signifies the enquiry conducted by the historian, should have been transferred by popular usage to the material in which he works – the series of events themselves; for this transferred usage encourages the fallacy that history is something that exists outside the mind of the historian and independently of it. This popular usage has also encouraged confusion of thought about the so-called 'pattern' in history.

Needless to say, I should reject absolutely the conception once put forward by H A L Fisher (and tacitly held, I suspect, by some other modern historians) of a 'patternless' history, that is to say of history as an inconsequential narration having no coherence and therefore no meaning for the present. But this does not commit me to the view of a pattern inherent in the events themselves – the view of Spengler and Toynbee; or of a pattern woven by an inscrutable providence – the view of Butterfield. For me the pattern in history is what is put there by the historian. History is itself the pattern into which the historian weaves his material; without pattern there can be no history. Pattern can only be the product of mind – the mind of the historian working on the events of the past.

The view that the pattern of history takes shape in the brain of the historian, and is fashioned not only by the events he is describing but also by the world in which he is living, is supported by an overwhelming weight of experience; and, although professional historians still sometimes put forward unguarded professions of objectivity, the 'conditioned' character of all historical writing has now become almost a commonplace. Creators of historical systems are not exempt from this rule. The idea of progress which inspired nineteenth-century systems and the idea of cyclical movement and decline which inspires more recent systems have been transparently derived not so much from a dispassionate analysis of the past as from the emotional impact of the current situation. Even in detail those systems reflect the particular bias of those who construct them. Hegel found the culmination of the historical process in the Prussian State, Spencer in the free trade, free competition and free contract of mid-Victorian England. Spengler owed the immense popularity of his work to the occasion which it provided for his compatriots to treat the downfall of Germany in 1918 as an integral part of the predestined 'decline of the West'. The deepening pessimism about the future of Western civilization which marks successive volumes of Professor Toynbee's *Study of History* reflects the increasing solicitude of the 1930s about the weaknesses and failures of British policy. Articulate human groups share a natural human inclination to attach universal significance to their own experiences. The pattern is not inherent in the events themselves; it is imposed upon them out of the consciousness and experience of the historian.

The pattern is, however, determined not so much by the historian's view of the present as by his view of the future. Past and future are the two essential time dimensions; the present is an infinitesimally small moving point on a continuous line consisting of past and future. It is thus the future prospect even more than the present reality which shapes the historian's view of the past. Macaulay and his nineteenth-century successors were influenced not so much by their satisfaction with what they saw around them as by their conviction that things would be even better in the future. Current theories of decline in history are prompted not so much by contemplation of our present difficulties as by the belief that things are going from bad to worse. It is the sense of direction which counts.

[...]

The historian is like an observer watching a moving procession from an aeroplane; since there is no constant or ascertainable relation between the speed, height and direction of the aircraft and the movement of the procession, changing and unfamiliar perspectives are juxtaposed in rapid succession, as in a cubist picture, none of them wholly false, none wholly true. Any static view of history purporting to be recorded from a fixed point by a stationary observer is fallacious.

Let me sum up, in the light of these reflections, what I mean by the historical approach and how I think it applicable to the problems which we have to face. History seeks to link the past with the future in a continuous line along which the historian himself is constantly moving. It is clear that we should not expect to extract from history any absolute judgments, either on the past or on the future. Such judgments it is not in its nature to give. All human judgment, like all human action, is involved in the logical dilemma of determinism and free will. The human being is indissolubly bound, in both his actions and his judgments, by a chain of causation reaching far back into the past; yet he has a qualified power to break the chain at a given point – the present – and so alter the future. In common-sense language, he can decide and judge for himself, but only up to a certain point; for the past limits and determines his decision and his judgment in innumerable ways. To admit that our judgments are wholly and irrevocably conditioned is to plead moral and intellectual bankruptcy. But to recognise the conditioned element in them is the best way to put us on our guard against too readily yielding to intellectual fashions – of which the nineteenth-century belief in progress and the twentieth-century belief in decadence are excellent examples.

[…]

If, however, we resist the temptations of determinism and scepticism, we must be cautious about yielding too readily to the blandishments of utopia. Utopianism means a rejection of the past. It denies the validity of history, substituting for it an indulgence in wish-dreams about what might have happened if only George III had not lost the American colonies, if only the internal combustion engine or the atom bomb had not been invented, if only Kerensky had beaten the Bolsheviks in 1917 – the sort of speculation that belongs not to serious history but to the competitions column of the weeklies. In its visions of the future, it constructs imaginary commonwealths having no lineal or causal connexion with the past, and therefore unrealisable. The sane student of history must reject these wish-dreams, these speculations, these castles in the air, even at the risk of being branded as a determinist. If somebody who believes that monarchy is the best possible form of government tells me that he proposes to start a campaign for the restoration of monarchy in the United States, I shall tell him that he is wasting his time, since the history of the last 150 years is against him. But that does not make me a determinist. The function of the historian is not to reshape or reform the past, but to accept it and to analyse what he finds significant in it, to isolate and illuminate the fundamental changes at work in the society in which we live and the perhaps age-old processes which lie behind them; and this will entail a view (which, since it will be present even if it is unconscious, had much better be consciously recognised and deliberately avowed) of the processes by which the problems set to the present generation by these changes can be resolved.

The historian undertakes a twofold operation: to analyse the past in the light of the present and the future which is growing out of it, and to cast the beam of the past over the issues which dominate present and future. His aims and purposes will ultimately be derived from values which have their source outside history; for without these history itself must become meaningless – a mere succession of action for the sake of action, and change for the sake of change. But the translation of these values into terms of policy is historically conditioned and subject to all the imperfections of the historical process; and the application of policy to a particular historical situation is also closely involved in the understanding and acceptance of that situation. Well-meaning reformers who propound utopian solutions of political problems commonly fail to recognise how far self-interest has intruded into the formulation of their ideal in terms of policy, and how complicated are the historical issues involved in its application. A historically minded generation is one which looks back, not indeed for solutions which cannot be found in the past, but for those critical insights which are necessary both to the understanding of its existing situation and to the realisation of the values which it holds.

E H CARR
WHAT IS HISTORY?

I often think it odd that it should be so dull,
for a great deal of it must be invention.
Catherine Morland on history (*Northanger Abbey,* ch. xiv)

[...]

First, it is alleged that history deals with the unique and particular, and science with the general and universal. This view may be said to start with Aristotle, who declared that poetry was 'more philosophical' and 'more serious' than history, since poetry was concerned with general truth and history with particular.[1] A host of later writers, down to Collingwood[2] inclusive, made a similar distinction between science and history. This seems to rest on a misunderstanding. Hobbes's famous dictum still stands: 'Nothing in the world is universal but names, for the things named are everyone of them individual and singular.'[3] This is certainly true of the physical sciences: no two geological formations, no two animals of the same species and no two atoms are identical. Similarly, no two historical events are identical. But insistence on the uniqueness of historical events has the same paralysing effect as the platitude taken over by Moore from Bishop Butler and at one time especially beloved by linguistic philosophers: 'Everything is what it is and not another thing.' Embarked on this course, you soon attain a sort of philosophical nirvana, in which nothing that matters can be said about anything.

The very use of language commits the historian, like the scientist, to generalisation. The Peloponnesian War and the Second

World War were very different, and both were unique. But the historian calls them both wars, and only the pedant will protest. When Gibbon wrote of both the establishment of Christianity by Constantine and the rise of Islam as revolutions,[4] he was generalising two unique events. Modern historians do the same when they write of the English, French, Russian and Chinese revolutions. The historian is not really interested in the unique, but in what is general in the unique. In the 1920s discussions by historians of the causes of the war of 1914 usually proceeded on the assumption that it was due either to the mismanagement of diplomats, working in secret and uncontrolled by public opinion, or to the unfortunate division of the world into territorial sovereign states. In the 1930s discussions proceeded on the assumption that it was due to rivalries between imperialist powers driven by the stresses of capitalism in decline to partition the world between them. These discussions all involved generalisation about the causes of war, or at any rate of war in twentieth-century conditions. The historian constantly uses generalisation to test his evidence. If the evidence is not clear whether Richard murdered the princes in the Tower, the historian will ask himself – perhaps unconsciously rather than consciously – whether it was a habit of rulers of the period to liquidate potential rivals to their throne; and his judgment will, quite rightly, be influenced by this generalisation.

The reader, as well as the writer, of history, is a chronic generaliser, applying the observation of the historian to other historical contexts with which he is familiar – or perhaps to his own time. When I read Carlyle's *French Revolution*, I find myself again and again generalizing his comments by applying them to my own special interest in the Russian Revolution. Take for instance this on the terror:

Horrible, in lands that had known equal justice – not so unnatural in lands that had never known it.

Or, more significantly, this:

> It is unfortunate, though very natural, that the history of this period has so generally been written in hysterics. Exaggeration abounds, execration, wailing; and on the whole, darkness.[5]

Or another, this time from Burckhardt on the growth of the modern state in the sixteenth century:

> The more recently power has originated, the less it can remain stationary – first because those who created it have become accustomed to rapid further movement and because they are and will remain innovators *per se*; secondly, because the forces aroused or subdued by them can be employed only through further acts of violence.[6]

It is nonsense to say that generalisation is foreign to history; history thrives on generalizations. As Mr. Elton neatly puts it in a volume of the new *Cambridge Modern History*, 'what distinguishes the historian from the collector of historical facts is generalization';[7] he might have added that the same thing distinguishes the natural scientist from the naturalist or collector of specimens. But do not suppose that generalisation permits us to construct some vast scheme of history into which specific events must be fitted. And, since Marx is one of those who is often accused of constructing, or believing in, such a scheme, I will quote by way of summing-up a passage from one of his letters which puts the matter in its right perspective:

> Events strikingly similar, but occurring in a different historical milieu, lead to completely dissimilar results. By studying each of these evolutions separately and then comparing them,

it is easy to find the key to the understanding of this phenomenon; but it is never possible to arrive at this understanding
by using the *passe-partout* of some historical-philosophical
theory whose great virtue is to stand above history.[8]

History is concerned with the relation between the unique and the
general. As a historian, you can no more separate them, or give
precedence to one over the other, than you can separate fact and
interpretation.

This is perhaps the place for a brief remark on the relations
between history and sociology. Sociology at present faces two
opposite dangers – the danger of becoming ultra-theoretical and
the danger of becoming ultra-empirical. The first is the danger of
losing itself in abstract and meaningless generalizations about
society in general. Society with a big S is as misleading a fallacy
as History with a big H. This danger is brought nearer by those
who assign to sociology the exclusive task of generalizing from
the unique events recorded by history: it has even been suggested
that sociology is distinguished from history by having 'laws'.[9]
The other danger is that foreseen by Karl Mannheim almost a
generation ago, and very much present today, of a sociology 'split
into a series of discrete technical problems of social readjustment'.[10] Sociology is concerned with historical societies, everyone of which is unique and moulded by specific historical
antecedents and conditions. But the attempt to avoid generalisation and interpretation by confining oneself to so-called 'technical' problems of enumeration and analysis is merely to become
the unconscious apologist of a static society. Sociology, if it is to
become a fruitful field of study, must, like history, concern itself
with the relation between the unique and the general. But it must
also become dynamic – a study not of society at rest (for no such
society exists) but of social change and development. For the
rest, I would only say that the more sociological history becomes,
and the more historical sociology becomes, the better for both.

Let the frontier between them be kept wide open for two-way traffic.

The question of generalisation is closely connected with my second question: the lessons of history. The real point about generalisation is that through it we attempt to learn from history, to apply the lesson drawn from one set of events to another set of events: when we generalize, we are consciously or unconsciously trying to do this. Those who reject generalisation and insist that history is concerned exclusively with the unique are, logically enough, those who deny that anything can be learned from history. But the assertion that men learn nothing from history is contradicted by a multitude of observable facts. No experience is more common. In 1919 I was present at the Paris Peace Conference as a junior member of the British delegation. Everyone in the delegation believed that we could learn from the lessons of the Vienna congress, the last great European peace congress a hundred years earlier. A certain Captain Webster, then employed in the War Office, now Sir Charles Webster and an eminent historian, wrote an essay telling us what those lessons were. Two of them have remained in my memory. One was that it was dangerous, when redrawing the map of Europe, to neglect the principle of self-determination. The other was that it was dangerous to throw secret documents into your wastepaper basket, the contents of which would certainly be bought by the secret service of some other delegation. These lessons of history were taken for gospel and influenced our behaviour. This example is recent and trivial. But it would be easy to trace in comparatively remote history the influence of the lessons of a still remoter past. Everyone knows about the impact of ancient Greece upon Rome. But I am not sure whether any historian has attempted to make a precise analysis of the lessons which the Romans learned, or believed themselves to have learned, from the history of Hellas. An examination of the lessons drawn in western Europe in the seventeenth, eighteenth and nineteenth centuries from Old

Testament history might yield rewarding results. The English Puritan revolution cannot be fully understood without it; and the conception of the chosen people was an important factor in the rise of modem nationalism. The stamp of a classical education was heavily imprinted in the nineteenth century on the new ruling class in Great Britain. Grote, as I have already noted, pointed to Athens as an exemplar for the new democracy; and I should like to see a study of the extensive and important lessons consciously or unconsciously imparted to British empire-builders by the history of the Roman Empire. In my own particular field, the makers of the Russian Revolution were profoundly impressed – one might almost say, obsessed – by the lessons of the French revolution, of the revolutions of 1848 and of the Paris Commune of 1871. But I shall recall here the qualification imposed by the dual character of history. Learning from history is never simply a one-way process. To learn about the present in the light of the past means also to learn about the past in the light of the present. The function of history is to promote a profounder understanding of both past and present through the interrelation between them.

My third point is the role of prediction in history: no lessons, it is said, can be learned from history because history, unlike science, cannot predict the future. This question is involved in a tissue of misunderstandings. As we have seen, scientists are no longer so eager as they used to be to talk about the laws of nature. The so-called laws of sciences which affect our ordinary life are in fact statements of tendency, statements of what will happen other things being equal or in laboratory conditions. They do not claim to predict what will happen in concrete cases. The law of gravity does not prove that that particular apple will fall to the ground; somebody may catch it in a basket. The law of optics that light travels in a straight line does not prove that a particular ray of light may not be refracted or scattered by some intervening object. But this does not mean that these laws are worthless, or not in principle valid. Modern physical theories, we are told, deal only with the probabilities of events taking place. Today science is more inclined to remember that induction can logically lead only to probabilities or to reasonable belief, and is more anxious to treat its pronouncements as general rules or guides, the validity of which can be tested only in specific action. *'Science, d'où prévoyance; prévoyance, d'où action'*, as Comte put it.[11] The clue to the question of prediction in history lies in this distinction between the general and the specific, between the universal and the unique. The historian, as we have seen, is bound to generalize; and, in so doing, he provides general guides for future action which, though not specific predictions, are both valid and useful. But he cannot predict specific events, because the specific is unique and because the element of accident enters into it. This distinction, which worries philosophers, is perfectly clear to the ordinary man. If two or three children in a school develop measles, you will conclude that the epidemic will spread; and this prediction, if you care to call it such, is based on a generalisation from past experience, and is a valid and useful guide to action. But you cannot make the specific prediction that Charles or Mary will catch measles. The historian proceeds in the same way. People do not expect the historian to predict that revolution will break out in Ruritania next month. The kind of conclusion which they will seek to draw, partly from specific knowledge of Ruritanian affairs and partly from a study of history, is that conditions in Ruritania are such that a revolution is likely to occur in the near future if somebody touches it off, or unless somebody on the government side does something to stop it; and this conclusion might be accompanied by estimates, based partly on the analogy of other revolutions, of the attitude which different sectors of the population may be expected to adopt. The prediction, if such it can be called, can be realised only through the occurrence of unique events, which cannot themselves be predicted. But this does not mean that inferences drawn from history about the future are worthless, or that they do not possess a conditional validity which serves both as a guide to action and a key to our understanding of how things happen. I do not wish to suggest that the inferences of the social scientist or of the historian can match those of the physical scientist in precision, or that their inferiority in this respect is due merely to the greater backwardness of the social sciences. The human being is on any view the most complex natural entity known to us and the study of his behaviour may well involve difficulties different in kind from those confronting the physical scientist. All I wish to establish is that their aims and methods are not fundamentally dissimilar.

1. Aristotle, *Poetics*, ch. ix.

2. R. G Collingwood, 'Historical Imagination: an Inaugural Lecture Delivered before the University of Oxford on 28 October 1935', 5.

3. Thomas Hobbes, *Leviathan* (London, 1651), I, iv.

4. Edward Gibbon, *The Decline and Fall of the Roman Empire*, ch. xx, ch. 1.

5. Thomas Carlyle, *The French Revolution: a History*, 3 vols (London, 1837), vol I, v, ch. 9; vol III, i, ch. 1.

6. J Burckhardt, *Judgements on History and Historians* (London, 1959), 34.

7. G Elton, *The New Cambridge Modern History: The Reformation 1520–1559*, ii (Cambridge University Press, Cambridge, 1958), 20.

8. K Marx and F Engels, *Works* (Russian ed), xv, 378; the letter from which this passage is quoted appeared in the Russian journal Otechestvennye Zapiski in 1877. Professor Popper appears to associate Marx with what he calls 'the central mistake of historicism', the belief that historical tendencies or trends 'can be immediately derived from universal laws alone' (*The Poverty of Historicism* [London, 1957]), 128–29): this is precisely what Marx denied.

9. This appears to be the view of Professor Popper (*The Open Society* [2nd edn, 1952], ii, 322). Unfortunately he gives an example of a sociological law: 'Wherever the freedom of thought, and of the communication of thought, is effectively protected by legal institutions and institutions ensuring the publicity of discussion, there will be scientific progress.' This was written in 1942 or 1943, and was evidently inspired by the belief that the Western democracies, in virtue of their institutional arrangements, would remain in the van of scientific progress – a belief since dispelled, or severely qualified, by developments in the Soviet Union. Far from being a law, it was not even a valid generalisation.

10. K Mannheim, *Ideology and Utopia: an Introduction to the Sociology of Knowledge*, trans Louis Wirth and Edward Shils (Routledge, New York, 1936), 228.

11. A Comte, *Cours de philosophie positive* (Paris, 1830), i, 51. The phrase can be translated as 'Science, hence foresight; foresight, hence action'.

PIETER GEYL:
A PASSIONATE APPLIED HISTORIAN

INTRODUCTION BY BEATRICE DE GRAAF

One could argue that Pieter Geyl's most important contribution to history is his famous dictum that 'one can consider history a never-ending argument.'[1] Yet there is far more to say about Geyl's work, and especially about his contribution to the field of applied history.

First of all, Geyl (1887–1966) staged himself as a public persona, and applied his wit to numerous contemporary discussions and controversies. According to contemporaries, Geyl used and abused history all the time. 'Vain, arrogant, brilliant, controversial, famous, notorious, sharp-witted, self-assured, shameless, innovative, hypercritical, a libertine: all of this can be said of Pieter Geyl,' Utrecht University states on the website listing its archival holdings of Geyl. Remarkably, Geyl himself was so convinced of his own importance that he had already started to collect and set up his own archive during his lifetime, amassing more than 40 linear metres of materials.[2]

Geyl studied history in Leiden, started his career as a teacher, then became a journalist and went to London, where he was appointed professor of Dutch History at the University of London in 1919. He participated in the consolidation of the Institute of Historical Research, challenged the existing historiography of the Low Countries internationally, and was appointed professor of Modern History in Utrecht in 1936. He spent the Second World

War in German hostage camps, but engaged himself even more strongly as a public intellectual after the war, in the Netherlands and abroad.

Secondly, Geyl gained fame (or notoriety) for applying his expertise on the Eighty Years' War to political activism on behalf of a 'Greater Netherlands' ideology. According to Geyl, this war had separated the 'Dutch tribe' in a Flemish and Dutch people, a situation that required revision in the twentieth century (after the intermitted reunion of the Netherlands and Belgium between 1815 and 1830). With this irredentist concept, Geyl argued that the Netherlands, Flanders and even Brussels could and should be reunited again, to provide a 'Greater Netherlands State' ('Dietsland', or 'Dutchland') that also could include parts of Dutchspeaking territories in Germany, France, South Africa and Suriname.[3] Although fervently anti-Nazi, Geyl saw his ideas being appropriated by Nazi and fascist groups in the 1920s and 1930s – something which he abhorred. After the war, his Greater Netherlands views had become tainted with the collaboration practices within nationalist circles in Belgium and the Netherlands.[4]

And thirdly, Geyl's theory of history, his views on 'the use and abuse of history' that propelled him to engage in various disputes, polemics and controversies with past and contemporary historians, was a very sharply delineated one. Geyl felt that the defence of reason and criticism as the basic principles of writing history should enjoy absolute priority. A true historian should devote themself to deconstructing past prejudices and biases. He demonstrated this view in his manifold contribution to Dutch history of the sixteenth and seventeenth centuries, where he time and again tried to debunk the 'legend' that the Dutch revolt was the product of noble ideals on freedom and protestant spirituality predominantly.[5] He also railed against the famous historian Arnold J Toynbee, whom he called out for reducing complexity and adhering to the ahistorical (since teleological and 'metaphysical') notions of 'laws' on rise and decline.[6]

If a historian, in the name of reason and with a critical mind, is to embark upon such a mission, this historian should always abide by the strictest rule of reason themselves, and should never let their judgement be clouded by emotions or passions.[7] The quote Geyl himself referred to in his chapter on the 'use and abuse of history' is a testimonial to this principle. In October 1945, Geyl described to his students:

> Our feeling of national solidarity and patriotism does not need the stimulus of hatred. Hatred of another nation is not a historical attitude of mind. Hatred of oppression and cruelty, yes; hatred of crime and deception. But the historian who uses reason and criticism will be able to make the necessary distinction, and the rejection of an entire nation, and of that nation's civilization, which has in so many ways intertwined itself with European civilization, cannot stand the test of true historical judgment.[8]

His main aim was to distinguish between writing history based on sound criticism and reason and abusing history by elevating instinct and passion and letting them prevail over such a methodological approach. The fallacy of national socialist ideology was its attack on criticism and reason. Yet he also denounced the flawed and overemotional manner in which, after the Second World War, the whole German population and civilisation was conflated with Nazism and collectively and indiscriminately condemned by many non-German, European historians.

In short, Geyl was as passionate about the prevalence of criticism and reason as he was hotly engaged in various political debates – making him even more of an enigma, and a supreme example of an applied historian in life and work.

Utrecht, September 2022

1. Pieter Geyl, *Napoleon. Voor en tegen in de Franse geschiedschrijving* (Utrecht, 1946), 5.
2. More information on the collection can be found at https:www.uu.nl/en/special-collections/the-treasury/private-collections/geylcollection.
3. Pieter Geyl, *De Groot-Nederlandsche gedachte. Historische en politieke beschouwingen* (Harlem, H.D. Tjeenk Willink & Zoon, 1925; 1930); *Geschiedenis van de Nederlandse Stam* (Amsterdam, Wereldbibliotheek 1948–1959; 1961); L Wils, 'De zogenaamde Grootnederlandse geschiedschrijving', in *Vlaanderen, België, Groot-Nederland. Mythe en geschiedenis. Historische opstellen, gebundeld en aangeboden aan de schrijver bij het bereiken van zijn emeritaat als hoogleraar aan de K.U. Leuven* (Davidsfonds, Leuven, 1994), 384–428.
4. See Jo Tollebeek, 'Begreep Geyl de Vlamingen?', in *Jaarboek van de Maatschappij der Nederlandse Letterkunde 2009–10* (Leiden, 2011), 67–80, https:www.dbnl.org/tekst/_jaa004201001_01/_jaa004201001_01_0005.php.
5. See Geyl, *The Revolt of the Netherlands, 1555–1609* (Barnes & Noble, New York, 1966).
6. See Geyl, 'Toynbee the Prophet', *Journal of the History of Ideas*, 16/2 (1955): 260–74.
7. William Bark, review, *History and Theory*, 4/1 (1964): 107–23, here 111.
8. See Geyl, *Use and Abuse of History* (Yale University Press, New Haven, CT, 1955), 3.

PIETER GEYL
USE AND ABUSE OF HISTORY

In what follows I write not as a philosopher but as a historian. If I venture to deal with some general aspects of history, I shall not feel compelled to analyse all my assumptions. No doubt a fundamental view of life in its relation to eternity directs my thinking, but I shall allow it to be deduced or guessed at from my treatment of the subject. As a matter of method I shall be practical and concrete, as befits my calling. I shall argue from my own experience and look at the problems as they have presented themselves to me in the course of a lengthening life spent, if I may say so, not merely in studying the past but in watching the world around me and occasionally, in a modest way, trying to take part in its struggles.

This does not mean that I am setting out to present a chapter of autobiography. I shall try to integrate my personal observations and pragmatic solutions with the general trends of historical thinking and practice.

[…]

History tries to fulfil certain of our permanent and profound needs as civilised and social beings. From the very beginning, as soon as groups of human beings freed themselves from the shackles of primitivity or began to dispute – however partially and tentatively – the despotism of custom, they took to noting down striking events and the names of leading members. These earliest monuments of history served more purposes than one. They were intended to glorify kings or priests or warriors and by their glory to shed lustre on the dynasty, the church or the state. But at the same time the bare facts which they helped to fix constituted a knowledge useful for the stability of society and its institutions.

There has been this antinomy from the beginning of history: change, movement were the indispensable conditions for its birth, yet one of the main purposes to which it was immediately put was the prevention of change and movement. Substitute 'regulation' for 'prevention' and you have the purpose of what was to develop eventually into a wealth of literature. In early times the epic, tempestuously bursting the bounds of reality, even of probability, is nevertheless a kind of history, and the one in which feelings of loyalty or communal pride take the lead. The chronicle is the form in which the idea of the usefulness of factual notation predominates. Both appeal to feelings, which they at the same time rouse to consciousness, not only of veneration or of awe but of disinterested delight in the spectacle of things past, a feeling of wonder, an aesthetic feeling.

There is another craving which the human mind since early times has attempted to satisfy by turning to history. Events are interpreted, or they are related into a significant whole, so as to throw light on the great mystery of man's fate on earth and the way it is influenced or directed by the divine powers. In both epic and chronicle this element is frequently found, and the holy books of many religions are replete with history. It is not always possible to draw a clear distinction between these various types of writings. The historical books of the Old Testament partake of the epic as well as the chronicle, while at the same time intend to reveal God's disposal of human affairs. But we have a motive here which has been fertile enough to bring forth a whole literature of its own. [...]

What I venture to say is that the discipline of history, the historical spirit, is a force for truth and against myth, and that, besides, insofar as it can make itself felt, it will exercise a restraining influence, an influence making for sanity. History studied in the way I indicated will make us realise that progress has never followed a straight line; that ideals, great motive forces that they are, will in practice always lead to compromise; that there is something to be said for the other side in every dispute. I have said that historism carried to excess, as it has often been and sometimes still is, leads to a boundless relativism and a position according to which patience, tolerance and acceptance are the only virtues. I hate every interpretation of history by which the moral issues become obscured and initiative and the personality smothered. But that is not the effect of the historical spirit as I outlined it. *Understanding* does not necessarily mean *forgiving*; the attention to the particular and the individual in spite of the idea, the Zeitgeist or the system leads to the very opposite of a flat picture of masses driven. Allied to it is the capacity for making distinctions. Nothing is further removed from my mind than the consideration of patience, tolerance and acceptance as the only virtues, but fortunately it is not only in them that a bar to passionate rejection or headlong enthusiasm can be found. Who will deny that the world stands in need of such a bar? The capacity for making distinctions will provide one.

In the little speech I made to my students in October 1945, I also said (immediately following the passage quoted above):

Our feeling of national solidarity and patriotism does not need the stimulus of hatred. Hatred of another nation is not a historical attitude of mind. Hatred of oppression and cruelty, yes; hatred of crime and deception. But the historian who uses reason and criticism will be able to make the necessary distinction, and the rejection of an entire nation, and of that nation's civilization, which has in so many ways intertwined itself with European civilization, cannot stand the test of true historical judgment.

A state of mind, then. But this is not, of course, all that history has to offer. Men can still be seen turning to it for the other purposes

I have mentioned. To almost everyone of them something will respond within the mind or heart of almost everyone of us. Along some of these ways, it is true, the questioner of the riddle of the past will be led more readily to myth than to history. At any rate we are still sensitive to the symbolism of historical parallels; the large view justifying the ways of God to men still exercises a fascination; the spectacle of the past can still charm our aesthetic sense; but we also find in it lessons for the practice of today, or it can be idealised in order to put the present to shame; precedents have not lost their force, and antiquity still seems venerable, so that a demonstration of it gives a feeling of security.

But if I ask myself which are the purposes that I and I suppose most modern scholars will place first when put on our mettle to justify our calling and our work, there present themselves in answer, first, the enrichment of civilization by the reanimation of old modes of existence and thought, of which I spoke in my first and especially in my second chapter; second, the cultivation of the historical attitude of mind, of which I have just spoken; third, the elucidation of the present and its problems by showing them in perspective; and about this last point I have something more to say.

In fact, the point is closely allied to the two others, at times almost indistinguishable from them. The present is not elucidated merely by connecting it with trends in the immediately preceding period, from which it may be seen to issue. The whole of history will help us understand the world we live in. A mind that has established contact with forms of life remote and unfamiliar, that has come to know great events and personalities of some particular period, pondering motives and evidence, watching the ever surprising shapes in which greatness and character appear, or studying the curious changes of social habits and the impact of economic factors – such a mind is likely to see more deeply into contemporary phenomena and movements, be it of culture or of politics. This is what Burckhardt meant when he said that history will make us wise; for although Bacon had said the same thing three centuries before, the great Swiss historian gave to the word a somewhat different conno-tation by adding, 'Wise for always; not clever for another time.'[1] He meant, of course, that history is not to be searched for practical lessons, the applicability of which will always be doubtful in view of the inexhaustible novelty of circumstances and combination of causes, but just this, that the mind will acquire a sensitiveness, an imaginative range.

Yet undoubtedly the history of the recent past of one's own coun-try or the group of countries belonging to the same sphere of civi-lization and power politics offers, for the purpose of understanding the present, a special and irreplaceable interest. There is here by universal consent[2] an immediate and practical use of history for anyone trying to find his way through the politics of his own or of a foreign country, or, of course, through international politics. The same might certainly be said of virtually every field of cultural or social or economic activity, but let me here limit the discussion to political history.

Politics do not start from today. They are rooted in the past. History plays its part in them, as it did in the world of the seven-teenth century. Contending views of great political issues of a cen-tury and longer ago are still live issues. But also the governments, the parties, the churches, even when not a word about history is spoken, consciously or unconsciously move along tracks or find bounds set to their action which are a legacy of the past.

Better consciously than unconsciously, and that is as much as to say: better to know something about history. You may think I am merely stating a truism. Do not secretaries of state and foreign secretaries thumb the volumes of war documents published by various governments? Do they not read the biographies or mem-oirs of their predecessors? Will not an ambassador sent out to a country begin by reading up that country's history?

Not that a course of reading before departure to the foreign cap-ital would be the ideal way to fit oneself for an ambassadorial post. We historians cannot give to anyone the knowledge required in capsules nicely dosed, effect guaranteed. The case of the literature about Napoleon is a propos. Always it is in the conflict of opinions, it is by comparing different views, by seeing the various aspects revolve as different minds reflect them, that history can be made to yield some of her more precious secrets. I may seem dangerously near the conclusion that only trained historians are fit to rule the world. In all sincerity that is not what I mean, although I can't deny that I have sometimes wished that, for instance, American statesmen, who now exercise so direct and profound an influence on the destinies of the world, knew more about the history of, for instance, Europe. They might not, in that case, talk so lightly about European federation. But then, many European statesmen talk lightly on that subject. Indeed, I could wish that they, too, knew their history better, or that they were gifted with a little more historical imagination.

In March 1953, I delivered a speech at Utrecht on the 317th anniversary of our university. In that speech I proclaimed my doubts about the wisdom, or even practicability, of the European federation scheme (in reality Little-European, for can one speak of Europe when England is not included?). I am relieved by what has happened since: the disappearance of the EDC from the scene of practical politics, the emergence of a combination in which England is to take her part and rash supranational experiments are eliminated. But in 1953 I soon met with the reproach that I had anticipated, namely that I was using history to advocate immobility and condemn Europe to an indefinite continuance of her plight. You see here the old conflict raising its head, the reformers denouncing history as the patron of 'no-change'. As it happened, I had replied to the charge beforehand in that very speech:

By no means. I too want to go in the direction of greater European unity. What I reject are schemes taking no account of the reality. Man is both free and in bonds. Free, for he must always move on; old forms are all the time decaying; man must, and he can, use his will and choose. In bonds, for he cannot use his will indiscriminately, nor choose according to the dictates of his constructive cunning or his fancy. We are incessantly freeing ourselves from our past, but at the same time it maintains a sway over us. It is not wise policy to ignore that sway, nor should the taking it into account be denounced as a sign of rigid conservatism.[3]

It is perhaps wrong of me to broach, towards the end of a disquisition on general aspects of history, a concrete example which requires more space than I have left to do justice to its complexity. I have stated my view about that problem categorically here, and indeed I hold it strongly. But the only point I am entitled to make when writing of use and abuse of history is that the problem shows the relevance for the present of a discussion of the past. It may be I was wrong on this question, although I think I was right. But by stating my view I took part in the discussion, the argument from which the future will emerge – the free, untrammelled argument which is what distinguishes Western civilization from that of the totalitarian states; one might almost say, which *is* Western civilisation.

And I think I may add that not I personally but all professional historians do possess a kind of familiarity with the past which should not be unheard in that great argument. We do not claim to have Clio's only authentic message, but we know that we devote ourselves to the deciphering of it with a single-minded devotion. Enthusiasm and abstract thinking, too, are stating their case, supported, most likely, by mythical readings of the past. Even if we wanted to, we could not suppress those voices or prevent others from listening to them; we shall ourselves at times find in them delight and inspiration. Meanwhile, events will proceed on their mysterious course as they have always done, and to the shaping of it how much the past contributes, and how much the urge that is in man's creative powers, we can only guess. But shall historians therefore keep silent? No, we must fulfil our function, which is, to

the best of our ability, to show up the myths and tell the world all
we can find about past reality – in short to promote legitimate use
and to check the abuse of history.

1. Jacob Burckhardt (1818–97); professor at the University of Basel 1858–93.
    The dictum quoted occurs in *Weltgeschichtliche Betrachtungen* (Leipzig, 1985,
    published posthumously).
2. If Huizinga denied this (*Verzamelde werken,* 7, 163), it was, I think, the reaction
    to the vogue of histories and collections of documents and memoirs relating
    to the First World War of a mind of exceptionally broad culture and little
    inclination towards politics. Now that I mention him only to indicate dissent,
    I feel I must add how enlightening as well as delightful I have always found
    his book *The Discipline of History: De wetenschap der geschiedenis* (1937), now in
    Verzamelde werken, vol 7.
3. Also reprinted in Pieter Geyl, *Historicus in de tijd* (1954).

J H HEXTER:
'HE ALSO SERVES WHO ONLY SITS AND THINKS'[1]

INTRODUCTION BY DAVID MARTIN JONES

J H Hexter (1910–96) was one of the most original and iconoclastic intellectual historians of the twentieth century. He taught at Washington University, St Louis, before becoming Charles Stille Professor of History at Yale in 1963. On retiring, in 1978, he returned to Washington as the founding director of the Centre for the History of Freedom, which was devoted to the study of the history of liberty. In a perceptive obituary, Donald R Kelley wrote: 'Jack Hexter was a great scholar, talented writer and polemicist, devoted baseball fan, and authentic American humorist, who made wit and facetiousness part of his historiographical tool-kit.'[2]

In *Reappraisals in History* (1961) and *The History Primer* (1971) Hexter questioned the endeavour to apply abstract scientific laws to a historical mode of inquiry. Mining documentary sources to find evidence to support speculative grand theories he considered a particularly egregious enterprise. He termed the practice 'lumping'. 'Lumpers' selectively choose evidence to fit predetermined historical patterns.

By contrast, 'splitters', like Hexter himself, emphasise contingency and complexity. Using everyday experiences instead of historicist theories like Marxism better captured the thoughts and actions of historical figures. Applying 'common language, common sense and credibility' to historical studies more effectively advanced historical knowledge and understanding. Hexter's historical method followed three basic rules: 'do not go off half cocked; get the story straight; keep prejudices about present-day issues out.'[3] He further insisted that words be carefully weighed, since the historical craft requires a distinct rhetorical voice. He particularly emphasised respect for the documents of the past and the contemporaries who composed them, and he strove to implement them often at personal cost. He held firm the primacy of political, constitutional and intellectual history; and he considered the evolution of liberty the central theme of the modern history of the West.

Hexter's admirers thought his particular strength was in writing *about* history rather than the writing *of* history, but as Gertrude Himmelfarb noted, these exercises are 'opposite sides of the same coin'.[4] Indeed, his methodological principles informed his pathfinding studies of sixteenth- and seventeenth-century thought and political languages.[5]

Several generations of graduate students learned what the historian's craft involved from 'The Historian and his Day' (1954), an essay that first appeared in *Encounter* after the *American Historical Review* rejected it. Hexter applied common sense and common experience to the question of whether the writing of history inevitably reflected present-mindedness or whether it could and should aspire to an ideal of past-mindedness. Must a historian always rewrite history in the context of his own day?

Hexter, with characteristic ingenuity, transcended the debate by offering an account of how one professional historian – himself – spent his day. From this quotidian perspective, Hexter showed that the historian spends more of his time engaging with the past than he does with the present.

This has important implications for applying history. The historian's time is necessarily oriented to the past. Far from anachronistically imposing the present on the past, he is more likely to do the reverse. Indeed, as Hexter himself argued, 'the unique vision of the historian's time is that he knows something of the results of the acts he deals with.'[6] Consequently, instead of the passions, prejudices and prepossessions of the present dominating the historian's view of the past, '*it is the other way about.*'[7] The passions, the events and the crises of early modern Europe might thus inform a historical perspective upon the present state of European disunion.

While men ordinarily try to connect the present with a future that is to be, the historian connects his present with a future that has already been. Each man in his own time tries to discover the motives and the causes of the actions of those people he has to deal with; and the historian does this with varying degrees of success. But unlike Everyman, the historian knows something of the results of the acts of those he deals with in the unique dimension of the historian's time. The historian rarely has no notion of the outcome of the events he is studying. He will know what happens after.

History, then, is a becoming, understood not only in terms of what came before but also of what comes after. Some significant and neglected conclusions emerge from this short excursus into the historian's day. Rewriting history reflects the lapsed time between the event written about and the present. It also reflects the rate of increase of actual data on the subject written about. We seek new sources and re-examine old ones to discover in them connections and relations that our predecessors may have missed. History also needs rewriting as knowledge about the human condition, its ways and waywardness, increases.

Nevertheless, Hexter warns, there has been a worrying tendency to exaggerate the speed with which knowledge increases. Many master ideas about historical development over the last 50 years exhibit an urge towards 'secular salvation in a shaky world' rather than a precise estimate of the cognitive value of the ideas in question, which often seek conformity with the latest intellectual fashion.[8] It is all too easy to mistake for progress a process that only involves skipping from recent to current errors – the end of history thesis and its troubled legacy springs to mind.

Cardiff, January 2022

1. J H Hexter, 'Factors in Modern History', in *Reappraisals in History* (Longmans, London, 1961) 44.
2. Donald R Kelley, 'J. H. Hexter 1910–96', *Journal of the History of Ideas* 58/2 (1997), 349–50.
3. J H Hexter, 'The Historian and his Day', in *Reappraisals in History*, 8.
4. Gertrude Himmelfarb, 'J. H. Hexter (1910–1996)', in *Proceedings of the American Philosophical Society* 143/2 (1999).
5. See interalia J H Hexter, *The Visions of Politics on the Eve of the Reformation: More Machiavelli and Seyssel* (Basic Books, New York, 1973) and Hexter, *More's Utopia the Biography of an Idea* (Princeton University Press, Princeton, NJ, 1952).
6. Hexter, 'The Historian', 11.
7. Italics in the original. Hexter, 'The Historian', 9.
8. Hexter, 'The Historian', 12.

J H HEXTER
THE HISTORIAN AND HIS DAY

For a good while now a fairly strenuous contest has been in progress between two opposed schools of historical thought. Accepting a classification proposed by one of the keenest though most courteous of the riders in the lists, the division lies roughly between the 'present-minded' and the 'history-minded' historians. In the course of time many historians have joined one side or the other in the controversy with the natural consequence that there has been some sense and a good deal of nonsense talked on both sides. In general, for some subtle psychological reason that I am unable to fathom, the kind of scholar who, distrustful of 'ideas' and 'theories', believes that history is all 'facts' has tended to take the side of the 'history-minded' historians. For more obvious reasons the chronic 'do-gooder', who believes that knowledge justifies itself only by a capacity to solve current problems, lines up with the 'present-minded' position.

[…]

Obviously it is not fair to judge either the history-minded or the present-minded historians by the vagaries of their respective lunatic fringes. Casting off the eccentric on both sides, there remains a real and serious divergence of opinion, as yet apparently irreconcilable, maintained on both sides by scholars whose achievements entitle their views to respectful consideration. The divergence is connected at least ostensibly with a fundamental difference in general outlook between the two parties to the argument. In a sense the present-minded are realists in the field of history, the history-minded are idealists.

[…]

The harsh fact of life is that, willy-nilly, the present-day historian lives not in the past but in the present, and this harsh fact cannot be altered by any pious resolve to be history-minded.

What we say about any historical epoch in some way reflects our experience and that experience was accumulated not in the fifteenth, in the sixteenth, or in any other century than the twentieth. When we look back on the past, we do so from the present. We are present-minded just as all earlier historians were present-minded in their day because for better or worse we happen to live in our own day. Indeed the very horrid examples cited by the proponents of history-mindedness afford irrefutable evidence that the best of former historians were in their day present-minded, and we can hardly hope to be different. So the best thing for us to do is to recognise that every generation reinterprets the past in terms of the exigencies of its own day. We can then cast aside our futile history-minded yearnings and qualms and deal with the past in terms of our day, only mildly regretting that, like all the words of man, our own words will be writ on water. By this intellectual stratagem the present-minded turn – or seek to turn – the flank of the history-minded.

We must admit, I believe, that some points in the argument of the present-minded are true beyond dispute. It is certainly true, for example, that all that we think is related to our experience somehow, and that all our experience is of our own day. But though this be true, it is also trivial. It is a plea in avoidance dressed up as an argument. Granting that we can have no experience beyond what we have acquired in the course of our own lives, the question is, does anything in that experience enable us to understand the past in its own terms rather than in terms of the prepossessions of our own day? Banal statements about the origin of our ideas in our own experience do not answer this question; they merely beg it.

In the second place, I think we must admit that in some respects all historians are present-minded, even the most determined proponents of history-mindedness. All historians are indeed engaged in rewriting past history in the light of at least one aspect of present experience, that aspect which has to do with the increments to our positive knowledge that are the fruit of scientific investigation.

[…]

It seems to me that the proponents of history-mindedness must, and in most cases probably do, concede the validity of this kind of present-mindedness in the writing of history; and if this is all that present-mindedness means, then every historian worth his salt is present-minded. No sane contemporary scientist in his investigations of the physical world would disregard nineteenth-century advances in field theory, and no sane historian in his work would rule out of consideration insights achieved in the past century concerning the connection of class conflict with historical occurrences. But this is only to say that all men who are professionally committed to the quest of that elusive entity – the Truth – use all the tracking devices available to them at the time, and in the nature of things cannot use any device before it exists. And of course the adequacy of the historical search at any time is in some degree limited by the adequacy of the tracking devices. In this, too, the historian's situation is no different from that of the scientist. Adequate investigation of optical isomers in organic chemistry, for example, had to wait on the development of the techniques of spectroscopy. If this is what present-mindedness means, then present-mindedness is not just the condition of historical knowledge. For *all* knowledge at any time is obviously limited by the limits of the means of gaining knowledge at that time; and historians are simply in the same boat as all others whose business it is to know.

Now I do not believe that the proponents of present-mindedness mean anything as bland and innocuous as this. On the contrary I am fairly sure they mean that the historian's boat is different from, and a great deal more leaky than, let us say, the physicist's or the geologist's boat. What then is supposed to be the *specific* trouble with the historian's boat? The trouble, as the present-minded see it, can be described fairly simply. The present-minded contend that in writing history no historian can free himself of his total experience and that that experience is inextricably involved not only in the limits of knowledge but also in the passions, prejudices, assumptions and prepossessions, in the events, crises and tensions of his own day. Therefore those passions, prejudices, assumptions, prepossessions, events, crises and tensions of the historian's own day inevitably permeate what he writes about the past. This is the crucial allegation of the present-minded, and if it is wholly correct, the issue must be settled in their favour and the history-minded pack up their apodictic and categorical-imperative baggage and depart in silence. Frequently discussions of this crucial issue have got bogged down because the history-minded keep trying to prove that the historian can counteract the influence of his own day, while the present-minded keep saying that this is utterly impossible. And of course on this question the latter are quite right. A historian has no day but his own, so what is he going to counteract it with? He is in the situation of Archimedes, who could find no fulcrum for the lever with which to move the earth. Clearly if the historian is to be history-minded rather than present-minded he must find the means of being so in his own day, not outside it. And thus at last we come up against the crucial question – what *is* the historian's own day?

As soon as we put the question this way we realise that there is no ideal Historian's Day; there are many days, all different, and each with a particular historian attached to it. Now since in actuality there is no such thing as The Historian's Day, no one can be qualified to say what it actually consists of.

[...]

I must insist emphatically that the history I write is, as the present-minded say, intimately connected with my own day and inextricably linked with my own experience; but I must insist with even stronger emphasis that my day is not someone else's day, or the ideal Day of Contemporary Man; it is just the way I happen to dispose of twenty four hours.

[…]

Now it may seem immodest or perhaps simply fantastic to take days spent as are mine – days so little attuned to the great harmonies, discords and issues of the present – and hold them up for contemplation. Yet I will dare to suggest that in this historian's own humdrum days there is one peculiarity that merits thought. The peculiarity lies in the curious relation that days so squandered seem to establish between the present and a rather remote sector of the past.

[…]

So for a small part of my day I live under a comfortable rule of bland intellectual irresponsibility vis-à-vis the Great Issues of the Contemporary World, a rule that permits me to go off half-cocked with only slight and occasional compunction. But during most of my day – that portion of it that I spend in dealing with the Great and Not-So-Great Issues of the World between 1450 and 1650 – I live under an altogether different rule. The commandments of that rule are:

1. Do not go off half cocked.
2. Get the story straight.
3. Keep prejudices about present-day issues out of this area.

[…]

The reviewing host seems largely to have lined up with the history-minded. This seems to be a consequence of their training. Whatever the theoretical biases of their individual members, the better departments of graduate study in history do not encourage those undergoing their novitiate to resolve research problems by reference to current ideological conflicts. Consequently most of us have been conditioned to feel that it is not quite proper to characterise

John Pym as a liberal, or Thomas More as a socialist, or Niccolò Macchiavelli as a proto-Fascist, and we tend to regard this sort of characterisation as at best a risky pedagogic device. Not only the characterisation but the thought process that leads to it lie under a psychological ban; and thus to the external sanction of the review columns is added the internal sanction of the still small voice that keeps saying, 'We really shouldn't do it that way.'[1]

The austere rule we live under as historians has some curious consequences. In my case one of the consequences is that my knowledge of the period around the sixteenth century in Europe is of a rather different order than my knowledge about current happenings. Those preponderant segments of my own day spent in the discussion, investigation and contemplation of that remote era may not be profitably spent but at least they are spent in an orderly, systematic, purposeful way. The contrast can be pointed up by a few details. I have never read the Social Security Act, but I have read the Elizabethan Poor Law in all its successive versions and moreover I have made some study of its application. I have never read the work of a single existentialist but I have read Calvin's *Institutes of the Christian Religion* from cover to cover. I know practically nothing for sure about the relation of the institutions of higher education in America to the social structure, but I know a fair bit about the relation between the two in France, England and the Netherlands in the fifteenth and sixteenth centuries. I have never studied the economic reports to the president that would enable me to appraise the state of the American nation in 1950, but I have studied closely Hales's *Discourse of the Commonwealth of England* and derived from it some reasonable coherent notions about the condition of England around 1550. Now the consequence of all this is inevitable. Instead of the passions, prejudices, assumptions and prepossessions, the events, crises and tensions of the present dominating my view of the past, *it is the other way about.* The passions, prejudices, assumptions and prepossessions, the events, crises and tensions of early modern Europe to a very considerable extent lend precision to my rather haphazard notions about the present. I make sense of present-day welfare state policy by thinking of it in connection with the 'commonwealth' policies of Elizabeth. I do the like with respect to the contemporary struggle for power and conflict of ideologies by throwing on them such light as I find in the Catholic–Calvinist struggle of the sixteenth century.

[…]

For our purposes the crucial fact about the ordinary time of all men, even of historians in their personal as against their professional capacity, is that in no man's time is he *really* sure what is going to happen next. This is true, obviously, not only of men of the present time but also of all men of all past times. Of course there are large routine areas of existence in which we can make pretty good guesses; and if this were not so, life would be unbearable. Thus, my guess, five evenings a week in term time, that I will be getting up the following morning to teach classes at my place of employment provides me with a useful operating rule; yet it has been wrong occasionally, and will be wrong again. With respect to many matters more important, all is uncertain. Will there be war or peace next year? Will my children turn out well or ill? Will I be alive or dead thirty years hence? three years hence? tomorrow?

[…]

Somewhat inaccurately we might say that while man's time ordinarily is oriented to the future, the historian's time is oriented to the past. It might be better to say that while men are ordinarily trying to connect the present with a future that is to be, the historian connects his present with a future that has already been.

The professional historian does not have a monopoly of his peculiar time, or rather, as Carl Becker once put it, every man is on occasion his own historian. But the historian alone lives systematically in the historian's own time. And from what we have been saying it is clear that this time has a unique dimension. Each man in his own time tries to discover the motives and the causes of the actions of those people he has to deal with; and the historian does the like with varying degrees of success. But, as other men do not and cannot, the historian knows something of the results of the acts of those he deals with: this is the unique dimension of the historian's time. If, in saying that the historian cannot escape his own time, the present-minded meant this peculiarly historical time – which they do not – they would be on solid ground. For the circumstances are rare indeed in which the historian has no notion whatever of the outcome of the events with which he is dealing. The very fact that he is a historian and that he has interested himself in a particular set of events fairly assures that at the outset he will have some knowledge of what happened afterward.

This knowledge makes it impossible for the historian to do merely what the history-minded say he should do – consider the past in its own terms, and envisage events as the men who lived through them did. Surely he should try to do that; just as certainly he must do more than that simply because he knows about those events what none of the men contemporary with them knew; he knows what their consequences were. [...] The historian who resolutely refused to use the insight that his own peculiar time gave him would not be superior to his fellows; he would be merely foolish, betraying a singular failure to grasp what history is. For history is a becoming, an ongoing, and it is to be understood not only in terms of what comes before but also of what comes after.

[...]

The history of the Treaty of Versailles of 1919 may indeed need to be written over a number of times in the next few generations as its consequences more completely unfold. But this is not true of the Treaty of Madrid of 1527. Its consequences for better or worse pretty well finished their unfolding a good while back. The need for rewriting history is also a function of the increase in actual data on the thing to be written about. Obviously any general estimate of the rate of increase of such data would be meaningless. History also must be rewritten as the relevant and usable knowledge about man, about his ways and his waywardness, increases. Here again there has been a tendency to exaggerate the speed with which that knowledge is increasing. The hosannahs that have greeted many 'master ideas' about man during the past fifty years seem more often than not to be a reflection of an urge towards secular salvation in a shaky world rather than a precise estimate of the cognitive value of the ideas in question. Frequently such 'master ideas' have turned out to be plain old notions in new fancy dress, or simply wrong. Perhaps the imperative, felt by the present-minded, to rewrite history every generation is less the fruit of a real necessity than of their own attempts to write it always in conformity with the latest intellectual mode. A little less haste might mean a little more speed. For the person engaged in the operation it is all too easy to mistake for progress a process that only involves skipping from recent to current errors.

If, instead of asking how often history *must* or ought to be rewritten, we ask how often it *will* be rewritten, the answer is that it will be rewritten, as it always has been, from day to day. This is so because the rewriting of history is inescapably what each working historian in fact does in his own day. That is precisely how he puts in his time. We seek new data. We re-examine old data to discover in them relations and connections that our honored predecessors may have missed. Onto these data we seek to bring to bear whatever may seem enlightening and relevant out of our own day. And what may be relevant is as wide as the full range of our own daily experience, intellectual, aesthetic, political, social, personal. Some current event may, of course, afford a historian an understanding of what men meant five hundred years ago when they said that a prince must rule through *amour et cremeur*, love and fear. But then so might his perusal of a socio-psychological investigation into the ambivalence of authority in Papua. So might his reading of Shakespeare's *Richard II.* And so might his relations with his own children.

For each historian brings to the rewriting of history the full range of the remembered experience of his own days, that unique array that he alone possesses and is. For some historians that sector of their experience which impinges on the Great Crises of the Contemporary World sets up the vibrations that attune them to the part of the past that is the object of their professional attention. Some of us, however, vibrate less readily to those crises. We feel our way towards the goals of our historic quest by lines of experience having precious little to do with the Great Crises of the Contemporary World. He would be bold indeed who would insist that all historians should follow one and the same line of experience in their quest, or who would venture to say what this single line is that all should follow. He would not only be bold; he would almost certainly be wrong. History does not thrive in measure, as the experience of each historian differs from that of his fellows. It is indeed the wide and varied range of experience covered by all the days of all historians that makes the rewriting of history – not in each generation but for each historian – at once necessary and inevitable.

---

1.   I do not for a moment intend to suggest that current dilemmas have not suggested *problems* for historical investigation. It is obvious that such dilemmas are among the numerous and entirely legitimate points of origin of historical study. The actual issue, however, has nothing to do with the point of origin of historical studies, but with the mode of treatment of historical problems.

ERNEST MAY:
THE CRITIQUE OF HISTORICAL MALPRACTICE

INTRODUCTION BY PHILIP ZELIKOW

For a half-century, from 1959 until his death in 2009, Ernest May was in the front rank of historians studying the interactions of the United States with the world. He left an enormous and fascinatingly readable body of work, of which the following passage is just one short excerpt.

Lean and crew-cut, often solitary and bookish, May grew up in Texas and had earned a PhD in history at the relatively new university, UCLA, when he was only 22. He served as a Navy officer, serving with the fleet on a ship ferrying soldiers and supplies into Korea during that war. Gifted with languages, he was comfortable researching sources in Spanish, French and German.

The Navy decided that this young officer might be better employed as a historian working for the Joint Chiefs of Staff and transferred him back to Washington. The experience there was formative. Among other things – such as a lifelong bemusement with the fatuousness of some leading lights in American government – May left the Pentagon with a continuing, probing wariness about the inner world of civil–military relations, along with lasting friendships among the remarkable group of historians then involved in the renowned official histories of the Second World War and other projects.

Coming out of the Navy in 1954, May had career options in the Foreign Service or in academia. He had offers from both Princeton and Harvard. His first book, an international history of America's entry into the First World War which built on his doctoral thesis, was already well advanced. May chose academia and Harvard, and he taught there for the rest of his life.

May was often called a 'diplomatic' historian, but in his case the adjective can mislead. May's methods were usually grounded in a broad analysis of prevailing culture, social trends, public or press opinion, the character of institutions, economic interests, and the precarious balance of politicised factions.

May's deepest interests were to understand the formation of personal and popular beliefs. In April 1995, I attended a memorable Harvard forum discussing former Secretary of Defense Robert McNamara's just-published memoir about the Vietnam War. McNamara watched as May went to the lectern. May commented with his usual courtesy about the value of the book. He then said:

His [McNamara's] reconstruction of what happened in the 60s is, I think, quite clinical and rational. And he looks back and explains the mistakes that were made in judgment and policy. I don't think that the book succeeds in recreating the frame of mind in which those decisions were made.

You take the episode that he was describing here [about Laos in 1961], which is described in some detail in the book: the transition from the Eisenhower to the Kennedy administrations. Here are the best and the brightest, not only of the Kennedy administration but of the Eisenhower administration. And they sit there and they believe, they say to each other and they believe, that the fate at least of Southeast Asia, and perhaps of the civilised world, hinges on what happens in *Laos* – a landlocked country of three million, in hamlets populated by people devoted primarily to singing songs, making love and raising opium.

And there's a *theology* around this, a set of beliefs which are not recaptured in the book. And it's a little bit like – if you'll forgive my saying so – it's a little bit like a Crusader's memoir written by someone who can't remember *why* he particularly *cared* about the fate of Jerusalem.

May's methods were sometimes those of the microhistorian, an approach which the discipline of history usually associates with social or cultural history, and which can overlap with anthropology. But May applied those tools to the reconstruction of pivotal political episodes. And by the mid 1960s, during his first decade at Harvard, May had formulated the main trajectories of scholarship that he would pursue during his next 40 years.

First, May contended that good historical scholarship tended to belie 'realist' and 'neo-realist' theories, either as generalisations about how and why governments actually behave as they do, or as prescriptions for how policy-makers realistically could or should behave in practice.

Second, May never abandoned his emphasis on using international methods to reconstruct international stories. To May, this cross-national empathy was a cardinal principle of professional practice for would-be policy-makers.

Third, May was devoted to raising consciousness about how policy beliefs – about reality, about values, or about prospective actions – form and turn into axioms. The opportunity to help students improve the quality of their thought was one of the pulls that drew May to splitting his teaching with the Harvard Kennedy School, working with friends there like Richard Neustadt and Graham Allison.

In the formation of axioms, the pernicious role of historical analogies loomed front and centre. Historical reasoning is the most common form of reasoning in public affairs. The following excerpt, written as May approached the midpoint of his long scholarly career, is from a book about the over-reliance on historical reasoning. It was a 1973 book on supposed 'lessons' of the past, on 'the use and misuse of history in American foreign policy'. It was a book spurred by the Vietnam War, but one that spends little time discussing that conflict. Instead, in the chapters that preceded this excerpt, May explained that:

- Planning the postwar future during the Second World War, American leaders 'were captives of an unanalyzed faith that the future would be like the recent past. They visualized World War II as parallel to World War I' and prepared for the last peace.
- Confronting their problems as the Second World War ended, American leaders were conditioned by their searing experience with Hitler to assess the 'totalitarian' Soviet Union through the lens of the challenge they had faced against the 'totalitarian' Axis powers.
- Startled by the North Korean invasion of South Korea in June 1950, American leaders threw aside their recent careful calculations of national interest and immediately fell back upon axioms about how the free world should have resisted Hitler's aggressions.

May does not necessarily condemn these choices. He does argue that the historical thinking enveloped the choices and distracted from sharper analysis of the real cases at hand.

Since such historical reasoning is bound to happen, May stresses in this excerpt that it might as well be more thoughtful and better informed. Good historians and deeper historical knowledge were, May explains, a kind of vaccination or antibiotic that leaders could inject into their deliberations, building resistance against dangerously infectious analogies and axiomatic beliefs.

Charlottesville, VA, April 2022

ERNEST MAY
TASKS FOR HISTORIANS

People in government who see value in more critical and systematic reasoning from past experience will need help from men and women who have studied history and given some thought to how work by professional historians can best be exploited.

In episodes recounted earlier in this book, an official or staff aide might have significantly influenced policy by eliciting from historians information about or interpretations of the past other than those in currency. An analysis of the economic history of the interwar years could have pointed out to the negotiators at Bretton Woods unique features of the period after World War I not likely to be reproduced after World War II. Some data about the 1920s could have made clear to the framers of the Acheson–Lilienthal and Baruch plans a dozen factors distinguishing Anglo–American–Japanese negotiations over naval limitations from American–Soviet negotiations over international control of nuclear weapons. Truman and his advisers in 1950 could have been cautioned of the many respects in which the North Korean invasion of South Korea differed from the Italian attack on Ethiopia or the Nazi conquest of Austria and Czechoslovakia. With assistance from scholars steeped in the sources, George Ball could have added counts in which Vietnam in the 1960s was unlike Korea in 1950 and perhaps made his memorandum more persuasive. By calling on historians to analyse the uproar over 'loss of China', Kennedy and Johnson could have discovered that many factors in it were unique and not likely to be duplicated.

It is not my contention that historians are specially well qualified as advisers on what to do. Like other humans, some may be and some may not. Arthur Schlesinger Jr appears to have been valued by Kennedy, and on occasion his usefulness was related to his background as a history professor. In 1961, for instance, when Kennedy was considering a settlement in Laos involving a coalition government, he was warned that such a government would be taken over by its communist members. Czechoslovakia stood as the prime example. Schlesinger was able to remind the president that this had not always occurred, France and Italy after World War II offered contrary instances, and Latin America provided others. When records of the Johnson administration come to light, they may show that Eric Goldman provided some special services by virtue of his expertness on American history. Although Henry Kissinger was a political scientist, he had done historical research on both Bismarck and Metternich, and it may be that this knowledge and experience contributed to his effectiveness as Nixon's de facto foreign minister. On the other hand, the example of Walt Rostow suggests that imprudent advisers are as frequently found among historians as among any other group.

In arguing that history ought to be more carefully used in policy-making, I would not even go so far as to claim that it is an arcanum, like economics or science, requiring a priesthood comparable to the Council of Economic Advisers or the President's Science Advisory Council. I do insist, however, that historians, like accountants or statisticians, have special credentials for dealing with particular data and that history is not likely to be better used in government unless those who advise on or make policy discover how better to use historians.

For one thing, historians ought to be asked to supply perspective on events in foreign countries. What they say may, of course, reflect bias. If asked in 1961 to account for the insurgency in Vietnam, a historian partial to Diem would not have told the same tale as one sympathetic to Ho Chi Minh. If honest craftsmen, however, each would have distinguished guesswork from verifiable fact and taken care that his generalizations fitted all the discoverable evidence. Neither could have left out of account either the hypothesis of civil war or the hypothesis of plotting in Hanoi to overthrow an independent government in Saigon. Through hearing or reading accounts by either or both, new members of the Kennedy administration might have been led to view with more skepticism the bureaucracy's description of South Vietnam as a free nation under assault by communists following a long-prepared timetable.

[...]

People in government should also look to historians for some information about past policies of the United States. Those who come into office from law firms, corporations or even universities often have to depend on careerists to explain the setting and context of their new business. Sometimes the careerists are capable of doing so; sometimes not. In State and Defense, where senior officers rotate from job to job every few years, few men have deep knowledge of any particular set of problems. In any case, their concerns tend to be immediate, and their efforts to provide perspective are coloured, wilfully or not, by their convictions about what ought to occur in future.

When Kennedy's appointees moved in, they were not told much about the past of Vietnam itself, but they were given to understand that the Eisenhower administration had made an iron commitment to maintaining a non-communist regime in Saigon. Belief that this was the case probably influenced their judgment. Later, in any event, Secretary McNamara was to cite as an important reason for upholding this commitment, no matter what the price, the alleged fact that ever since 1954 Vietnam had been 'a test case of U.S. capacity to help a nation meet a Communist "war of liberation".'[1] In reality, the Eisenhower administration had probably moved only gradually to such a stance. Its leaders possibly never regarded their obligations to South Vietnam as unlimited. Since little evidence has come to light, even in the *Pentagon Papers*, one cannot be sure. A career official familiar with the record, George Carver of the CIA, was later to urge Johnson, however, to *return* to Eisenhower's policy, and he characterised that policy as limited support for South Vietnam conditioned on Saigon's demonstrating ability to win, primarily with its own resources.[2] Convinced that the American commitment should be clear, the Southeast Asia specialists in the bureaucracy refrained from informing the new men of past ambiguities. It might have been well if some historian had been on hand to ensure that those ambiguities were not forgotten.

[...]

As previous chapters have suggested, the most important function for the historian as historian is analysis of those instances which men in government are most likely to see as parallels, analogies or precedents. Such analysis may not in itself help officials perceive what to do. They might well decide that their general rule was right even if the precise historical example they had in mind was not adequate proof of its validity. At least, however, the challenge to the example would have compelled closer thought about the inherent logic of the rule; and if it ever turned out that the example was the source of the rule rather than a mere illustration, the challenge might prompt fresh thinking.

Conceivably, historians as such might be asked to identify and analyse a range of possible analogies, such as those arrayed in the chapter above on bombing for peace. In preparation for the Paris Peace Conference of 1919, the British government commissioned studies of previous peace conferences. During World War II, had scholars been asked to re-examine Utrecht and Vienna as well as Versailles as possible parallels for the peacemaking to come, they might have worked out the implications of comparing Stalin not with Hitler but with Peter the Great or Alexander I or Lenin. In 1950, a historian certainly could have made the point that the North Korean invasion, if instigated by the Soviet Union, might bear less resemblance to the Japanese conquest of Manchuria or the Italian attack on Ethiopia than to Russian efforts to gain control of Korea prior to 1905.

Historians as such could even be enlisted for forecasting exercises comparable to that in the preceding chapter. By and large, they disclaim special qualifications for foretelling what will happen. It was Hegel who framed the maxim that we learn from history that we do not learn from history; and Santayana, that those who do not know the past are condemned to repeat it. Both were philosophers who had had no practice in reconstructing the uncertain complexities of the past. Impressed, in H A L Fisher's famous phrase, with the role of the contingent and the unforeseen, professional historians tend to argue that, if history teaches anything, it is how uncertain and unpredictable are the consequences of what men do. And this book illustrates how often statesmen misguess because they expect patterns of the past to repeat themselves. Most historians would agree with Arthur Schlesinger Jr that 'Santayana's aphorism must be reversed: too often it is those who *can* remember the past who are condemned to repeat it'.[3] Yet it may be that historians come closer than most scholars to engaging systematically in prophecy. For they predict backward. They construct hypotheses about the forces that produced change or continuity in some past period. In the process, they may develop some skill at least in identifying questions to be asked by those who look ahead. [...]

Perhaps even more important are the potential costs in time. To people high in government, nothing is more valuable. They are deluged by paper. On almost any day, they have to set aside some seemingly urgent matters in order to deal with others still more urgent. While many might accept the abstract argument that they should have fuller and more precise historical information, it does not follow that, in practice, they would judge reading or hearing history the most profitable way to employ a marginal hour.

The problem is all the greater because history is not easily condensed. The historian's generalizations explain evidence, and they are seldom meaningful unless at least some of the evidence is presented along with them. Moreover, most historians by training and perhaps temperament tend to err on the side of giving too much detail and introducing too many qualifications. Expressing doubt that historians could in practice be helpful to him, one State Department officer remarked, 'Historians refuse to generalize… to give up detail and to give up shadings.'[4] If history is to be better used in government, nothing is more important than that professional historians discover means of addressing directly, succinctly and promptly the needs of people who govern.

Having singled out some services that historians might perform, some ways in which they might become better equipped to do so, and some obstacles to their actually being called upon to serve, I obviously ought to conclude with some programmatic recommendations. I shall not do so. The reasonableness of federal support for foreign area studies, freer opening of archives and an increase in historical studies permitted or sponsored by the government seems to me self-evident. On the other hand, I have too much the perspective of a scholar and the academy to perceive more than superficially the problems visible to budget-framers, Congressmen, bureaucrats and preoccupied men and women high up in the executive branch.

Earlier chapters attempted to establish the point that history is important to people in government. Men and women making decisions under conditions of high uncertainty necessarily envision the future partly in terms of what they believe to have happened in the past. Their understanding of the present is shaped by what they think to have gone before. Often, their knowledge of what in fact occurred earlier is shallow or faulty, and deficiencies in information breed greater deficiencies in reasoning. Having learned not to trust inexpert guesswork where numbers, economic models, or scientific formulas are concerned, perhaps they will see that they also need clearer understanding of the history that so often imprisons them.

1. *The Pentagon Papers: The Defense Department History of United States Decisionmaking on Vietnam*, 4 vols (Senator Gravel edn; Beacon Press, Boston, 1971), iii, 500.
2. *The Pentagon Papers*, iv, 89–90.
3. Arthur M. Schlesinger Jr, *The Bitter Heritage: Vietnam and American Democracy* (Houghton Mifflin, Boston, 1966), 91.
4. Berkman interview.

MICHAEL HOWARD:
NOT PROMISING LESSONS

INTRODUCTION BY LAWRENCE FREEDMAN

These two pieces topped and tailed Sir Michael Howard's period as the Regius Professor of Modern History at Oxford University. In the first, his inaugural lecture from 1981, he was setting out why it was important to study history. The second, from May 1989, was his valedictory, in which he wanted to explain why history had become an essential part of the education of civilised people. He then left Oxford, a year away from the university's retirement age, to teach at Yale University, an institution which worried less about the seniority of its faculty.

The Regius Chair was an unusual post, and Howard was a surprising choice to fill it. It was the historical profession's premier position in the UK. But it was also one that was curiously a Crown appointment in the gift of the prime minister of the day, then Margaret Thatcher, on the basis of names put to her by the university. In his self-deprecating memoir, he surmised that he was chosen as a matter of financial and administrative convenience from the university perspective, because he already had a chair in the faculty, so there would be no new cost, and that he was one of the few historians of whom Thatcher was aware. He was, however, being too modest: he had already made his mark as an original scholar and a brilliant communicator.

The appointment was also unusual because military history was generally considered to be marginal to the mainstream of the academic study of history, although Howard had done as much as anyone to give it respectability with a landmark book on the Franco-Prussian War. More importantly, other than his previous post – the Chichele Chair in the History of War which he had only held for a couple of years – he had not been part of a history faculty since the 1950s. In 1954, while in his first job as a lecturer in history at King's College London, he was appointed by the university to teach military studies. This led to a falling-out with his head of department, who wanted him to continue with his established duties. The dispute led him to go his own way until, in 1961, he had his own Department of War Studies at King's.

Over this period, he took as much interest in the contemporary as the historical and became a commentator on issues connected with nuclear deterrence and foreign policy. He was also instrumental in setting up the International Institute for Strategic Studies, a think tank based in London. He appreciated interdisciplinary endeavours, having worked with social scientists, and he also understood how the important policy issues of the day were addressed by those in government, the military, think tanks and the media. Importantly, Howard knew how much they were inclined to use 'the lessons of history' to make their points.

Howard was an elegant and theatrical speaker, whose lectures were crafted so that they could also serve as published essays. Much of his published work originated as public lectures, including these two pieces.

Howard explained in his memoir what he wanted to do in his inaugural lecture:

> Now I had to explain why I considered history itself to be important. There was no problem in persuading my colleagues that they were not wasting their time in doing what to them came naturally. But why should anyone pay them to do it or subsidise undergraduates to study it at the taxpayer's expense?

In answering this question, he stressed the importance of not promising 'lessons of history'. History did not speak; only historians spoke, and they were products of their time. What appeared to be a reasonable point based on one set of events might no longer look so valid once those events had been reinterpreted and then reinterpreted again. Moreover, the events studied were unique, the result of circumstances that were unlikely to be replicated. If there was a lesson, reinforced by his own wartime experiences, it was that events did not follow their expected course. Even social scientists attempting to generate laws of international affairs were thwarted by having to work with incomplete data and too many variables.

Making sense of the past, however, was part of thinking about the present and the future, and it was important that the history was as full and accurate as possible and not just a form of convenient mythology. As they explore the past, historians must examine their own countries honestly, and they must also broaden their perspectives to engage with other countries and cultures, including those with whom they might be locked in conflict. Howard worried that attempts to understand the Soviet Union, for example, by reading Marx while ignoring Dostoevsky, would fall short. This approach risked the same mistake as Chamberlain had made about Hitler at Munich. The problem was not just the obvious error about not standing up to dictators but a failure to understand the culture and preoccupations that produced a character such as Hitler, difficult for a man who had grown up in Victorian England.

Historians were themselves products of historical circumstances which enabled them to follow their scholarly instincts. It was a privilege enjoyed by Western historians that they were not obliged to celebrate the greatness of their nations while ignoring any failings. Their ability to research freely and without favour, to challenge and reinterpret, to reveal and expose, could not be taken for granted. They must always beware, he warned, of how 'fragile and fortuitous these circumstances can be'.

In his valedictory, Howard returned to the idea of lessons. Here he was keen to challenge the idea that the study of history was about discovering the line of progression to an improved society. He noted the utilitarian approach developed during the Enlightenment whereby history had to be studied not for its own sake but to illustrate 'the natural laws which governed the conduct of mankind'. Instead, he argued for a 'perception of history as a continual movement from the realm of necessity to that of a choice', with the belief that more knowledge better spread would provide the necessary equipment to make those choices.

History was not the product of impersonal forces working through their intrinsic logic but of free-willed human activities. It engendered both its own criteria for judgement and its own imperatives for action. It was an argument for studying history as a process, even though this did not necessarily point to comforting conclusions but instead to continuing problems and conflicts. But returning to the conditions under which the best historical scholarship flourished, it led him to favour those 'political regimes in which free discourse is favoured over those in which it is not'. Good outcomes depended not on an 'abstract concept of historical development', let alone the 'random play of chance' or the 'providence of an almighty God' but instead on that capacity for 'reason and judgement both educated and *created* by historical experience'.

Howard approached history as a classic liberal – mistrustful of dogma and approved national myths, while celebrating critical, independent thought and free choice. It was only under liberal conditions that historical scholarship could flourish.

London, February 2022

MICHAEL HOWARD
THE LESSONS OF HISTORY

An Inaugural Lecture Given in the University of Oxford

in March 1981

Only a tiny minority of students come to universities to learn how to be professional historians, and it is not primarily for them that our History Schools should be organised. The state now provides the money, and students are encouraged to find the time to read history – the three most formative years of their lives, when they could be learning a trade or a profession far more lucrative, of far more immediate 'relevance' to social needs – because it is still believed that a knowledge of the past is prerequisite to an understanding of the present; an understanding equally necessary to the elites who conduct the business of the state and the electorate to whom they are responsible. It is still believed that an understanding of the past is a necessary part of that self-awareness, that understanding of ourselves, that is the true object of a liberal education. To know the way in which our society came to be formed, to have some understanding of the conflicting forces within it, is not only an advantage in the conduct and understanding of public affairs: it is indispensable. No amount of technical expertise, no degree of professional competence, can ever take its place.

This understanding is of so broad, so general, and often of so incommunicable a kind, that social scientists often and understandably lose patience with historians who are reluctant to translate it into precise recommendations or formulate from it specific laws, and themselves seek to provide more direct techniques of guidance. Often their insights have brilliantly illuminated our understanding of both past and present: Max Weber, for one, did not write as a historian, but no historian, of any era, can now afford to neglect his work. But in formulating laws that will be either predictive or normative social scientists have been no more successful than historians; for the number of variables is so incalculable, the data inevitably so incomplete. The theories they formulate are at best explanatory or heuristic. They can never be predictive. Even the most convincing of their theories should be regarded as tentative hypotheses to be critically re-examined as new data become available. Even the most persuasive will eventually be displaced and relegated to the museum of historiographical curiosities. They may illuminate our judgement, but they can never take its place.

As a historian specialising in military affairs I was beset at an early age by sheep hungry for food that I did not feel competent to provide. I had to deliver, to a class of young army officers, a lecture on the Italian campaign of 1943–5. I sketched as best I could its rationale, its course and its consequences, with some deeply felt comments on the quality of the leadership on both sides. At the end there was a silence which I correctly gauged to be disapproving. It was broken by a young man in the front row asking impatiently, 'But what were its *lessons?*' And well might he ask. What was the point in all this if it did not have a direct professional relevance? They were busy men. But it was a question that nothing in my historical training here or in the University of London had equipped me to deal with and which I deeply, and absurdly, resented having to answer.

In fact of course one could derive many 'lessons' from that campaign for the military professional, who was likely to be confronted again with comparable if not identical problems of tactics, supply, intelligence and morale; and sharply focused questions directed to such specific issues could indeed produce valuable answers. But as a historian I was conscious above all of the unique quality of an experience that resulted from circumstances that would never, that *could* never, be precisely replicated. The lesson that most of those involved in the campaign on either side would agree about, is that if one wants to conquer Italy, the southern end of the peninsula is not the best place to begin. But the historian now knows that when the Allies landed at Salerno no such campaign was visualised and no such object intended. The Allied leaders were responding to the unforeseen circumstances created by the collapse of Mussolini's regime in the only way that seemed open to them; and the only 'lesson' that a historian would be justified in deriving from these events is that in war, in *any* war, this is the kind of thing that armed forces may find themselves having to do; not necessarily through the miscalculations or the stupidity of their leaders, but because all other options seem to be foreclosed or appear demonstrably worse. Subsequent generations of historians will deepen our understanding of the circumstances that shaped the decisions and set them in their social and economic framework. The Allied obsession with firepower and air power, the reluctance to accept heavy casualties, their lack of combat skills in comparison with their adversary, the excellence of their supply and welfare services and the determination to maintain them at whatever cost to mobility: all this may, in the long run, be of greater interest to the historian than the events, or even the outcome of the campaign itself. But what lesson can this teach, except that armed forces reflect the societies that produce them, and within the limits these impose on them they can only be expected to produce a finite range of results?

It is safer to start with the assumption that history, whatever its value in educating the judgement, teaches no 'lessons', and the professional historians will be as sceptical of those who claim that it does as professional doctors are of their colleagues who peddle patent medicines guaranteeing instant cures. The past is infinitely various, an inexhaustible storehouse of events from which we can prove anything or its contrary. Do arms races always end in war? The longest and perhaps the bitterest arms race in modern history was that between the French and British navies between 1815 and

1904, a period of 90 years in which peace was successfully preserved between two powers who had for 125 years before that been engaged in virtually continuous official or unofficial conflict. Does 'appeasement' never pay? It paid off handsomely enough when the British settled their differences with the French in Africa in 1904 and with Russia in Central Asia three years later. Does neutrality, or nonalignment, enhance national and international security? The example of Switzerland and Sweden argues one way, that of Belgium, of Holland, and of the smaller Italian states in the eighteenth century quite another. In short, historians may claim to teach lessons, and often they teach very wisely. But 'history' as such does not.

The trouble is that there is no such thing as 'history'. History is what historians write, and historians are part or the process they are writing about. We may seek for what Jakob Burckhardt described as the 'Archimedean point outside events' which would enable us to make truly dispassionate judgments and evaluations, but we know we cannot find it, and I am afraid we mistrust those of our colleagues in the social sciences who believe that they can. We know that our work, if it survives at all, will be read as evidence about our own *mentalité* and the thought processes of our own time rather than for anything we say about the times about which we write, however careful our scholarship and cautious our conclusions. We also know – or ought to know – how incomplete at best our knowledge of the past is bound to be: either because we have so little to go on or, for more recent times, because we have so much and have to be rigorously selective if we are going to make any sense of it at all. New evidence is constantly suggesting fresh perspectives and fresh conclusions, and historical controversies normally end because the participants are tired of them rather than because a consensus has been reached on which all can agree and which provides a firm platform for the proclamation of reliable conclusions. Was there, or was there not, a general crisis in the seventeenth century? Were the governing classes of the Second

German Reich or were they not determined on world war? On these great questions no certainty has been reached and none can be expected. But how much better we understand the past because they have been so exhaustively discussed!

The professional historian thus tends to be impatient of the layman who seeks guidance from him in dealing with the questions of his own day, let alone the future. His time is cut out trying to discover as best he can not only what 'really happened' in the past, but, increasingly, what the past was really *like*; in recreating the intellectual and social structures which will enable him to 'explain' events; trying, for example, to understand the social and intellectual framework that made the war of 1914 or the Revolution of 1789 *possible*, rather than tracing the course of events that led to them or allocating 'responsibility' among the participants; much less generalizing from them about wars and revolutions in our own day. And this, for the layman, is maddening. He looks for wise teachers who will use their knowledge of the past to explain the present and guide him as to the future. What does he find? Workmen, busily engaged in tearing up what he had regarded as a perfectly decent highway; doing their best to discourage him from proceeding along it at all; and warning him, if he does, that the surface is temporary, that they have no idea when it will be completed, nor where it leads, and that he proceeds at his own risk.

Well, the roadworks have to be done, and of course they are never complete. Even if no new evidence about the past, archaeological or documentary, compelled us to review our ideas about it; even if technology provided us with no new tools; the continual reshaping of our own minds by the events and social processes of our own times would make us ask new questions and discard earlier interpretations as inadequate if not false. None the less all this work must have some object, some aspiration in view. It cannot be simply the study of the past 'for its own sake', for outside the minds and writings of historians the past has no independent reality. If we as historians demand considerable sums of public money and battle for our quota of students it is not to enable us solipsistically to cultivate and refine our own perceptions and sensibilities. It is because we can, and should, claim to serve a more fundamental social purpose; and if we do not fulfil it things can go very wrong with our society indeed.

I am very well aware that the argument that historians have a social function – indeed a social obligation – is likely to be no more welcome among scholars today than it was when the first holder of this Chair was appointed over two and a half centuries ago. Professor Galbraith himself sounded from this very rostrum a trumpet blast against the conversion of the study of history to 'mere propaganda, resting on a narrow basis of civic usefulness', and we know what he meant. 'Socially useful' or 'relevant' history, whether consciously or unconsciously selected or tailored to meet contemporary social or political needs, has no place in a university or anywhere else. But there is a danger that this is the kind of history that almost automatically would get taught, or at least learned, if the historical profession did not exist to prevent it. For all societies have *some* view of the past; one that shapes and is shaped by their collective consciousness, that both reflects and reinforces the value-systems which guide their actions and judgments; and if professional historians do not provide this, others less scrupulous or less well qualified will. Far more than poets can historians claim to be the unacknowledged legislators of mankind; for all we believe about the present depends on what we believe about the past.

Certainly the historian cannot escape from the present. The more ambitious he is in attempting to create great comprehensive patterns of historical development, as did Marx, or Toynbee, or Spengler, or Sorokhin, the more evidently will he betray the moods and preoccupations of his own day. But he can, even within the limits imposed by his own cultural environment, ensure that our view of the past is not distorted by fraud, by evident prejudice or by simple error. Our primary professional responsibility is to keep clear and untainted those springs of knowledge that ultimately feed the great public reservoirs of popular histories and school textbooks and are now piped to every household in the country through the television screens. It is not an indifferent matter, or one of purely scholarly interest, to choose examples from recent history if it is widely believed that Adolf Hitler had no special responsibility for the Second World War; or that 120,000 people were killed in the Allied bombing of Dresden; or that Churchill connived in the murder of General Sikorski, or deliberately allowed Coventry to be bombed in order to protect the ultra secret; or that the United States deliberately destroyed Hiroshima and Nagasaki not in order to forward their military operations against Japan but as a demonstration intended to overawe the Soviet Union. Such beliefs about the past, however indirectly, shape attitudes and guide judgement for the present. It is important to be sure that they are correct.

So the first lesson that historians are entitled to teach is the austere one: not to generalize from false premises based on inadequate evidence. The second is no more comforting: the past is a foreign country; there is very little we can say about it until we have learned its language and understood its assumptions; and in deriving conclusions about the processes which occurred in it and applying them to our own day we must be very careful indeed. The *understanding* of the past, particularly of the beliefs and assumptions that held societies together and determined those activities on the level of high politics that are normally regarded as 'history', is the most rewarding, as it is the most difficult, of the historian's tasks. And it is here that he needs that quality of imagination so properly called for by my predecessor in his valedictory lecture. Yet it is a quality best used not in creating alternative 'scenarios' of the past but in recreating the structure of beliefs that determined action and perhaps made some actions more likely than others. It would indeed be fascinating and not illegitimate to ask what would have happened if Hitler had shown more interest in sea power; or had spared more resources for the Mediterranean theatre; or had above all shown more knowledge and understanding of the United States. But perhaps it is more useful to understand the prejudices and the order of priorities likely to exist in the mind of an autodidact whose formative years were spent in Vienna, where the great issues of the day related not to the rivalry of distant seaborne empires but to the clash between Teuton and Slav, between German and Czech, between Western and Russian power and – with horrible implications for the future – between Gentile and Jew.

For this quality of historical imagination is needed as much in dealing with the recent as it is with the more remote past. No one can be under any illusions about the difficulties of comprehending the world of Charlemagne, or of Frederick Barbarossa, or even of Napoleon Bonaparte. But is it really any easier for us today to understand the world of High Victorian imperialism or of Edwardian England? And how many historians can claim to have comprehended not so much the motives and intentions of Adolf Hitler, over which so much ink has been spilled, but the world outlook and the value systems that held the Third Reich together and kept the entire German people working and fighting until the very framework of their society had been destroyed over their heads? It is only if we have achieved such an understanding that we can plausibly answer such hypothetical questions as whether the Second World War could have been averted or curtailed if we had 'stood up to' Hitler sooner; of if we had given greater encouragement to the clandestine opposition within Germany; or if we had not demanded unconditional surrender. What was the *society* that we were dealing with, and how could it have reacted to these events?

If it is difficult for historians in retrospect, with all the wisdom of hindsight and all the time in the world, to comprehend the complex processes that went to the creation of the Third Reich and the nature of the society to which it gave political expression, we should not be too quick to condemn those contemporary British statesmen who so tragically misunderstood the phenomenon in their own day. For their perceptions were also constrained by their cultural framework. Neville Chamberlain and his closest colleagues had been brought up in the England of Queen Victoria and were middle-aged when the First World War began. Their world was that of the British Empire. The problems posed by the Congress Party in India, by the Wafd movement in Egypt, and by the relations of Briton and Boer in South Africa were more immediate to them, more real, more urgent, than were the racial antagonisms of Central Europe. How could they be expected to see the significance of that populist nationalism, fuelled invariably by anti-Semitism, that was seeping up everywhere in the Continent like so much sewage through the cracks in the old order; the *anomie* that ravaged societies where traditional values had been destroyed by war and revolution? The works on European history on which they had been brought up had been written before the turn of the century in a spirit of optimistic liberalism, seeing in the unification of Germany and of Italy the happy climax to a long struggle for freedom and self-expression and taking little account of anything that had happened after that. Even those of their Foreign Office advisers who saw the dangers of National Socialism saw them in traditional terms: the revival of the power and the pretensions of the German, indeed the *Prussian* state, which they had known in their youth. Few if any comprehended the full challenge posed by the 'Revolution of Nihilism' which enabled the Nazis to find willing collaborators in every country they conquered; and made of Nazism a popular, indeed a *populist* movement, of a kind that both liberal and Marxist historians have found difficult to explain away.

When we consider the insularity of our attitude to our continental neighbours after 1945, the patronising aloofness displayed by so many British statesmen and senior civil servants towards the birth of the European Community, their reluctance to give that lead in the remaking of Europe which was for so many years ours for the asking, we may wonder how far this attitude was rooted in a historical consciousness nurtured by university history teachers who for generations had seen the Continent as an area of concern for specialists, the study of whose problems was an interesting option but no more. It is significant that in the Oxford history syllabus in the 1920s there was only one special subject available in modern continental history – that on Congress diplomacy between 1815 and 1822. Others available included British rule in India, the development of Canada and the revolt of the American colonies. Admirable as it was that the horizons of undergraduates should have been extended to the other side of the Atlantic, the contribution that the Oxford History School made to our understanding of our nearest neighbours was, for that generation, notably small.

And this perhaps indicates that the value of history as a training of the judgement and of the imagination is very limited if it is exercised only in recreating our own past, with little reference to the total context within which our society developed and, more particularly, the often very divergent structures of other societies whose development may have been of yet greater importance to the making of the world in which we live today. If it is, indeed, one of the major functions of the historian to explain the present by deepening our understanding of the past, then a study simply of our own society will not get us very far. Our awareness of the world and our capacity to deal intelligently with its problems are shaped not only by the history we know but by what we do *not* know. Ignorance, especially the ignorance of educated men, can be a more powerful force than knowledge. Ethnocentrism in historical studies, whatever its advantages in scholarly training, is likely to feed parochialism in the societies which those historians serve; and such parochialism can have pretty disastrous results.

Am I now suggesting that the history taught in universities and schools should, in spite of all I said a few moments ago, be 'relevant', and guided by some criterion of civic usefulness? In a sense I must admit that I am. But we must distinguish between *how* history is studied by the professional historians and *what* history is taught to the laity. The range of the historical profession must be universal, and universities exist to make possible that universality. In the eyes of the scholar, as in the eyes of God, all ages are of equal significance. It is as important to understand Byzantium as it is to understand the Soviet Union (and unless one understands Byzantium how can one understand the Soviet Union?). It is as important to understand the pre-Columbian societies of Central America as it is to understand Moghul dynastic rule in India, or the system of land tenure in fifteenth-century Franconia, or the development of municipal government in Leeds. The past is a vast chain, every link of which must be kept in good repair. The links that lie chronologically or geographically near us can claim no special priority from the professional historian, and one of the things we have to teach the laity is that this is so.

But if our object in teaching history to the laity is to enable them to understand the present by explaining the past, and we have only three years in which to do this, then we cannot avoid making hard decisions about what we are going to select from the illimitable range offered by the past; what aspects of it we allocate for the compulsory and what for optional study. If a valid definition can be given to the term 'Modern History' – and I sometimes doubt whether it can – then it must be the history concerned with the world in which we live today and with the processes that have gone to form it. We are therefore justified in asking how far the subjects we prescribe for study will enhance that understanding, and in giving some priority to those for which a case can most easily be made. Of course it is true that for a full understanding of the contemporary world it is as important to understand the causes of the decline of the Roman Empire as those for the rise and fall of the Third Reich. The academic snobbery that disdains the history of the recent past precisely because it relates so obviously to the present is as indefensible as the lay impatience with a remote past because on the face of it it does not. But the layman has every right to ask the historian not how his own researches contribute to our understanding of the contemporary world, but how do the studies that he, the layman, is required to pursue? And there is a certain obligation on our part to provide a convincing answer.

In the eighteenth century the world of classical antiquity provided a model whose 'relevance' to contemporary issues was unquestioned, or only just beginning to be questioned. In the nineteenth century the historian was expected to show only how his society had reached its existing state of perfection or – for the less easily satisfied – might be expected to progress to a future state of perfection. But the demands of our own tumultuous century have been more complex. To explain 'the modern world', the historian has to involve himself and his pupils in the study of societies sometimes very different from his own. And he may find himself forced to adopt a standpoint, from which the history of his own society will appear to be of secondary importance.

The range of the Oxford History School has been commendably extended since the Second World War. Special Subjects and Further Subjects have splendidly proliferated, bringing every corner of the world within the purview of any student who wants to take advantage of them. But the Anglocentric core remains – and I use the prefix 'Anglo' advisedly. The Irish dimension is still peripheral, studied only insofar as it affects the fortunes of the political parties in Westminster; and again one may wonder how far its absence has contributed to the neglect shown by the British public and the incompetence displayed by successive British administrations in dealing with the Irish problem over so many years. It is still possible here to study nothing that has happened beyond these shores save for a period of 'General History' covering a couple of centuries; which effectively means the history of Europe and of Western Europe at that; and woe betide the naive examiner who demands any broader knowledge from the candidates who take this paper! As for the history of the United States, a society which more than any other is likely to shape our lives, if not our deaths, that is regarded as a matter for specialist study, and the great bulk of undergraduates leave the Oxford History School as ignorant of it as they were when they arrived.

If we are properly to educate the laity it is not enough to awaken an interest in the past to provide them with an agreeable leisure occupation. It is not enough to provide for them scholarly exercise in the handling of evidence on which they can sharpen their wits. We have to teach them how to step outside their own cultural skins and enter the minds of others; the minds not only of our own for-bears, enormously valuable though this is, but of those of our con-temporaries who have inherited a different experience from the past. And important as is the contribution of our colleagues the geographers and anthropologists, on whose insights we increas-ingly draw, the study of history alone can teach how to do this; history and the subject so properly associated with it when this Chair was founded: modern languages. As Burckhardt said, we cannot know too many languages. We need them not so much in order to make ourselves understood but in order to understand. Without knowing the languages that shape and express their thought our comprehension of other cultural communities will be dim and unreliable, however great in the abstract may be our knowledge of their past. Lord Dacre, in his farewell to his col-leagues, congratulated us on having resisted up till now the general decline into 'monoglot illiteracy'. If we do not continue to resist it, and more, if we do not fight hard to reverse it, we shall find our range not being extended but narrowed, and our contribution to the understanding of both the past and present reduced to the level of parochial trivia.

And this is the third 'lesson' that historians must teach: the importance of comprehending cultural diversity and equipping oneself to cope with it. Much has properly been made of Neville Chamberlain's failure to understand Hitler, as of Roosevelt's fail-ure to understand Stalin; but these disastrous misunderstandings are often depicted as cases of honest men being outwitted by crooks. Alas, the misunderstanding was at a far deeper level than that, and it is one that is constantly recurring as new elites, almost boastfully ignorant of their knowledge of any world save their own, acquire authority in some of the most powerful states in the world. We have seen so much of this since the Second World War: people often of masterful intelligence, trained usually in law or economics or perhaps in political science, who have led their governments into disastrous decisions and miscalculations because they have no awareness whatever of the historical background, the cultural universe, of the foreign societies with which they have to deal. It is an awareness for which no amount of strategic or economic analysis, no techniques of crisis management or conflict resolution and certainly no professed understanding of the 'objective historical process of the international class struggle' can provide a substitute. Such miscalculations are always dangerous. In our own day they may be lethal on a very large scale indeed.

This brings me to the last and most sombre 'lesson' that the study of history has to impart; and that is, how vulnerable may be the social framework which permits the historian to ply his trade at all. I am not referring to the fact of which we are all uncomfortably aware, or should be; that if the statesmen of the world do not conduct their affairs with prudence, I might well be the last occupant of this Chair. Our own generation knows from experience that no society has a dispensation from catastrophe, and that history provides no sure formula for avoiding one. This knowledge is in itself the beginning of wisdom. Bur there are other, more subtle, dangers to which societies have succumbed; dangers which, by destroying the insights that historical studies can provide, could make catastrophe more likely. Sir Maurice Powicke, one of the most learned and humane scholars ever to hold this chair, once proclaimed confidently, 'Nobody can abolish the past'. Today, if he attended many international historical congresses, he might be less sure. There are countries in the world where it is precisely the duty of historians to abolish the past, and their own professional survival depends on their success in keeping it abolished and erecting in its place a socially convenient myth which it is their function to defend, embellish and generally keep up to date.

Such a role is nothing new for historians. In most societies, in most eras, they have received official countenance only on condition they subscribed to and reinforced the reigning dogmas. The emergence of bourgeois liberal societies in which historians are free to publish what *had* 'really happened' in the past, at whatever embarrassment to the authorities of the present, to demolish myths rather than create them, is only a few centuries old. Such 'bourgeois objectivism' does not flourish in totalitarian societies, nor is it very helpful to the nation-building elites in the Third World. The freedom of historians to teach, study and publish as their scholarly instincts dictate, and to treat professors intruded by the Crown with the genial tolerance they deserve, is itself the result of historical circumstances which historians themselves should understand very well; as they can understand how fragile and fortuitous these circumstances can be. And this is a matter of which no historian can afford to be simply a dispassionate chronicler and analyst. However great his intellectual and moral detachment, in the last resort he is committed to the values, and to the society, that enables him to remain so detached. He is a member of the polis and cannot watch its destruction without himself being destroyed. However impatient the historian may be of lay requirements for guidance, however diffident he may be in claiming a wisdom he knows he does not possess, this is the one thing he *should* know. This is the one 'lesson of history' he must never allow himself to forget.

MICHAEL HOWARD
STRUCTURE AND PROCESS IN HISTORY

A Valedictory Lecture given in the University of Oxford

in May 1989

Eight years have passed since I gave an inaugural lecture in these schools, and expressed my views as to why history should be studied and how it should be taught. It was a fairly routine apologia and a declaration of intent which I have since done all too little to implement.

It is not my purpose in this valedictory lecture to give an account of my stewardship, nor to provide yet another justification for the study of history. I want rather to consider why the study of history *has* been seen, throughout the evolution of Western society, as an intrinsic and essential part of the education of all civilised men and women, and what they have expected to acquire from that study.

Today most of us would argue that only a knowledge of the past enables us fully to understand the present, and that a failure to read the past correctly warps our capacity to act intelligently in the contemporary world. But for most of the past millennium, expectations of what historians can contribute to the common weal have been even higher. The study of history has been believed to provide a guide, not simply to passive understanding of the world, but to active political and moral action within it. Today few of us – certainly few non-Marxists – would have the temerity to make such a claim, but it was not always so. For the best part of a thousand years Western man has studied the past in the expectation that he would receive both political and moral guidance from doing so, and historians have been on the whole only too happy to oblige.

Almost from earliest times history was expected to 'teach lessons'; to provide guidance as to how to act or not to act; to furnish examples of virtue rewarded and evil punished. The laws of moral and political behaviour were generally regarded as immutable and invariable in all ages and all societies. Each new generation was joining in an activity of which the rules were well established and whose skills could only be learned by studying the techniques of past masters. Even in the picture of the past painted by medieval scholars, directed though this was to depicting God's eschatological purposes for mankind, both Old and New Testaments are used to define patterns of behaviour and provide examples of virtue rewarded and evil punished – and the need for remaining virtuous even if, in the unknowable purposes of God, good behaviour was not rewarded but resulted, as it did for most of mankind throughout most of its history, only in suffering; the reward for which lay in the hereafter and whose purpose would be understood only in the fulness of time.

For the humanists of the Renaissance and the classical historians on whom they commented, virtue was not necessarily rewarded either: only *virtù*, which was a very different matter. History was a manual of statecraft. But it was also a guide to conduct. It was defended, in the 1579 translation of Plutarch's *Lives*, as 'a certain rule and instruction which by examples past, teacheth us to judge of things present and to foresee things to come, so as we may know what to like of and what to follow, what to mislike, and what to eschew'. Thucydides had already made the same point nearly two thousand years before: history was 'philosophy teaching by example'. What was exemplified were the challenges which all generations had in turn to confront in conducting their affairs; and the qualities required to meet those challenges – courage, equanimity, moderation, loyalty, magnanimity, foresight, all the prudent skills of the statesman and the warrior – were considered to be as 'relevant' for the moderns as they had been for the ancients.

Gentlemen in the eighteenth century filled their libraries with the classics and sent their sons to the universities to read 'more humane letters' in the belief that these still provided the best preparation for public, as the study of the Scriptures provided the best preparation for private life.

The impact of the Enlightenment strengthened this belief in the uniformity of human behaviour with its assumption that man governed his own destiny by the use of his own judgement and reason, and that, in all ages, rational and intelligent behaviour led to felicity, and foolish passion or unreasoning superstition to disaster. The past was to be studied in the same spirit, and for the same reasons, as scientists studied the natural world. The chief use of historical study, taught Hume, 'is only to discover the constant and universal principles of human nature'; and in the eighteenth century historians maintained that only such history should be studied as did possess such utility. Anything that was not so relevant was simply antiquarianism; a respectable enough way of passing the time, but an activity that had little in common with the writing of history. No utility was seen, in that pre-Romantic era, in studying the past 'for its own sake'. The men of the Enlightenment therefore read history to find not, as in the Renaissance, models for appropriate behaviour, but illustration of the natural laws which governed the conduct of mankind.

[…]

This is the position in which we find ourselves if we reject that whole school of historical thought, from Kant to Marx, which saw history not only as process but as *progress*; if we do not believe that in spite of all setbacks, 'a seed of enlightenment' does survive and prepare the way for continual improvement, so that the standards by which we judge ourselves and others are, in a sense at once absolute and historical, an improvement on those which prevailed in the past; standards which entitle us to condemn slavery or persecution or torture or genocide wherever or whenever we find it, however justifiable it appeared to other ages or other cultures.

If we really cannot make any such claim, all moral judgement sinks to an undifferentiated level of cultural relativism, in which we have no 'standard of rectitude' to judge either the past or the present.

To accept such a position seems to me perverse. The fact of the historical process over the last two hundred years is self-evident, whether or not we regard it as 'progress'. Fernand Braudel, that great architect of historical structures, could in his giant study *Civilization and Capitalism, 15th–18th Century* take a *longue durée* of three hundred years in which the structure apparently remained stable and change incremental. He might for an earlier epoch have chosen an even longer period. But from the end of the eighteenth century until our own day we have been witnessing the progressive and infectious *disintegration* of traditional social structures, and history has become the record of ever more rapid and bewildering change throughout the world. That change has been discontinuous and uneven, faster and earlier in some areas than in others, and it is precisely the contrast in the speed and the incidence of that change that has caused most of the social and political tensions which have underlain the very *évènementielle* history of the past two centuries. (And if anyone tries to write the history of the twentieth century without dealing with 'events', I can only say, good luck to them.)

Earlier generations had no hesitation in describing as 'progress' or 'the march of civilization' that process of economic transformation which, originating in Britain in the eighteenth century, spread to the whole of Europe and North America in the nineteenth century, and the rest of the world in the twentieth. Later, less loaded words were used: 'industrialisation', or more often 'modernisation'. Now I think that the accepted term is 'development'; one which, interestingly, returns to the original Kantian concept of the unfolding of potential, of seed germinating and growing towards fulfilment.

It is this process of modernisation that confounds purely cyclical theories of history. It is indeed possible that agrarian societies were constrained by the structural limitations of their environment to follow certain common patterns of growth and decline; but the chain reaction of modernisation has transformed the range of opportunities available to mankind, creating a situation for which there exists literally no historical parallel.

The benefits of this process are easy to list. The increase in life expectancy, of surviving beyond childbirth and infancy and living to see one's fiftieth, even one's eightieth birthday; the elimination of the plagues and famines which so regularly decimated the population of Europe; the drastic reduction, in the incidence of *pain* – that pain – which had accompanied men, and even more, women, like an evil shadow throughout their brief lives; emancipation from the bonds of law or custom that had bound men to their masters or to the soil for so many centuries; the alleviation, through the application of technology, of the day-long, year-long, back-breaking toil in field or factory that made a mockery of political freedom; the increase in the universal provision of the necessities of life, and of luxuries that rapidly came to be regarded as necessities – necessities not just for the rich but for the entire population, not just for developed countries but increasingly for the entire world; the growth of literacy and with it access to knowledge, and with knowledge, power. The list is infinite and the process far from complete. We are indeed quite properly conscious of how much further we have to go rather than how far we have already come. But the distance that we have already travelled during the past two hundred years, especially in the northern hemisphere, is already so great that it is not surprising if we have to study the earlier history even of our own societies as if it were that of some remote age in the past. Is it really so naive to call this process 'Progress'?

[...]

But Reason is not a Thing, or a Person, much less a God. It is an *activity,* and a highly individual one. It is *people* thinking and judging: more, it is individual *persons* thinking and judging. Neither is

History a Thing: it is what people think, write and believe about the past. A knowledge of the past is essential in making political or moral judgments, but 'History' as such does not judge. That is done by people; and best done by people free to think, read, inform themselves and debate before they decide; and having decided, be free to change their minds. They may be free to do so only within the constraints imposed by historical structures, but those structures are themselves created by human thoughts and actions, and are constantly being modified by them.

[…]

Such a perspective at least provides us with a framework for moral judgement which is not divorced from history but derived from our understanding of it. It rescues us from, on the one hand, the desert of sterile cultural relativism and arid professional 'neutrality', and, on the other, the lush self-indulgence of escapist nostalgia – 'The Heritage Industry'. It is rooted in a perception of history as a continual movement from the realm of necessity to that of choice, and a belief that the growth and diffusion of knowledge increasingly equips us with the opportunity, and the capability, to make those choices.

This movement, this historical dynamic, consists of freely willed human activities. It engenders both its own criteria for judgement and its own imperatives for action. These enable us, however successfully we may 'empathise' with past generations, to judge them if necessary with Actonian rigour. They lead us in our own generation to favour political regimes in which free discourse is favoured and encouraged over those in which it is not. They further lay on us the continuing obligation to ensure that nowhere in the world should poverty, illiteracy and grinding hardship deprive peoples of those opportunities for physical improvement and moral growth which the historical process has provided for the fortunate societies of the West.

This imperative provides indeed the real justification for the study of history as process; for it is only from that study that we can discover what we have been, understand what we are, and gain intimations of what we might become. The study is not comforting. It holds out hope of nothing but continuing problems, continuing conflicts – conflicts which may become yet more bitter as more of mankind become conscious of the gap that separates potential from fulfilment, aspiration from achievement, and, once they have achieved their immediate goals, reach out for more. But it is only by such conflicts that growth can take place at all and that mankind can move on to higher levels of aspiration and achievement.

There is, as I have said, no assurance of a happy ending: all may disintegrate into ruin and chaos on a scale never before seen. But whether it does so or not depends not on any abstract concept of historical development, nor on the random play of chance, nor on the providence of an almighty God. It depends on our skill in using that capacity for reason and judgement which has already brought us so far; reason and judgement both educated and *created* by historical experience. On the whole we have done quite well in avoiding or recovering from catastrophe, but we must continue to do well: *for ever*. We have no justification for looking forward to a time when we can sit back and say, 'That is it: now we are safe: now there is peace.' If such a time were indeed to come it would be the end of history, since we would all be dead.

Let me in conclusion again quote Kant: 'Nature does not seem to have been concerned with seeing that man should live agreeably, but that he should work his way onward to make himself by his own conduct worthy of life and well-being.' That is what we have continually to do. The historical process, through the very challenges it poses and the responses it evokes, itself creates the morality of mankind. That seems to me a very good reason for studying it.

JOHN LEWIS GADDIS:
THE LANDSCAPE OF HISTORY

INTRODUCTION BY THE AUTHOR

The Landscape of History originated in an invitation from Oxford University to spend the 2000/1 academic year there as the George Eastman Visiting Professor at Balliol College. My letter of appointment required only 'participation in twenty-four academic functions during the three terms of the academic year'. It then added, accurately enough, that 'the Eastman Professor enjoys considerable scope for flexibility in adjusting...pedagogical activities in combination with scholarly projects which the holder may wish to pursue.'

Confronted with so much latitude in so congenial a setting, I was at first at a loss to know how to use my time. One possibility would have been simply to dine: high table at Oxford is definitely an 'academic function'. Another would have been to spend the year doing research, but this would have disappointed my hosts, who clearly expected some sort of visibility. A third would have been to lecture on Cold War history, but I'd done that as Harmsworth professor eight years earlier and had since published the lectures.[1] Even in that rapidly changing field, there might not be much new to say.

So I settled on a set of lectures, delivered as before in the Examination Schools building on High St, on the admittedly ambitious subject of how historians think. I had several purposes in mind in doing so, the first of which was to pay homage to scholars now dead and to students very much alive, both of whom had taught me. The scholars, in particular, were Marc Bloch and E H Carr, whose respective introductions to the historical method, *The Historian's Craft* and *What Is History?*, first forced me to consider what historians do. The students were my own, undergraduates and graduates at Ohio, Yale and Oxford universities, with whom I'd spent a good deal of time discussing these and other less familiar works on historical methodology.

A second purpose derived from the first. I'd begun to worry that all this reading and talking might soon begin to produce, in my own mind, something like what Cervantes describes Don Quixote as doing after reading too many books on knight-errantry: 'He so bewildered himself in this kind of study that…his brain…dried up, [and] he came at last to lose his wits.'[2] I felt the need to avoid that dismal prospect.

My third purpose – whether or not I'd dodged the dangers implied in the second – was to do some updating. A lot had happened since the Nazis executed Bloch in 1944, leaving us with a classic that breaks off, like Thucydides, in mid-sentence; and since the more fortunate Carr completed his George Macaulay Trevelyan lectures, which became his classic, at Cambridge in 1961. My impression, though, was that it was not so much they as we who needed the updating. For Bloch and Carr had anticipated certain developments in the physical and biological sciences that brought those disciplines closer to what historians had been doing all along. Most social scientists had hardly noticed these trends, and most historians, even as they read and taught Bloch and Carr, had neglected what these authors were suggesting about a convergence of the historical method with those of the so-called 'hard' sciences.

That suggests my fourth purpose, which was to encourage my fellow historians to make their methods more explicit. We normally resist doing this. We work within a wide variety of styles, but we prefer in all of them that form conceal function. We recoil from the notion that our writing should replicate, say, the design of the

Pompidou Centre in Paris, which proudly places its escalators, plumbing, wiring and ductwork on the *outside* of the building, so that they're there for all to see. We don't question the need for such structures, only the impulse to exhibit them. Our reluctance to reveal our own workings, however, too often confuses our students – even, at times, ourselves – as to just what it is we do.

Bloch and Carr had little patience with such methodological modesty,[3] and that brought me to my final purpose, which had to do with teaching. It is striking that, with all the time that had passed since their introductions to the historical method came out, no better ones for use in the classroom had yet appeared. The reason was not just that Bloch and Carr were accomplished methodologists: we'd had many since, and some more skilled. What distinguished them was the clarity, brevity and wit – in a word, the elegance – with which they expressed themselves. They showed that you can discuss ductwork gracefully. Few methodologists attempt this even today, which is why they speak mostly to themselves and not to the rest of us.

Landscape never became a bestseller, alas, but it has remained in print and continues, gratifyingly, to be used in classrooms. I'm grateful also to the editors of this volume for their use of this preface as their introduction.

New Haven, CT, March 2022

---

1. John Lewis Gaddis, *We Now Know: Rethinking Cold War History* (Oxford University Press, New York, 1997).
2. Miguel de Cervantes, *Don Quixote de la Mancha*, tr. Charles Jarvis (Oxford University Press, New York, 1992), 23.
3. See for example, Marc Bloch, *The Historian's Craft*, tr. Peter Putnam (Manchester University Press, Manchester, 1992), 8, 59; and E H Carr, *What Is History?*, (1961; 2nd edn, Penguin, New York, 1987), 19–20.

The Wanderer above the Sea of Fog,
Caspar David Friedrich, *c.* 1818.

JOHN LEWIS GADDIS
HOW HISTORIANS MAP
THE PAST

A young man stands hatless in a black coat on a high rocky point. His back is turned towards us, and he is bracing himself with a walking stick against the wind that blows his hair in tangles. Before him lies a fog-shrouded landscape in which the fantastic shapes of more distant promontories are only partly visible. The far horizon reveals mountains off to the left, plains to the right, and perhaps very far away – one can't be sure – an ocean. But maybe it's just more fog, merging imperceptibly into clouds. The painting, which dates from 1818, is a familiar one: Caspar David Friedrich's *The Wanderer above the Sea of Fog.* The impression it leaves is contradictory, suggesting at once mastery over a landscape and the insignificance of an individual within it. We see no face, so it's impossible to know whether the prospect confronting the young man is exhilarating, or terrifying, or both.

Paul Johnson used Friedrich's painting some years ago as the cover for his book *The Birth of the Modern,* to evoke the rise of romanticism and the advent of the Industrial Revolution.[1] I should like to use it here to summon up something more personal, which is my own sense – admittedly idiosyncratic – of what historical consciousness is all about. The logic of beginning with a landscape may not be immediately obvious. But consider the power of metaphor, on the one hand, and the particular combination of economy and intensity with which visual images can express metaphors, on the other.

The best introduction I know to the scientific method, John Ziman's *Reliable Knowledge in Science*, points out that scientific insights often arise from such realisations as 'that the behavior of an electron in an atom is "like" the vibration of air in a spherical container, or that the random configuration of the long chain of atoms in a polymer molecule is "like" the motion of a drunkard across a village green'.[2] 'Reality is still to be embraced and reported without flinching,' the sociobiologist Edward O Wilson has added. 'But it is also best delivered the same way it was discovered, retaining a comparable vividness and play of the emotions.'[3] It's here, I think, that science, history and art have something in common: they all depend on metaphor, on the recognition of patterns, on the realisation that something is 'like' something else.

For me, the posture of Friedrich's wanderer – this striking image of a back turned towards the artist and all who have since seen his work – is 'like' that of historians. Most of us consider it our business, after all, to turn our back on wherever it is we may be going, and to focus our attention, from whatever vantage point we can find, on where we've been. We pride ourselves on *not* trying to predict the future, as our colleagues in economics, sociology and political science attempt to do. We resist letting contemporary concerns influence us – the term 'presentism', among historians, is no compliment. We advance bravely into the future with our eyes fixed firmly on the past: the image we present to the world is, to put it bluntly, that of a rear end.[4]

I.

Historians do, to be sure, assume *some* things about what's to come. It's a good bet, for example, that time will continue to pass, that gravity will continue to extend itself through space, and that Michaelmas term at Oxford will continue to be, as it has been for well over seven hundred years, dreary, dark and damp. But we know these things about the future only from having learned about the past: without it we'd have no sense of even these fundamental truths, to say nothing of the words with which to express them, or even of who or where or what we are. We know the future only by the past we project into it. History, in this sense, is all we have.

But the past, in another sense, is something we can never have. For by the time we've become aware of what has happened it's already inaccessible to us: we cannot relive, retrieve or rerun it as we might some laboratory experiment or computer simulation. We can only *represent* it. We can portray the past as a near or distant landscape, much as Friedrich has depicted what his wanderer sees from his lofty perch. We can perceive shapes through the fog and mist, we can speculate as to their significance, and sometimes we can even agree among ourselves as to what these are. Barring the invention of a time machine, though, we can never go back there to see for sure.

Science fiction, of course, has invented time machines. Indeed, two recent novels, Connie Willis's *Doomsday Book* and Michael Crichton's *Timeline*, feature graduate students in history at, respectively, Oxford and Yale, who use these devices to project themselves back to England and France in the fourteenth century for the purpose of researching their dissertations.[5] Both authors suggest some things time travel might do for us. It could, for example, give us a 'feel' for a particular time and place: the novels evoke the denser forests, clearer air and much louder singing birds of medieval Europe, as well as the muddy roads, rotting food and smelly people. What they don't show is that we could easily detect the larger patterns of a period by visiting it, because the characters keep getting caught up in complications of everyday life that tend to limit perspective. Like catching the plague, or being burned at the stake, or getting their heads chopped off.

Maybe this is just what it takes to keep the novel exciting, or to make the movie rights marketable. I'm inclined to think, though, that there's a larger point lurking here: it is that the direct experience of events isn't necessarily the best path towards understanding them, because your field of vision extends no further than your own immediate senses. You lack the capacity, when trying to figure out how to survive a famine, or flee a band of brigands, or fight from within a suit of armour, to function as a historian might do. You're not likely to take the time to contrast conditions in fourteenth-century France with those under Charlemagne or the Romans, or to compare what might have been parallels in Ming China or pre-Columbian Peru. Because the individual is 'narrowly restricted by his senses and power of concentration', Marc Bloch writes in *The Historian's Craft*, he 'never perceives more than a tiny patch of the vast tapestry of events…In this respect, the student of the present is scarcely any better off than the historian of the past.'[6]

I'd argue, indeed, that the historian of the past is *much better off* than the participant in the present, from the simple fact of having an expanded horizon. Gertrude Stein got close to the reason in her brief 1938 biography of Picasso:

> When I was in America I for the first time travelled pretty much all the time in an airplane and when I looked at the earth I saw all the lines of cubism made at a time when not any painter had ever gone up in an airplane. I saw there on earth the mingling lines of Picasso, coming and going, developing and destroying themselves.[7]

What was happening here, quite literally, was detachment from, and consequent elevation above, a landscape: a departure from the normal that provided a new perception of what was real. It was what the Montgolfier brothers saw from their balloon over Paris in 1783, or the Wright brothers from their first 'Flyer' in 1903, or the Apollo astronauts when they flew around the moon at Christmas 1968, thus becoming the first humans to view the earth set against the darkness of space. It's also, of course, what Friedrich's wanderer sees from his mountaintop, as have countless others for whom elevation, by shifting perspective, has enlarged experience.

This brings us around, then, to one of the things historians do. For if you think of the past as a landscape, then history is the way we represent it, and it's that act of representation that lifts us above the familiar to let us experience vicariously what we can't experience directly: a wider view.

II.

What, though, do we gain from such a view? Several things, I think, the first of which is a sense of identity that parallels the process of growing up. Taking off in an airplane makes you feel both large and small at the same time. You can't help but have a sense of mastery as your airline of choice detaches you from the ground, lifts you above the traffic jams surrounding the airport and reveals vast horizons stretching out beyond it – assuming, of course, that you have a window seat, it isn't a cloudy day, and you aren't one of those people whose fear of flying causes them to keep their eyes clamped shut from take-off to landing. But as you gain altitude, you also can't help noticing how small you are in relation to the landscape that lies before you. The experience is at once exhilarating and terrifying.

So is life. We are born, each of us, with such self-centredness that only the fact of being babies, and therefore cute, saves us. Growing up is largely a matter of growing out of that condition: we soak in impressions, and as we do so we dethrone ourselves – or at least most of us do – from our original position at the centre of the universe. It's like taking off in an airplane: the establishment of identity requires recognising our relative insignificance in the larger scheme of things. Remember how it felt to have your parents unexpectedly produce a younger sibling, or abandon you to the tender mercies of kindergarten? Or what it was like to enter your first public or private school, or to arrive at places like Oxford, or Yale, or the Hogwarts School of Witchcraft and Wizardry?[8] Or as a teacher to confront your first classroom filled with sullen, squirmy, slumbering, solipsistic students? Just as you've cleared one hurdle another is set before you. Each event diminishes your authority at just the moment at which you think you've become an authority.

If that's what maturity means in human relationships – the arrival at identity by way of insignificance – then I would define historical consciousness as the projection of that maturity through time. We understand how much has preceded us, and how unimportant we are in relation to it. We learn our place, and we come to realise that it isn't a large one. 'Even a superficial acquaintance with the existence, through millennia of time, of numberless human beings,' the historian Geoffrey Elton has pointed out, 'helps to correct the normal adolescent inclination to relate the world to oneself instead of relating oneself to the world.' History teaches 'those adjustments and insights which help the adolescent to become adult, surely a worthy service in the education of youth'.[9] Mark Twain put it even better:

> That it took a hundred million years to prepare the world for [man] is proof that that is what it was done for. I suppose it is. I dunno. If the Eiffel Tower were now representing the world's age, the skin of paint on the pinnacle knob at its summit would represent man's share of that age; and anybody would perceive that the skin was what the tower was built for. I reckon they would, I dunno.[10]

Here too, though, there's a paradox, for although the discovery of geologic or 'deep' time diminished the significance of human beings in the overall history of the universe, it also, in the eyes of Charles Darwin, T H Huxley, Mark Twain and many others, dethroned God from his position, at its centre – which left no one else around but man.[11] The recognition of human insignificance did not, as one might have expected, enhance the role of divine agency in explaining human affairs: it had just the opposite effect.

It gave rise to a secular consciousness that, for better or for worse, placed the responsibility for what happens in history squarely on the people who live through history.

What I'm suggesting, therefore, is that just as historical consciousness demands detachment from – or if you prefer, elevation above – the landscape that is the past, so it also requires a certain displacement: an ability to shift back and forth between humility and mastery. Niccolò Machiavelli made the point precisely in his famous preface to *The Prince*: how was it, he asked his patron Lorenzo de' Medici, that 'a man from a low and mean state dares to discuss and give rules for the governments of princes?' Being Machiavelli, he then answered his own question:

> For just as those who sketch landscapes place themselves down in the plain to consider the nature of mountains and high places and to consider the nature of low places place themselves high atop mountains, similarly to know well the nature of peoples one needs to be [a] prince, and to know well the nature of princes one needs to be of the people.[12]

You feel small, whether as a courtier or an artist or a historian, because you recognise your insignificance in an infinite universe. You know you can never yourself rule a kingdom, or capture on canvas everything you see on a distant horizon, or recapture in your books and lectures everything that's happened in even the most particular part of the past. The best you can do, whether with a prince or a landscape or the past, is to *represent* reality: to smooth over the details, to look for larger patterns, to consider how you can use what you see for your own purposes.

That very act of representation, though, makes you feel large, because you yourself are in charge of the representation: it's you who must make complexity comprehensible, first to yourself, then to others. And the power that resides in representation can be great indeed, as Machiavelli certainly understood. For how much influence today does Lorenzo de' Medici have, compared to the man who applied to be his tutor?

Historical consciousness therefore leaves you, as does maturity itself, with a simultaneous sense of your own significance and insignificance. Like Friedrich's wanderer, you dominate a landscape even as you're diminished by it. You're suspended between sensibilities that are at odds with one another; but it's precisely within that suspension that your own identity – whether as a person or a historian – tends to reside. Self-doubt must always precede self-confidence. It should never, however, cease to accompany, challenge, and by these means discipline self-confidence.

III.

Machiavelli, who so strikingly combined both qualities, wrote *The Prince*, as he immodestly informed Lorenzo de' Medici, 'considering that no greater gift could be made by me than to give you the capacity to be able to understand in a very short time all that I have learned and understood in so many years and with so many hardships and dangers for myself'. The purpose of his representation was distillation: he sought to 'package' a large body of information into a compact usable form so that his patron could quickly master it. It's no accident that the book is a short one. What Machiavelli offered was a compression of historical experience that would vicariously enlarge personal experience. 'For since men almost always walk on paths beaten by others…a prudent man should always…imitate those who have been most excellent, so that if his own virtue does not reach that far, it is at least in the odor of it.'[13]

This is as good a summary of the uses of historical consciousness as I have found. I like it because it makes two points: first, that we're bound to learn from the past whether or not we make the effort, since it's the only database we have; and second, that we might as well try to do so systematically. E H Carr elaborated on the first of these arguments when he observed in *What Is History?*

that the size and reasoning capacity of the human brain are probably no greater now than they were five thousand years ago, but that
very few human beings live now as they did then. The effectiveness
of human thinking, he continued, 'has been multiplied many times
by learning and incorporating…the experience of the intervening
generations'. The inheritance of acquired characteristics may not
work in biology, but it does in human affairs: 'History is progress
through the transmission of acquired skills from one generation to
another.'[14]

As his biographer Jonathan Haslam has pointed out, Carr's idea
of 'progress' in twentieth-century history tended disconcertingly
to associate that quality with the accumulation of power in the
hands of the state.[15] But in *What Is History?* Carr was making a
larger and less controversial argument: that if we can widen the
range of experience beyond what we as individuals have encountered, if we can draw upon the experiences of others who've had to
confront comparable situations in the past, then – although there
are no guarantees – our chances of acting wisely should increase
proportionately.

This brings us to Machiavelli's second point, which is that we
should learn from the past systematically. Historians ought not to
delude themselves into thinking that they provide the *only* means
by which acquired skills – and ideas – are transmitted from one
generation to the next. Culture, religion, technology, environment
and tradition can all do this. But history is arguably the best
method of enlarging experience in such a way as to command the
widest possible consensus on what the significance of that experience might be.[16]

I know that statement will raise eyebrows, because historians so
often and so visibly disagree with one another. We relish revision-
ism and distrust orthodoxy not least because were we to do otherwise we might put ourselves out of business. We have, in recent
years, embraced postmodernist insights about the relative character of all historical judgments – the inseparability of the observer

from that which is being observed – although some of us feel that we've known this all along.[17] Historians appear, in short, to have only squishy ground upon which to stand, and hence little basis for claiming any consensus at all on what the past might tell us with respect to the present and future.

Except when you ask the question: compared to what? No other mode of inquiry comes any closer to producing such a consensus, and most fall far short of it. The very fact that orthodoxies so dominate the realms of religion and culture suggests the absence of agreement from below, and hence the need to impose it from above. People adapt to technology and environment in so many different ways as to defy generalisation. Traditions manifest themselves so variously across such diverse institutions and cultures that they provide hardly any consistency on what the past should signify. The historical method, in this sense, beats all the others.

Nor does it demand agreement, among its practitioners, as to precisely what the 'lessons' of history are: a consensus can incorporate contradictions. It's part of growing up to learn that there are competing versions of truth, and that you yourself must choose which to embrace. It's part of historical consciousness to learn the same thing: that there is no 'correct' interpretation of the past, but that the act of interpreting is itself a vicarious enlargement of experience from which you can benefit. It would ill serve any prince to be told that the past offers simple lessons – or even, for some situations, any lessons at all. 'The prince can gain the people to himself in many modes,' Machiavelli wrote at one point, 'for which one cannot give certain rules because the modes vary according to circumstances.' The general proposition still holds, though, that 'for a prince it is necessary to have the people friendly; otherwise he has no remedy in adversity.'[18]

This gets us close to what historians do – or at least, to echo Machiavelli, should have the odour of doing: it is to interpret the past for the purposes of the present with a view to managing the future, but to do so without suspending the capacity to assess the particular circumstances in which one might have to act, or the relevance of past actions to them. To accumulate experience is not to endorse its automatic application, for part of historical consciousness is the ability to see differences as well as similarities, to understand that generalizations do not always hold in particular circumstances.

That sounds pretty daunting – until you consider another arena of human activity in which this distinction between the general and the particular is so ubiquitous that we hardly even think about it: it's the wide world of sports. To achieve proficiency in basketball, baseball or even bridge, you have to know the rules of the game, and you have to practise. But these rules, together with what your coach can teach you about applying them, are nothing more than a distillation of accumulated experience: they serve the same function that Machiavelli intended *The Prince* to serve for Lorenzo de' Medici. They're generalizations: compressions and distillations of the past in order to make it usable in the future.

Each game you play, however, will have its own characteristics: the skill of your opponent, the adequacy of your own preparation, the circumstances in which the competition takes place. No competent coach would lay out a plan to be mechanically followed throughout the game: you have to leave a lot to the discretion – and the good judgment – of the individual players. The fascination of sports resides in the intersection of the general with the particular. The practice of life is much the same.

Studying the past is no sure guide to predicting the future. What it does do, though, is *prepare* you for the future by expanding experience, so that you can increase your skills, your stamina – and, if all goes well, your wisdom. For while it may be true, as Machiavelli estimated, 'that fortune is the arbiter of half our actions', it's also the case that 'she leaves the other half, or close to it, for us to govern.' Or, as he also put it, 'God does not want to do everything.'[19]

Two representations of the same subject, one
from a particular time and the other for all time.
The Arnolfini Portrait, Jan van Eyck, 1434,
and *The Lovers*, Pablo Picasso, 1904.

IV.

Just how, though, do you present historical experience for the purpose of enlarging personal experience? To include too little information can render the whole exercise irrelevant. To include too much can overload the circuits and crash the system. The historian has got to strike a balance, and that means recognising a trade-off between literal and abstract representation. Let me illustrate this with two well-known artistic portrayals of the same subject.

The first is Jan van Eyck's great double portrait The Arnolfini Portrait, from 1434, which documents a relationship between a man and a woman in such precise detail that we can see every fold in their clothes, every frill in the lace, the apples on the windowsill, the shoes on the floor, the individual hairs on the little dog, and even the artist himself reflected in the mirror. The picture is striking because it's as close as anything we have to photographic realism four hundred years before photography was invented. This can only have been 1434, these can only have been the Arnolfinis, and they can only have been painted in Bruges. We get the vicarious experience of a distant but very particular time and place.

Now, contrast this with Picasso's *The Lovers*, an ink, watercolour, and charcoal drawing dashed off quickly in 1904. The image, like van Eyck's, leaves little doubt as to the subject. But here everything has been stripped away: background, furnishings, shoes, dog, even clothes, and we're down to the essence of the matter. What we have is a transmission of vicarious experience so generic that anyone from Adam and Eve onward would immediately understand it. The very point of this drawing is the abstraction that flows from its absence of context, and it's this that projects it so effectively across time and space.

Switch now, if you can manage this leap, to Thucydides, in whom I find both the particularity of a van Eyck and the generality of a Picasso. He is, at times, so photographic in his narrative that he could be writing a modern screenplay. He tells us, for example, of a Plataean attempt against a Peloponnesian wall in which the soldiers advanced with only their left feet shod to keep from slipping in the mud, and in which the inadvertent dislodgment of a single roof tile raised the alarm. He places us in the middle of the Athenian attack on Pylos in 425 BC just as precisely as those remarkable first moments of Steven Spielberg's film *Saving Private Ryan* place us on the Normandy beaches in 1944 AD He makes us hear the sick and wounded Athenians on Sicily 'loudly calling to each individual comrade or relative whom they could see, hanging upon the necks of their tent-fellows in the act of departure, and following as far as they could, and when their bodily strength failed them, calling again and again upon heaven and shrieking aloud as they were left behind'.[20] There is, in short, an authenticity in this particularity that puts us there at least as effectively as one of Michael Crichton's time machines.

But Thucydides, unlike Crichton, is also a great generaliser. He meant his work, he tells us, for those inquirers 'who desire an exact knowledge of the past as an aid to the interpretation of the future, which in the course of human things must resemble if it does not reflect it'. He knew that abstraction – we might even call it a Picasso-like separation from context – is what makes generalizations hold up over time. Hence he has the Athenians telling the rebellious Melians, as a timeless principle, that 'the strong do what they can and the weak suffer what they must': it follows that the Athenians 'put to death all the grown men whom they took, and sold the women and children for slaves, and subsequently sent out five hundred colonists and inhabited the place themselves'. Thucydides also shows us, though, that there are exceptions to any rule: when the Mityleneans rebel and the Athenians conquer them, the strong suddenly have second thoughts and send out a second ship to overtake the first, countermanding the order to slaughter or enslave the weak.[21]

This tension between particularisation and generalisation – between literal and abstract representation – comes with the territory, I think, when you're transmitting vicarious experience. A simple chronicle of details, however graphic, locks you into a particular time and place. You move beyond it by abstracting, but abstracting is an artificial exercise, involving an oversimplification of complex realities. It's analogous to what happened in the world of art once it began, in the late nineteenth century, to depart from the literal representation of reality. One objective of impressionism, cubism and Futurism was to find a way to represent motion from within the necessarily static media of paint, canvas and frame. Abstraction arose as a form of liberation, a new view of reality that suggested something of the flow of time.[22] It worked, though, only by distorting space.

Historians, in contrast, employ abstraction to overcome a different constraint, which is their separation in time from their subjects. Artists coexist with the objects they're representing, which means that it's always possible for them to shift the view, adjust the light or move the model.[23] Historians can't do this: because what they represent is in the past, they can never alter it. But they can, by that means of the particular form of abstraction we know as *narrative*, portray movement through time, something an artist can only hint at.

There's always a balance to be struck, though, for the more time the narrative covers, the less detail it can provide. It's like the Heisenberg uncertainty principle, in which the precise measurement of one variable renders another one imprecise.[24] This, then, is yet another of the polarities involved in historical consciousness: the tension between the literal and the abstract, between the detailed depiction of what lies at some point in the past, on the one hand, and the sweeping sketch of what extends over long stretches of it, on the other.

V.

Which brings me back to Friedrich's *Wanderer*, a representation in art that comes close to suggesting visually what historical consciousness is all about. The back turned towards us. Elevation from, not immersion in, a distant landscape. The tension between significance and insignificance, the way you feel both large and small at the same time. The polarities of generalisation and particularisation, the gap between abstract and literal representation. But there's something else here as well: a sense of curiosity mixed with awe mixed with a determination to find things out – to penetrate the fog, to distil experience, to depict reality – that is as much an artistic vision as a scientific sensibility.

Harold Bloom has written of Shakespeare that he created our concept of ourselves by discovering ways – never before achieved – of portraying human nature on the stage.[25] John Madden's film *Shakespeare in Love*, I think, shows that actually happening: it's the moment when Romeo and Juliet has been staged for the first time, when the last lines have been delivered, and when the audience, utterly amazed, sits silently with eyes bulging and mouths agape, unsure of what to do. Confronting uncharted territory, whether in theatre, history or human affairs, produces something like that sense of wonder. Which is probably why *Shakespeare in Love* ends at the beginning of *Twelfth Night*, with Viola shipwrecked on an uncharted continent, filled with dangers but also with infinite possibilities. And as in Friedrich's *Wanderer*, it's a backside we see in that last long shot as she wades ashore.

Now, I don't mean to suggest that historians can, with any credibility, play the role of Gwyneth Paltrow. We're supposed to be solid, dispassionate chroniclers of events, not given to allowing our emotions and our intuitions to affect what we do, or so we've traditionally been taught. I worry, though, that if we don't allow for these things, and for the sense of excitement and wonder they bring to the doing of history, then we're missing much of what the field is all about. The first lines Shakespeare has Viola speak, filled as they are with intelligence, curiosity and some dread, could well be the starting point for any historian contemplating the landscape of history: 'What country, friends, is this?'

1. Paul Johnson, *The Birth of the Modern: World Society, 1815–1830* (HarperCollins, New York, 1991). For his discussion of the painting, see 998.
2. John Ziman, *Reliable Knowledge: an Exploration of the Grounds for Belief in Science* (Cambridge University Press, New York, 1978), 21. See also the economist Brian Arthur's short history of modern science as metaphor, quoted in M Mitchell Waldrop, *Complexity: the Emerging Science at the Edge of Order and Chaos* (Simon & Schuster, New York, 1992), 327–30; as well as Stephan Berry, 'On the Problem of Laws in Nature and History: a Comparison', *History and Theory*, 38 (1999), 122, 132.
3. Edward O Wilson, *Consilience: the Unity of Knowledge* (Knopf, New York, 1998), 26. R G Collingwood, *The Idea of History* (Oxford University Press, New York, 1956), 95–96, provides a sophisticated defence of the use of metaphor, based on Kantian philosophy.
4. For a comparable artistic metaphor, see Walter Benjamin, *Illuminations*, tr. Harry Zohn (Schocken Books, New York, 1968), 257.
5. Connie Willis, *Doomsday Book* (Bantam, New York, 1992); Michael Crichton, *Timelines* (Knopf, New York, 1999).
6. Marc Bloch, *The Historian's Craft*, tr. Peter Putnam (1953; Manchester University Press, Manchester, 1992), 42.
7. Gertrude Stein, *Picasso* (Beacon Press, Boston, 1959), 50. See also Gertrude Stein, *Everybody's Autobiography* (Exact Change, Cambridge, MA, 1993), 197–98; and, for a similar point about the writings of Garrett Mattingly, R J Evans, *In Defence of History* (Granta, London, 1997), 143–44.
8. J K Rowling's description of the latter institution in *Harry Potter and the Philosopher's Stone* (Bloomsbury, London, 1997) will resonate with students at the first two.
9. G R Elton, 'Putting the Past Before Us,' in Stephen Vaughan, ed., *The Vital Past: Writings on the Uses of History*, (University of Georgia Press, Athens, GA, 1985), 42. See also Elton, *The Practice of History* (Crowell, New York, 1967),145–46; and Elton, *Return to Essentials: Some Reflections on the Present State of Historical Study* (Cambridge University Press, Cambridge, 1991), 43–45, 73.
10. Mark Twain, 'Was the World Made for Man?' quoted in Stephen Jay

Gould, *Wonderful Life: the Burgess Shale and the Nature of History* (Norton, New York,1989), 45.

11. See Stephen Jay Gould, Time's Arrow, *Time's Cycle: Myth and Metaphor in the Discovery of Geologic Time* (Harvard University Press, Cambridge, MA, 1987).

12. Niccolò Machiavelli, *The Prince*, tr. Harvey C Mansfield (2nd edn (University of Chicago Press, Chicago, 1998), 4. Collingwood, *The Idea of History*, 59–60, cites Descartes and Kant on the necessity of displacement for historians.

13. Machiavelli, *The Prince*, 3–4, 22.

14. E H Carr, *What Is History?* (1961; 2nd edn, Penguin, New York, 1987) 114. See also Collingwood, *The Idea of History*, 333–34. For three (at the time of writing this text) recent elaborations on this argument, see Jared Diamond, *Guns, Germs, and Steel: the Fates of Human Societies* (Norton, New York,c1999); Robert Wright, *Non-Zero: the Logic of Human Destiny* (Pantheon, New York, 2000); and, from a methodological point of view, Martin Stuart-Fox, 'Evolutionary Theory of History', *History and Theory*, 38 (1999), 33–51.

15. Jonathan Haslam, *The Vices of Integrity: E. H. Carr, 1892–1982* (Versa, New York, 1999). See also Michael Cox, ed., *E. H. Carr: a Critical Appraisal* (Palgrave, New York, 2000), especially 9–10, 91.

16. For a comparable view of the importance of 'consensibility' in science, see Ziman, *Reliable Knowledge*, 3.

17. The point is made in Evans, *In Defence of History*, 103–05; Niall Ferguson, 'Virtual History', 65–66; and Joyce Appleby, Lynn Hunt and Margaret Jacob, *Telling the Truth about History* (Norton, New York, 1994), 216–17. See also Bloch, *The Historian's Craft*, 120–22, and Carr, *What Is History?*, 73, 82.

18. Machiavelli, *The Prince*, 40–41.

19. Machiavelli, *The Prince*, 98, 103.

20. Thucydides, *The Peloponnesian War*, tr. Richard Crawley (Random House, New York, 1982) 164–65, 240, 472.

21. Thucydides, *The Peloponnesian War*, 98, 103.

22. See, on this point, Stephen Kern, *The Culture of Time and Space, 1880–1918* (Harvard University Press, Cambridge, MA, 1983), especially 21–24, 87, 119.

23. Collingwood, *The Idea of History*, 246. Tracy Chevalier's novel *Girl with a Pearl Earring* (Dutton, New York, 1999) makes the point elegantly with respect to Johannes Vermeer.

24. Michael Frayn provides as clear an explanation as is probably possible for a lay audience in the postscript to his play *Copenhagen* (Methuen, London, 1998), 98. See also, within the text of the play, 24 and 67–68, as well as Collingwood, *The Idea of History*, 141; and for the problem as it relates to the 'new' social history, Appleby, Hunt and Jacob, *Telling the Truth aboutHistory*, 158, 223.

25. Harold Bloom, *Shakespeare: Invention of the Human* (Penguin Putnam, New York, 1998).

MARGARET MACMILLAN:
THE POWER OF HISTORY

If I were writing about the uses and abuses of history today, I would probably produce a much longer book given the many ways that history crops up in so many of our public debates and our concerns, and how much we argue about the past and its impact on the present. I would have trouble, too, choosing among all the many examples that the past decades and the present have produced of the uses and abuses of history. I sometimes wonder if we talk so much today about history as a judge or guide, or worry about being on its 'right side', because other sources of authority – religions, tradition, political leaders – have dwindled in our estimation.

In the 21st century, history still shapes our identities and our relations with others, which is why many citizens and governments continue to take it so seriously. We have seen renewed history wars, for example in the United States, with angry scenes at school board meetings where parents clash over what their children should be taught about American history. In a number of countries, governments are attempting to mould citizens through what schools teach about the past, such as Hungary's National Core Curriculum, where great victories are featured and defeats ignored.

The past is used more than ever to support claims in the present. Britain is being challenged to confront and make good the sins of the past from the slave trade to imperialism. Governments and institutions draw up policies to rectify inequalities among groups which, it can be argued, are the consequences of past discrimination and injustice. Around the world Indigenous peoples are bringing out old treaties or collecting oral histories to demand restitution for land or the loss of their culture. Nikole Hannah-Jones, the creator of the *New York Times'* '1619 Project' which argues that slavery and racism were the foundation on which the United States was founded, says, 'the project is an argument for reparations. You can't read it and not understand that something is owed.'[1]

Two other things strike me about history as it is being used today. First, the resurgence of iconoclasm. We have seen it often before, of course, in the destruction of the icons in the Byzantine Empire, the smashing of statues and stained glass in the Puritan Revolution, or much more recently the removal of statues of Lenin or Stalin throughout central Europe after 1989. Yet erasing symbols of the past has a new urgency, particularly in many democratic countries. Monuments which once were simply part of the landscape have become targets for those who want to show how much they deplore certain aspects of the past. The statute of the slave owner Sir Edward Colston has fallen in Bristol and that of the great imperialist Cecil Rhodes may go in Oxford, while across the American South monuments to Civil War generals are being removed. In Canada and Scotland, roads and squares named after Lord Dundas are being changed on the grounds that he supported slavery.

Secondly, history increasingly is used as a justification for territorial claims. China claims dominance in the South China Sea on the basis of history and is taking steps such as occupying rocky shoals to enforce its argument. Its claim to Taiwan also rests on history. Even though since 1945 there has been a general, largely unspoken international consensus that borders should not be changed by force, history is being used as an excuse to breach that. In 2014, when Russia seized Crimea by force, President Putin argued that it had been part of Russia since the time of Catherine the Great and should never have been incorporated into Ukraine in 1954. He subsequently sent his forces into the east of Ukraine, virtually annexing much of the Donbass. In late 2021, Russia started to move up significant forces to its borders with Ukraine. Putin's justification for trying to bring Ukraine under Russia's sway is largely based on history. Ukrainians and Russians, he claimed in a long essay published in the summer of 2021, have always been one people, only divided from each other by the machinations of outsiders. As he has said repeatedly, Ukraine must never become a member of NATO and indeed the countries of the former Eastern bloc such as Poland, the Czech Republic and Hungary should never have been allowed to join. The West, Putin claims, lied to Russia at the end of the Cold War and promised in 1990 that NATO would not move 'one inch eastwards'. It may not matter if his history is wrong if it persuades his own domestic opinion and enough of the rest of the world.

While I would use different examples in writing my book today and perhaps emphasise different issues, I would not change the title. We can use history well to better understand ourselves, others, and our world and its challenges. And we need to be wary of how much history can be abused. So I would still offer the same contents warning: handle with care.

Toronto, January 2022

Editor's note: Written one month before Russia's invasion of Ukraine.

---

1.   Darcel Rockett, '5 minutes with Nikole Hannah-Jones, the architect
     behind the New York Times' "1619 Project"' (10 Oct 2019),
     https:www.chicagotribune.com/lifestyles/ct-life-nikole-hannah-jones-1619-
     project-20191009-20191010-m3rym2hxyncj7ihcn67q2gekdq-story.html

MARGARET MACMILLAN
THE USES AND ABUSES OF HISTORY

History as a Guide and Friend

History, as we have seen, is much used, but is it much use? On that, opinion has been divided ever since the fifth century BC when Thucydides declared that the past was an aid in the interpretation of the future. Gibbon regarded it rather as 'the register of the crimes, follies, and misfortunes of mankind'. A J P Taylor, contrarian in this as in so much else, believed that history was an enjoyable exercise that had no use whatsoever beyond helping us to understand the past. 'Of course,' he said dismissively, 'you can learn certain commonplaces, such as that all men die or that one day, the deterrent, whatever it may be, will fail to deter.' Perhaps it is best to ask if we would be worse off in the present if we did not know any history at all. I think the answer would probably be yes.

To begin with, history helps us to understand: first, those with whom we have to deal and second, and this is equally important, ourselves. As the American historian John Lewis Gaddis put it, it is like looking in a rear-view mirror: if you only look back, you will land in the ditch, but it helps to know where you have come from and who else is on the road. One of the factors that made the Cold War so dangerous to both sides is that they simply did not understand each other. The Americans took the Soviets' rhetoric at face value and took for granted that their leadership really was out for world domination. The Communists, whether Soviet or Chinese, assumed that capitalist countries such as the United States and Britain would inevitably come to blows in their increasingly ruthless struggle for profits, and the winner would then attack Communism.

Michael Howard, the British military historian, despaired of the attitude that prevailed in Washington for much of the Cold War: 'The Soviet Union was seen in the United States as a force of cosmic evil whose policy and intentions could be divined simply by multiplying Marxist dogma by Soviet military capacity.' Many of the Soviet goals were, in fact, traditional Russian ones, dictated by geography and history. Russia has few natural borders and has suffered repeated invasions; its governments have always sought buffer zones to protect the Russian heartland. When Stalin took the opportunity to move into Eastern Europe at the end of World War II, he was as much motivated by a desire for security as he was by ideology and by national pride; Russian national pride, for all that he came from Georgia. During the war he created new military honours named not after Marx or Lenin but great czarist generals and admirals. One evening at the end of the war, after a dinner with his intimates, Stalin spread a map out on a table and happily pointed to all the old czarist territory he had regained.

American strategists also assumed that the Kremlin was prepared to risk all-out war in pursuit of its goals. In fact, given the Soviet Union's huge losses in both world wars and the enormous job of reconstruction that lay before it after 1945, it was equally likely that the Soviet leadership would do a great deal to avoid war. We now know that was, in fact, often the case. When Nikita Khrushchev put nuclear-tipped missiles into Cuba in 1962, part of his motive was to let the United States feel what it was like to fear direct attack and the devastation of its land, something the Soviets knew so well. And when he pulled them out, it was because he did not want to live through another even more deadly war than the two he had already survived.

[...]

If you do not know the history of another people, you will not understand their values, their fears, and their hopes or how they are likely to react to something you do. There is another way of getting things wrong, and that is to assume that other peoples are just like you. Robert McNamara has spent much of his life trying to come to terms with what went wrong with the American war in Vietnam. In his memoir, *In Retrospect*, he came up with lessons he hoped future leaders might heed. 'We viewed,' he says in one, 'the people and leaders of South Vietnam in terms of our own experience. We saw in them a thirst for – and a determination to fight for – freedom and democracy.' The United States failed equally to understand the determination of the North Vietnamese. Time and again, it assumed that it could raise the pain it was inflicting on the north to the point where its leadership would do a cost–benefit analysis and decide that the time had come to throw in the towel. Yet these were the people who had fought for seven years to defeat the French. 'Our misjudgements of friend and foe alike,' McNamara concluded sadly, 'reflected our profound ignorance of the history, culture, and politics of the people in the area and the personalities and habits of their leaders.'

It is not a lesson the Bush White House of recent years appeared to have learned. You believe in studying reality, a senior adviser said contemptuously to the journalist Ron Suskind in 2002. 'That's not the way the world really works any more', he continued. 'We're an empire now, and when we act, we create our own reality. And while you're studying that reality – judiciously, as you will – we'll act again, creating other new realities, which you can study too, and that's how things will sort out. We're history's actors…and you, all of you, will be left to just study what we do.' If the White House had studied reality a bit more, the president might not have used the word *crusade* two days after September 11 to refer to how he intended to deal with terrorists. Muslims, even moderate ones, tend to react viscerally to being reminded of much earlier attacks from the West. If some attention had been paid to reality, the

United States and the United Kingdom might not have been quite so surprised that the Iraqis failed to welcome them or appreciate foreign control of their oil.

[…]

Knowing history can help us avoid lazy generalizations as well. It would be folly to take on the Serbs, said the pessimists as Yugoslavia was falling to pieces; look how they fought off the Nazis in World War II. In fact, if you look more closely at what happened, as an American army researcher did a few years ago, the German divisions were not the cream of the German army and most were seriously under strength. And looking even further back, at World War I, the Serbian army was defeated and forced into exile and Serbia itself was occupied until the end of the war by German and Austrian troops. Afghanistan comes in for much the same rhetoric of despair; it has never, the pundits say, been conquered by an outside power. That would come as a surprise to Alexander the Great as much as to Genghis Khan. Today, we hear that the Western powers cannot interfere in the increasing chaos and misery of Zimbabwe because it would only rouse memories of colonialism among the population. It is a pity that such considerations were not taken into account when the United States went into Vietnam or, more recently, into Iraq.

History can also help in self-knowledge. The favourable light we so often see ourselves in can cast shadows as well. Canadians see themselves as a benevolent force in the world; they tend to overlook the fact that, among rich countries, ours has provided a surprisingly small amount of foreign aid in past decades. We pride ourselves on being peacekeepers; Canadians often do not know that Canada fought in four major wars in the twentieth century, from the South African one to the Korean. Americans tend to think of themselves as a peace-loving people who have never willingly picked a fight. 'Our country has never started a war,' President Ronald Reagan said in 1983. 'Our sole objective is deterrence, the strength and capability it takes to prevent war.' That is not how it might seem to the Mexicans or the Nicaraguans or the Cubans or, today, to the Iraqis.

George Santayana's famous 'Those who cannot remember the past are condemned to repeat it' is one of those overused dictums politicians and others offer up when they want to sound profound. It is true, however, that history reminds us usefully about the sorts of situations that have caused trouble in the past. Allied leaders in World War II were determined that, this time, Germany and the other Axis powers would not be able to claim that they had never been defeated on the battlefield. Allied policy was one of unconditional surrender, and Germany, Japan and Italy were all occupied at the end of the war and serious attempts, largely successful, were made to remodel their societies so that they would no longer be undemocratic and militaristic. When someone complained that such treatment was like the savage peace the Romans imposed on Carthage, the American general Mark Clark remarked that no one heard much of the Carthaginians these days.

When President Franklin Delano Roosevelt and other Western leaders were starting to plan for the post-war world, they had the recent past very much in their minds in other ways. They wanted to build a robust world order that would prevent the world from sliding, yet again, into another deadly conflict. The interwar years had been unstable ones, partly because the League of Nations had not been strong enough. Key powers, the United States in particular, had not joined or, like Germany and Japan, had dropped out. This time, Roosevelt was determined that the United States should be a member of the new United Nations. He was also prepared to do a good deal to keep the Soviet Union in. What had been a precariously balanced international order was put under further strain in the 1930s by the Great Depression, which encouraged countries to turn inward, throwing up tariff walls to protect their own workers and their own industries. What may have made sense for individual nations was disastrous for the world as a whole. Trade and investment dropped off sharply and national rivalries were exacerbated. To avoid that happening again, the Allies, with the Soviet Union's grudging acquiescence, created the economic institutions known collectively as the Bretton Woods system. The World Bank, the International Monetary Fund and the International Trade Organisation (this last did not materialise as the World Trade Organisation until much later) were designed to provide stability to the world's economy and to encourage free trade among nations. How much difference these all made to the international order after 1945 will always be a matter of debate, but the world did not get a repeat of the 1930s.

[...]

Two groups in particular in our society have always taken history seriously as a guide. People in business and the military want to know what their chances of success are if they take a particular course of action. Will they lose their investment or, in the case of the military, the war? One way of narrowing the odds is to study similar situations in the past. That, after all, is what the case study is. Why was the Edsel a failure and the Volkswagen a success? In 2008, as the effects of the sub-prime mortgage crisis rippled through the world's economies, market analysts turned to history to try to determine how long the downturn in the stock markets would last. (In the past fifty years, apparently, we have had nine bear markets and they have lasted on average just over a year.)

Investors may experience several bad patches; the military often never see a war, and it is the rare senior officer who fights in more than one. It is possible to practise war, in exercises, but those cannot replicate the actuality of war itself, with its real violence and death, and in all its confusion and unpredictability. So history becomes all the more important a tool for learning about possible reasons for victory and, equally important, for defeat. The weapons and uniforms are very different, yet military academies and staff colleges still find some utility in setting their students to studying the Peloponnesian Wars or Nelson's battles. After exercises and actual campaigns, the military study what happened and try to draw lessons from it. The official histories of World War II were meant to help governments and their military learn from successes and mistakes.

[…]

History can help us to be wise; it can also suggest to us what the likely outcome of our actions might be. There are no clear blueprints to be discovered in history that can help us shape the future as we wish. Each historical event is a unique congeries of factors, people or chronology. Yet by examining the past we can get some useful lessons about how to proceed and some warning about what is or is not likely to happen. We do have to be careful to cast our gaze as widely as possible. If we look only for the lessons that reinforce decisions we have already made, we will run into trouble. In May 1941, as warnings poured in from all quarters that the Germans were getting ready to attack the Soviet Union, Stalin refused to listen to them. He did not want a war with Germany because he knew just how ill-prepared the Soviet Union was. And so he persuaded himself that Germany would not move until it had made peace with Great Britain. 'Hitler and his generals are not so stupid as to fight at the same time on two fronts,' Stalin told his inner circle. 'That broke the neck of the Germans in the First World War.' A month later, German troops overran the Soviet forces that had been told to take up defensive positions back from the borders. Stalin could have found other lessons from the past if he had wanted. Hitler had shown himself a gambler before when he had seized Austria and Czechoslovakia. His rapid and stunning victory over France in 1940 had served only to convince him that he was always right. Moreover, he had made no secret of his long-term goal of moving eastward to obtain territory for the German people.

History, if it is used with care, can present us with alternatives, help us to form the questions we need to ask of the present, and warn us about what might go wrong. In the 1920s, T E Lawrence criticised the British government for its involvement in what had become the new country of Iraq:

The people of England have been led in Mesopotamia into a trap from which it will be hard to escape with dignity and honour. They have been tricked into it by a steady withholding of information. The Baghdad communiques are belated, insincere, incomplete. Things have been far worse than we have been told, our administration more bloody and inefficient than the public knows. It is a disgrace to our imperial record and may soon be too inflamed for any ordinary cure. We are today not far from a disaster. Our unfortunate troops, Indian and British, under hard conditions of climate and supply, are policing an immense area, paying dearly every day in lives for the willfully wrong policy of the civil administration in Baghdad but the responsibility, in this case, is not on the army which has acted only upon the request of the civil authorities.

[…]

If we had wanted to know in 2002 how Iraqis would respond to a foreign invasion and occupation, then we might have found some instructive ideas and warnings in the British experience there or in other occupations, such as the ones of Germany and Japan at the end of World War II. When we are trying to make sense of a situation (and may well have more information than we can absorb) to come to a decision, we use analogies to try to discern a pattern and to sort out what is important from what is not. If we decide that a dictator, say Saddam Hussein, is rather like Hitler, then that suggests ways we might want to deal with him. If the economic crisis of 2008 is like the start of the Great Depression, then governments and central banks may decide to stimulate the economy. If it is more like the crash of the dot.com bubble in the 1990s, it may be wiser to treat it as a short-term correction in the markets. We may not always get the right analogy, but we are almost certainly bound to try to use one.

[…]

Analogies from history must, of course, be treated with care. Using the wrong one not only can present an oversimplified picture of a complex situation in the present but can also lead to wrong decisions. After September 11, it became fashionable, especially among neoconservatives, to talk about how the West finds itself engaged in World War IV. Norman Podhoretz, a leading neocon thinker, argued that the Cold War was really World War III and that now, after a too-brief period of peace in the 1990s, we are engaged in an equally massive and deadly struggle against Islamic fundamentalism.

[…]

Another analogy that has had a good airing over the years is Munich, shorthand for the appeasement policies the democracies used in the 1930s with the dictators in a vain effort to prevent another war. Named after the Munich conference of 1938 when Britain and France agreed that Hitler's Germany should have the German-speaking parts of Czechoslovakia, Munich has become the symbol of weakness in the face of aggression. If the democracies had stood up to Hitler, better still even earlier in the 1930s before Germany had rearmed, and to Italy and Japan, they could have prevented, so the critics of appeasement say, World War II. That is a matter for historians and others to argue over.

What is undeniable is that the Munich analogy has had a strong hold over statesmen and -women ever since and has been applied liberally to justify a whole range of policies.

[…]

When the new Bush administration focused on Iraq after September 11, it too used the Munich analogy, but its relevance was much more tenuous. In the 1930s, Hitler headed one of the most powerful countries in the world. As the American scholar Jeffrey Record put it, 'Hitler was neither weak nor deterred; Saddam was nothing but weak and deterred.' In 1991, Operation Desert Storm was over almost before it started. In 2003, it took three weeks to defeat Hussein completely with a relatively small force; four years to defeat

Hitler with the combined forces of the British Empire, the Soviet Union and the United States. Although both the Bush and Blair administrations tried to portray Hussein as a menace to the world in the lead-up to the invasion, their evidence, as we now know, that he possessed weapons of mass destruction was flimsy at best. And the assertion that Hussein was somehow allied with Osama bin Laden was absurd to anyone who knew history. Hussein was a secularist, Bin Laden a religious fanatic. There had been no love lost between the two men and, indeed, Bin Laden had repeatedly called upon Iraqis to overthrow Hussein. We can learn from history, but we also deceive ourselves when we selectively take evidence from the past to justify what we have already made up our minds to do.

[…]

Conclusion

History can help us to make sense of a complicated world, but we must always be careful if it offers explanations that are too simple. And we must always be prepared to consider alternatives and to raise questions. We should not be impressed when our leaders say firmly 'history teaches us' or 'history will show that we were right'. They can oversimplify and force inexact comparisons just as much as any of us can. Even the very clever and the powerful (and the two are not necessarily the same) go confidently off down the wrong paths. It is useful, too, to be reminded, as a citizen, that those in positions of authority do not always know better.

In 1893, the British naval commander in the Mediterranean, Vice-Admiral George Tryon, decided to take personal command of the summer naval manoeuvres. When he ordered an about-face of two parallel rows of battleships, his officers tried to point out that there would be a collision. A relatively simple calculation demonstrated that the combined turning circles of the ships were greater than the distance between them. While his officers watched in dismay, his flagship *Victoria* was rammed by the *Camperdown*. Tryon refused to believe that the damage was serious and ordered the nearby vessels not to send their lifeboats. The *Victoria* sank, taking him and 357 sailors with it. The Charge of the Light Brigade, when the flower of the British cavalry rode straight into the mouths of the Russian guns, is an equal reminder of human folly, not just of Lord Cardigan, who led the charge, but of the system that allowed him to be in command. As David Halberstam, the American journalist, said in the last piece he ever wrote, 'It is a story from the past we read again and again, that the most dangerous time for any nation may be that moment in its history when things are going unusually well, because its leaders become carried away with hubris and a sense of entitlement cloaked as rectitude.'

Nor should we think that we will always be right. As John Carey, the distinguished British man of letters, puts it, 'One of history's most useful tasks is to bring home to us how keenly, honestly and painfully, past generations pursued aims that now seem to us wrong or disgraceful.' Think of the arguments over the position of the earth and the sun, of the conviction, apparently supported by science, that so many Victorians had that there were superior and inferior races, or the calm assumptions even a few decades ago that women and Black people could not make good engineers or doctors.

If the study of history does nothing more than teach us humility and scepticism, then it has done something useful. We must continue to examine our own assumptions and those of others and ask, where's the evidence? Or, is there another explanation? We should be wary of grand claims in history's name or those who claim to have uncovered the truth once and for all. In the end, my only advice is use it, enjoy it, but always handle history with care.

PHILIP ZELIKOW:
FABLE AND FACT

Developing the Historical Mind

INTRODUCTION BY BOB QU

The tortoise and the hare. The ant and the grasshopper. The boy who cried wolf.

In just a few words, each of these phrases conjures up a story, a moral, and a whole set of normative judgments. The language of parable is a powerful one. It should be no surprise, then, that it is the language most commonly used in historical analogies. This language distils history into easily digestible lessons, neatly packaged for consumption by decision makers.

The problem is that, for the most part, the lessons are wrong. Flattened of detail, they have a troublesome tendency to lead astray those who assume naively that history repeats itself. No amount of regressions, correlations or simplifications can produce a precept that is universally reliable. History does not, it turns out, follow such rules, and past performance is no guarantee of future results.

So how, then, is one supposed to learn from it? In 'The Nature of History's Lessons', Philip Zelikow outlines a much more rewarding method for turning history into usable knowledge. This is a method that embraces historical complexity as an asset to be used, not a nuisance to be simplified away. It is a method that focuses on the importance of human choices as a motive force of change, and the importance of reconstructing these choices with as much texture as possible.

Critically, this reconstruction needs to avoid being the proverbial man looking for his keys under the lamp post, and recreate the decisions *not* taken as well as the one that ultimately was. These decisions are constrained by what scientists might call 'degrees of freedom', a term the historian Rebecca Scott has borrowed to capture 'the process by which, as values for different elements of a system are fixed on each of its dimensions, the range of possibilities for the total state of the system narrows'.[1] At each stage, there are certain choices available – certain 'degrees of freedom'. As choices are made, some possibilities close off – but also new ones open, giving way to the next set of choices.

This method is not designed to produce easy answers. Rather, it is designed to improve our ability to understand the problems that confront us in the present through studying the problems of the past. If anything, it is a method that helps produce more *questions*, since knowing the right questions to ask in any given situation is infinitely more useful than having a bank of canned answers. These questions, driven by our historical study, can illuminate options in the present that we may not have considered, or drive better evaluation of the ones that we have.

Zelikow is well-positioned to understand how history can provide meaningful lessons for policymakers. His method is one developed over a long, distinguished, and somewhat eclectic career. A high-level debater in college, his natural first career was as a promising young lawyer, cutting his teeth in criminal and civil rights law in Texas in the late 1970s and early 1980s. But in 1982, he made the fateful decision to return to graduate school with an eye towards working in foreign policy, enrolling in the Fletcher School at Tufts University. In 1984, with a master's degree and the beginnings of a dissertation, he began teaching at the Naval Postgraduate School in Monterey.

Then came another turn: in 1985, he was offered entry into the Foreign Service. It was a heady time to be in diplomacy; the Cold War was entering a new phase of unprecedented possibilities, spurred by the new leader of the Soviet Union, Mikhail Gorbachev. By 1989, Zelikow had been seconded to the staff of the National Security Council (NSC), where, with another young staffer named Condoleezza Rice, he had the opportunity to observe and shape the decisions that ushered in the end of the Cold War.[2]

Zelikow's stint on the NSC was followed by a move that was just as formative: teaching at the Harvard Kennedy School of Government, where he worked with Richard Neustadt and Ernest May, becoming close friends with both. Momentarily relieved from the pressure cooker of government, here was an opportunity to reflect on how policy was made and executed, and what history could offer to improve that process.[3] In 1998, he left Harvard for the University of Virginia (UVA), where he helped develop the Miller Centre of Public Affairs into one of the country's premier institutions for the study of decision-making at the highest level of American government.

It was while at UVA that Zelikow was called upon to undertake his most challenging duty yet: executive director of the 9/11 Commission. He began work in January 2003, in a nation still reeling from the shock of the attacks of September 2001. Through the next year and a half, he steered the commission through an investigative effort that was breathtaking in its scope, all amidst a fraught political environment and non-trivial frictions with the White House. Its final report received both literary acclaim and bestseller status – uncommon for a work of history, nearly unprecedented for a government report. More importantly, it helped the country understand and cope with its collective trauma, and spurred legislation that has helped ensure that the US has suffered no major terrorist attacks by Muslim extremists in the intervening two decades. As Zelikow points out, people tend to notice the things that *do* happen; rarely do they notice the things that don't. Especially in this case, we should.

Zelikow is a leading example of what it means to cross between worlds at the highest levels. He has worked at all levels of American government, without sacrificing one iota of his scholarly rigour as a historian. His most recent book, on the secret peace negotiations between Britain, Germany and the US in 1916, is a major contribution to the historiography of the First World War.[4] At the same time, he co-wrote a report on Taiwan for the Council on Foreign Relations that is a masterclass in how to integrate historical thinking into policymaking in a useful and analytically rigorous way.[5]

Through these dual careers, he has personally modelled how these modes of thinking can complement and refine each other. The method he has developed takes a good deal more effort than simply treating history as a lode of parables to be mined. It requires active analysis, empathy and a command of historical detail – in other words, hard work. The moral of the story is that the results are all the more rewarding for it.

Annapolis, MD, March 2022

---

1. R J Scott, *Degrees of Freedom: Louisiana and Cuba after Slavery* (Harvard University Press, Cambridge, MA, 2005), 10.
2. These decisions have been ably recounted in P Zelikow and C Rice, *To Build a Better World: Choices to End the Cold War and Create a Global Commonwealth* (Twelve, New York, 2019).
3. Some of the fruits of that work include P Zelikow and C Rice, *Germany Unified and Europe Transformed: a Study in Statecraft* (Harvard University Press, Cambridge, MA, 1995); P Zelikow, *The Kennedy Tapes: Inside the White House During the Cuban Missile Crisis* (Harvard University Press, Cambridge, MA, 1997); and, eventually, G Allison and P Zelikow, *Essence of Decision: Explaining the Cuban Missile Crisis* (rev. ed.; Longman, New York, 1999) and P Zelikow, E May, and the Harvard Suez Team, *Suez Deconstructed: an Interactive Study in Crisis, War, and Peacemaking)* Brookings Institution, Washington, DC, 2018).
4. P Zelikow, *The Road Less Traveled: the Secret Battle to end the Great War, 1916–1917* (Public Affairs, New York, 2021).
5. R Blackwill and P Zelikow, 'The United States, China, and Taiwan: a Strategy to Prevent War', Council on Foreign Relations Special Report No. 90, February 2021.

PHILIP ZELIKOW
THE NATURE OF HISTORY'S LESSONS

What happened in the past can be very complicated, as is life. One way to learn from the past is to simplify the record of what happened: distil and distil until, at last, the final essence offers a usable generalisation, a parable.

Another way is to accept how difficult it is to understand the past, that foreign country. Accept the complexity and try to master some of it: struggle and struggle until, at last, growing comprehension provides the satisfactions of knowledge.

This essay argues for the second way. Embrace the complexity! It is the more reliable path to knowledge.

More than two hundred years ago Edmund Burke warned princes not 'to be led into error' by a false use of history. 'Not that I derogate from the use of history,' Burke assured his audience, 'it is a great improver of the understanding, by showing both men and affairs in a great variety of views. From this source much political wisdom may be learned.'

But Burke cautioned his listeners as strongly as he could that the wisdom came not from converting history into 'precept'. Historical study could be 'an exercise to strengthen the mind, as furnishing materials to enlarge and enrich it'. But there is great danger if it is used as 'a repertory of cases and precedents'. If history is thus misused, 'better would it be that a statesman had never learned to read'.[1]

Yet the way of simplification is so much easier. The reader or listener does not need much background information or special training. The simpler the points, the easier they are to explain. And many simple generalizations do have obvious value along with the value of being, well, obvious.

The second way, however, offers greater and more lasting yields. In medicine, for example, there have long been many rewards from studying gross anatomy, examining what anyone could see. It might have seemed simpler not to bother with microscopes. After all, few people had microscopes or could use them. And it may have seemed as if so much could be understood without bothering about the significance of things like germs, genes or molecules. Hardly anyone could see those things; they were hard to understand.

[…]

Only closer examinations that welcome complexity can decode such strange doings. Only thus can we prepare ourselves through such vicarious experiences for the ways these challenges actually arise, the kinds of faces they really present. The path of complexity is difficult, but the rewards include more lifelike fitness training for the intellect.

Seen through a historian's microscope the world can be far stranger and more fascinating than anything that can be seen by the unaided eye.

[…]

Life Cycles of Historical Belief
Those who consider the matter for a minute or two realise that historical reasoning is as common in public affairs as oxygen is in water. People catalogue past experiences to inform their present choices. Sometimes they do this quickly, intuitively, half consciously. Every so often someone will even try to do this more formally, taking an inventory of or classifying the past experiences in

some scheme through which they think they can estimate future probabilities.

These habits are natural for humans. Histories envelop us. Personal, institutional, local, national, tribal: there are so many stories. But history does not automatically convert itself into usable stories.

Lived moments are jumbles of experiences and impressions: heels clicking on the marble floor of a palace while hastening to the next meeting. Hot, dry air and the smell of smoke blasting through the helicopter amid the thudding roar of the rotors. The startling comment by the Defense Secretary, punctuating another tedious meeting in a handsome, sterile, windowless White House conference room while everyone pretends not to notice. The blood-soaked Humvee from which the dead and wounded have just been extracted. Struggles to stay awake, jet-lagged, three days into the latest transcontinental hopscotch. The memo full of concentrated passion, filed unread, and a week later forgotten.

Later, recalled for 'history', anecdotes – once the stuff of corridor talk and dinner parties – are reassembled. The detritus of related documents are collected, if they can be found. Composing, simplifying, the melange is turned into a narrative, and the narrative becomes a tellable, recallable story.

From such stories, further distilled, the usual path is to further simplification. The more universally known the stories, the more they supply common reference points. So distil, distil. Turn the stories into a shorthand for instant communication. Shared narratives about history become tokens of identity. When this work is done, often only a word or a phrase is needed, the invoked narrative becomes the word picture that is worth a thousand other words. One need do no more, in the right context, than pronounce *appeasement, Pearl Harbor, Vietnam, Great Depression, 9/11, American empire* or *Iraq* and, presto, a whole world view can instantly be shared.

This progression can be diagrammed:

History, unrefined…
Relatable stories…
Mass cult shorthand…
Flowing into judgment

And the cumulative judgments flow again into history's stream.

This cycle is a human process. Historical beliefs are not inherited in some national DNA. They are transmitted through culture and environment, learned through experience, direct or vicarious. One person's experience is idiosyncrasy. A nation's common trauma is a touchstone.

[…]

Some reigning lessons become so well known, taught and retaught that they ossify into one of the small number of master scripts that can mould public policies across whole eras. These ageing shibboleths can go on for quite a long time until they are overthrown. There is a similar evolution that happens in the life cycle of paradigms in science.[2] When the shibboleths are finally toppled, it may not be because the historians have got better or the history readers have become wiser. More often, some new collective trauma – a war, a depression – has displaced them, swept them away with compelling needs for fresh social constructions.

[…]

How to Dissect Choices

[…]

So May was always inclined to put policy episodes under a microscope. His consistent objective was to examine more carefully the beliefs that drove the action. Where did these beliefs come from? Through what filters did people see the situation they were in?

Of course, May found that these prisms were usually constructed from historical experiences, personal or vicarious. He analysed how people use analogies. He studied public opinions, how they arise. He looked harder at the nature of the press and opinion leaders and where they derived their views. Such investigations also led him to a lifelong interest in the way governments prepare and use intelligence assessments.[3]

To dissect sovereign beliefs, the analyst has to cut them up. One hundred and fifty years ago, Alexis de Tocqueville speculated about the course of the February 1848 overthrow of France's monarchy. De Tocqueville had been an important participant in the turmoil and, as he reflected later on the experience, 'The Revolution of February, in common with all other great events of this class, sprang from general causes, impregnated, if I am permitted the expression, by accidents.'

Regarding 'general causes', he nicely summarised, 'Antecedent facts, the nature of institutions, the cast of minds and the state of morals'. But de Tocqueville was drawn back to those small causes. He had begun by calling them 'accidents', but they were more than that.

De Tocqueville despised the 'narrow' theories, 'false beneath their air of mathematical exactness', that would not grant the disproportionate importance of small events. Vexed with 'the writers who have invented these sublime theories in order to feed their vanity and facilitate their work', he insisted that many important historical events could only be explained by accidental circumstances, to the extent that they could be explained at all.

Yet, de Tocqueville added, these accidental circumstances were not, in fact, really accidents at all. 'Chance' was really 'that tangle of secondary causes which we call chance, for want of the knowledge how to unravel it.'[4]

In biology, specimens are cut up for examination under the microscope; they are 'fixed' in lifelike condition and sliced, 'sectioned'. In history, where the specimens are metaphysical, the 'sectioning' of the specimens is conceptual. The analyst can try to identify the sequence of distinct choices and the possibilities attendant at each stage. So as May and I tried to learn how to dissect choices for the historian's microscope, we eventually found it was helpful to cut them up into three sorts of interacting judgments.[5]

1. Value judgments. What do they care about?
2. Reality judgments. What is going on?
3. Action judgments. What can they do?

Each of these kinds of judgment constantly inform and interact with the others. It is hard to overstate the importance of this point.

For instance, suppose your friend Alex cares about the crisis in Syria because he feels that he, or perhaps his country, can do something about it. This would be a value judgment influenced by an action judgment. Or suppose Alex pays more attention to what is going on in Syria because he cares about it. This would be a reality judgment influenced by a value judgment. In turn, he might be more likely to act – even the act of voicing an opinion – because he felt he knew more about what was going on. Thus an action judgment is influenced by a reality judgment. There are many possible combinations.

[…]

Generalizations, Hard and Soft
Inside every judgment there are generalizations. These are the pithy summaries, the relatable stories refined from the raw ore of history.

A hard generalisation is the kind that presents a factual statement. This thing happened; that was its cause. For example, someone could say that America suffered a great depression that began in 1929. This depression was caused by constrained monetary policies, a pinched supply of money, which in turn was induced by adherence to the gold standard.

A soft generalisation is not so direct and it is not so factual. It might be a presumption. It might be an inference. For example, having considered the depression story, someone could say that in a financial crisis, leaders should loosen monetary policies. This loosening will counter the ebb of ordinary credit flows.[6] That is a kind of soft generalisation, the kind that attempts to build a bridge, a bridge from the past to the future.

A hard generalisation is one that says: 'This *is* true, you may rely on it.' A soft generalisation says, in effect, 'This *might* be true.'

Historians rarely do enough to harden the first kind of generalisation – about what happened and why in a particular case. They can usually do very well, professionally, by suggesting a fresh and sufficiently plausible additional explanation. They can succeed in academia by making what might have already seemed a soft account softer still.

Social scientists, on the other hand, often do too much to harden soft inferences. They can do well in academia by discovering systematic patterns and probabilities.

These two professional tendencies combine in unfortunate ways. The historians are weakening, not shoring up, the factual foundation. The social scientists are eagerly building ever higher towers atop this soft soil.

[…]

The Representation of Experience

To generalize about how people behaved in a historical episode we need to be able to relate to recognisable experiences of actual people, not relate to choices made by symbols or abstractions. That is the purpose of trying to dissect their choices. One could, for example, classify the Soviet invasion of Afghanistan in 1979 as an example of 'power-seeking'. And one could also classify the American invasion of Iraq in 2003 as an example of more 'power-seeking'. But these labels are so detached from an actual description of the interactive judgments in play that they become empty and artificial.

In other words, 'If appropriate representations [of reality] come presupplied [by labels], the hard part of the analogy-making task has already been accomplished.'[7] The similarity comes from attaching similar labels. Histories are bound to be profoundly misrepresented whenever they are extracted from their original context of place and time.[8] A battery of historians demonstrated the enormity of these distortions, using as their test case a well-known treatment of 'neorealism' and 'power-seeking' by the political scientist, John Mearsheimer.[9]

The more a writer converts an episode from detailed historical narrative into a typecast or generic event, the more the connection to a description of reality will be lost.[10] What actually happened gets converted into 'irreducibly alien terms'. Indeed, such high concepts become so far divorced from natural realism that there is a case, the philosopher Willard Van Ormond Quine explained, for barring such terms from our language as meaningless. Quine would consign them to the limbo of 'nonsentences' in order to prevent 'an encroachment of coherence considerations upon standards of truth'.[11]

[…]

Generic laws only explain generic situations. There are few of these. 'Things are made to look the same only when we fail to examine them too closely.'[12]

Meanwhile, some social scientists have become more dogmatic in prescribing more novel statistical or scientific methods for their disciplines – though, as I have discussed, these representations of reality are founded on philosophical principles far less secure than those underlying physics or biology.[13]

King, Keohane and Verba concede that there is a mix of systematic and non-systematic variables in historical episodes. This produces what they call, quoting Paul Holland, the 'fundamental problem of causal inference'. To contain this problem, students are taught methods to try and separate, pull out, the variables that are systematic from those that are not.

The philosophical problem, though, as William James once put it, is that 'novelty, as empirically found, doesn't arrive by jumps and jolts, it leaks in insensibly'.

[…]

These philosophical problems may help explain why, in the case of scholarship on international relations, 'several decades of empirical research…has failed to produce a single meaningful lawlike generalization in international relations research'. As prominent scholars of international relations theory John Mearsheimer and Stephen Walt have acknowledged, 'None of the existing IR theories has enormous explanatory or predictive power.'[14] Or, as Achen put it, 'we have had difficulty with the real task of quantitative work – the discovery of reliable empirical generalizations.'[15]

Statistical methods *can* produce important inferences about well-structured mass behaviour. Take voting in American elections: there are many thousands or millions of data points, and research can validly look for likely patterns among further thousands or millions of such occurrences. In other words, quantitative methods seem useful in analyzing quantitative behaviour. But the aggregate behaviour of governments, or individual leaders, is not as easily converted into such large and comparable data sets.[16]

[…]

History as a Re-enactment of Possibilities

To untangle what did happen, to unpack de Tocqueville's 'accidents', the historian needs to consider too what was *not* chosen, what did *not* happen. And why.

Fixing only on what actually did happen in a past experience is what can convert the past episode from a menu of mind-opening options into a mind-closing axiom.[17] These axioms are almost always carried in the vehicle of some historical analogy, relating a present circumstance to some past outcome.[18]

Instead, 'history teaches us about human nature and our future best choices by teaching us about *possibilities* rather than *regularities*'.[19] We should not try too hard to use the past to build dikes 'to contain [the] future's uncertainty', because 'the more we trust these "dikes", the less they provoke our curiosity'.[20]

Naturally, people are tempted to boil down their experiences into pat lessons. One former Secretary of Defense even published a little book of his aphorisms, *Rumsfeld's Rules.* They seem like the sort of lessons that Isaiah Berlin once scorned as 'a very thin, generalized residue, and one far too unspecific to be of much help in a practical dilemma'.[21]

But knowledge, like life, really does not need to be reduced to such precepts in order to communicate it. In fact, such distillations impair real communication of the knowledge by divorcing it even further from the contextual details that enrich the experience with real-life educational nutrients.[22]

Historical literature, like fictional literature, can be a path to understanding human nature and the possibilities that lie within it. What can be learned from any literature at all? People read stories because they are drawn to the depictions of people in situations. What was it like? How did they respond?

British historian and philosopher Robin Collingwood found in history a form of instructive re-enactment. Consider Julius Caesar's decision to take his army 'cross the Rubicon' and challenge his Roman Republic. To understand Caesar's choice, to add it to the reservoir of knowledge about human nature and political judgments, Collingwood urged the use of critical judgment to enter Caesar's world with whatever evidence could be found: 'This implies envisaging for himself the situation in which Caesar stood, and thinking for himself what Caesar thought about the situation and the possible ways of dealing with it.'[23]

The work of the historian in this case is not mere reproduction or description. To offer insight, 'this re-enactment is only accomplished…so far as the historian brings to bear on the problem all the powers of his own mind and all his knowledge of philosophy and politics. It is not a passive surrender to another's mind; it is a labour of active and therefore critical thinking'. Such critical analysis 'is not something secondary to tracing the history of it. It is an indispensable condition of the historical knowledge itself.'[24]

The method I recommend has only a couple of steps. The first is to break the puzzling decision/outcome into its sequence of successive, different choices.

Then, for each, consider the possibilities attendant at each stage. Not only might this method improve the explanation; it makes the explanation a good deal more interesting for the reader. This is a kind of counterfactual analysis, constrained by contemporary evidence of plausibility. It analyzes roads not taken to see the turns that were.[25]

[…]

Hindsight is not 20/20. In fact, as the 9/11 Commission report observed, hindsight blinds. It blinds because the path of what happened is so brightly lit that all the other possibilities are cast even more deeply into shadow. History lessons should try to overcome that blindness.

My method does dig a little deeper into a critical set of choices, requiring more of an effort to recover – to 're-enact', in Collingwood's term – the choices as perceived by people at the time. The method will certainly be recognisable to those who study social history, where some of the best scholars have painstakingly reconstructed microhistories to recover the uncertainties and curious little worlds of the past. But the study of a White House in any particular presidency is not so different from the study of a medieval village. Each has its folkways, its routines and its votaries.

Political judgment, for Isaiah Berlin, was a 'gift' that seemed to mean that 'above all, a capacity for integrating a vast amalgam of constantly changing, multicolored, evanescent, perpetually overlapping data, too many, too swift, too intermingled to be caught and pinned down and labeled like so many individual butterflies'. To Berlin it was this knowledge of the varied capacities inherent in a situation that great statesmen seem to have 'in common with the great psychological novelists'.[26]

To revisit these strange other worlds in the past, breaking down how some puzzling choices actually happened, does require some imagination. Our senses now sharpened to the 'changing, multicolored, evanescent' beliefs that once held sway, we are that much better equipped for the amalgam we encounter every day.

---

1. Burke then elaborated that: 'This method [turning history into precepts] turns [statesmen's] understanding from the object before them, and from the present exigencies of the world, to comparisons with former times, of which, after all, we can know very little and very imperfectly; and our guides, the historians, who are to give us their true interpretation, are often prejudiced, often ignorant, often fonder of system than of truth.' From Burke's remarks on the policy of the Allies with respect to France, begun in October 1793, in *The Writings & Speeches of Edmund Burke*, vol. 4 (Little, Brown & Company, Boston, MA, 1901), 468. I am indebted to Hiroshi Nakanishi of Kyoto University for calling my attention to this address by Burke.

2. See Thomas Kuhn, *The Structure of Scientific Revolutions*, (University of Chicago Press, Chicago, IL, 1962; repr. 2012), especially 1–9.

3. A seminal essay is Ernest May, 'The Nature of Foreign Policy: the Calculated versus the Axiomatic,' *Daedalus*, 91 (1962), 653–67. This was followed by *'Lessons' of the Past: the Use and Misuse of History in American Foreign Policy* (Oxford University Press, Oxford, 1973). Neustadt and May published illustrations and suggestions for better use of historical reasoning in *Thinking in Time: the Uses of History for Decision Makers* (Free Press, New York, 1986). May's groundbreaking study of public and elite opinion, an aim that was unfortunately veiled by his book's title, is *American Imperialism: a Speculative Essay* (Imprint, Chicago, IL, 1991); originally published in 1968, the 1991 edition added a useful introductory essay. Some illustrations of the way May turned his inquiry to the study of intelligence assessments are *Knowing One's*

Enemies: Intelligence Assessment before the Two World Wars (Princeton University Press, Princeton, NJ, 1986); Philip Zelikow, *Dealing with Dictators: Dilemmas of U.S. Diplomacy and Intelligence Analysis, 1945–1990* (Cambridge University Press, Cambridge, 2006); and key aspects of his landmark study of the 1940 fall of France, *Strange Victory: Hitler's Conquest of France* (Hill and Wang, New York, 2000).

4. The definitive French text is Alexis de Tocqueville, *Oeuvres Completes*, xii: *Souvenirs*, ed. J P Mayer (Gallimard, Paris, 1964); for an English translation, see *Recollections*, ed. J P Mayer and tr. by Alexander Teixeira de Mattos (Greenwood, Westport, CT, 1948), 67–68. Stephen Jay Gould, *Wonderful Life: the Burgess Shale and the Nature of History* (W.W. Norton & Company, New York, 1989), 289–90, makes a rather similar point in its discussion of natural history: 'Invariant laws of nature impact the general forms and functions of organisms; they set the channels in which organic design must evolve. But the channels are so broad relative to the details that fascinate us! The physical channels do not specify arthropods, annelids, mollusks, and vertebrates, but, at most, bilaterally symmetrical organisms based on repeated parts. The boundaries of the channels retreat even further into the distance when we ask the essential questions about our own origin… When we set our focus upon the level of detail that regulates most common questions about the history of life, contingency dominates and the predictability of general form recedes to an irrelevant background.'

5. May and I developed this template for our teaching during the 1990s. It is based on a framework persuasively articulated by a British lawyer, philosopher and occasional public servant named Geoffrey Vickers in his book *The Art of Judgment* (1965; SAGE Publications, Beverly Hills, CA, 1995). An early elaboration of this template appears in the introduction May and I wrote for our edited volume, Dealing with Dictators, 1–17.

6. For scholars who work on theories of history, this distinction between particular explanations and generalised inference is sometimes described, following Wilhelm Windelband's 1894 formulation, as a contrast between 'idiographic' and 'nomothetic' sciences. There is a temptation even among historians to slight rigorous explanation of particular episodes as they embed their descriptions in some more universal generalization. See Allan Megill, *Historical Knowledge, Historical Error: a Contemporary Guide to Practice* (University of Chicago Press, Chicago, IL, 2007), 83–88. Megill is trying to attract more respect for particular descriptions. He also rightly urges historians to use more rigorous methods in explaining these particulars.

7. David Chalmers, Robert French and Douglas Hofstadter, 'High-Level Perception, Representation, and Analogy,' in Douglas Hofstadter and the Fluid Analogies Research Group, Fluid Concepts and Creative Analogies: Computer Models of the Fundamental Mechanisms of Thought (Basic Books, New York, 1995), 182.

8. Drawing from arguments made centuries ago by Immanuel Kant, see Ernest R May, 'History-theory-action,' *Diplomatic History*, 18 (1994), 589–603.

9. See Ernest May, Richard Rosecrance and Zara Steiner, eds., *History and Neorealism* (Cambridge University Press, Cambridge, 2010).

10. See William James, *Essays in Radical Empiricism*, ed. R. B. Perry (Longmans, New York, 1912; 1938), 40–41. James's principle of 'radical empiricism' argues that philosophers should only debate 'things definable in terms drawn from experience'. See also William James, *The Meaning of Truth: a Sequel to 'Pragmatism'* (Cambridge, Cambridge University Press, 1909; 1978), 6–7. A corollary principle is one of 'natural realism'. See Hilary and Ruth Anna Putnam, 'What the Spilled Beans Can Spell: the Difficult and Deep Realism of William James', *Times Literary Supplement* (21 June 1996). The James position is attacked by some as holding that it makes all reality either subjective or instrumental, as suits the observer, but such an attack misunderstands James. For more elaboration, especially on the 'interpenetration', not indistinguishability, of fact and value, see Hilary Putnam, *Pragmatism: An Open Question* (Cambridge University Press, Cambridge, 1995), 7–23; see also John Searle, *The Construction of Social Reality* (Free Press, New York, 1995).

11. W V Quine, *Pursuit of Truth*, rev. ed. (rev. edn. Cambridge University Press, Cambridge, 1990), 98. The artificiality of the categories is a necessary by-product of the quest to produce scientific generalizations in a manner that emulates the natural sciences. In the natural sciences, the use of sharply defined categories of phenomena is justified because the method is 'applied only to carefully chosen subject matter under highly contrived conditions'. The social domain also has categories, but their delineations are rarely as sharp as those in which 'deductive argument can be applied with reasonable certainty. Without such categories, conventional scientific method is hamstrung'. John Ziman, *Reliable Knowledge: an Exploration of the Grounds for Belief in Science* (Cambridge University Press, Cambridge, 1978), 160–62. See also the related argument in the works of Nelson Goodman, especially *Fact, Fiction, and Forecast* (4th edn., Cambridge University Press, Cambridge, 1983). Hence the search for measurable choices of a highly repetitive character (in voting, for example, or in consumer purchases) among utility theorists in the social sciences. For a sceptical view of the possibilities, see Ziman, Reliable Knowledge, 158–86.

12. Nancy Cartwright, *How the Laws of Physics Lie* (Oxford University Press, Oxford, 1983), 13, 11, 19. 'Fundamental laws,' she adds, 'do not govern objects in reality, they govern only objects in models.' See 18, 109. For her discussion of the descriptive weaknesses of one of the strongest law-like generalizations in all of natural science, the law of gravity, see 56–67.

13. See John Lewis Gaddis, 'History, Science, and the Study of International Relations,' in Ngaire Woods, ed., *Explaining International Relations since 1945*

(Oxford University Press, Oxford, 1996).

14. John Mearsheimer and Stephen Walt, 'Leaving Theory Behind: Why Hypothesis Testing Has Become Bad for IR,' Faculty Research Working Paper RW13-001 (John F. Kennedy School of Government, Cambridge, MA, 2013)

15. Some, like C H Achen, think the 'democratic peace' hypothesis may have made the cut; see 'Toward a New Political Methodology,' : Microfoundations and Art', *Annual Review of Political Science*, 5 (2002), 423–50. Though, in that illustration, other critics of statistical uses have pointed out that the democratic peace hypothesis was more about correlation. There had actually not been good tests for any particular theory about just what the cause might be that explained these correlations. Bear Braumoeller and Anne Sartori, 'The Promise and Perils of Statistics in International Relations', in *Models, Numbers, and Cases: Methods for Studying International Relations* (University of Michigan Press, Ann Arbor, MI, 2004), 134. On the democratic peace hypothesis Achen also acknowledges that it would be helpful if the labellers knew better just 'what "democracy" meant' in the way they typecast different governments across history; Achen, 'Toward a New Political Methodology', 442.

16. Philosophically, the compared behaviours must be scientifically homogeneous. This comparability will be greatest in situations that are epistemically objective, so that the facts making up the situation do not depend for their existence on a particular person's attitude toward them, and where the reactions to the situations have a structured, repetitive quality that can be measured in ways that are also epistemically objective; see the discussion of ontological and epistemic objectivity in Searle, *Construction of Social Reality*, 7–23. This is why, in the natural sciences, there is so much emphasis on physical observations that can be perceived identically by independent observers. Ziman, *Reliable Knowledge*, 42–56; see also Ziman's earlier point (28) that the science of physics actually defines itself as being concerned only with those aspects of reality that are amenable to mathematical analysis. On the problems of using statistical associations to assess more subjective behavior, see, for example, Albert S Yee, 'The Causal Effects of Ideas on Policies,' *International Organization*, 50 (1996), 69, 71–76.

17. See May, 'The Nature of Foreign Policy'.

18. May, later joined by Richard Neustadt, thus naturally moved from writing about axioms to writing about analogies. He eventually came to a position that comprehensively rejected the use of historical cases to establish structured, predictive models of probable behavior; see May, 'History-theory-action'. On the temptations and dangers of analogical reasoning, see also Yuen Foong Khong, *Analogies at War: Korea, Munich, Dien Bien Phu, and the Vietnam Decisions of 1965* (Princeton University Press, Princeton, NJ, 1992); Robert Jervis, *Perception and Misperception in International Politics*

(Princeton University Press, Princeton, NJ, 1976); and Daniel Kahneman, Paul Slovic and Amos Tversky, *Judgment under Uncertainty: Heuristics and Biases* (Cambridge University Press, Cambridge, 1982).

19. Michael Scriven, 'Causes, Connections and Conditions in History', in William Dray, ed., *Philosophical Analysis and History* (Greenwood, Westport, CT, 1978), 250, emphasis in the original. For the sympathetic argument that generalizations about regularities can yield plausible association, but that these produce only a hypothesis of appropriateness, see Rex Martin, *Historical Explanation: Re-enactment and Practical Inference* (Cornell University Press, Ithaca, NY, 1977). Megill, *Historical Knowledge*, 154–55, posits that 'the only view of explanation that works for historians is one that focuses on counterfactuality and that allows the regularity criterion to recede into the background'. I am not sure that most historians adhere to this view, however.

20. Bertrand de Jouvenel, The Art of Conjecture, tr. Nikita Lary (Basic books, New York, 1967), 47. To similar effect, see Harvey Brooks, 'The Typology of Surprises in Technology, Institutions, and Development,' in W C Clark and R E Munn, eds, *Sustainable Development of the Biosphere* (Cambridge University Press, Cambridge, 1986), especially 326, 335–39.

21. Isaiah Berlin, 'On Political Judgment', *New York Review of Books* (3 October 1996), 26, 27.

22. Michael Polanyi, *Personal Knowledge: Towards a Post-Critical Philosophy* (rev. edn. University of Chicago Press, Chicago, IL, 1962), 33–37, 49–65, 69–124; see also Max Black, *Models and Metaphors: Studies in Language and Philosophy* (Cornell University Press, Ithaca, NY, 1962), 25–47, 219–43.

23. Robin G. Collingwood, *The Idea of History*, ed. Jan van der Dussen (Cambridge University Press, Cambridge, 1994; essays originally published between 1936 and 1940), 215.

24. Collingwood, *Idea of History*. See also William Dray, *History as Re-enactment: R.G. Collingwood's Idea of History* (Oxford University Press, Oxford, 1995).

25. As Megill, *Historical Knowledge, Historical Error*, 153, notes, 'In imagining how things might have been different, the restrained counterfactualist tries to understand better what actually did happen.' Following on work by James Fearon more than twenty years ago, Robert Jervis, 'Counterfactuals, Causation, and Complexity', in hilip E Tetlock and Aaron Belkin, eds., *Counterfactual Thought Experiments in World Politics* (Princeton University Press, Princeton, NJ, 1996), 309–16, notes that there is also growing acceptance in political science that 'counterfactuals can alert us to the possible operation of dynamics and pathways that we would otherwise be prone to ignore.' Jervis, 'Counterfactuals', 308.

26. Berlin, 'On Political Judgment,' 27–28.

FRANCIS J GAVIN: HISTORY FOR POLICY?

INTRODUCTION BY THE AUTHOR

This essay was based on a lecture I gave in Washington DC, in 2016, just two days after Donald Trump's surprising election as the 45th president of the United States. I was exhausted – like millions of Americans, I watched with deep anxiety as the *New York Times* reporter Nate Silver's online probability needle shifted unexpectedly against Senator Hillary Clinton during the late evening of 8 November 2016. The bottle of expensive, chilled champagne, acquired to celebrate the election of the first female president with my wife and daughters, stayed unopened.

As I walked from my hotel to the lecture on 10 November, it was as if Washington was in mourning. No-one was smiling, or even looking up, and everything seemed like it was moving in slow motion.

Arriving at the School of Advanced International Studies before the lecture, everyone still seemed shaken. A friend of mine who was a high-level national security official from the Obama administration came from the White House to attend. When I saw him in a long hug with a colleague who was a well-known neoconservative who had served in the George W Bush administration, I thought it was a sign of the end of days. This lecture was an attempt to explain how historical thinking could make sense of things that, in real time, made little sense to us.

It was not the first nor the last time that history would provide, if not comfort, then perspective on contemporary events. I have attempted, throughout my academic and teaching career, to separate my scholarly assessments and personal political beliefs. This was hard to achieve in November 2016, as I thought then – and continue to believe – that Donald Trump was both unqualified to be president and an especially poisonous political actor. Still, thinking historically reminded me that the world takes uncertain, unpredictable paths, and often the true drivers of what matters are deeper forces – and not necessarily those that dominate cable television news programmes or the front page of the newspapers. It also reminded me that deeply contested, polarised, even ugly politics had been a character of American elections since the founding – perhaps none uglier than the battle between John Adams and Thomas Jefferson to replace George Washington in 1800. The 2016 election and its outcome were less unprecedented than we wanted to believe.

Since writing this essay, I have tried to think more about what it means to think historically, or to develop a historical sensibility. It is not always easy. Unlike other disciplines or epistemologies, the study of – and efforts to use – history can be frustrating. History offers no predictions, it dismisses efforts to make generalisations over space or time, and it promotes complexity over parsimony. Ask a historian for an answer, and they are likely to respond: 'It's complicated.' History offers no off-the-shelf lessons, and indeed, it is likely to criticise those who rustle through the past like a grab bag, seeking the insight or historical example that best suits them.

History is often abused, at times for unwarranted nostalgia, and at its worst to fuel bitter resentments. Its own identity as a discipline is often uncertain, as history seems unsure of whether it is a part of the social sciences or the humanities. Unlike the social sciences, historians are often unclear about why they choose the historical questions they research and what their assumptions are about historical agency and causality. As Peter Novick chronicled over

30 years ago in his masterpiece, *That Noble Dream*, the profession of history fought viciously amongst itself over the question of whether an objective past exists and whether it can be accessed and presented to the world. Unlike social sciences such as economics and political science, history has been uncertain as to whether and how to engage the state and other institutions of power. In a world drowning in data and new technologies, the study of the past seems old-fashioned, even irrelevant. For these and many other reasons, university enrolments in history courses and programmes have dropped precipitously in the United States since the 1970s.

Despite these challenges, I believe that thinking historically provides powerful and unique insights into understanding and navigating a complex world. As I try to explain in this essay, it is especially comforting to decision makers having to make consequential choices about an unknowable and uncertain future. It induces humility, epistemological modesty and an appreciation and understanding, if not acceptance, of diverging temporal, cultural and geographical perspectives. These are qualities that are much needed in this complex, confusing world.

Washington, DC, July 2022

FRANCIS J GAVIN
THINKING HISTORICALLY

A Guide for Strategy and Statecraft

On 22 November 2011, the *New York Times* published a short Errol Morris op-doc, 'Umbrella Man', to mark the 48th anniversary of the assassination of President John F Kennedy in Dallas, Texas. In the six-and-a-half-minute video, Morris employs his Interrotron camera to create his trademark intimacy while interviewing Josiah 'Tink' Thompson, author of a book on the famous Zapruder film titled *Six Seconds in Dallas*. Backed by a haunting score arranged by minimalist composer Arvo Pärt and spliced with snippets of video from the fateful day, Thompson tells the mysterious story of a shadowy figure called the 'umbrella man'.

Who was the umbrella man? During the Zapruder and other films and photographs from that fateful day in Dallas, an upright figure can be seen standing on the so-called grassy knoll, holding an open black umbrella, moments before the assassin's bullets are fired into the president's motorcade. The image is arresting: the weather in Dallas was sunny and warm.

The sight of a lone man under the umbrella would have been disconcerting even if Kennedy's murder had not taken place right in front of the man seconds later. As Thompson says: 'In all of Dallas, there appears to be exactly one person standing under an open black umbrella… Can anyone come up with a non-sinister explanation for this?'

Writing in the *New Yorker's* 'Talk of the Town' series in December 1967, writer John Updike suggested that the mystery surrounding who the umbrella man was and what he was doing on the grassy knoll 'dangles around history's neck like a fetish'. None of the authorities — the Dallas police, the Secret Service, the FBI or the Warren Commission — ever located or even identified him or could explain his baffling appearance.

Given all the mystery surrounding the assassination, it was only natural to concoct all sorts of ominous motives animating this sinister character and his menacing umbrella. Who was the umbrella man and what was he doing? Clearly he played a key role in the conspiracy to kill the president. Perhaps the umbrella was a gun device of some sort, firing a flechette into the president's throat. Or maybe it was a way to signal to the actual shooter to go ahead with the assassination. Into the vacuum of uncertainty, it did not seem unreasonable to make a causal link between the shadowy figure, his umbrella, and the fateful events of that day.

Or not. In 1978, Louie Steven Witt reluctantly came forward to the House Select Committee on Assassinations to admit he was the umbrella man and explain himself. In 1963, Witt worked near the Dealey Plaza and took a walk every day during his lunch hour: 'I was going to use this umbrella to heckle the President's motorcade… Being a conservative-type fellow, I sort of placed him in the liberal camp and I was just going to kind of do a little heckling.' The umbrella was a symbolic protest:

It had something to do with the—when the senior Mr. Kennedy was Ambassador to England, and the Prime Minister, some activity they had had in appeasing Hitler. The umbrella that the Prime Minister of England came back with got to be a symbol in some manner with the British people. By association, it got transferred to the Kennedy family, and, as I understood, it was a sore spot with the Kennedy family.[1]

When asked if his protest had anything to do with the president's 'posture with; say, the Russians', Witt replied 'No. No. No. That was not it at all.'

As Thompson points out, this explanation 'is just wacky enough to be true'. It was a stark reminder to anyone looking to the past:

> [I]f you have any fact which you think is really sinister, is really obviously a fact that can point to some sinister under-pinning, hey forget it man. Because you can never on your own think up all the non-sinister, perfectly valid explanations for that fact. A cautionary tale.

Talking about the film, Morris argued that his interest in the assassination emerged from his curiosity about the nature of historical investigation and how to assess evidence:

> Why, after 48 years, are people still quarrelling and quibbling about this case? What is it about this case that has led not to a solution, but to the endless proliferation of possible solutions?

Thompson, summarising Updike, says that historical research may have two parts — the macro level 'where things obey natural laws and usual things happen and unusual things don't happen' and the world 'under a microscope' where you will find 'a whole dimension of weird, incredible things going on'.

This essay is about thinking historically. It is not a history of a particular event, person, place or process. Nor is it strictly a presentation about methodology or how to do historical work effectively. There are many excellent books and articles that can help you become a good historian. What I hope to do is explore something I call 'historical sensibility', which I believe can be a powerful tool to understand and aid making policy, especially foreign, foreign economic, and national security policy.

This may strike many as odd or problematic. First, there are many who assume that the main role of the historian is to unearth, collect and present facts. These facts are then strung together to create a linear narrative, with a clear beginning, middle and end. For many in the 'harder' social sciences, however, this is often seen as little more than storytelling. For true knowledge to appear, many facts have to be collected, shaved down to look alike, then aggregated and analysed to discover generalisable laws of the universe.

To be sure, historians are dogged pursuers of evidence and will travel the world over to find a document or conduct an interview that might shed light on the past. They also construct stories to help us understand worlds gone by. But the facts do not speak for themselves, and the linear, surface narrative that so appeals to our brains is often misleading. Immersing oneself in the past sensitises you to how unusual, unexpected and non-linear history can be. Historians traffic in ironies, unintended consequence, and are often the ambulance chasers of surprise. We live in that gap that Thompson identifies, between a world structured by discoverable natural laws and the dimension where 'weird, incredible things' are happening. We try to make sense of both and bring these worlds together. We try to understand and explain the origins and consequences of seismic events like the assassinations of presidents, while trying to understand if that man with the black umbrella should worry us at all.

What do I mean by a 'historical sensibility'? It goes beyond our notions as to what historians do: collecting evidence, largely from archives, to tell stories about the past. I define it as a familiarity with the past and its powerful and often unpredictable rhythms. A historical sensibility is less a method than a practice, a mental awareness, discernment, responsiveness to the past and how it unfolded into our present world. Developing this sensibility can provide many benefits and insights to the decision-maker facing complex issues and radical uncertainty about the future, not the least of which is humility and prudence. Scholar and policymaker Eliot Cohen has termed it the 'historical mind', which he aptly describes as a 'way of thinking shaped by one's reading of history and by using history as a mode of inquiry and a framework for thinking about problems'.

What are the qualities to this orientation and how can one obtain it? A historical sensibility includes several characteristics. First, this sensibility demonstrates a toleration and even appreciation of uncertainty, surprise and unintended consequences in human affairs, and a comfort with indeterminacy and multi-causal explanations. It makes the unfamiliar familiar, while revealing the unfamiliar in what was believed was well-understood. Furthermore, the historical sensibility provides an empathy (though not necessarily a sympathy) for the past — a willingness to understand historical subjects on their own terms and as products of a particular time and place. This also means developing a consciousness of the powerful hold that history exerts on other cultures, leaders and nations. It also acknowledges the fundamental importance of the perspective of the observer. Though the historian strives for an elusive objectivity, she admits that the who, what and when of the historian matters quite a bit when reconstructing the past. Finally, a historical sensibility recognises and appreciates complexity and, though willing to be proven wrong, casts a skeptical eye on claims of parsimonious models that claim to explain, generalize and predict complex social, cultural and political behaviour. As Gordon Wood eloquently stated,

> To possess a historical sense does not mean simply to possess information about the past. It means to have a different consciousness, a historical consciousness, to have incorporated into our minds a mode of understanding that profoundly influences the say we look at the world.

Or, to quote the historian and policymaker Philip Zelikow:

The path of complexity is difficult, but the rewards include more lifelike fitness training for the intellect. And seen through a microscope, including a historian's microscope, the world can be far stranger and more fascinating than anything that can be seen by the unaided eye.

The best historical work, and the adept historical sensibility, combines and integrates these insights and methods to develop both a better understanding of the past and what it can tell us — and not tell us — about the choices and circumstances we face today. Sympathetic to the concerns of both the social scientist and the decision-maker, I identified nine tools, lessons and advantages a historical approach might provide to a policymaker.

I will not go through them all here. Some are obvious, like 'vertical history', which is assessing the temporal, or short, medium and long term causes of an event, and how they interact. Or 'horizontal history', which looks at the spatial dimension of history, or how different issues are interconnected and related. Another tool of the historical sensibility is teasing out the unintended consequences of actions. When President Eisenhower approved financing for dams and irrigation canals in Afghanistan in the 1950s, he hoped to improve agricultural productivity in a developing nation. He did not aim to make possible the creation of one of the world's largest opium fields.

A less obvious lesson from this sensibility is that history teaches decision makers about something I call 'chronological proportionality', or the weight of historical events. The issues that most grab our attention today and dominate the headlines of newspapers are not likely to be the questions that have the most important long-term consequences. In 1967 and 1968, for example, American newspapers had far more print on the war in Vietnam than on the nuclear non-proliferation treaty, the Six-Day War in the Middle East or political changes in China and Eastern Europe, but what event mattered most to long-term US and global interests from our current perspective? Or consider historian Erez Manela's path-breaking work on US policy towards global efforts to eradicate smallpox during the same period. During the first seven decades of the twentieth century, 300 million people died of smallpox, twice the number killed by wars during the same period. In 1967 alone, two million people fell to smallpox. Less than a decade later, the disease was eradicated. Manela demonstrates how a combination of factors and actors came together, far below the level of high policy but still the result of discrete decisions, to generate policy outcomes that had profound global consequences that few recognised at the time or since.

It is not always clear in real time what matters most, though a historical sensibility can sensitise us to look for real-world consequences in unusual places. Will the recent US presidential election seem like the key issue we faced 30 or 40 years from now, when perhaps some deeper, more fundamental shifts (the climate or demographics, for example) or a completely unexpected event shapes the realities of that future world? We don't know, but it is worth considering.

Relatedly, history conditions decision makers to understand that policy decisions made in world capitals are often far less important in shaping what matters in the world than other, often less visible historical forces. Culture, technology, demographics and geography, for example — all are critical forces that are less pliable to policy than we often think.

My favourite examples are three events that took place within a very short period of time: the sale of the early Apple personal computer, the release of Star Wars — the highest grossing motion picture of all time, and the famous 1976 'Judgment of Paris' in which previously unknown wines from Napa Valley bested established French wines in a blind taste test. In other words, policymakers in Washington in the mid 1970s who were poring over economic data, looking at crime statistics and urban crisis, witnessing political chaos abroad, and fearing a Soviet military behemoth that appeared to be winning the arms race had little reason to be optimistic about the future.

But the future was being made elsewhere and in different ways than policymakers understood, in places like California, where deep and often obscure historical forces were working to transform the US economy, society, technological base and culture in ways that would have profound effects on American power and world history.

A deep historical perspective should also allow the decision-maker to avoid outcome or retrospective bias, or fall into the trap of what I call 'understanding the Third Balkan War'. As former national security adviser Sandy Berger pointed out: 'History is written through a rear-view mirror but it unfolds through a foggy windshield.' If the past is to be of use to policymakers, it must be exploited in a way that avoids what economists call 'the curse of knowledge', or that cognitive bias that emerges that in hindsight, the outcome of a historical event was more predictable than was likely the case. Since we know how past events have turned out, we can easily assume that the causal path that led to the event was inevitable. But most complex and difficult policy choices involve what former Secretary of State Henry Kissinger has called '51/49' decisions: in other words, it is very difficult to know, a priori, whether a difficult policy choice will turn out correctly, even if in retrospect it seemed obvious. This is true for good policies as well as bad, which an immersion in history and an understanding of the past should tell us.

This point relates to why we should be careful not to cherry-pick events from the past or be unaware of horizontal connections, as mentioned above. During what Fredrik Logevall has called the 'long 1964', the Johnson administration made what was, in retrospect, a tragic and unwise decision to escalate America's role in the war in Southeast Asia. Looked at both in hindsight (we know the outcome) and in isolation (just focusing on American policy in Southeast Asia), President Johnson and his advisers look inept.

At the same time, however, the same administration carried out an impressive debate and discussion of how to respond to what was seen as a far greater long-term danger — the People's Republic of China's detonation of an atomic device in October 1964. This process led to a sophisticated and successful nuclear non-proliferation policy that resulted in the 1968 Treaty on the Non-Proliferation of Nuclear Weapons and established the principles that guide US policy to this day. Did the same people who crafted these complex strategies simply lose 20 IQ points when the discussion turned to Vietnam? In fact, making policy in real time is extraordinarily difficult. History should avoid simplistic judgments based solely on future outcomes that could not be anticipated.

Finally, a historical sensibility conditions the observer to recognise perspective. We know that it is important to understand how others view and understand the past. But there is also a temporal aspect to perspective. Let me give you an example: imagine a country that possessed the world's eight- or ninth-largest economy, which was politically dominated by its aggressive military and surrounded by seemingly insurmountable security challenges. Let's say you told the leaders of that country: 'Follow the grand strategy I suggest, and in a very short period of time, from a historical perspective, you will possess the world's second largest economy, built on a thriving technological base, be relatively secure, and develop a healthy democracy and a civic culture that was largely pacifistic.'

A country would have to be crazy to pass up that deal, but it effectively describes a Japan in 1940 compared to 1970. Japan pursued a disastrous war that left its country in ruin. Only decades later, however, the country had transformed its economy, governance and security situation in ways that were the envy of the world. History is full of surprises and unintended consequences, and intent only rarely produces the obvious and desired outcome. Or imagine this exercise: a publisher provides a scholar with 300 pages to write the history of the world between 1945 and 1990.

Even though the subject and end date would remain the same, we can easily imagine that the book chapters might look much different when revised in 2000, 2020 or 2045, than they would when originally published in 1990. History reveals that how you assess the past does not only involve who is involved, but when the question is asked.

Perspective also encourages the policymaker to challenge their assumptions and constantly revise their understanding of the past. Many things that we believe to be true are often not. How many of you think you know the story of the famous baseball player, Ty Cobb? Baseball fans recognise Cobb as the greatest hitter who ever lived, but they also grew up with stories of his mean-spiritedness, cheating, violence and racism, and how he was hated by his fellow baseball players.

This image was repeated in various fora over the years and accepted as gospel truth, until Charles Leerhsen started researching a biography and soon recognised that the received wisdom was completely wrong. It turns out that Cobb was an avid student of history descended from a long line of abolitionists who enjoyed acting on the stage. While he was a passionate and aggressive ballplayer, Cobb was well respected and liked by his contemporaries and demonstrated a racial sensitivity unusual for the age. Leehrsen highlights why the myth of the terrible Cobb emerged – an unscrupulous biography by Al Stump simply made up sensational stories to sell books – and why it persisted for decades. Leerhsen explains, 'It is easy to understand why this is the prevailing view. People have been told that Cobb was a bad man over and over, all of their lives. The repetition felt like evidence.'

The benefits of history to policy are not obvious. As a discipline, it sits awkwardly but proudly between the humanities and the social sciences. History provides few 'off-the-shelf' lessons, makes no predictions, and easily resists generalisation. It is better at demonstrating what an event or phenomena is not than identifying what it is. History is as likely to be misused than provide lessons, and it often resists efforts to become 'applied'. Compared to its other, more muscular cousins in the social sciences, history can look anaemic. As Gordon Wood points out,

> Unlike sociology, political science, psychology, and the other social sciences, which tend to breed confidence in managing the future, history tends to inculcate skepticism about our ability to manipulate and control purposefully our destiny.

Historians are also strange people, very different from policymakers, at times intellectually chaste and at others times wildly promiscuous. Chaste in their obsession to uncover every last shred of evidence, no matter how small or seemingly insignificant; promiscuous in their ability to create whole worlds and civilisations on the written page largely from their imaginations. What other avocation could obsessively fight over the precise timing of a telegram sent between two political leaders on the eve of war in 1914 but boldly and out of thin air name and define whole historical periods? It is easy to forget that categories such as the Middle Ages or the Renaissance or the Modern World do not exist in nature but are instead the creative result of the historian's imagination, or that, as the great historian Simon Schama points out, the very concept of a 'French Revolution' was not completely solidified until established by historians almost half a century after the event. Bringing this world of history together with policy is not easy or natural.

Unfortunately, knowledge is no guarantee of success. The double firsts Sir Anthony Eden earned in Persian and Arabic while at Oxford did not prevent him from pursuing disastrous policies towards Iran and Egypt when he was the prime minister of Great Britain. History can offer lessons, insights and even methods, though they are often meagre and must be used cautiously and with care. The most important quality of a historical sensibility, the most valuable gift provided by an immersion in the past, is humility. From the world of social science, where bold predictions and generalizations are the coin of the realm, and from the universe of policymakers, where difficult choices demand clear answers and decision can have enormous consequences, this may not seem like much. Perhaps that is the point — making difficult decisions facing complexity and the radical uncertainty of the future is very hard. Even the best ideas will only help so much, though given the stakes, even those marginal improvements are well worth seeking. Perhaps it is helpful to remember the words of Sir Michael Howard: 'The true use of history, whether civil or military, is not to make man clever for the next time, it is to make him wise forever.'

---

1   AARC Assasination Archives and Research Center. HSCA Hearings –
    Volume IV. https://aarclibrary.org/publib/jfk/hsca/reportvols/vol4/html/
    HSCA_Vol4_0222a.htm

GRAHAM ALLISON AND NIALL FERGUSON:
THE RETURN OF APPLIED HISTORY

INTRODUCTION BY GRAHAM ALLISON

In 2012, Henry Kissinger returned to Harvard after an absence of four decades. At an event I hosted, he was asked by a student what someone hoping for a career like his should study. He answered 'history and philosophy' – two subjects notable for their absence in most American schools of public policy. As my colleague Niall Ferguson and I observed, both were also prominent in their absence at the highest levels of American decision-making.

Far from the 'end' of history heralded by scholars and analysts when the Soviet Union disintegrated, we are now caught up in its vengeful 'return'. Today, foreign policy elites have woken to the meteoric rise of an authoritarian China, which now rivals the United States in many domains, and the resurgence of an assertive, authoritarian Russian nuclear superpower that is willing to use its military forces to change borders in Europe. In attempting to understand the challenge China poses, policy analysts have rediscovered the dynamics of rivalries between rapidly rising and established ruling powers that have been chronicled by historians since Thucydides. In attempting to address Russia's war against Ukraine and its threat to the European order, analysts have been forced to read carefully not only what Putin has said (for example, his 2007 speech at the Munich Security Conference and his 5,000-word essay published just six months before his forces invaded Ukraine) but also the record of Imperial Russia in which the Czars' greatness was measured by their success in expanding Russian territory. Moreover, Putin's threats to conduct tactical nuclear strikes in his war against Ukraine have sent policymakers back to the Cuban Missile Crisis of 1962 and the playbook that President Kennedy used to bring that standoff to a peaceful resolution.

As policymakers were reawakening to the continuing relevance of history, it dawned on my colleague Niall and me that this might be a propitious time to revive an effort to 'apply history' as more rigorous, disciplined analysis. Building on the solid foundation laid by our former colleagues Ernest May and Richard Neustadt in their core course at the Kennedy School and their classic 1986 book *Thinking in Time*, we imagined a next wave of 'applied history' both as a discipline in the university and as a tool in the practice of statecraft. To that end, in 2015, we published an 'Applied History Manifesto' in *The Atlantic* and launched Harvard's Applied History Project. The manifesto defines applied history as 'the explicit attempt to illuminate current challenges and choices by reasoning from history, analysing precedents and analogues'. What medical practice is to biology, applied history should be to mainstream history. Mainstream historians begin with an event or era and attempt to provide an account of what happened and why. Applied historians begin with a current choice or predicament and analyse the historical record to provide perspective, stimulate imagination, find clues about what is likely to happen, suggest possible interventions, and assess probable consequences. Enlisting colleagues from Harvard's History Department, Kennedy School, Business School and beyond, the Applied History Project began a series of working group meetings. We also established the Ernest May Fellowship for select pre- and postdoctoral students, and are proud of the more than 25 alumni May Fellows who are now advancing the subject.

From the outset, we thought of this undertaking not as a hierarchical organisation – but as a movement. We hoped that like-minded historians and public policy analysts would take initiatives of their own, exploring and demonstrating ways in which historical reasoning about the past can provide clues about the future. Ten years on, we have been gratified by the ways in which this movement has taken flight. Today, the Applied History Network includes more than 200 leading thinkers at 50 major institutions around the world. The proposal we made in the manifesto for the White House to create a Council of Historical Advisers analogous to the Council of Economic Advisers has not yet materialised. But in the United Kingdom, Prime Minister Boris Johnson enlisted a distinguished member of the network from King's College London, John Bew, as his in-house Applied Historian and chief foreign policy advisor. And President Biden now regularly consults with historians, led by Vanderbilt professor Jon Meacham, who has convened a series of small group meetings at the White House to provide historical perspective on policy challenges.

When asked recently where I now see applied history today, I responded pointedly by answering directly three questions: Can we learn lessons from history that policymakers can apply to today's challenges? Do statesmen learn lessons from history that they pass to their successors who face similar challenges? And, lastly, are President Biden and his national security team applying lessons from what JFK did in the Cuban Missile Crisis in attempting to meet the challenge posed by Putin's invasion of Ukraine and his nuclear threats?

First, when asked whether we can learn lessons from history that policymakers can apply to illuminate current challenges and inform current choices, mainstream historians often respond in ways that suggest the answer is no. Even here at the Harvard Kennedy School, for followers of Ernest May, we recognise that in the last years of his life he occasionally despaired of finding ways to help policymakers use history more effectively. My colleague Fredrik Logevall, who is now teaching a revised version of the basic May-Neustadt course on applied history at the Kennedy School, has written that we can be 'bamboozled by analogies' and that 'lessons of the past are too easy' and encourage the 'misuse of history'. Our former colleague Moshik Temkin went much further in an often-cited *New York Times* op-ed entitled 'Historians Shouldn't Be Pundits'. In his punchline, 'analogies are more than useless; they can be dangerous' because 'things rarely repeat themselves'.

While I'm reluctant to disagree with my colleagues, nonetheless, my answer is: of course we can learn lessons from history. Analogies, proffered lessons and claims that 'history teaches' can be misused and abused. But so can – and are – all forms of evidence and analysis. Political leaders are advocates. Many convert whatever they can get their hands on into ammunition that they use in trying to persuade others to support their proposals. But that is no more reason for historians to retreat from the policy arena than it is for statisticians, economists or scientists. Careful, disciplined analysis of history can illuminate the road ahead, inform choices and improve understanding of their consequences.

Second, do statesmen learn lessons from history that they recommend as advice for successors facing analogous challenges? Again my answer is unambiguously yes. In facing what is agreed to have been the most dangerous crisis in recorded history – the Cuban Missile Crisis of 1962 – President Kennedy certainly did. As grace or fortune had it, just two months before the Missile Crisis, JFK had read Barbara Tuchman's *The Guns of August*, a succinct, brilliant analysis of the ways in which early-twentieth century European leaders were dragged by the rush of events into the First World War. Repeatedly during the fateful 13 days of the Cuban Missile Crisis, Kennedy asked how he could be sure Tuchman's successors would never be able to write a book called *The Missiles of October*. He reflected on mistakes predecessors made in 1914 and attempted to ensure that his government was not sleepwalking in their footsteps.

Third, facing the challenge posed by Putin's invasion of Ukraine and repeated threats to conduct tactical nuclear strikes, are

President Biden and his national security team reviewing what JFK did in the Cuban Missile Crisis? Again, my answer is most certainly yes. In his most important foreign policy speech delivered at the American University in Washington DC just five months before his assassination, JFK drew what he said was the central lesson from the Cuban Missile Crisis – a lesson he urged successors to ponder and apply. In his words: 'Above all, while defending our own vital interests, nuclear powers must avert those confrontations which bring an adversary to a choice of either a humiliating retreat or a nuclear war.' Clearly Biden was thinking about this when he acknowledged that he had been exploring 'Putin's off-ramp…Where does he find himself in a position he does not only lose face but lose significant power in Russia?'

The same speech contains another paragraph that I had read many times but only come to appreciate in the past decade as I've been wrestling with the China challenge. JFK said: 'If we cannot end now our differences, at least we can help make the world safe for diversity.' He recognised the necessity for coexistence – since the alternative would be co-destruction. Ronald Reagan captured this imperative incandescently in his favourite one-liner: 'A nuclear war cannot be won and therefore must never be fought.' How that lesson can be adapted and applied in constructing a sustainable strategy for the rivalry with a China that now has a robust nuclear arsenal is a timely question for applied historians.

Cambridge, MA, November 2022

GRAHAM ALLISON AND NIALL FERGUSON
APPLIED HISTORY MANIFESTO

Applied history is the explicit attempt to illuminate current challenges and choices by analyzing historical precedents and analogues. Mainstream historians begin with a past event or era and attempt to provide an account of what happened and why. Applied historians begin with a current choice or predicament and attempt to analyse the historical record to provide perspective, stimulate imagination, find clues about what is likely to happen, suggest possible policy interventions, and assess probable consequences. It might be said that applied history is to mainstream history as medical practice is to biochemistry, or engineering to physics. But that analogy is not quite right, as in the realm of science there is mutual respect between practitioners and theorists. In the realm of policy, by contrast, one finds a culture of mutual contempt between practitioners and historians. Applied history is an attempt to address that.

The Applied History Project at Harvard's Kennedy School seeks to revitalise the study and practice of history in the tradition of two twentieth-century giants: the modern historian Ernest May and the leading analyst of the American presidency, Richard Neustadt. Their book *Thinking in Time*, published in 1986, provides the foundation on which we intend to build. An urgently needed companion volume might be titled *Acting in Time*. Over the past decade, particularly as one of us was engaged in research for a biography of Henry Kissinger, we shared a humbling epiphany. It has been said that most Americans live in the 'United States of Amnesia'. What we had not fully appreciated is how often this includes American policymakers as well. Reflecting on a wide range of administrations, we have come to realise the crucial importance in American foreign policymaking of the history deficit: the fact that key decision makers know alarmingly little not just of other countries' pasts, but also of their own.

Speaking about his book, *Doomed to Succeed: the U.S.–Israel Relationship from Truman to Obama*, veteran US diplomat Dennis Ross recently noted that 'almost no administration's leading figures know the history of what we have done in the Middle East'. Neither do they know the history of the region itself. In 2003, when President George Bush chose to topple Saddam Hussein and replace his regime with an elected government that represented the majority of Iraqis, he did not appear to appreciate either the difference between Sunni and Shiite Muslims or the significance of the fact that Saddam's regime had been led by a Sunni minority that had suppressed the Shiite majority. He failed to heed warnings that the predictable consequence of this choice would be a Shiite-dominated Baghdad beholden to the Shiite champion in the Middle East – Iran. Indeed, in attempting to explain the consequences of this fateful choice, one of the leaders from the region is reported to have told President Bush that if he cut down the tallest tree in the region (Saddam), he should not be surprised when he found the second tallest tree towering over the others.

The problem is by no means limited to the Middle East or to Bush. The Obama administration's inability or unwillingness to recognise the deep historical relationship between Russia and Ukraine left it blind to the predictable consequences of European Union initiatives in late 2013 and early 2014 to lead Ukraine down a path to membership in the EU and, in time, NATO. 'I don't really even need George Kennan right now', Obama told the editor of the *New Yorker* in an interview published in January 2014, referring to one of the great applied historians of the early Cold War. Within two months Russia had annexed Crimea.

Even more remarkable, however, is the apparent ignorance of the Republican candidate for the presidency of the historical significance of his own foreign policy mantra, 'America First'.

While this history deficit is only one of the weaknesses in the foreign policy of recent administrations of both parties, it is one that is more amenable to repair than most. Yet to address this deficit it is not enough for a president occasionally to invite friendly historians to dinner, as Obama has been known to do. Nor is it enough to appoint a court historian, as John F Kennedy did with Arthur M Schlesinger Jr.

We urge the candidates currently running for president to announce now that, if elected, they will establish a White House Council of Historical Advisers analogous to the Council of Economic Advisers established after World War II. Several eminent historians made similar recommendations to Presidents Carter and Reagan during their administrations: the chequered record of US foreign policy since 1977 suggests that, in failing to do so, Carter and Reagan missed a great opportunity. We suggest that this council's charter begin with Thucydides' observation that 'events of future history will be of the same nature – or nearly so – as the history of the past, so long as men are men'. While applied historians will never be clairvoyants with an unclouded crystal ball, we agree with Winston Churchill that 'the longer you can look back, the farther you can look forward'. The next president's charge to this council should be to provide historical perspectives on contemporary problems.

Imagine that President Obama had such a council today. What assignments could he give them? How could their responses help inform choices he now faces?

Start with the most intractable issue the president and his national security team have been debating recently: what to do about ISIS? He could ask his applied historians whether or not we have even seen anything like this before, and if so, which precedents seem most similar? He could ask further what happened in those cases, and thus what clues they offer about what might happen in this one. We infer from recent statements that the administration tends to see ISIS as essentially a new version of al-Qaeda, and the goal of policy is to decapitate it, as al-Qaeda was decapitated with the assassination of Osama bin Laden in 2011. But there is good reason to believe that ISIS is quite different in structure from al-Qaeda and may in fact be a classic acephalous network.

Our initial search for precedents and analogues for ISIS includes 50 prior cases of similarly brutal, fanatical, purpose-driven groups, including the Bolsheviks of the Russian Revolution. Deciding which characteristics of ISIS we consider most salient – for example, its revolutionary politics or its religious millenarianism – helps us to narrow this list to the most instructive analogues. A systematic study of these other cases could help steer the president away from a potentially erroneous equation of ISIS with its most recent forerunner.

That this kind of approach can be invaluable is illustrated by the US government's response to the Great Recession of 2008. That September saw the biggest shock to the US economy since the Great Depression. In 24 hours, the Dow Jones industrial average plummeted, credit swaps among major banks froze, and the shock spread almost instantly to international markets. In the words of then-Secretary of the Treasury Hank Paulson, 'the "system-wide" crisis was more severe and unpredictable than any in our lifetimes'. For that reason, historical knowledge of earlier financial crises – and particularly the Great Depression that began in 1929 – was at a premium. It was sheer good luck that the chairman of the Federal Reserve from 2006 to 2014 was also a serious student of economic history. As Ben Bernanke wrote in his 2015 memoir, 'understanding what was happening in the context of history proved invaluable' because 'the crisis of 2007–2009 was best understood as a descendant of the classic financial panics of the nineteenth and early twentieth centuries'. The spectre that haunted Bernanke most was the Great Depression of 1929. While some criticised his 'obsession' with the post-1929 depression, there can be no doubt about his commitment not to repeat the mistakes that contributed to that catastrophe.

In a 2010 speech, Bernanke identified lessons from the Great Depression for policy makers today: 'First, economic prosperity depends on financial stability; second, policy makers must respond forcefully, creatively and decisively to severe financial crises; third, crises that are international in scope require an international response.' Bernanke's Fed acted decisively, inventing unprecedented initiatives that stretched – if not exceeded – the Fed's legal powers, such as purchasing not only bonds issued by the federal government but also mortgage-backed and other securities in what was called 'quantitative easing'. The speed of the Fed's international initiatives to backstop other central banks and persuade them to collaborate in cutting short-term interest rates so as to enhance stability can also be traced back to Bernanke's knowledge of mistakes made in the Great Depression. Although the recent crisis took place in a radically different financial and economic context, Bernanke wrote in the conclusion of his memoir, 'it rhymed with past panics'.

Just as the financial storm was gathering, our colleagues Carmen Reinhart and Kenneth Rogoff were just completing a decade of research during which they had assembled a database of 350 financial crises over the past eight centuries. Their book *This Time Is Different: Eight Centuries of Financial Folly* explicitly analysed 'precedents and analogues' with a view to illuminating current events. In testimony to Congress and a series of op-eds in late 2008 and early 2009, they argued that recessions caused by financial crises tend to persist for much longer than business-cycle recessions. Indeed, they opined that the 'current crisis could mean stunted U.S. growth for at least five to seven more years', and that it would leave behind a legacy of significantly higher public debt.

Though hotly contested at the time by those who claimed that monetary and fiscal stimulus would achieve a rapid 'v-shaped' recovery, their historically derived insights have proven prescient.

While Western economies stagnated, China continued its meteoric growth and increasingly realised its ability to reap geopolitical benefits from its new-found financial power. Will China's rise result in war with the United States? In a chapter written for the 2009 volume *Power and Restraint*, Ernest May offered an instructive demonstration of how the analysis of analogues and precedents can provide clues about 'alternative patterns that might play out in U.S.–Chinese relationships'. To do this, he considered 'experience at the turn of the century and in the 1920s that can be instructive in suggesting some of the processes that engendered enmity or friendship across national boundaries'. Specifically, he compared and contrasted interactions between Britain and two rising powers: Germany on the one hand, and the United States on the other. Britain and Germany, he notes, could have remained at peace since they 'were essentially similar in culture, values, and institutions'. 'Why,' then, 'did the next two decades see Britain and Germany instead become enemies? Why did Britain not react to America's challenges as to those from Germany?'

May's analysis is subtle and nuanced, as always. In the first case, he concluded that 'most of the blame has to go to Germany and its wilful ruler, Kaiser Wilhelm II.' Indeed, he argued that 'the central reason for Germany's self-destructive behaviour was that the kaiser and his ministers were preoccupied with their own domestic politics'. 'Wilhelm and his ministers found it useful – almost necessary – to have trouble abroad in order to maintain quiet at home.' Reflecting on the consequences, he drew a telling lesson for China: 'The example of Imperial Germany clearly warns how dangerous it can be for a rising power to use foreign policy as a means of satisfying domestic political needs.'

In contrast, by finding ways to accommodate a rising United States, Britain demonstrated 'how a great nation can benefit from swallowing its pride and being guided by long-term calculations of interest, both international and domestic'. In the shaping of British foreign policy, 'a chain of British decision-makers calculated coldly that the cost of resisting American pretensions would be too high'. May thus applauded the British government's wise choice 'to make a virtue of necessity and to yield to the Americans in every dispute with as good grace as was permitted'. When a Liberal government came to power in 1906, British policy culminated in the new Foreign Secretary's declaration that 'the pursuit and maintenance of American friendship was and would be a "cardinal policy" of the United Kingdom'.

As one of us has argued, another analogy for the US–China relationship can be found as early as the tensions between ancient Athens and Sparta. As the Athenian historian Thucydides explained brilliantly in his account of the Peloponnesian War, 'What made war inevitable was the growth of Athenian power and the fear which this caused in Sparta.' The Thucydides Trap – the inevitable structural stress that occurs when a rapidly rising power threatens to displace a ruling power – serves as the best framework available for thinking about US-China relations today and in the years ahead. One of us has led a team of researchers at Harvard Kennedy School's Belfer Centre that reviewed the leading historical accounts of the last 500 years and identified 16 cases when this occurred. In 12 of those cases, the outcome was war. The study represents one possible answer a Council of Historical Advisers could give to the president if he asked whether or not precedents exist for the current US-China relationship.

To be sure, as Ernest May repeatedly reminded students and policy makers alike, historical analogies are easy to get wrong. Amateur analogies were commonplace in the wake of the 9/11 attacks, ranging from the then president's own comparison with Pearl Harbor to the even worse parallels drawn by some members of his administration between Saddam Hussein and the leaders of the World War II Axis powers. To guard against such errors, May counselled that when considering a historical analogy, one should always follow a simple procedure: put the analogy as the headline on a sheet of paper; draw a straight line down the middle of the page; write 'similar' at the top of one column and 'different' at the top of the other; and then set to work. If you are unable to list at least three points of similarity and three of difference, then you should consult a historian.

To apply this 'May Method' amid the flurry of analogising on the 100th anniversary of the outbreak of World War I, one of us compared challenges facing US and Chinese leaders today with those faced by European leaders in 1914. That analysis highlighted seven salient similarities as well as seven instructive differences, and concluded that

> the probability of war between the United States and China in the decade ahead is higher than I imagined before examining the analogy – but still unlikely. Indeed, if statesmen in both countries reflect on what happened a century ago, perspective and insights from this past can be applied now to make risks of war even lower.

As the most consequential modern practitioner of applied history, Henry Kissinger, put it, 'History is not a cookbook offering pre-tested recipes. It teaches by analogy, not by maxims.' History 'illuminates the consequences of actions in comparable situations'. But – and here is the art that requires both imagination and judgment – for it to do so, 'each generation must discover for itself what situations are in fact comparable'.

'Is it unprecedented?' is just one of a number of questions or assignments that we propose the president could give their Council of Historical Advisers. Others include:

- What lessons of statecraft from a former president's handling of another crisis could be applied to a current challenge? (What would X have done?)

- What is the significance of a historical anniversary for the present (a common topic for presidential speeches)?
- What is the relevant history of the state, institution or issue at hand?
- What if some action had not been taken (the kind of question too seldom asked after a policy failure)?
- Grand strategic questions like 'Can the United States avoid decline?'
- Speculative questions about seemingly improbable future scenarios.

Most presidents have a favourite predecessor. In developing his strategy for meeting Iran's nuclear challenge, President Obama is reported to have reflected on WWKD? (What Would Kennedy Do?) His choice of an 'ugly deal' to stop the advance of Iran's nuclear programme rather than the bombing of its uranium enrichment plants (as Israeli prime minister Benjamin Netanyahu hoped he might) or acquiescing in an Iranian fait accompli (as some of his advisers thought inevitable) had some parallels with Kennedy's choices in the Cuban Missile Crisis to strike a deal with Nikita Khrushchev rather than risk an invasion of Cuba or learn to live with Soviet missiles off the Florida coast. Two key points were that the successful deal in 1962 was based on secret negotiations with Moscow – even though that unsettled some American allies – and that there was a middle ground between complete capitulation and nuclear war.

A third type of assignment the president could give his historians would be to take the anniversary of a major historical event as an occasion to reflect on current challenges. The ongoing centennial of World War I has provided leaders with an important opportunity to speak about its significance. Despite the fact that a general European war seemed to many contemporaries unthinkable, and despite the fact that the economies of Britain and Germany were so heavily interdependent, war broke out and proved impossible to end by diplomatic means. When it ended four years later with the disintegration of the Central Powers, more than ten million men had lost their lives prematurely and Europe had been severely weakened.

In the decade before this war, the major governments had made a series of commitments to each other that created what Kissinger has called a 'diplomatic doomsday machine'. As the strategic competition between the United States and China in the South and East China Seas intensifies, applied historians could usefully carry out a serious review of US commitments to Japan, the Philippines and others that might one day function as a modern-day equivalent.

A fourth type of assignment suitable for the president's historians would be to determine the relevant history of the state, institution or issue at hand, and how foreign counterparts understand that history. In dealing with foreign nations, we should never forget Henry Kissinger's observation that 'history is the memory of states' and that 'for nations, history plays the role that character confers on human beings'. Learning the history of other nations, and honing the skills of historical enquiry in general, can help to promote cultural empathy. As Sir Michael Howard argued thirty-five years ago, any proper historical education must teach its students 'how to step outside their own cultural skins and enter the minds of others; the minds not only of our own forebears, enormously valuable though this is, but of those of our contemporaries who have inherited a different experience from the past'. Unfortunately, many of our elites can be, as Sir Michael put it,

> people often of masterful intelligence, trained usually in law or economics or perhaps in political science, who have led their governments into disastrous decisions and miscalculations because they have no awareness whatsoever of the historical background, the cultural universe, of the foreign societies with which they have to deal.

We cannot understand the decisions of key players in foreign nations without grasping how they themselves understand their nation's history, for, in Sir Michael's words, 'all we believe about the present depends on what we believe about the past'.

Therefore, in preparing to engage China's leaders, what might the next president ask their council? A useful starting assignment would be: How does Xi Jinping understand the arc of Chinese history and his role in China's future? Does he see his mission simply as rounding out China's economic development and restoring it to its historically 'normal' role as the biggest country in the world after its 'century of humiliation'? If so, we could expect to see the emergence of a richer and more confident China, but probably embedded in a 'status quo' system still fundamentally shaped by US power and institutions. Or does he also seek to revise the international order by displacing the United States as the predominant Asian and perhaps global power in the foreseeable future? In answering this assignment, the applied historians could draw on the recorded wisdom of a man who perhaps understood the world view and historical consciousness of China's leaders better than anyone: the late leader of Singapore, Lee Kuan Yew. Lee – whom every Chinese leader since Deng Xiaoping, including Xi, has called a 'mentor' – argued that 'the size of China's displacement of the world balance is such that the world must find a new balance,' and that China 'wants to be China and accepted as such – not as an honorary member of the West'. When asked if China's leaders wish to supplant the United States, Lee responded: 'Of course. Why not? How could [the Chinese] not aspire to be number one in Asia and, in time, the world?'

One clear example of how the history deficit can be dangerous becomes apparent when considering America's dealings in the Middle East. If the president who takes office in 2017 were preparing to engage the leaders of Israel and the leading Arab nations on the Israeli–Palestinian conundrum, what might they ask the applied historians? A good start would be to ask them what the most significant US policies and actions in the region have been in recent decades and how key players in Israel, the Palestinian territories, Jordan, Saudi Arabia, Egypt and Iran interpret and remember those decisions. As Dennis Ross has noted, while US leaders are usually ignorant of our previous actions in the Middle East, 'those in the region know the history very well'. How does the experience they have inherited from the past differ from ours? What lessons have they drawn from US behaviour?

A fifth type of assignment for applied historians is to pose and answer 'what if?' questions designed to analyse past decision making. Addressing such questions requires disciplined counterfactual reasoning. While many mainstream historians have voiced reservations about counterfactual analysis, this method lies at the heart of every historical account. As one of us argued in 'Virtual History', 'it is a logical necessity when asking questions about causation to pose "but for" questions, and to try to imagine what would have happened if our supposed cause had been absent'.

When assessing the relative importance of various possible causes of World War I, historians make judgments about what would have happened in the absence of these factors. Methods developed for doing this systematically can be employed by applied historians in considering current policy choices. Thus, President Obama's successor could ask his Council of Historical Advisers to replay 2013. What if Obama had opted to enforce the 'red line' in Syria against the Assad regime, rather than delegating the removal of chemical weapons from Syria to the Russian government? And what if, in January 2014, the EU had not offered Ukraine an economic association agreement that was clearly designed to pull Kiev westward? Would President Putin still have intervened militarily in Ukraine?

A sixth kind of question for the Council of Historical Advisers would be of a fundamentally strategic nature. Is the United States in irreversible decline? Can it overcome the challenges facing it to lead a new 'American century', or will the coming decades see the steady erosion of American power? Applied historians would begin by noting the recurring streak in American political culture of what Sam Huntington labelled 'declinism'. Many people were convinced that the United States was being overtaken by the Soviet Union in the late 1950s and 1960s, or by Japan in the 1980s. But in none of the earlier cases had the majority of Americans lost faith in the American dream: the belief that if one works hard and plays by the rules, one's children will have more opportunities and a higher standard of living than their parents. In the past generation, as middle-class incomes have stagnated, that belief has been eroded. Bismarck defined a statesman as 'a politician who thinks of his grandchildren'. It is unclear whether the current American political system would allow such a statesman to enact the far-sighted policies required to address the growing problem of inter-generation inequity – or indeed to be elected in the first place. The current generation is the first in the history of the United States to have asked, in essence, 'What have our children and grandchildren ever done for us?' A truly visionary president would revive the importance of our posterity as the most important constituent of a well-governed republic.

Finally, a more speculative assignment, but still a vital one, would be to ask the council: 'What unlikely but possible strategic upheavals might we face in the medium-term?'

- Will ISIS buy or steal a nuclear weapon?
- Will Chinese and Japanese forces clash in the East China Sea, sparking a wider war?
- Will the Saudi royal family be deposed?
- Will the European Union disintegrate?
- Will Russia invade a Baltic state?

While some of these scenarios may seem far-fetched, recall this time six years ago: how many pundits would have predicted the timing or speed of the Arab Spring, or that Syria would now lie in ruins? Two and a half years ago, how many believed it probable that Vladimir Putin would invade Crimea, that his proxies would shoot down a Dutch airliner, or that he would commit combat forces to Syria?

Of course, building future scenarios is part of what intelligence agencies do. Yet, currently, historians play a very small part in this process. Applied historians do not have crystal balls. But they do have certain advantages over those who would try to answer such questions with models and regression analysis. They know that dramatic events that were dismissed as implausible before the fact are in hindsight frequently described as inevitable. Their study of previous sharp discontinuities encourages a 'historical sensibility' that is attuned to the long-term rhythms, strategic surprise and daring *coups de main* that run through history.

This historical sensibility can prove invaluable. One applied historian, now well known for discerning and profiting from long-term historical cycles in markets, developed so much of a historical sensibility while writing a doctoral dissertation on the relationship between commodities and the grand strategy of the British Empire that he was able to anticipate Iraq's seizure of Kuwait's oil fields a full two years before Saddam made his move.

For too long, history has been disparaged as a 'soft' subject, often by social scientists offering spuriously hard certainty. We believe it is time for a new and rigorous applied history to close America's history deficit. Not only do we want to see it incorporated into the Executive Office of the president, alongside the economic expertise that has so long been seen as indispensable to the executive branch, but we also want to see it develop as a discipline in its own right in our universities, beginning at Harvard.

Harvard's Applied History Project is taking a 'big tent' approach to revitalising applied history in the academy and promoting its use in government, business and other sectors of society. We stake no claim to inventing the concept: indeed, we trace its origins back at least to Thucydides and acknowledge that it had been a major strand in mainstream history until recent decades. We make no claim to exclusivity: indeed, we applaud colleagues – and mentors – such as Sir Michael Howard of Oxford or Paul Kennedy of Yale, whose contributions in this domain we celebrate and hope to emulate.

We encourage journalists to ask candidates for the presidency how they intend to eliminate the history deficit in American policy making. The slogan 'America First' has a bad history. A better slogan – which has no past to speak of in the United States – might be 'History First'.

CONTRIBUTORS

LORD ACTON (1834–1902) was a liberal historian, politician, and philosopher of resistance to the state. He was Regius Professor of Modern History at University of Cambridge, where he taught two courses of lectures on the French Revolution and on Modern History. In 1869, he was raised to the peerage by Queen Victoria.

GRAHAM ALLISON is the Douglas Dillon Professor of Government at Harvard University, where he served as Dean of Harvard Kennedy School of Government and, until 2017, Director of the Belfer Center for Science and International Affairs. He is the author of *Destined for War: Can America and China Escape Thucydides's trap?* and *Essence of Decision: Explaining the Cuban Missile Crisis.* As Assistant Secretary of Defense for President Clinton, he received the Defense Department's highest civilian award and in 2009 he received the Award for Behavioral Research Relevant to the Prevention of Nuclear War from the National Academy of Sciences.

CARL BECKER (1873–1945) was an American historian known for his work on early American intellectual history and on the eighteenth-century Enlightenment in Europe. In 1923, he was elected fellow of the American Academy of Arts and Sciences. His best-known work is *The Heavenly City of the Eighteenth-Century Philosophers* (1932), four lectures on the Enlightenment delivered at Yale University.

PHILIP BOBBITT is the Herbert Wechsler Professor of Federal Jurisprudence at Columbia University, and Distinguished Senior

Lecturer at the University of Texas. He has served in the US government during seven administrations, including in the post of senior director for strategic planning at the National Security Council. Bobbitt's books include *The Shield of Achilles: War, Peace and the Course of History* and *Impeachment: a Handbook* (with Charles Black Jr).

KATHLEEN BURK is Professor Emerita at University College London. She is a specialist on Anglo-American relations, the founder of the journal *Contemporary European History* and a fellow of the Norwegian Academy of Science and Letters. Her books include *Old World, New World: the Story of Britain and America* and *The Lion and the Eagle: the Interaction of the British and American Empires, 1783–1972*.

J B BURY (1861–1927) was a classical scholar and historian who wrote several books on theory and philosophy of history, Ancient Greece and Byzantine history among other topics. Bury was Erasmus Smith's Professor of Modern History at Trinity College Dublin and Regius Professor of Modern History at the University of Cambridge.

HERBERT BUTTERFIELD (1900 –1979) was a British historian and Regius Professor of Modern History at the University of Cambridge. He is best known for *The Whig Interpretation of History* (1931), which denunciates the teleological aspects of the 'Whig' approach to history. He received thirteen honorary degrees, one of which was a DLitt from Cambridge in 1974.

E H CARR (1892–1982) is best known for *What Is History?* in which he opposes empiricism within historiography and casts lights on the proper functions of historians. He was educated at the Merchant Taylorss School in London and later at Trinity College, Cambridge, where he was awarded a first class degree in Classics in 1916. After resigning from the Foreign Office in 1936 he began his academic career.

CHRISTOPHER COKER is director of LSE IDEAS, a foreign policy think tank at the London School of Economics and Political Science. He is a former member of the Council of the Royal United Services Institute, for whom he wrote the monograph *Empires in Conflict: the Growing Rift Between Europe and the United States*. He is also a former editor of the *Atlantic Quarterly* and the *European Security Analyst*.

ALBERTO R COLL is the Vincent de Paul Professor of Law and United States Foreign Relations at De Paul University, Chicago. He is the author of *The Wisdom of Statecraft: Sir Herbert Butterfield and the Philosophy of International Politics*. He has taught at Georgetown, Brown University, and the U.S. Naval War College, where he was also Dean. At the University of Virginia, where he received his JD and PhD, Coll worked closely with Butterfield collaborators Adam Watson and Kenneth Thompson. The author of numerous publications on international politics and law, Coll also has served as Principal Deputy Assistant Secretary of Defense.

MICHAEL COX is Emeritus Professor of International Relations at the London School of Economics (LSE) and Founding Director of LSE IDEAS. He joined the LSE in 2002 having previously held a Chair in the Department of International Politics at the University of Wales, Aberystwyth. His most recent books include *The Post-Cold War World*, a centennial edition of John Maynard Keynes's *The Economic Consequences of the Peace*, as well as *Agonies of Empire: American Power from Clinton to Biden* and *Afghanistan: Long War – Forgotten Peace*.

ROBERT CROWCROFT is Senior Lecturer in History at the University of Edinburgh. His books include *The End is Nigh: British Politics, Power, and the Road to the Second World War*, *Attlee's War: World War II and the Making of a Labour Leader* and, as co-editor, *The Oxford Handbook of Modern British Political History, 1800–2000*.

JOHANN GUSTAV DROYSEN (1808–1884) was a German historian. His work on Alexander the Great was the first in a new school of German historical thought in which history can be explained by the impact of highly influential individuals. He studied at Humboldt-Universität zu Berlin, where he later gave lectures. In 1848 Droysen was elected a member of the Frankfurt parliament.

NIALL FERGUSON is the Milbank Family Senior Fellow at the Hoover Institution, Stanford University, and a senior faculty fellow of the Belfer Center for Science and International Affairs at Harvard University, where he served for twelve years as the Laurence A. Tisch Professor of History. He is a columnist for *Bloomberg Opinion*, and his books include *Kissinger, 1923–1968: the Idealist* and *The Square and the Tower: Networks, Hierarchies and the Struggle for Global Power.*

LAWRENCE FREEDMAN was Professor of War Studies at King's College London from 1982 to 2014 and vice principal from 2003 to 2013. Elected a fellow of the British Academy in 1995, he was appointed official historian of the Falklands campaign in 1997 and a member of the Privy Council of the UK in 2009, when he was called to take part in the inquiry into the Iraq War. His books include *Strategy: a History* and *The Future of War: a History.*

JOHN LEWIS GADDIS is Robert A. Lovett Professor of Military and Naval History at Yale University, where he currently teaches courses on grand strategy, biography, historical methods and time travel. His most recent books are *George F. Kennan: an American Life* and *On Grand Strategy.*

FRANCIS J GAVIN is the Giovanni Agnelli Distinguished Professor and the inaugural director of the Henry A Kissinger Center for Global Affairs at Johns Hopkins SAIS. In 2021, Professor Gavin was named a 2021–2022 Ernest May Senior Visiting Fellow of the Applied History Project at Harvard's Belfer Center for Science and International Affairs. Gavin is the author of *Gold, Dollars, and Power: the Politics of International Monetary Relations, 1958–1971* and *Nuclear Weapons and American Grand Strategy.*

PIETER GEYL (1887–1966) was a Dutch historian. After teaching in the Netherlands, he went on to work as a correspondent in London for the Dutch newspaper *Nieuwe Rotterdamsche Courant.* He then taught Dutch history at the University of London before returning home and being appointed professor of Modern History at Universiteit Utrecht in 1936.

BEATRICE DE GRAAF is a Distinguished Professor at the Department of History and Art History at Universiteit Utrecht. Her research focus is on history of security, (counter)terrorism and international relations. With her monograph *Fighting Terror after Napoleon. How Europe Became Secure after 1815* she was awarded the Arenberg Prize for European History in 2022.

MATTIAS HESSÉRUS is the Director of the Ax:son Johnson Institute for Statecraft and Diplomacy and sits on the committee of the Engelsberg Applied History Programme at the University of Cambridge and King's College London. Hessérus received a PhD from Uppsala University. He was a Fulbright Visiting Scholar at Columbia University in New York City, and held a Swedish Institute Scholarship at the École des hautes études en sciences sociales in Paris. He has worked for radio and TV and spent three years as review editor of *Axess Magazine.* He is part of the Engelsberg Ideas team and host of its podcast *History Lessons.*

J H HEXTER (1910–1996) was an American historian, specialising in British history, who taught at several major American universities such as Yale and Washington University. In 1966 he organised the founding of the Yale Center for Parliamentary History, and later went on to found Washington University's Center for the History of Freedom.

MICHAEL HOWARD (1922–2019) was a British military historian. He taught at King's College London, where he developed the strategic studies of military history to assess defence and national security more broadly rather than focusing on specific battles. He was knighted in 1986 for his academic work.

KATJA HOYER is a German-British historian and journalist. She is a Visiting Research Fellow at King's College London and a Fellow of the Royal Historical Society. Katja is a columnist for *The Washington Post* and writes for *The Spectator, The Telegraph, Die Welt* and other newspapers on current political affairs in Germany and Europe. She is the author of the bestselling *Blood and Iron.* Her latest book is *Beyond the Wall: East Germany, 1949–1990.*

DAVID MARTIN JONES is a Visiting Professor in War Studies, King's College London, Visiting Professor in the Humanities Research Institute, University of Buckingham and Honorary Professor at the University of Technology, Sydney, Australia. He is amongst other things the author of *History's Fools: the Pursuit of Idealism and the Revenge of Politics.*

ANDREW LAMBERT is the Laughton Professor of Naval History in the Department of War Studies at King's College London. His work has addressed a range of issues, including technology, policy-making, regional security, deterrence, historiography, crisis management and conflict. He received the 2014 Anderson Medal for the book *The Challenge: Britain against America in the Naval War of 1812.*

NICCOLÒ MACHIAVELLI (1469–1527) was an Italian diplomat, philosopher, and historian. His experiences as a diplomat had great influence on his political penmanship. He is often called the father of modern political science. His most famous work is *The Prince,* an analysis of how to acquire and maintain political power, which coined the term Machiavellism.

MARGARET MACMILLAN is emeritus Professor of History at the University of Toronto and emeritus Professor of International History and the former Warden of St. Antony's College at the University of Oxford. Her books include *Paris 1919: Six Months that Changed the World*, *The Uses and Abuses of History* and *The War that Ended Peace: How Europe Abandoned Peace for the First World War*. Her most recent book is *War: How Conflict Shaped Us*.

ERNEST MAY (1928–2009) was an American historian specialising in international relations, chiefly American foreign policy. He taught at Harvard University for 55 years until his death. He also served on the faculty at the John F. Kennedy School of Government. He wrote several books studying historical decision-making in the hopes of illuminating the policy- and decision-making of politicians.

FRIEDRICH NIETZSCHE (1844–1900) was a German philosopher and writer. He was one of the twentieth century's most influential thinkers, known for his statement expressing the death of God. At 24 years old Nietzsche became professor of classical philology at the University of Basel.

T G OTTE is Professor of Diplomatic History at the University of East Anglia and is currently a Leverhulme Major Research Fellow. He is the author or editor of some twenty-one books, among them *Statesman of Europe: a Life of Sir Edward Grey*. He has also been an adviser to the Foreign and Commonwealth Office.

POLYBIUS (200 BC–118 BC) was a Greek historian, known for his analysis of the separation of powers. His reputation rests on *The Histories*, consisting of 40 books, in which he covered Roman history, focusing on it becoming a dominant world power.

BOB QU is an instructor in the History Department at the U.S. Naval Academy and an infantry officer in the U.S. Marine Corps. He received a BA with distinction in History from Yale University and a MA in History from the University of Virginia, where he is currently completing his PhD. His scholarship focuses on the post-Cold War order and the NATO response to the war in Bosnia-Herzegovina.

LEOPOLD VON RANKE (1795–1886) was a German historian and professor of history. He was critical of sources and focused on archival research and analysis of historical documents. This was prominent in his book *History of the Latin and Teutonic Peoples from 1494 to 1514*, based on a wide variety of sources such as memoirs, government documents and diaries.

ISKANDER REHMAN is an Ax:son Johnson Fellow at the Henry A. Kissinger Center for Global Affairs, and the Senior Fellow for Strategic Studies at the American Foreign Policy Council.

KORI SCHAKE is Director of Foreign and Defense policy at the American Enterprise Institute. She has worked in the Departments of State and Defense, the National Security Council, on the 2008 McCain presidential campaign, and taught at Stanford, Johns Hopkins SAIS, West Point, and in War Studies at Kings College. She is the author of *Safe Passage: the Transition from British to American Hegemony* and a contributing writer at *The Atlantic*.

JOHN ROBERT SEELEY (1834–1895) was a British historian. He is known for his book *The Expansion of England*, in which he advocates the British Empire. He was made Regius Professor of Modern History at the University of Cambridge in 1869.

BENJAMIN F SHAMBAUGH (1871–1940) was an American historian, and professor of political science at the University of Iowa. He was later made founding chair of the Department of Political Science. He coined the term 'applied history' in 1909, which he defined as the use of scientific knowledge of history to solve present issues.

BRENDAN SIMMS obtained his PhD from the University of Cambridge, where he is a Fellow of Peterhouse and director of the Centre for Geopolitics. He is founder and president of the Henry Jackson Society, a London-based think tank devoted to the spread of democracy and human rights, and president of the Project for Democratic Union, a Munich-based student-organised think tank. His books include *Britain's Europe: a Thousand Years of Conflict and Cooperation* and (co-authored with Steve McGregor) *The Silver Waterfall: How America Won the Pacific War at Midway.*

THUCYDIDES (*c.* 460 BC–405 BC) was a Greek historian and is foremost known for his work on the *History of the Peloponnesian War*, which portrays the struggles between Athens and Sparta. His work was the first recorded political and moral analysis of a nation's war policies.

PHILIP ZELIKOW is the White Burkett Miller Professor of History at the University of Virginia. His scholarship focuses on critical episodes in American and world history. His most recent book is *The Road Less Traveled: the Secret Battle to End the Great War, 1916–17.* He has also held government posts in five administrations and was the director of the 9/11 Commission.

Literature and copyright ©

Classics of Applied History

Published by Bokförlaget Stolpe, Stockholm, Sweden, 2023

Edited by
John Bew, Professor in History and Foreign Policy at the Department of War
Studies, King's College London
Andrew Ehrhardt, Ax:son Johnson Institute Postdoctoral Fellow at the Kissinger
Centre, Johns Hopkins University
Mattias Hessérus, Director of the Ax:son Johnson Institute for Statecraft and
Diplomacy

Text editor: Andrew Mackenzie
Design: Patric Leo
Layout: Petra Ahston Inkapööl
Prepress and print coordinator: Italgraf Media AB, Sweden
Print: Printon, Estonia, via Italgraf Media, 2023
First edition, first printing
ISBN: 978-91-89425-06-4

Bokförlaget Stolpe is a part of Axel and Margaret Ax:son Johnson Foundation for
Public Benefit.

BOKFÖRLAGET STOLPE

AXEL AND MARGARET AX:SON JOHNSON
FOUNDATION FOR PUBLIC BENEFIT